Cracking the
SAT®

Math 1 & 2
Subject Tests

2013–2014 Edition

Cracking the

SAT®

Math 1 & 2
Subject Tests

2013–2014 Edition

Jonathan Spaihts
Revised by Tom Watts

PrincetonReview.com

Random House, Inc. New York

The Princeton Review, Inc.
111 Speen Street, Suite 550
Framingham, MA 01701
E-mail: editorialsupport@review.com

ISBN: 978-0-307-94554-9
ISSN: 1556-7095

SAT is a registered trademark of the College Board,
which does not sponsor or endorse this product.

The Princeton Review is not affiliated with Princeton
University.

Editor: Liz Rutzel
Production Editor: Jim Melloan
Production Assistant: Craig Patches
Illustrations by: The Production Department of
    The Princeton Review

Printed in the United States of America on partially
recycled paper.

10 9 8 7 6 5 4 3 2 1

2013–2014 Edition

Editorial
Rob Franek, Senior VP, Publisher
Selena Coppock, Senior Editor
Calvin Cato, Editor
Kristen O'Toole, Editor
Meave Shelton, Editor

Random House Publishing Team
Tom Russell, Publisher
Nicole Benhabib, Publishing Director
Ellen L. Reed, Production Manager
Alison Stoltzfus, Managing Editor

Acknowledgments

Thanks to Tom Watts for his work on this year's revision, as well as to reviewers Morgan Chase and Alexandra Schaffer, and the production team of The Princeton Review.

Special thanks to Adam Robinson, who conceived of and perfected the Joe Bloggs approach to standardized tests, and many other techniques in the book.

Contents

Chapter 1
Introduction

Welcome to the world of the SAT Math Level 1 and Level 2 Subject Tests. This chapter will help you get familiar with this book and show you how to use it most effectively. We will also talk about when to take a Math Subject Test and which test is best for you. Let's get started!

WHAT ARE THE MATH SUBJECT TESTS?

The Math Subject Tests are standardized tests in mathematics. Colleges use these tests to assist in admissions decisions and to place incoming students in classes at the right level. The Subject Tests are written by ETS, a company in the business of writing tests like these. ETS makes money by charging students to take the SAT and SAT Subject Tests, and charging again to send the scores to colleges. You'll also run into ETS exams if you ever apply to graduate school.

Each Math Subject Test has 50 multiple-choice questions and is one hour long. The tests are scored from 200 to 800 points. Math Level 1 and Math Level 2 test a range of mathematical topics, from basic algebra to trigonometry and statistics. There is substantial overlap between the subjects of the two tests, but they are nevertheless very different.

Many colleges require some SAT Subject Tests (frequently two, but occasionally one or three). The subjects available are varied: two in mathematics, three in science, two in history, one in English, and twelve in foreign languages. Different schools have different preferences and requirements for which tests to take, too. For example, an engineering program may want to see the Math Level 2 and a science. Check each school's website to determine how many tests you must take and which ones (if any) are preferred.

What's on These Tests?

The content of each Mathematics test is approximately as follows:

Topic	Math Level 1	Math Level 2
Functions	6 questions	12 questions
Trigonometry	4 questions	10 questions
Algebra	15 questions	9 questions
Plane Geometry	10 questions	0 questions
Coordinate Geometry	5 questions	6 questions
Solid Geometry	3 questions	3 questions
Statistics	4 questions	4 questions
Miscellaneous	3 questions	6 questions
TOTAL	50 questions	50 questions

The Math Level 1 focuses on Algebra I, Geometry, and Algebra II, while the Math Level 2 focuses on Geometry, Algebra II, and Precalculus. The tests overlap, but the Math Level 2 tests more advanced material, and it tests basic material in greater depth.

For example, while both tests cover trigonometry, the Math Level 2 has more than twice as many questions on trigonometry, so it asks about many more different trigonometry topics than the Math Level 1 does. Similarly, the Math Level 2 rarely tests geometry except in the coordinate plane or in three dimensions, so that it can combine a geometry question (say, about triangles) with a *xy*-plane question (say, about slope).

Don't worry if you don't recognize some of the topic headings. Students taking the Math Subject Tests are not expected to have spent time on every one of these topics in school. What's more, you can do quite well on these tests even if you haven't studied *everything* on them.

Which Test Should I Take?

Taking the Math Level 1 is a fine idea for most students applying to more selective schools. You should base that decision on the admission requirements of the schools that interest you. The Math Level 2, on the other hand, is not for just anyone—it's a much harder test. The great majority of students who take a Math Subject Test choose to take the Math Level 1.

Taking the Math Level 2 test is appropriate for high school students who have had a year of trigonometry or precalculus and have done well in the class. You should also be comfortable using a scientific or graphing calculator. If you hate math, do poorly on math tests, or have not yet studied Trigonometry or Precalculus, the Math Level 2 test is probably not for you. It's worth noting, however, that while the Math Level 2 test is difficult, the test is scored on a comparatively generous curve. If you find yourself making random (or "silly") mistakes more than anything else, the Math Level 2's scoring grid may work in your favor.

Colleges also receive your percentile (comparing you to other test takers), as well as your scaled (200–800) score. For the most part, they pay attention to the scaled score and ignore the percentile. However, to the small extent that percentiles matter, the Math Level 1 has considerably more forgiving percentiles. People who take the Math Level 2 are generally really good at math; about 13% of them get a perfect score! Less than 1% of Math Level 1 test-takers get a perfect score, though. As a result, a 790 on the Math Level 2 is only in the 85th percentile (about 13% get an 800 and 2% get a 790), while a 790 on the Math Level 1 is still 99th percentile. The disparity between the percentiles continues down the entire score range.

If you are very unsure about which test to take, even after working practice questions and taking practice tests, you can take both tests.

WHEN SHOULD I TAKE A MATH SUBJECT TEST?

The right time to take a Math Subject Test varies from person to person. Many students take the test at the end of a Precalculus class in school. (Precalculus also goes by many other names, such as Trigonometry or other less recognizable names.) Some students take Math Level 2 during or at the end of an AP Calculus course. A few students take Math Level 1 after taking Algebra II, especially if they will not take another math class in high school; such timing must be chosen with caution, because some students who have not taken Precalculus have not seen enough trigonometry to answer some questions on the Math Level 1.

The SAT Subject Tests are offered six times per year, and no test date is easier or harder than any other test date. The most popular test dates are in May and June, because these are at the end of a school year when the material is freshest in the student's mind. Whenever you choose to take the test, make sure you have time to do some practice beforehand, so that you can do your best (and not have to take the thing again!).

The Calculator

The Math Level 1 and Math Level 2 Subject Tests are designed to be taken with the aid of a calculator. Students taking either test should have a scientific or graphing calculator and know how to use it. A "scientific" calculator is one that has keys for the following functions:

- the values of π and e
- square roots
- raising to an exponent
- sine, cosine, and tangent
- logarithms

Calculators without these functions will not be as useful. Graphing calculators are allowed on both Math Subject Tests. The graphing features on a graphing calculator are helpful on a fairly small number of questions per test, and they are necessary for about 0–1 questions per test. If you're going to take a graphing calculator to the test, make sure you know how to use it. Fumbling over your calculator trying to figure something out during the test is just not a productive use of your time!

This book is going to focus on the TI-83. If you have another family member of the TI-80 series, know that these comments still apply to you with minor adjustments. Check with your manual for specific key stroke changes. If you have a scientific calculator, we'll be showing you your key stroke changes in the sidebars throughout the manual.

The ETS Predictor
ETS says that for the Math Level 1, a calculator is useful or necessary for about 40–50 percent of the questions. For Math Level 2, ETS says that a calculator may be useful or necessary for about 55–65 percent of the questions.

Certain kinds of calculators are not allowed. For example, a calculator with a QWERTY keyboard (like a computer keyboard) is not allowed. Your calculator must not require a wall outlet for power and must not make noise or produce paper printouts. There will be no replacements at the test center for malfunctioning or forgotten calculators, though you're welcome to take a spare, as well as spare batteries. Laptops, tablets, and cell phones are also not allowed as calculators.

Bottom line: You need a calculator for this test, but it doesn't have to be fancy. A $10 scientific calculator is certainly good enough.

HOW TO USE THIS BOOK

It's best to work through the chapters of this book in sequence, since the later chapters build on the techniques introduced in earlier chapters. If you want an overall review of the material on the SAT Math Subject Tests, just start at the beginning and cruise through to the end. This book will give you all the techniques and knowledge you need to do well on either of the Math Subject Tests. If you feel a little shaky in certain areas of math and want to review specific topics, the chapter headings and subheadings will also allow you to zero in on your own problem topics. As with any subject, pay particular attention to the math topics you don't like—otherwise, those are the ones that will burn you on the real test.

If you really want to get your money's worth out of this book, you'll follow this study plan.

Need More?
You can also visit collegeboard.com for more information and test questions.

- Read through a lesson carefully until you feel that you understand it.
- Try the practice questions at the end of that lesson.
- Check your answers, and review any questions you got wrong until you understand your mistakes.
- Try a sample test at the end of the book when you feel prepared to do so.
- Score your test and review it to see where your strengths and weaknesses lie.
- Review any test questions you got wrong until you understand your mistakes.
- Take the second test. Then score and review it.

Many study books for the Math Subject Tests are much thicker than this one and contain lots of unnecessary material. Instead of making you wade through hundreds of extra pages, we've stripped our book down to the bare necessities. Each section contains just a few practice questions that focus on the rules and techniques tested by ETS—nothing extra. If you make sure you understand all of the practice questions, you'll understand the questions on the real test.

Math Level 2–Only Material

Because the Math Level 2 Subject Test contains harder material than the Math Level 1 Subject Test, you'll sometimes run into material in this book that will never show up on the Math Level 1—it's too complicated. Such material will be marked with the following button:

Level 2 Only

Hmm…Which Test to Take?
If you're still not sure whether you should be taking the Math Level 2 Subject Test, use the Math Level 2 Only material as a qualifying quiz. If you get more than half of the Math Level 2 Only questions wrong, the Math Level 2 Subject Test is probably not for you.

If you're planning to take only the Math Level 1 (and that's most of you), ignore all sections and questions marked with the Level 2 Only button, and don't worry about them.

If you're planning to take the Math Level 2 Subject Test, this whole book is for you. Do everything.

Question Numbers   As you cruise through this strangely stimulating math book, you'll run into practice questions that seem to be numbered out of order. That's because the numbers of the practice questions tell you what position those questions would occupy on a 50-question Math Level 1 Subject Test. The question number gives you an idea of how difficult ETS considers a given question to be.

Curious about where a question would fall on the Math Level 2 Subject Test? Simple. Just subtract 15 from the given question number. You may notice that questions numbered 1–15 then seem not to exist on the Math Level 2 Subject Test. You're right. There are no questions that easy on the Math Level 2 Subject Test. They're still useful practice for you, but keep in mind that the Math Level 2 Subject Test starts out tricky and stays that way.

Chapter 2
Strategy

It's easy to get the impression that the only way to do well on the Math Subject Tests is to become a master of a huge number of math topics. However, there are many effective strategies that you can use on the Math Subject Tests. From Pacing and Process of Elimination to how to use your calculator, this chapter takes you through the most important general strategies, so you can start practicing them right away.

CRACKING THE MATH SUBJECT TESTS

It's true that you have to know some math to do well, but there's a great deal you can do to improve your score without staring into math books until you go blind.

Several important strategies will help you increase your scoring power. There are a few characteristics of the Math Subject Tests that you can use to your advantage.

- The questions on Math Subject Tests are arranged in order of difficulty. You can think of a test as being divided roughly into thirds, containing easy, medium, and difficult questions, in that order.
- The Math Subject Tests are multiple-choice tests. That means that every time you look at a question on the test, the correct answer is on the paper right in front of you.
- ETS writes incorrect answers on the Math Subject Tests by studying errors commonly made by students. These are common errors that you can learn to recognize.

The next few pages will introduce you to test-taking techniques that use these features of the Math Subject Tests to your advantage, which will increase your score. These strategies come in two basic types: Section strategies, which help you determine which questions to do and how much time to spend on them, and question strategies, which help you solve an individual question once you've chosen to do it.

SECTION STRATEGY

The following represents a sample scoring grid for the Math Subject Tests. The grids vary somewhat from test to test, so this is just a general guide.

Math Level 1

Raw Score	Scaled Score	Percentile	Raw Score	Scaled Score	Percentile
50	800	99	25	560	31
49	790	99	24	550	29
47–48	780	99	23	540	27
46	770	98	22	530	24
45	750	95	21	520	22
43–44	740	97	20	510	20
42	730	93	19	500	18
41	720	86	18	490	16
39–40	710	83	17	480	14
38	700	80	16	470	13
37	690	76	14–15	460	11
36	680	72	13	450	10
35	670	69	12	440	8
34	660	66	11	430	7
33	650	62	9–10	420	6
32	640	59	8	410	5
31	630	55	7	400	4
30	620	51	6	390	4
29	600	43	4–5	380	2
28	590	40	3	370	2
27	580	37	2	360	1
26	570	34	1	350	1

Math Level 2

Raw Score	Scaled Score	Percentile	Raw Score	Scaled Score	Percentile
43–50	800	87	17	570	22
42	790	85	15–16	560	20
41	780	82	—	550	18
40	770	79	14	540	15
39	760	77	13	530	14
38	750	73	12	520	12
37	740	71	—	510	10
36	730	68	11	500	8
35	720	66	10	490	7
34	710	62	—	480	6
33	700	61	9	470	4
31–32	690	58	8	460	3
30	680	56	—	450	3
29	670	53	7	440	2
28	660	50	6	430	2
27	650	47	—	420	1
26	640	44	—	410	1
24–25	630	40	4–5	400	1
23	620	37	—	390	1-
22	610	33	3	380	1-
21	600	31	2	370	1-
19–20	590	28	1	360	1-
18	580	25			

A few points are notable:

- While it is theoretically possible to score below a 350 on the tests, it usually requires a negative raw score (getting more than 4 times as many questions wrong as right). In practice, the tests are scored 350-800.
- On some test dates, some scores are not possible (such as 420 on the Math Level 2 scoring given above).
- The Math Level 2 scoring grid is very forgiving. Approximately 43 raw points scores an 800, and approximately 33 raw points (out of 50) scores a 700. The percentiles are tough, though; a 700 is only 61st percentile! The Math Level 1 has a more conventional score distribution.

Pacing

The first step to improving your performance on a Math Subject Test is *slowing down.* That's right: You'll score better if you do fewer questions. It may sound strange, but it works. That's because the test-taking habits you've developed in high school are poorly suited to a Math Subject Test. It's a different kind of test.

Think about a free-response math test. If you work a question and get the wrong answer, but you do most of the question right, show your work, and make a mistake that lots of other students in the class make (so the grader can easily recognize it), you'll probably get partial credit. If you do the same thing on the Math Subject Tests, you get one of the four wrong answers. But you don't get partial credit for choosing one of the listed wrong answers; you lose a quarter-point. That's the *opposite* of partial credit! Because the Math Subject Tests give the opposite of partial credit, there is a huge premium on accuracy in these tests.

> One Point Over Another?
> A hard question on the Math Subject Tests isn't worth more points than an easy question. It just takes longer to do, and it's harder to get right. It makes no sense to rush through a test if all that's waiting for you are tougher and tougher questions—especially if rushing worsens your performance on the easy questions.

How Many Questions Should I Do?

Use the following charts to determine how many questions to do on your next practice test.

Math Level 1

On your last test, you scored:	On your next test, attempt:	If you get this many raw points...	You'll get a score near:
200–500	30	24	550
510–550	35	29	600
560–600	40	33	650
610–650	45	38	700
660–700	49	45	750
710–800	50	50	800

Math Level 2

On your last test, you scored:	On your next test, attempt:	If you get this many raw points...	You'll get a score near:
200–550	30	23	600
560–600	35	28	650
610–650	40	33	700
660–700	45	38	750
710–800	50	44	800

As you improve, your pacing goals will also get more aggressive. Once you take your next practice test and score it, come back to this chart and adjust your pacing accordingly. For example, if you initially scored a 550, but on your second test you scored a 610, then use the 610–650 line for your third test, and you may score a 700 (or even higher!).

Personal Order of Difficulty (POOD)

You probably noticed that the previous chart doesn't tell you *which* questions to do on the Subject Tests, only how many. That's because students aren't all the same. Even if a certain question is easy for most students, if you don't know how to do it, it's hard for you. Conversely, if a question is hard for most students but you see exactly how to do it, it's easy for you. Most of the time, you'll find lower-numbered questions easy for you and higher-numbered questions harder for you, but not always, and you should always listen to your POOD.

Develop a Pacing Plan

The following is an example of an aggressive pacing plan. You should begin by trying this plan, and then you should adapt it to your own needs.

First, do questions 1–20 in 20 minutes. They are mostly easy, and you should be able to do each one in about a minute. (As noted above, though, you must not go so quickly that you sacrifice accuracy.) If there is a question that looks more time-consuming, but you know how to do it, mark it so that you can come back to it later, but move on.

Second, pick and choose among questions 21–50. Do only questions that you are sure you can get right quickly. Mark questions that are more time-consuming (but you still know how to do them!) so that you can come back to them later. Cross out questions that you do not know how to do; you shouldn't waste any more time on them.

Third, once you've seen every question on the test at least once and gotten all the quick points that you can get, go back to the more time-consuming questions. Make good choices about which questions to do; at this point, you will be low on time and need to make realistic decisions about which questions you will be able to finish and which questions you should give up for lost.

This pacing plan takes advantage of the test's built-in order of difficulty and your POOD. You should move at a brisk but not breakneck pace through the easy questions so that you have enough time to get them right but not waste time. You should make sure that you get to the end of the test and evaluate every question, because you never know if you happen to know how to do question 50; it may be harder for most students than question 30, but it just may test a math topic that you remember very well from class (or this book). Delaying more time-consuming questions until after you've gotten the quick and easy points maximizes your score and gives you a better sense of how long you have to complete those longer questions, and, after some practice, it will take only a few seconds to recognize a time-consuming question.

QUESTION STRATEGY

It's true that the math on the Math Subject Tests gets difficult. But what exactly does that mean? Well, it *doesn't* mean that you'll be doing 20-step calculations, or huge, crazy exponential expansions that your calculator can't handle. Difficult questions on the Math Subject Tests require you to understand some slippery mathematical *concepts,* and sometimes to recognize familiar math rules in strange situations.

This means that if you find yourself doing a 20-step calculation, stop. There's a shortcut, and it probably involves using one of our techniques. Find it.

Process of Elimination (POE)

It's helpful that the Math Subject Tests contain only multiple-choice questions. After all, this means that eliminating four answers that cannot possibly be right is just as good as knowing what the right answer is, and it's often easier. Eliminating four answers and choosing the fifth is called the Process of Elimination (POE).

POE can also be helpful even when you can't get down to a single answer. Because of the way the SAT is scored (plus one raw point for a correct answer and minus a quarter-point for an incorrect answer), if you can eliminate at least one answer, it is to your advantage to guess.

So, the bottom line:

> To increase your score on the Math Subject Tests, eliminate wrong answer choices whenever possible, and guess aggressively whenever you can eliminate anything.

There are two major elimination techniques you should rely on as you move through a Math Subject Test: Approximation and Joe Bloggs.

Approximation

Sometimes, you can approximate an answer:

> You can eliminate answer choices by approximation whenever you have a general idea of the correct answer. Answer choices that aren't even in the right ballpark can be crossed out.

Random Guessing
If you randomly guess on five questions, you can expect to get one right and four wrong.
Your score for those five questions will be:
$$+1 - \frac{4}{4} = 0$$
This isn't very helpful.

POE Guessing
If you correctly eliminate two answer choices and guess among the remaining three, you have a one-in-three chance of getting the right answer. If you do this on six questions, you can expect to get two right and four wrong.
Your score will be :
$$+2 - \frac{4}{4} = 1$$
That's not a lot for six questions, but every point helps.

Take a look at the following three questions. In each question, at least one answer choice can be eliminated by approximation. See whether you can make eliminations yourself. For now, don't worry about how to do these questions—just concentrate on eliminating answer choices.

---

21. If $x^{\frac{3}{5}} = 1.84$, then $x^2 =$

  (A) −10.40
  (B) −3.74
  (C)   7.63
  (D) 10.40
  (E) 21.15

Here's How to Crack It

You may not have been sure how to work with that ugly fractional exponent. But if you realized that x^2 can't be negative, no matter what x is, then you could eliminate (A) and (B)—the negative answers, and then guess from the remaining answer choices.

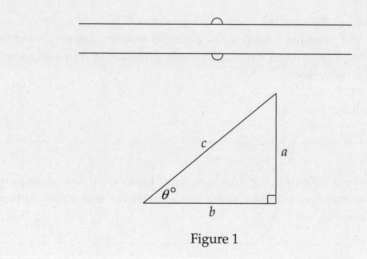

Figure 1

28. In Figure 1, if $c = 7$ and $\theta = 42°$, what is the value of a ?

  (A) 0.3
  (B) 1.2
  (C) 4.7
  (D) 5.2
  (E) 6.0

Here's How to Crack It

Unless you're told otherwise, the figures that the Math Subject Tests give you are drawn accurately, and you can use them to approximate. In this example, even if you weren't sure how to apply trigonometric functions to the triangle, you could still approximate based on the diagram provided. If c is 7, then a looks like, say, 5. That's not specific enough to let you decide between (C), (D), and (E), but you can eliminate (A) and (B). They're not even close to 5. At the very least, that gets you down to a 1-in-3 guess—much better odds.

For some reason, sometimes ETS inserts figures that are deliberately inaccurate and misleading. When the figure is wrong, ETS will print underneath, "Note: Figure not drawn to scale." When you see this note, trust the text of the problem, but don't believe the figure, because the figure is just there to trick you.

---

37. The average (arithmetic mean) cost of Simon's math textbooks was $55.00, and the average cost of his history textbooks was $65.00. If Simon bought 3 math textbooks and 2 history textbooks, what was the average cost of the 5 textbooks?

    (A) $57.00
    (B) $59.00
    (C) $60.00
    (D) $63.50
    (E) $67.00

Here's How to Crack It

Here, once again, you might not be sure how to relate all those averages. However, you could realize that the average value of a group can't be bigger than the value of the biggest member of the group, so you could eliminate (E). You might also realize that, since there are more $55 books than $65 books, the average must be closer to $55.00 than to $65.00, so you could eliminate (C) and (D). That gets you down to only two answer choices, a 50/50 chance. Those are excellent odds.

These are all fairly basic questions. By the time you've finished this book, you won't need to rely on approximation to answer them. The technique of approximation will still work for you, however, whenever you're looking for an answer you can't figure out with actual math.

Joe Bloggs

What makes a question hard? Sometimes a hard question tests more advanced material. For example, on the Math Level 1, trig questions are relatively rare before about question 20. Sometimes a hard question requires more steps, four or five rather than one or two. But more often, a hard question has trickier wording and better trap answers than an easy question.

ETS designs its test around a person we like to call Joe Bloggs. (Joe Bloggs isn't really a person; he's a statistical construct. But don't hold that against him.) When ETS writes a question that mentions "a number," it counts on students to think of numbers like 2 or 3, not numbers like −44.76 or 4π. That instinct to think of the most obvious thing, like 2 or 3 instead of −44.76 or 4π, is called "Joe Bloggs," and this instinct—your inner Joe Bloggs—is dangerous but useful on the Math Subject Tests.

Joe Bloggs is dangerous because he gets a lot of questions wrong on the Math Subject Tests, especially on the hard questions. After all, these tests are testing students on math that they've already learned, but it somehow has to make students get wrong answers. It does that by offering answers that are too good to be true: Tempting oversimplifications, obvious answers to subtle questions, and all sorts of other answers that seem comforting and familiar. Joe Bloggs falls for these every time. Don't be Joe Bloggs! Instead, eliminate answers that Joe Bloggs would choose, and pick something else!

---

43. Ramona cycles from her house to school at 15 miles per hour. Upon arriving, she realizes that it is Saturday and immediately cycles home at 25 miles per hour. If the entire round-trip takes her 32 minutes, then what is her average speed, in miles per hour, for the entire round-trip?

    (A) 17.0
    (B) 18.75
    (C) 20.0
    (D) 21.25
    (E) 22.0

Here's How to Crack It

This is a tricky problem, and you may not be sure how to solve it. You can, however, see that there's a very tempting answer among the answer choices. If someone goes somewhere at 15 mph and returns at 25 mph, then it seems reasonable that the average speed for the trip should be 20 mph. For question 43, however, that's far too obvious to be right. Eliminate (C). It's a Joe Bloggs answer.

---

49. If θ represents an angle such that
   $\sin 2\theta = \tan\theta - \cos 2\theta$, then $\sin\theta - \cos\theta =$

   (A) $-\sqrt{2}$
   (B) 0
   (C) 1
   (D) $2\sqrt{2}$
   (E) It cannot be determined from the information given.

Here's How to Crack It

On a question like this one, you might have no idea how to go about finding the answer. That "It cannot be determined" answer choice may look awfully tempting. You can be sure, however, that (E) will look tempting to *many* students. It's too tempting to be right on a question this hard. You can eliminate (E). It's a Joe Bloggs answer.

Keep Joe Bloggs in mind whenever you're looking to eliminate answer choices and guess, especially on hard questions.

SO DO I HAVE TO KNOW MATH AT ALL?

The techniques in this book will go a long way toward increasing your score, but there's a certain minimum amount of mathematical knowledge you'll need in order to do well on the Math Subject Tests. We've collected the most important rules and formulas into lists. As you move through the book, you'll find these lists at the end of each chapter.

The strategies in this chapter, and the techniques in the rest of this book, are powerful tools. They will make you a better test taker and improve your performance. Nevertheless, memorizing the formulas on our lists is as important as learning techniques. Memorize those rules and formulas, and make sure you understand them.

Using That Calculator

Behold the First Rule of Intelligent Calculator Use:

> Your calculator is only as smart as you are.

Scientific or Graphing?

ETS says that the tests are designed with the assumption that most test takers have graphing calculators. ETS also says that a graphing calculator may give you an advantage on a handful of questions. If you have access to a graphing calculator and know how to use it, you may want to choose it instead of a scientific calculator.

It's worth remembering. Some test takers have a dangerous tendency to rely too much on their calculators. They try to use them on every question and start punching numbers in even before they've finished reading a question. That's a good way to make a question take twice as long as it has to.

The most important part of problem solving is done in your head. You need to read a question, decide which techniques will be helpful in answering it, and set up the question. Using a calculator before you really need to do so will keep you from seeing the shortcut solution to a problem.

When you do use your calculator, follow these simple procedures to avoid the most common calculator errors.

- Check your calculator's operating manual to make sure that you know how to use *all* of your calculator's scientific functions (such as the exponent and trigonometric functions).
- Clear the calculator at the beginning of each problem to make sure it's not still holding information from a previous calculation.
- Whenever possible, do long calculations one step at a time. It makes errors easier to catch.
- Write out your work! Label everything, and write down the steps in your solution after each calculation. That way, if you get stuck, you won't need to do the entire problem over again. Writing things down will also prevent you from making careless errors.
- Keep an eye on the answer choices to see if ETS has included a partial answer designed to tempt you away from the final answer. Eliminate it!

Set It Up!

Some questions on the Math Subject Tests can be answered without much calculation—the setup itself makes the answer clear. Remember: Figure out *how* to do the problem with your brain; then *do* the problem with your calculator.

Above all, remember that your brain is your main problem-solving tool. Your calculator is useful only when you've figured out exactly what you need to do to solve a problem.

Chapter 3
Arithmetic

You've been doing arithmetic as long as you've been studying math. This chapter will review basic arithmetic used on the Math Subject Tests, such as factors, multiples, fractions, percents, and exponents. It will also give you some techniques to better assist you in tackling certain arithmetic questions. Don't forget your calculator!

DEFINITIONS

There are a number of mathematical terms that will be thrown around freely on the test, and you'll want to recognize and understand them. Here are some of the most common terms:

Integers	Positive and negative whole numbers, and zero; NOT fractions or decimals.
Prime Number	An integer that has exactly two distinct factors: itself and 1. All prime numbers are positive; the smallest prime number is 2. Two is also the only even prime number. One is not prime.
Rational Numbers	All positive and negative integers, fractions, and decimal numbers; technically, any number that can be expressed as a fraction of two integers—which means everything except numbers containing weird radicals (such as $\sqrt{2}$), π, or e.
Irrational Numbers	Any number that does not end or repeat (in other words, any number that isn't rational). This includes all numbers with radicals that can't be simplified, such as $\sqrt{2}$ (perfect squares with radicals, such as $\sqrt{16}$, don't count because they can be simplified to integers, such as 4). Also, all numbers containing π or e. Note that repeating decimals like .33333… are rational (they're equivalent to fractions, such as $\frac{1}{3}$).
Real Numbers	Any number on the number line; everything except imaginary numbers (see below).
Imaginary Numbers	The square roots of negative numbers, that is, any numbers containing i, which represents $\sqrt{-1}$.
Consecutive Numbers	The members of a set listed in order, without skipping any; consecutive integers: −3, −2, −1, 0, 1, 2; consecutive positive multiples of 3: 3, 6, 9, 12.
Distinct Numbers	Numbers that are different from each other.
Sum	The result of adding numbers.
Difference	The result of subtracting numbers.
Product	The result of multiplying numbers.
Quotient	The result of dividing numbers.

Remainder	The integer left over after dividing two numbers. For example, when 17 is divided by 2, the remainder is 1. Remember: On the Math Subject Tests, a remainder is ALWAYS an integer.
Reciprocal	The result when 1 is divided by a number. For example, the reciprocal of $\frac{3}{4}$ is $\frac{4}{3}$, and the reciprocal of $\frac{1}{16}$ is 16.
Positive Difference	Just what it sounds like—the number you get by subtracting the smaller of two numbers from the bigger one. You can also think of it as the distance between two numbers on the number line.
Absolute Value	The positive version of a number. You just strike the negative sign if there is one. You can also think of it as the distance on the number line between a number and zero.
Arithmetic Mean	The average of a list of values; also simply referred to as the "mean."
Median	The middle value in a list when arranged in increasing order; in a list with an even number of members, the average of the *two* middle values.
Mode	The value that occurs most often in a list. If no value appears more often than all the others in a list, then that list has no mode.

At the beginning of each chapter in this book, you may see additional definitions that pertain to the material in that chapter. Every time you see such definitions listed, be sure that you know them well. One way to memorize the definitions is to make flash cards for them.

FACTORS AND MULTIPLES

The "factors" of a number are all of the numbers by which it can be divided evenly. ETS sometimes refers to factors as "divisors." Some questions on the Math Subject Tests will specifically require you to identify the factors of a given number. You may find factorizations useful for solving other questions, even if they don't specifically talk about factorizations. There are two forms of factorization: plain old factorization and prime factorization.

Factors

The factorization of a number is a complete list of its factors. The best way to compile a list of all of a number's factors is to write them in pairs, beginning with 1 and the number itself. Then count upward through the integers from 1, checking at each integer to see whether the number you're factoring is divisible by that integer. If it is, add that integer to the list of factors, and complete the pair.

Remember that the largest factor of a number is that number!

Here is the factorization of 60:

1	60
2	30
3	20
4	15
5	12
6	10

Start with 1 and the original number as your first pair and move up (2, 3, 4, etc.) to ensure that you won't miss any. You'll know your list is complete when the two columns of factors meet or pass each other. Here, the next integer after 6 that goes into 60 is 10, so you can be sure that the factorization is complete. This is the most efficient way to get a complete list of a number's factors.

Prime Factors

The other kind of factorization is prime factorization. The prime factorization of a number is the unique group of prime numbers that can be multiplied together to produce that number. For example, the prime factorization of 8 is $2 \times 2 \times 2$. The prime factorization of 30 is $2 \times 3 \times 5$.

Prime factorizations are found by pulling a prime number out of a number again and again until you can't anymore. The prime factorization of 75, for example, would be found as follows:

$$75 =$$

$$3 \times 25 =$$

$$3 \times 5 \times 5$$

Notice that it doesn't matter which prime number you see first as a factor of the original. When you've got nothing but prime numbers left, you're done. Here's the prime factorization of 78.

$$78 =$$

$$2 \times 39 =$$

$$2 \times 3 \times 13$$

Because they're often useful on the Math Subject Tests, you should be able to take prime factorizations quickly.

DRILL

Find the prime factorizations of the following numbers. Answers can be found in Chapter 12.

1. 64 = _____
2. 70 = _____
3. 18 = _____
4. 98 = _____
5. 68 = _____
6. 51 = _____

Prime factorizations are useful in many questions dealing with divisibility. For example:

What is the smallest number divisible by both 14 and 12 ?

To find the smallest number that both numbers will go into, look at the prime factorizations of 12 and 14: $12 = 2 \times 2 \times 3$, and $14 = 2 \times 7$, so it's easy to build the factorization of the smallest number divisible by both 12 and 14. It must contain at least two 2s, a 3, and a 7. That's $2 \times 2 \times 3 \times 7$, or 84. That's the smallest number you can divide evenly by 12 ($2 \times 2 \times 3$) and 14 (2×7).

Multiples

ETS also expects you to know the definition of a "multiple." The multiples of a number are simply all the numbers that are evenly divisible by your original number. An easy way to think of multiples is to recite the times tables for a number. For example, the "positive integer multiples of 6" are simply 6×1, 6×2, 6×3, and so forth, that is, 6, 12, 18…. If ETS asks you for the "fifth positive integer multiple of 6," that just means 6×5, or 30. It's easy to confuse factors and multiples (ETS hopes you will), so here's a way to keep the two straight. If you look back at the factorization of 60, you'll see that there are only 12 factors of 60, which is few. But 60 has as many multiples as you like. So think "factors are few, multiples are many."

Also notice that factors are smaller than or equal to your original number, whereas multiples are larger than or equal to your original number.

What is the largest factor of 180 that is NOT a multiple of 15 ?

Remember that the smallest multiple of a number is that number!

To answer the question, just make the biggest number you can, using the prime factors of 180. The prime factorization of 180 is $2 \times 2 \times 3 \times 3 \times 5$. Since 15 is the same as 3×5, just make sure your number doesn't have 3 *and* 5 as factors. The factor $2 \times 2 \times 5$ may look tempting, but the largest number that fits the bill is $2 \times 2 \times 3 \times 3$, or 36.

DRILL

Try the following practice questions. The answers to these questions can be found in Chapter 12.

3. What is the smallest integer divisible by both 21 and 18 ?

   (A) 42
   (B) 126
   (C) 189
   (D) 252
   (E) 378

7. If ¥x is defined as the largest prime factor of x, then for which of the following values of x would ¥x have the greatest value?

   (A) 170
   (B) 117
   (C) 88
   (D) 62
   (E) 53

9. If $x \, \Omega \, y$ is defined as the smallest integer of which both x and y are factors, then $10 \, \Omega \, 32$ is how much greater than $6 \, \Omega \, 20$?

   (A)   0
   (B)   70
   (C) 100
   (D) 160
   (E) 200

EVEN AND ODD, POSITIVE AND NEGATIVE

Some questions on the Math Subject Tests deal with the way numbers change when they're combined by addition and subtraction, or multiplication and division. The questions usually focus on changes in even and odd numbers, and positive and negative numbers.

Even and Odd Numbers

Even and odd numbers are governed by the following rules:

Addition and Subtraction
even + even = even
even − even = even
odd + odd = even
odd − odd = even
even + odd = odd
even − odd = odd

Multiplication
even × even = even
even × odd = even
odd × odd = odd

Division does not have neat rules. For example, 8 divided by 4 is 2 (an even divided by an even can be an even), but 8 divided by 8 is 1 (an even divided by an even can be an odd), and 8 divided by 16 is 0.5 (an even divided by an even may not be an integer). Only integers can be even or odd; fractions and decimals are neither even nor odd.

Positive and Negative Numbers

There are fewer firm rules for positive and negative numbers. Only the rules for multiplication and division are easily stated.

Multiplication and Division
positive × positive = positive
positive ÷ positive = positive
negative × negative = positive
negative ÷ negative = positive
positive × negative = negative
positive ÷ negative = negative

These rules are true for all numbers, because all real numbers except zero—including fractions, decimals, and even irrational numbers—are either positive or negative. Addition and subtraction for positive and negative numbers are a little more complicated—it's best simply to use common sense.

The one important rule to remember is that subtracting a negative is the same as adding a positive. So,

$$x - (-5) = x + 5$$
$$9 - (-6) = 9 + 6 = 15$$

If you remember this rule, adding and subtracting negative numbers should be simple.

Your understanding of these rules will be tested in questions that show you simple mathematical operations and ask you about the answers they'll produce.

DRILL

Try the following practice questions. The answers to these drills can be found in Chapter 12.

15. If n and m are odd integers, then which of the following must also be an odd integer?

    I. mn

    II. $\dfrac{m}{n}$

    III. $(mn + 1)^2$

(A) I only
(B) III only
(C) I and II only
(D) I and III only
(E) I, II, and III

18. If c and d are integers and $cd < 0$, then which of the following statements must be true?

(A) $\dfrac{cd}{d} > 0$

(B) $c + d = 0$

(C) $c^2 d > 0$

(D) $3cd^2 \neq 0$

(E) $cd(3 + cd) < 0$

20. If x is a positive even integer and y is a negative odd integer, then which of the following must be a positive odd integer?

(A) x^3y^2

(B) $(xy + 2)^2$

(C) $xy^2 - 1$

(D) $x + y$

(E) $\dfrac{x + y}{xy}$

DOING ARITHMETIC

This chapter deals with the basic manipulations of numbers: averages, word problems, exponents, and so on. Most of these operations can be greatly simplified by the use of a calculator, so you should practice them with your calculator in order to increase your speed and efficiency. Remember the points about calculator use from Chapter 2, however. If you use your calculator incorrectly, you'll get questions wrong. If you use it on every question without thinking, it will slow you down. Keep your calculator near at hand, but think before you use it.

The Order of Operations

You remember the Order of Operations, right? PEMDAS (or Please Excuse My Dear Aunt Sally). This is the order you must use to correctly solve an arithmetic problem. PEMDAS stands for Parentheses, Exponents (and roots), Multiplication and Division, Addition and Subtraction.

When using PEMDAS, it's important to remember that exponents and roots should be calculated from left to right, just as multiplication, division, addition and subtraction should be. You can think of PEMDAS in the following way:

> **PEMDAS**
> Parentheses
> Exponents and roots
> Multiplication and Division
> Addition and Subtraction

PEMDAS and Your Calculator

The safest way to do multistep problems like this on a calculator is one step at a time.

Left to Right

If you know what you're doing, you can compute left to right or right to left, but you have to be careful. For example, consider the expression $2 - 3 + 4$. If you evaluate this left to right, you do $2 - 3$ first, and it becomes $(-1) + 4$, which is 3. If you evaluate from right to left, you have to interpret it as $-3 + 4$, which is 1, and then $2 + 1$ is 3. You can't say that $3 + 4$ is 7, so it's $2 - 7$, because that gives you the wrong answer. If that sounds confusing, just evaluate left to right and you'll be fine..

Pretty Print
Some calculators can display calculations the way that they would be written by hand (for example, using a horizontal bar with a numerator above and a denominator below to represent a fraction). This feature is called Pretty Print, and if you don't have a calculator, it may be worth buying a calculator that has this feature. It may also be possible to install an add-on or change the settings in your calculator to add this feature. It's makes it easier to check if you've made a mistake, which is valuable!.

On scientific and graphing calculators, it's possible to type complex expressions into your calculator all at once and let your calculator do the work of grinding out a number. But in order for your calculator to produce the right answer, the expression must be entered in exactly the right way—and that takes an understanding of the order of operations.

For example, the expression $\dfrac{2\sqrt{3^3 - 2}}{5}$ would have to be typed into some calculators this way:

$$(2 \times \sqrt{(3 \wedge 3 - 2)}) \div 5 =$$

On other calculators, it would have to look like the following:

$$(2(3\wedge3 - 2)\wedge(1/2))/5 =$$

Any mistake in either pattern would produce an incorrect answer. On other calculators, the equation might have to be typed in in still another way. If you intend to make your calculator do your work for you, check your calculator's operating manual, and practice. In general, use lots of parentheses to make sure the calculator does the arithmetic in the right order. If you use too many parentheses, the calculator will still give you the right answer, but if you don't use enough, you may get the wrong answer. And remember, the safest way to use your calculator is one step at a time.

DRILL

Check your PEMDAS skills by working through the following complicated calculations with your calculator (answers can be found in Chapter 12):

1. $0.2 \times \left[\dfrac{15^2 - 75}{6}\right] =$

2. $\dfrac{5\sqrt{6^3 - 20}}{2} =$

3. $\sqrt{\dfrac{(7^2 - 9)(.375 \times 16)^2}{10}} =$

4. $\sqrt{5\left[(13 \times 18) + \sqrt{121}\right]} =$

5. $\sqrt{\dfrac{2025^{0.5}}{0.2}} - \dfrac{5}{\frac{1}{3}} =$

FRACTIONS, DECIMALS, AND PERCENTAGES

On arithmetic questions, you will often be called upon to change fractions to decimal numbers, or decimal numbers to percentages, and so on. Be careful whenever you change the form of a number.

You turn fractions into decimals by doing the division represented by the fraction bar.

$$\frac{1}{8} = 1 \div 8 = .125$$

To turn a decimal number into a fraction, count the number of decimal places (digits to the right of the decimal point) in the number. Then place the number over a 1 with the same number of zeros, get rid of the decimal point, and reduce.

$$.125 = \frac{125}{1000} = \frac{25}{200} = \frac{1}{8}$$

Decimal numbers and percentages are essentially the same. The difference is the percent sign (%), which means "÷ 100." To turn a decimal number into a percentage, just move the decimal point two places to the right, and add the percent sign.

$$.125 = 12.5\%$$

To turn percentages into decimal numbers, do the reverse; get rid of the percent sign and move the decimal point two places to the left.

$$0.3\% = 0.003$$

It's important to understand these conversions, and to be able to do them in your head as much as possible. Don't rely on the percent key on your calculator; it's far too easy to become confused and use it when converting in the wrong direction.

Watch out for conversions between percentages and decimal numbers—especially ones involving percentages with decimal points already in them (like .15%). Converting these numbers is simple, but this step is still the source of many careless errors.

Word-Problem Translation

Most of the common careless errors made in answering math questions are made in the very first step: reading the question. All your skill in arithmetic does you no good if you're not solving the right problem, and all the power of your calculator can't help you if you've entered the wrong equation. Reading errors are particularly common in word problems.

The safest way to extract equations from long-winded word problems is to translate, word for word, from English to math. All of the following words have direct math equivalents:

English	Math
what what fraction how many	x, y, etc. (a variable)
a, an	1 (one)
percent	÷ 100
of	• (multiplied by)
is, are, was, were	=
per (creates a ratio)	÷ (divided by)
x is how much more than y	$x - y$
x is how many times (more than) y	$x \div y$
x is how much less than y	$y - x$

Don't Get Tripped Up
Start writing your multiplication sign as a dot, not an ×, if you haven't already. Using an × can get very confusing, especially if your variable is an x. Make it easy and don't trip yourself up!

Using this table as a guide, you can translate any English sentence in a word problem into an equation. For example:

3. If the bar of a barbell weighs 15 pounds, and the entire barbell weighs 75 pounds, then the weight of the bar is what percent of the weight of the entire barbell?

The question at the end of the problem can be translated into:

$$15 = \frac{x}{100} \bullet 75$$

Solve this equation, and the question is answered. You'll find that x is equal to 20, and 20% is the correct answer.

DRILL

For each of the following exercises, translate the information in English into an equation and solve. The answers to this drill can be found in Chapter 12.

1. 6.5 is what percent of 260?
2. If there are 20 honors students at Pittman High and 180 students at the school in all, then the number of honors students at Pittman High is what percentage of the total number of students?
3. Thirty percent of 40 percent of 25 marbles is how many marbles?
4. What is the square root of one-third of 48?
5. The square root of what positive number is equal to one-eighth of that number?

Word for Word
Use the English to math conversion chart to translate each word into math.

Percent Change

"Percent change" is a way of talking about increasing or decreasing a number. The percent change is just the amount of the increase or decrease, expressed as a percentage of the starting amount.

For example, if you took a $100.00 item and increased its price by $2.00, that would be a 2% change, because the amount of the increase, $2.00, is 2% of the original amount, $100.00. On the other hand, if you increased the price of a $5.00 item by the same $2.00, that would be a 40% increase—because $2.00 is 40% of $5.00. If you ever lose track of your numbers when computing a percent change, just use this formula:

$$\% \, \text{Change} = \frac{\text{Amount Change}}{\text{Original}} \times 100$$

Whenever you work with percent change, be careful not to confuse the *amount of the change* with the total *after* you've worked out the percent change. Just concern yourself with the original amount and the amount of the increase or decrease. The new total doesn't matter.

DRILL

Test your understanding of percent change with the following practice questions. The answers to these drills can be found in Chapter 12.

2. A 25-gallon addition to a pond containing 150 gallons constitutes an increase of approximately what percent?

    (A) 14.29%
    (B) 16.67%
    (C) 17.25%
    (D) 20.00%
    (E) 25.00%

Your Calculator Is Your Friend

Here's a great place to test out how you're putting equations in your calculator.

5. The percent decrease from 5 to 4 is how much less than the percent increase from 4 to 5 ?

    (A) 0%
    (B) 5%
    (C) 15%
    (D) 20%
    (E) 25%

12. Nicoletta deposits $150.00 in her savings account. If this deposit represents a 12 percent increase in Nicoletta's savings, then how much does her savings account contain after the deposit?

    (A) $1,100.00
    (B) $1,250.00
    (C) $1,400.00
    (D) $1,680.00
    (E) $1,800.00

Percent change shows up in many different problem types on the Math Subject Tests—it can be brought into almost any kind of math question. Here's one of the most common math question types that deals with percent change.

The Change-Up, Change-Down   It's a classic trick question to ask what happens if you increase something by a percent and then decrease it by the same percent, as follows:

---

9. The price of a bicycle that usually sells for $250.00 is marked up 30 percent. If this new price is subsequently discounted by 30 percent, then the final price of the bicycle is

    (A) $200.50
    (B) $216.75
    (C) $227.50
    (D) $250.00
    (E) $265.30

Here's How to Crack It

The easy mistake on this problem type is to assume that the price (after increasing by 30% and then decreasing by 30%) has returned to $250.00, the original amount. Nope! It doesn't actually work out that way, as you'll see if you try it step by step. First, you increase the original price by 30%.

$$\$250.00 + \left(\frac{30}{100} \times \$250.00\right) =$$

$$\$250.00 + \$75.00 =$$

$$\$325.00$$

Then, discount this price by 30%.

$$\$325.00 - \left(\frac{30}{100} \times \$325.00\right) =$$

$$\$325.00 - \$97.50 =$$

$$\$227.50$$

The answer is (C). As you can see, the final amount isn't equal to the starting amount. The reason for the difference is that you're increasing the price by 30% of the starting number, and then decreasing by 30% of a *different* number—the new, higher price. The changes will never be of the same *amount*—just the same percent. You end up with a number smaller than your starting number, because the decrease was bigger than the increase. In fact, if you'd done the decrease *first* and then the increase, you would still have gotten the same number, $227.50.

———————◯———————

Remember this tip whenever you increase a quantity by a percent and then *decrease* by the same percent. Your final result will always be a bit smaller than your original amount. The same thing is true if you *decrease* a quantity by a percent and then increase by the same percent. You'll get a number a bit lower than your starting number.

REPEATED PERCENT CHANGE

On one common question type you'll have to work with percent change and exponents together. Occasionally, you'll be required to increase or decrease something by a percent again and again. Such questions often deal with growing populations or bank accounts collecting interest. Here's an example:

40. Ruby had $1,250.00 in a bank account at the end of 1990. If Ruby deposits no further money in the account, and the money in the account earns 5 percent interest every year, then to the nearest dollar, how much money will be in the account at the end of 2000 ?

   (A) $1,632.00
   (B) $1,786.00
   (C) $1,875.00
   (D) $2,025.00
   (E) $2,036.00

Here's How to Crack It

The easy mistake here is to find 5% of the original amount, which in this case would be $62.50. Add $62.50 for each of the ten years from 1990 to 2000 and you've got an increase of $625.00, right? Wrong. That would give you a final total of $1,875.00, but that's not the right answer. Here's the problem—the interest for the first year is $62.50, which is 5% of $1,250. But that means that now there's $1,312.50 in the bank account, so the interest for the second year will be something different. As you can see, this could get messy.

Here's the easy way. The first year's interest can be computed like any ordinary percent change, by adding the percent change to the original amount.

$$\$1,250.00 + \left(\frac{5}{100} \times \$1,250.00\right) = \text{total after one year}$$

But there's another way to write that. Just factor out the $1,250.00.

$$\$1,250.00 \times \left(1 + \frac{5}{100}\right) = \text{total after one year}$$

$$\$1,250.00 \times (1.05) = \text{total after one year}$$

You can get the total after one year by converting the percent change to a decimal number, adding 1, and multiplying the original amount by this number. To get the total after two years, just multiply by that number again.

$$\$1,250.00 \times (1.05) \times (1.05) = \text{total after two years}$$

> **Remember to Keep an Eye Out for Traps**
> Notice that $1,875.00 is in the answers. Remember that ETS *loves* to put in numbers that look familiar to you. You'll see partial answers; you'll see answers to a question that wasn't even asked. A test question numbered 40 is going to be a difficult one. Always remember to keep an eye out for answers that you can eliminate.

And so on. So, to figure out how much money Ruby will have after 10 years, all you have to do is multiply her original deposit by 1.05, 10 times. That means multiplying Ruby's original deposit by 1.05 to the 10th power.

$$\$1{,}250.00 \times (1.05)^{10} = \text{total after 10 years}$$

$$\$1{,}250.00 \times 1.629 = \text{total after 10 years}$$

$$\$2{,}036.25 = \text{total after 10 years}$$

So, to the nearest dollar, Ruby will have $2,036.00 after 10 years. The answer is (E).

There's a simple formula you can use to solve repeated percent-increase problems.

Final amount = Original × (1 + Rate)$^{\text{number of changes}}$

The formula for repeated percent-decrease problems is almost identical. The only difference is that you'll be subtracting the percentage change from 1 rather than adding it.

Final amount = Original × (1 − Rate)$^{\text{number of changes}}$

Just remember that you've got to convert the rate of change (like an interest rate) from a percentage to a decimal number.

Here's another one. Try it yourself, and then check the explanation below.

43. The weight of a bar of hand soap decreases by 2.5 percent each time it is used. If the bar weighs 100 grams when it is new, what is its weight in grams after 20 uses?

(A) 50.00
(B) 52.52
(C) 57.43
(D) 60.27
(E) 77.85

Here's How to Crack It

You've got all of your starting numbers. The original amount is 100 grams, and the rate of change is 2.5%, or 0.025 (remember to subtract it, because it's a decrease). You'll be going through 20 decreases, so the exponent will be 20. This is how you'd plug these numbers into the formula.

$$\begin{aligned} \text{Final amount} &= 100 \times (1 - .025)^{20} \\ &= 100 \times (.975)^{20} \\ &= 100 \times (.60269) \\ \text{Final amount} &= 60.27 \end{aligned}$$

The answer is (D). This is an excellent example of a question type that is difficult if you've never seen it before, and easy if you're prepared for it. Memorize the repeated percent-change formulas and practice using them.

To Memorize or Not to Memorize?

So, at this point, you're probably starting to get nervous about how many formulas we're giving you and how much you have to memorize. But remember: We're also showing you how to get there. Formulas are designed to save you time. If you ever can't remember a formula, you can still figure out how to do the problem. Notice for repeated percent change, you *can* do it the long way and still get to the right answer accurately. And don't forget your techniques like approximation and POE . . . and there's still more to come!

DRILL

Try the following practice questions. The answers to these drills can be found in Chapter 12.

35. At a certain bank, savings accounts earn 5 percent interest per year. If a savings account is opened with a $1,000.00 deposit and no further deposits are made, how much money will the account contain after 12 years?

    (A) $ 1,333.33
    (B) $ 1,166.67
    (C) $ 1,600.00
    (D) $ 1,795.86
    (E) $12,600.00

40. In 1900, the population of Malthusia was 120,000. Since then, the population has increased by exactly 8 percent per year. What was the population in the year 2000 ?

    (A) 216,000
    (B) 2,599,070
    (C) 1,080,000
    (D) 5.4×10^7
    (E) 2.6×10^8

43. In 1995, Ebenezer Bosticle created a salt sculpture that weighed 2,000 pounds. If this sculpture loses 4 percent of its mass each year to rain erosion, what is the last year in which the statue will weigh more than 1,000 pounds?

    (A) 2008
    (B) 2009
    (C) 2011
    (D) 2012
    (E) 2013

AVERAGES

The tests use averages in a variety of question types. Remember, the average is the sum of all the values divided by the number of values you're adding up. Looking at this definition, you can see that every average involves three quantities: the total, the number of things being added, and the average itself.

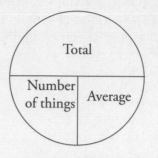

Ways to Remember
Remember that in order to find the average, you divide the total by the number of things. Think of the horizontal line in the average pie as one big division bar!

The chart above is called an average pie. It's The Princeton Review way of organizing the information found in an average problem. Cover up the "average" section with your thumb. In order to find the average, you divide the total by the "number of things." Now cover up the "number of things" section. You can find it by dividing the total by the average. Finally, you can find the total by multiplying the number of things by the average.

When you run into an average in a Math Subject Test question, you'll be given two of the three numbers involved. Usually, solving the problem will depend on your supplying the missing number in the average pie.

DRILL

Test your understanding of averages with the following questions. The answers to these drills can be found in Chapter 12.

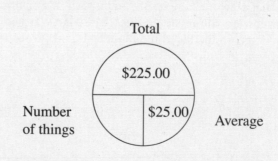

1. People at a dinner paid an average of $25.00 each. The total bill for dinner was $225.00.

   What else do you know? _____

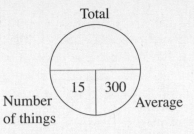

2. The average fruit picker on Wilbury Ranch picked 300 apples on Tuesday. There are 15 fruit pickers at Wilbury Ranch.

   What else do you know? _____

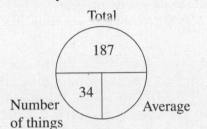

3. If the 34 students in the chess club lie down end to end, they would form a line 187 feet long.

   What else do you know? _____

The average pie becomes most useful when you're tackling a multiple-average question—one that requires you to manipulate several averages in order to find an answer. Here's an example:

—————————————○—————————————

32. Sydney's average score on the first 5 math tests of the year was 82. If she ended the year with a math test average of 88, and a total of 8 math tests were administered that year, what was her average on the last three math tests?

   (A) 99.5
   (B) 98.75
   (C) 98.0
   (D) 96.25
   (E) 94.0

Here's How to Crack It

In this question, there are three separate averages to deal with: Sydney's average on the first five tests, her average on the last three tests, and her final average for all eight. In order to avoid confusion, take these one at a time. Draw the first average pie.

Average Pies and Variables, Never the Twain Shall Meet
There should never be a variable in your average pie. You will always be given two of the three numbers you need in your pie. If you can't find two of the three numbers, that means you've missed a step somewhere.

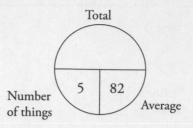

You have the number of things and the average, so you can find the total. You know that Sydney's total for the first test is 410. Fill in that information and draw another pie. For your second pie, the question tells you that Sydney's average on all 8 tests was 88, so you can multiply those numbers to find the total of her 8 scores, or 704. Fill in your second average pie below.

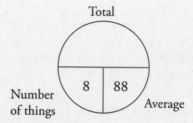

Since you know the total of all 8 tests and the total of the first 5 tests, you can figure out the total of the last three tests:

$$704 - 410 = 294$$

Draw one last pie, using the information that you have:

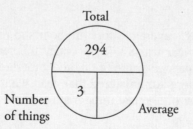

As it turns out, Sydney averaged a 98 on her last three math tests; so the answer is (C).

Multiple-average questions are never terribly difficult. Just draw an average pie every time you see the word *average* in the question. Organization is everything on these questions. It's easy to make careless errors if you get your numbers scrambled, so make sure you label the parts of the average pie. Notice that you can always add or subtract totals and numbers of things, but you can never add or subtract averages.

DRILL

Try these problems. The answers can be found in Chapter 12.

33. At a charity fund-raiser, the average of the first 19 donations is $485.00. In order for the average of the first 20 donations to be $500.00, what must the amount of the twentieth donation be, in dollars?

    (A) $300
    (B) $515
    (C) $650
    (D) $785
    (E) $800

35. During the first 20 days of September, the *Tribune* received an average of 4 complaint letters per day. During the last 10 days of September, the *Tribune* received an average of 7 complaint letters per day. What was the *Tribune's* average number of complaint letters per day for the entire month of September?

    (A) 5.0
    (B) 5.33
    (C) 5.67
    (D) 6.0
    (E) 6.25

36. Over a year, Brendan sold an average of 12 umbrellas per day on rainy days, and an average of 3 umbrellas per day on clear days. If the weather was rainy one day in five, and this was not a leap year, what was Brendan's average daily umbrella sales for the year?

    (A) 4.8
    (B) 5.2
    (C) 6.75
    (D) 7.3
    (E) 9.0

EXPONENTS

An exponent is a simple way of expressing repeated multiplication. You can think of 5^3, for example, as $5 \times 5 \times 5$. In this exponential expression, 5 is referred to as the "base," while 3 is the "exponent." Sometimes a third number is also present, called a "coefficient." In the expression $4b^2$, b is the base, 2 is the exponent, and 4 is the coefficient. Here, b is being squared, but the coefficient, 4, is not affected by the exponent.

For certain Math Subject Test questions, you'll need to do some algebraic calculations using exponents. To work with exponents in equations, you just need to remember a few basic rules.

Rules Come from Somewhere

If you ever forget the rules of exponents, remember that you can always expand and cancel. So if you're ever unclear, write it out. Here's a great example:

$$x^2 \bullet x^4 = (x \bullet x)(x \bullet x \bullet x \bullet x)$$

You have six x's. So the answer is x^6.

This also works with dividing:

$$\frac{m^5}{m^3} = \frac{mmmmm}{mmm}$$

Now cancel and you get mm or m^2.

You *never* have to stress about forgetting your rules. They make it easier to get through the problem more quickly, but if you forget, there's always another way!

Multiplying Exponents When Bases Are the Same

Exponential terms can be multiplied when their bases are the same. Just leave the bases unchanged and add the exponents.

$$n^3 \times n^5 = n^8 \qquad\qquad 3 \times 3^4 = 3^5$$

Coefficients, if they are present, are multiplied normally.

$$2b \times 3b^5 = 6b^6 \qquad\qquad \frac{1}{2}c^3 \times 6c^5 = 3c^8$$

Dividing Exponents When Bases Are the Same

Exponential terms can also be divided when their bases are the same. Once again, the bases remain the same, and the exponents are subtracted.

$$x^8 \div x^6 = x^2 \qquad\qquad 7^5 \div 7 = 7^4$$

Coefficients, if they are present, are divided normally.

$$6b^5 \div 3b = 2b^4 \qquad\qquad 5a^8 \div 3a^2 = \frac{5}{3}a^6$$

Multiplying and Dividing Exponents When Exponents Are the Same

There's one special case in which you can multiply and divide terms with different bases—when the exponents are the same. In this case you can multiply or divide the different bases. Then the bases change and the exponents remain the same.

For multiplication:

$$3^3 \times 5^3 = 15^3 \qquad\qquad x^8 \times y^8 = (xy)^8$$

And for division:

$$33^2 \div 3^2 = 11^2 \qquad\qquad x^{20} \div y^{20} = \left(\frac{x}{y}\right)^{20}$$

If exponential terms have different bases and different exponents, then there's no way to combine them by adding, subtracting, dividing, or multiplying.

Adding and Subtracting When Bases and Exponents Are the Same

Terms with exponents can be added or subtracted only when they have the same base and exponent.

$$2a^3 + a^3 = 3a^3 \qquad\qquad 5x^2 - 4x^2 = x^2$$

If they don't have the same base and exponent, exponential terms can never be combined by addition or subtraction.

Raising Powers to Powers

When an exponential term is raised to another power, the exponents are multiplied.

$$(x^2)^8 = x^{16} \qquad\qquad (7^5)^4 = 7^{20}$$

If there is a coefficient included in the term, then the coefficient is also raised to that power.

$$(3c^4)^3 = 27c^{12} \qquad\qquad (5g^3)^2 = 25g^6$$

Using these rules, you should be able to manipulate exponents wherever you find them.

ROOTS

A Horse of a Different Color
Square roots are sometimes called roots of the second power. It's yet another way ETS tries to throw you. It makes a simple concept sound very complicated. But you know better!

Roots are exponents in reverse. For example, $4 \times 4 = 16$. That means that $4^2 = 16$. It also means that $\sqrt{16} = 4$. Square roots are by far the most common roots on the Math Subject Tests. The square root of a number is simply whatever you would square to get that number.

You may also encounter other roots: cube roots, fourth roots, fifth roots, and so on. Each of these roots is represented by a radical with a number attached, like $\sqrt[3]{x}$, which means the cube root of x. Roots of higher degrees work just as square roots do. The expression $\sqrt[4]{81}$, for example, equals 3—the number that you'd raise to the 4th power to get 81. Similarly, $\sqrt[5]{32}$ is the number that, raised to the 5th power, equals 32—in this case, 2.

The Principal Idea

Remember how both 2 and -2 raised to the 4th power equal 16? Well, for the Math Subject Tests, a radical refers only to the *principal* root of an expression. When there is only one root, that's the principal root. An example of this is $\sqrt[3]{27}$. The only root of this expression is 3. When you have both a positive *and* a negative root, the positive root is considered to be the principal root and is the only root symbolized by the radical sign. So, even though $2^4 = 16$ and $(-2)^4 = 16$, $\sqrt[4]{16}$ means 2 only, and not -2.

When the number under a radical has a factor whose root is an integer, then the radical can be *simplified*. This means that the root can be pulled out. For example, $\sqrt{48}$ is equal to $\sqrt{16 \times 3}$. Because 16 is a perfect square, its root can be pulled out, leaving the 3 under the radical sign, as $4\sqrt{3}$. That's the simplified version of $\sqrt{48}$.

Working with Roots

The rules for manipulating roots when they appear in equations are the same as the rules for manipulating exponents. Roots can be combined by addition and subtraction only when they are roots of the same order and roots of the same number.

$$3\sqrt{5} - \sqrt{5} = 2\sqrt{5} \qquad\qquad 3\sqrt[3]{x} + 2\sqrt[3]{x} = 5\sqrt[3]{x}$$

Roots can be multiplied and divided freely as long as all the roots are of the same order—all square roots, or all cube roots, and so on. The answer must also be kept under the radical.

$$\sqrt{a} \times \sqrt{b} = \sqrt{ab} \qquad\qquad \sqrt[3]{24} \div \sqrt[3]{3} = \sqrt[3]{8} = 2$$

$$\sqrt{18} \times \sqrt{2} = \sqrt{36} = 6 \qquad\qquad \sqrt[4]{5} \div \sqrt[4]{2} = \sqrt[4]{\frac{5}{2}}$$

Be sure to memorize these rules before working with roots.

Fractional Exponents

A fractional exponent is a way of raising a number to a power and taking a root of the number at the same time. The number on top is the normal exponent. The number on the bottom is the root—you can think of it as being in the "root cellar."

So, in order to raise a number to the $\frac{2}{3}$ power, you would square the number and then take the cube root of your result. You could also take the cube root first and then square the result—it doesn't matter which one you do first, as long as you realize that 2 is the exponent and 3 is the order of the root.

Remember that an exponent of 1 means the number itself, so $x^{\frac{1}{2}}$ is equal to $\sqrt{x}$, the square root of x to the first power. Knowing this will help you handle roots with your calculator. For example, $17^{\frac{1}{3}}$ can be entered into your calculator as 17^(1/3).

Calculator Tip
Some scientific calculators have an exponent key that looks like y^x, x^y, or x^n instead of ^.

$$27^{\frac{1}{3}} = \sqrt[3]{27} = 3 \qquad\qquad b^{\frac{5}{2}} = \sqrt{b^5}$$

$$8^{\frac{2}{3}} = \sqrt[3]{8^2} = \sqrt[3]{64} = 4 \qquad\qquad x^{\frac{4}{3}} = \sqrt[3]{x^4}$$

SPECIAL EXPONENTS

There are some exponents on the Math Subject Tests that you've got to treat a little differently. Below are some unusual exponents with which you should be familiar.

Zero

Any number (except zero) raised to the power of zero is equal to 1, no matter what you start with. It's a pretty simple rule.

$$5^0 = 1 \qquad\qquad x^0 = 1$$

One

Any number raised to the first power is itself—it doesn't change. In fact, ordinary numbers, written without exponents, are numbers to the first power. You can think of them as having an invisible exponent of 1. That's useful when using the basic exponent rules you've just reviewed. It means that $(x^4 \div x)$ can be written as $(x^4 \div x^1)$, which can prevent confusion when you're subtracting exponents.

$$x = x^1 \qquad\qquad 4^1 = 4$$

Negative Exponents

Treat a negative exponent exactly like a positive exponent, with one extra step. After you have applied the exponent, flip the number over—that is, you turn the number into its reciprocal.

$$a^{-4} = \frac{1}{a^4} \qquad\qquad 3^{-2} = \frac{1}{3^2} = \frac{1}{9}$$

$$x^{-1} = \frac{1}{x} \qquad\qquad \left(\frac{2}{3}\right)^{-1} = \frac{3}{2}$$

The negative sign works the same way on fractional exponents. First you apply the exponent as you would if it were positive, and then flip it over.

$$x^{-\frac{1}{2}} = \frac{1}{\sqrt{x}} \qquad\qquad a^{-\frac{3}{2}} = \frac{1}{\sqrt{a^3}}$$

MORE IMPORTANT EXPONENT STUFF

There are a few important things to remember about the effects of exponents on various numbers:

- A positive number raised to any power remains positive. No exponent can make a positive number negative.
- A negative number raised to an odd power remains negative.
- A negative number raised to an even power becomes positive.

In other words, anything raised to an odd power keeps its sign. If a^3 is negative, then a is negative; if a^3 is positive, then a is positive. A term with an odd exponent has only one root. For example, if $a^3 = -27$, there's only one value of a that makes it true: $a = -3$.

On the other hand, anything raised to an even power becomes positive, regardless of its original sign. This means that an equation with an even exponent has two roots. For example, if $b^2 = 25$, then b has two possible values: 5 and −5. It's important to remember that two roots exist for any equation with an even exponent (the only exception is when $b^2 = 0$, in which case b can equal only 0, and b^2 has only one root).

One last thing to remember—since any real number becomes positive when raised to an even exponent, certain equations will have no real roots. For example, the equation $x^2 = -9$ has no real roots. There's no integer or fraction, positive or negative, that can be squared to produce a negative number. In this equation, x is said to be an imaginary number. The equation is considered to have no real solution.

Drill

In the following exercises, find the roots of the exponential expression given. Specify whether each expression has one root, two roots, or no real roots. The answers to these drills can be found in Chapter 12.

1. $b^3 = 27$; $b =$
2. $x^2 = 121$; $x =$
3. $n^5 = 32$; $n =$
4. $c^2 = 10$; $c =$
5. $x^4 = 81$; $x =$
6. $x^3 = -8$; $x =$
7. $d^6 = 729$; $d =$
8. $n^0 = 1$ (for $n \neq 0$); $n =$

Now try some multiple-choice questions. In the following exercises, expand the exponential expressions. Where the bases are numbers, find the numerical values of the expressions. The answers to these drills can be found in Chapter 12.

1. $4^{\frac{3}{2}} =$

   (A)   2.52
   (B)   3.64
   (C)   8.00
   (D)   16.00
   (E)   18.67

2. $x^{-\frac{3}{4}} =$

   (A) $-\sqrt[5]{x} \cdot x^4$

   (B) $-\dfrac{x^3}{x^4}$

   (C) $\dfrac{x^4}{x^3}$

   (D) $\dfrac{1}{\sqrt[4]{x^3}}$

   (E) $-\sqrt[4]{x^3}$

3. $\left(\dfrac{2}{3}\right)^{-2} =$

   (A)   2.25
   (B)   1.67
   (C)   0.44
   (D)   −1.50
   (E)   −0.44

4. $\left(\dfrac{1}{a}\right)^{-\frac{1}{3}} =$

   (A) $-\dfrac{1}{\sqrt[3]{a}}$

   (B) $\sqrt[-3]{a}$

   (C) $\dfrac{1}{a^3}$

   (D) $-a^3$

   (E) $\sqrt[3]{a}$

5. $5^{\frac{2}{3}} =$

   (A)   2.92
   (B)   5.00
   (C)   6.25
   (D)   8.67
   (E)   11.18

6. $\left(-\dfrac{5}{6}\right)^0 =$

   (A)   −1.2
   (B)   −0.8
   (C)   0.0
   (D)   1.0
   (E)   1.2

Summary

o   Factors are numbers that divide into your original number. Multiples are numbers that your original number divides into.
   *   Factors are smaller than or equal to your original number.
   *   Multiples are larger than or equal to your original number.

o   Make sure that you have a good grasp of PEMDAS and the rules involving even, odd, positive, and negative numbers:
   *   even ± even = even
   *   even ± odd = odd
   *   odd ± odd = even
   *   even × even = even
   *   even × odd = even
   *   odd × odd = odd
   *   positive × or ÷ positive = positive
   *   negative × or ÷ negative = positive
   *   positive × or ÷ negative = negative

o   If you have a question that asks for the average, mean, or arithmetic mean, use the average pie:

o   There are two formulas for percent change:
   *   The basic formula for percent change is:

$$\% \, \text{Change} = \frac{\text{Amount Change}}{\text{Original}} \times 100$$

   *   The formula for repeated percent change is: Final = Original × (1 ± Rate)$^{\text{\# of changes}}$. If it's a repeated percent increase, you add Rate. If it's a decrease, you subtract Rate.

o   Special exponents:
  • Any number, except 0, raised to the 0 power is 1.
  • Raising a number to the first power does not change the number.
  • A negative exponent means take the reciprocal of the number (divide 1 by the number), and then apply the exponent.
  • Fractional exponents are a way of writing exponents and roots together: The top of the fraction is the exponent and the bottom of the fraction is the root.

o   For exponents and roots, if you're adding or subtracting, the bases (what's under the root sign) must be the same.

Chapter 4
Algebra

Algebra questions ask you to solve for an unknown amount. In this chapter, we'll show you how ETS uses algebra (and often tries to trick you with it). You'll learn some great techniques to help you avoid ETS traps. We'll also review concepts, such as solving for *x*, inequalities, factoring, simultaneous equations, and quadratic equations.

ALGEBRA ON THE SUBJECT TESTS

Algebra questions will make up about 30 percent of the questions on the Math Level 1 Subject Test and about 20 percent of the questions on the Math Level 2 Subject Test. Many of these questions are best answered by using the simple algebra rules outlined in this chapter. Others can be shortcut with The Princeton Review techniques, which you'll also find in the following pages.

Definitions

Here are some algebraic terms that will appear on the Math Subject Tests. Make sure you're familiar with them. If the meaning of any of these vocabulary words keeps slipping your mind, add those words to your flash cards.

Variable	An unknown quantity in an equation represented by a letter (usually from the end of the alphabet), for example, x, y, or z.
Constant	An unchanging numerical quantity—either a number or a letter that represents a number (usually from the beginning of the alphabet), for example, 5, 7.31, a, b, or k.
Term	An algebraic unit consisting of constants and variables multiplied together, such as $5x$ or $9x^2$.
Coefficient	In a term, the constant before the variable. In ax^2, a is the coefficient. In $7x$, 7 is the coefficient.
Polynomial	An algebraic expression consisting of more than one term joined by addition or subtraction. For example, $x^2 - 3x^2 + 4x - 5$ is a polynomial with four terms.
Binomial	A polynomial with exactly two terms, such as $(x - 5)$.
Quadratic	A quadratic expression is a polynomial with one variable whose largest exponent is a 2, for example, $x^2 - 5x + 6$ or $y = x^2 + 4$.
Root	A root of a polynomial is a value of the variable that makes the polynomial equal to zero. More generally, the roots of an equation are the values that make the equation true. Roots are also known as zeros, solutions, and x-intercepts.

SOLVING EQUATIONS

Many questions on the Math Subject Tests will require you to solve simple algebraic equations. Often these algebraic questions are in the form of word problems. Setting up an equation from the information contained in a word problem is the first step to finding the solution, and is the step at which many careless mistakes are made. The translation chart on page 30 is very useful for setting up equations from information given in English.

An algebraic equation is an equation that contains at least one unknown—a variable. "Solving" for an unknown means figuring out its value. Generally, the way to solve for an unknown is to isolate the variable—that is, manipulate the equation until the unknown is alone on one side of the equal sign. Whatever's on the other side of the equal sign is the value of the unknown. Take a look at this example.

$$5(3x^3 - 16) - 22 = 18$$

In this equation, x is the unknown. To solve for x, you need to get x alone. You isolate x by undoing everything that's being done to x in the equation. If x is being squared, you need to take a square root; if x is being multiplied by 3, you need to divide by 3; if x is being decreased by 4, you need to add 4, and so on. The trick is to do these things in the right order. Basically, you should follow PEMDAS in reverse. Start by undoing addition and subtraction, then multiplication and division, then exponents and roots, and, last, what's in parentheses.

The other thing to remember is that any time you do something to one side of an equation, you've got to do it to the other side also. Otherwise you'd be changing the equation, and you're trying to rearrange it, not change it. In this example, you'd start by undoing the subtraction.

$$5(3x^3 - 16) - 22 = 18$$
$$+22 \quad +22$$
$$5(3x^3 - 16) = 40$$

Then undo the multiplication by 5, saving what's in the parentheses for last.

$$5(3x^3 - 16) = 40$$
$$\div 5 \qquad\qquad \div 5$$
$$3x^3 - 16 = 8$$

Once you've gotten down to what's in the parentheses, follow PEMDAS in reverse again—first the subtraction, then the multiplication, and the exponent last.

$$3x^3 - 16 = 8$$
$$+16 \quad +16$$
$$3x^3 = 24$$
$$\div 3 \qquad \div 3$$
$$x^3 = 8$$
$$x = 2$$

At this point, you've solved the equation. You have found that the value of x must be 2. Another way of saying this is that 2 is the root of the equation $5(3x^3 - 16) - 22 = 18$. Equations containing exponents may have more than one root (see pages 42–43, "Exponents," in the last chapter).

Solving Equations with Absolute Value

The rules for solving equations with absolute value are the same. The only difference is that, because what's inside the absolute value signs can be positive or negative, you're solving for two different results.

Let's look at an example:

$$20. \quad |x - 2| = 17$$

Now, we know that either $(x - 2)$ is a negative number or a non-negative number. When a number is negative, the absolute value makes it the inverse, or multiplies it by -1 to yield a positive result. If the number is positive, it remains the same after being sent through the absolute value machine. So when we remove the absolute value bars, we're left with two different equations:

$$x - 2 = 17 \qquad \text{or} \qquad -(x - 2) = 17$$

Now simply solve both equations:

$$
\begin{array}{cccc}
x - 2 = 17 & & \text{or} & -(x - 2) = 17 \\
\underline{+2 \quad +2} & & & x - 2 \ = -17 \\
& & & \underline{+2 \ = +2} \\
x \quad = 19 & & \text{or} & x \qquad = -15
\end{array}
$$

And that's all there is to it!

Vocab Review
Remember that a non-negative number can be either a positive number or zero. Since zero is neither positive nor negative, if we said "positive number" that wouldn't include zero.

DRILL

Practice solving equations in the following examples. Remember that some equations may have more than one root. The answers to these drills can be found in Chapter 12.

1. If $\dfrac{\left(3x^2 - 7\right)}{17} = 4$, then $x =$

2. If $n^2 = 5n$, then $n =$

3. If $\dfrac{2a - 3}{3} = -\dfrac{1}{2}$, then $a =$

4. If $\dfrac{5s + 3}{3} = 21$, then $s =$

5. If $\dfrac{3(8x - 2) + 5}{5} = 4$, then $x =$

6. If $|2m + 5| = 23$, then $m =$

7. If $\left|\dfrac{r - 7}{5}\right| = 4$, then $r =$

FACTORING AND DISTRIBUTING

When manipulating algebraic equations, you'll need to use the tools of factoring and distributing. These are simply ways of rearranging equations to make them easier to work with.

Factoring

Factoring simply means finding some factor that is in every term of an expression and "pulling it out." By "pulling it out," we mean dividing each individual term by that factor, and then placing the whole expression in parentheses with that factor on the outside. Here's an example:

$$x^3 - 5x^2 + 6x = 0$$

On the left side of this equation, every term contains at least one x—that is, x is a factor of every term in the expression. That means you can factor out an x:

$$x^3 - 5x^2 + 6x = 0$$

$$x(x^2 - 5x + 6) = 0$$

The new expression has exactly the same value as the old one; it's just written differently, in a way that might make your calculations easier. Numbers as well as variables can be factored out, as seen in the example below.

$$17c - 51 = 0$$

On the left side of this equation, every term is a multiple of 17. Because 17 is a factor of each term, you can pull it out.

$$17c - 51 = 0$$

$$17(c - 3) = 0$$

$$c - 3 = 0$$

$$c = 3$$

As you can see, factoring can make equations easier to solve.

Distributing

Distributing is factoring in reverse. When an entire expression in parentheses is being multiplied by some factor, you can "distribute" the factor into each term, and get rid of the parentheses. For example:

$$3x(4 + 2x) = 6x^2 + 36$$

On the left side of this equation the parentheses make it difficult to combine terms and simplify the equation. You can get rid of the parentheses by distributing.

$$3x(4 + 2x) = 6x^2 + 36$$

$$12x + 6x^2 = 6x^2 + 36$$

And suddenly, the equation is much easier to solve.

$$12x + 6x^2 = 6x^2 + 36$$

$$-6x^2 \quad -6x^2$$

$$12x = 36$$

$$x = 3$$

DRILL

Practice a little factoring and distributing in the following examples, and keep an eye out for equations that could be simplified by this kind of rearrangement. The answers to these drills can be found in Chapter 12.

3. If $(11x)(50) + (50x)(29) = 4,000$, then $x =$

   (A) 2,000
   (B)   200
   (C)   20
   (D)   2
   (E)   0.2

17. If $ab \neq 0$, $\dfrac{-3b(a+2)+6b}{-ab} =$

   (A) -3
   (B) -2
   (C)   0
   (D)   1
   (E)   3

36. If $x \neq -1$, $\dfrac{x^5 + x^4 + x^3 + x^2}{x^3 + x^2 + x + 1} =$

(A) $4x^2$

(B) x^2

(C) $4x$

(D) x

(E) 4

PLUGGING IN

Plugging In is a technique for short-cutting algebra questions. It works on a certain class of algebra questions in which relationships are defined, but no real numbers are introduced. For example:

11. The use of a neighborhood car wash costs n dollars for a membership and p cents for each wash. If a membership includes a bonus of 4 free washes, which of the following reflects the cost, in dollars, of getting a membership at the car wash and washing a car q times, if q is greater than 4 ?

(A) $100n + pq - 4p$

(B) $n + 100pq - 25p$

(C) $n + pq - \dfrac{p}{25}$

(D) $n + \dfrac{pq}{100} - \dfrac{p}{25}$

(E) $n + \dfrac{p}{100} - \dfrac{q}{4}$

To Number or Not to Number?

Let's say you walk into a candy store. The store is selling certain pieces of candy for 5 cents and 10 cents each. You want to get 3 pieces of the 5 cent candy and 6 pieces of the 10 cent candy. You give the cashier a $5 bill. What's your change?

Ok, now let's say you walk into a candy store run by ETS. This store is selling certain pieces of candy for x cents and y cents each. You want to get m pieces of the x cent candy and n pieces of the y cent candy. You give the cashier a z bill. What's your change?

Which problem would be easier to solve? The one with the numbers! Numbers make everything easier. So why bother with variables when you don't have to?

Here's How to Crack It

In this problem you see a lot of variables in the question and in the answer choices. That's a big clue!

> When you see variables in the answer choices, PLUG IN!

Let's try Plugging In with this problem. We'll start with *n*, the **membership fee.**

Plug In an easy number like 3, so that a membership costs $3.00.

Then, Plug In a number for *p*, the charge per wash. Since this number is in cents, and we'll need to convert it to dollars in the answers, choose a number that can be converted easily to dollars, like 200. Let's make *p* = 200, so a wash costs $2.00.

Last, let's say that *q*, the number of washes, is 5. That's as easy as it gets. With 4 free washes, you're paying for only 1.

Then, just work out the answer to the question using your numbers. How much does it cost for a membership and 5 washes? Well, that's $3.00 for a membership, 4 washes free, and 1 wash for $2.00. The total is $5.00. That means that if you plug your numbers into the answer choices, the right answer should give you 5. We call that your target number—the number you are looking for in the answer choices. Put a double circle around your target number, so that it stands out from all the other numbers you've written down. It looks like a bull's-eye that you're trying to hit:

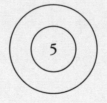

When you plug *n* = 3, *p* = 200, and *q* = 5 into the answer choices, the only answer choice that gives you 5 is (D). That means you've hit your target number, and you're done.

A Big Clue

There will be times when ETS will give you questions that include variables and the phrase "in terms of" (for example, "in terms of *x*"). This is a big clue that you can Plug In. Cross off the phrase "in terms of *x*," because you don't need it to solve the problem.

Take a look at one more:

---○---

13. The size of an art collection is tripled, and then 70 percent of the collection is sold. Acquisitions then increase the size of the collection by 10 percent. The size of the art collection is then what percent of its size before these three changes?

(A) 240%
(B) 210%
(C) 111%
(D) 99%
(E) 21%

Here's How to Crack It

Here's another question in which you aren't given numbers. In this case, you don't know the original size of the art collection. Instead of variables, though, the question and answers contain percents. This is another sign that you can Plug In whatever numbers you like. Because you're working with percentages, 100 is a good number to Plug In—it'll make your math easier.

You start with a collection of 100 items. It's tripled, meaning it increases to 300. Then it's decreased by 70%. That's a decrease of 210, so the collection's size decreases to 90. Then, finally, it increases by 10%. That's an increase of 9, for a final collection size of 99. Since the collection began at 100, it's now at 99% of its original size. The answer is (D). It doesn't matter what number you choose for the original size of the collection—you'll always get the right answer. The trick to choosing numbers is picking ones that make your math easier.

---○---

The idea behind Plugging In is that if these relationships are true, then it doesn't matter what numbers you put into the question; you'll always arrive at the same answer choice. So the easiest way to get through the question is to Plug In easy numbers, follow them through the question, and see which answer choice they lead you to.

Occasionally, more than one answer choice will produce the correct answer. This often occurs when the question asks for something that "must be true." When that happens, eliminate the answer choices that didn't work out, and Plug In some different kinds of numbers. Some numbers you might try are odd and even integers, positive and negative numbers, fractions, zero, positive or

Not Sure When to Plug In? Here Are Some Hints

- The answer choices contain variables, percentages, fractions, or ratios.
- There are unknown quantities or variables in the question.
- The question seems to call for an algebraic equation.
- You see the phrase "in terms of" followed by a variable (for example "in terms of p"). Cross off the phrase "in terms of p," because you don't need it to solve the problem.

negative one, and really big or really small numbers, like 1,000 or −1,000. The new numbers will produce a new target number. Use this new target number to eliminate the remaining incorrect answer choices. You will rarely have to Plug In more than two sets of numbers.

When using Plugging In, keep a few simple rules in mind:

- Avoid Plugging In 1 or 0, which often makes more than one answer choice produce the same number. For the same reason, avoid Plugging In numbers that appear in the answer choices—they're more likely to cause several answer choices to produce your target number.
- Plug In numbers that make your math easy—2, 3, and 5 are good choices in ordinary algebra. Multiples of 100 are good in percentage questions, and multiples of 60 are good in questions dealing with seconds, minutes, and hours.

Plugging In can be an incredibly useful technique. By Plugging In numbers, you're checking your math as you do the problem. When you use algebra, it takes an extra step to check your work with numbers. Also, there are fewer chances to mess up when you Plug In. And you can Plug In even when you don't know how to set up an algebraic equation.

Plugging In is often safer because ETS designs the answer choices so that, if you mess up the algebra, your result will be one of the wrong answers. When your answer matches one of the choices, you think it must be right. Very tempting. Furthermore, all of the answer choices look very similar, algebraically. This is how ETS camouflages correct answers. But when you Plug In, the answers often look very different. Often you'll be able to approximate to eliminate numbers that are obviously too big or too small, without doing a lot of calculation, and that will save you lots of time!

Drill

Try solving the following practice questions by Plugging In. Remember to check all your answer choices, and Plug In a second set of numbers if more than one answer choice produces your target number. The answers to these drills can be found in Chapter 12.

5. The price of an item in a store is p dollars. If the tax on the item is $t\%$, what is the total cost in dollars of n such items, including tax?

   (A) npt

   (B) $npt + 1$

   (C) $\dfrac{np(t+1)}{100}$

   (D) $100n(p + pt)$

   (E) $\dfrac{np(t+100)}{100}$

8. Vehicle A travels at x miles per hour for x hours. Vehicle B travels a miles per hour faster than Vehicle A, and travels b hours longer than Vehicle A. Vehicle B travels how much farther than Vehicle A, in miles?

   (A) $x^2 - ab$
   (B) $a^2 + b^2$
   (C) $ax + bx + ab$
   (D) $x^2 + abx + ab$
   (E) $2x^2 + (a + b)x + ab$

17. For any real number n, $|5-n|-|n-5| =$

    (A) -2
    (B) -1
    (C) 0
    (D) 1
    (E) 2

20. If Company A builds a skateboards per week, and Company B builds b skateboards per day, then in m weeks, Company A builds how many more skateboards than Company B ?

    (A) $7bm$

    (B) $m(a - 7b)$

    (C) $7(ma - mb)$

    (D) $7m(a - b)$

    (E) $\dfrac{m(a-b)}{7}$

23. If $a > 3$ and $b < 3$, then which of the following could be true?

    I. $a - b > 3$
    II. $a + b < 3$
    III. $|a + b| < 3$

    (A) I only
    (B) III only
    (C) I and II only
    (D) II and III only
    (E) I, II, and III

30. For all real numbers, $x^3 < y^3$. Which of the following must be true?

    I. $x < y$
    II. $x^2 < y^2$
    III. $|x| < |y|$

    (A) I only
    (B) III only
    (C) I and II only
    (D) II and III only
    (E) I, II, and III

PLUGGING IN THE ANSWERS (PITA)

Plugging In the Answers (PITA) is another approach to solving algebra questions. It uses numbers instead of algebra to find the answer. As you've just seen, Plugging In is useful on questions whose answer choices contain variables, percentages, fractions, or ratios—not actual numbers. PITA, on the other hand, is useful on questions whose answer choices do contain actual numbers.

ETS always organizes answers in numerical order—usually from least to greatest. You can use this to your advantage by combining PITA and POE.

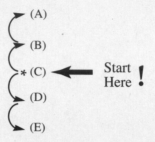

To use PITA on an algebra question, take (C), the middle answer choice, and stick it back into the problem. If it makes all of the statements in the question true, then it's the right answer. If it doesn't, eliminate (C) and try another answer choice. Usually, you'll know from your experience with (C) whether you want to try a smaller or larger answer choice. If (C) is too small, you can eliminate the smaller two choices and try again with the remaining two.

Like Plugging In, PITA can open doors for you when you're unsure how to approach a question with algebra. Also, like Plugging In, it checks your answers as you pick them, eliminating careless errors. Particularly at the tough end of a Math Subject Test, where you're getting into hard material, Plugging In and PITA can enable you to solve problems that would otherwise stump you.

Let's take a look at a PITA example.

─────────○─────────

10. A duck travels from point A to point B. If the duck flies $\frac{3}{4}$ of the way, walks $\frac{1}{9}$ of the way, and swims the remaining 10 kilometers of her trip, what is the total distance in kilometers traveled by the duck?

(A) 36
(B) 45
(C) 56
(D) 72
(E) 108

Here's How to Crack It

To use PITA on this question, you'd start with answer choice (C). The answer choices represent the quantity asked for in the question—in this case, the total distance traveled by the duck. Always know what question you're answering. Answer choice (C), therefore, means that the duck traveled a total distance of 56 kilometers. Follow this information through the problem.

The duck flies $\frac{3}{4}$ of the way. $\frac{3}{4}$ of 56 is 42 kilometers.

The duck walks $\frac{1}{9}$ of the way. $\frac{1}{9}$ of 56 is 6.22 kilometers.

That makes 48.22 kilometers, which leaves 7.78 kilometers in the trip.

BUT the duck swims 10 kilometers!

That means that (C) isn't the right answer. It also tells you that you need a longer trip to fit in all that flying, walking, and swimming; move down to (D), the next largest answer, and try again. At this point, you can also eliminate (A), (B), and (C) because they are too small.

The duck flies $\frac{3}{4}$ of the way. $\frac{3}{4}$ of 72 is 54 kilometers.

The duck walks $\frac{1}{9}$ of the way. $\frac{1}{9}$ of 72 is 8 kilometers.

That makes 62 kilometers, which leaves 10 kilometers in the trip.

And THAT'S exactly how far the duck swims, 10 kilometers. Right answer.

Generally, you'll never have to try more than two answer choices when using PITA thanks to POE—and sometimes, the first answer you try, (C), will be correct. Keep your eyes open for PITA opportunities on the Math Subject Tests, particularly when you run into an algebra question that you're not sure how to solve.

You Should Try PITA Whenever

- there is an unknown or variable in the question, the question asks for an actual value, and the answer choices are all numbers arranged in increasing or decreasing order
- you have the bizarre urge to translate a word problem into a complicated algebraic equation
- you find yourself reading a long, convoluted story about some number, and you don't even know what the number is
- you have no idea how to solve the problem

If, after you Plug In answer choice (C), you're not sure which way to go in the answer choices, don't haggle for too long. Just eliminate (C), pick a direction, and go! If you go the wrong way, you'll know pretty quickly, and then you can head the other way.

DRILL

Solve the following questions by using PITA. Remember to start with (C), the middle answer choice. The answers to these drills can be found in Chapter 12.

11. Matt has 4 more hats than Aaron and half as many hats as Michael. If the three together have 24 hats, how many hats does Michael have?

(A) 7
(B) 9
(C) 12
(D) 14
(E) 18

17. A shipment of 3,200 items is divided into 2 portions so that the difference between the portions is one-half of their average. What is the ratio of the smaller to the larger portion?

(A) 1 : 2
(B) 1 : 3
(C) 2 : 5
(D) 3 : 5
(E) 5 : 8

27. Three distinct positive integers have a sum of 15 and a product of 45. What is the largest of these integers?

(A) 1
(B) 3
(C) 5
(D) 9
(E) 15

Reading Inequality Signs

Here's how you should read the four basic inequality signs:

$a < b$ a is less than b

$a > b$ a is greater than b

$a \leq b$ a is less than or equal to b

$a \geq b$ a is greater than or equal to b

INEQUALITIES

Inequalities can be treated just like equations. You can add, subtract, multiply, and divide on both sides of the inequality sign. And you still solve by isolating the variable. There is one major difference between solving an equation and solving an inequality.

Whenever you multiply or divide both sides of an inequality by a negative, flip the inequality sign.

Multiplying across an inequality by a negative flips the signs of all of the terms in the inequality. The inequality sign itself must also flip.

$$-1(4n - 20 > -3n + 15) \qquad\qquad -1(x \geq 5)$$

$$-4n + 20 < 3n - 15 \qquad\qquad\qquad -x \leq -5$$

As long as you remember this rule, you can treat inequalities just like equations and use all of your algebra tools to solve them.

DRILL

Practice solving inequalities in the following exercises. The answers to these drills can be found in Chapter 12.

1. If $\dfrac{6(5-n)}{4} \leq 3$, then _____

2. If $\dfrac{r+3}{2} < 5$, then _____

3. If $\dfrac{4(1-x)+9}{3} \leq 5$, then _____

4. If $8(3x + 1) + 4 < 15$, then _____

5. If $23 - 4t \geq 11$, then _____

6. If $4n - 25 \leq 19 - 7n$, then _____

7. If $-5(p+2) < 10p - 13$, then _____

8. If $\dfrac{23s+7}{10} \geq 2s + 1$, then _____

9. If $-3x - 16 \leq 2x + 19$, then _____

10. If $\dfrac{14s-11}{9} \geq s - 1$, then _____

WORKING WITH RANGES

Inequalities are also used when discussing the range of possible values a variable could equal. Sometimes you'll see an algebraic phrase in which there are two inequality signs. These are called ranges. Your variable can be any number within a range of numbers. For example: $2 < x < 10$. This means that x can be any number between, but not equal to, 2 and 10. Let's look at this next example:

> At a certain amusement park, anyone under 12 years of age is not permitted to ride the Stupendous Hurlcoaster, because the person could easily lose his or her mind due to the ride's extreme funkiness. Anyone over 60 years of age is also prohibited from the ride, as the incredible velocity of the Hurlcoaster may cause spontaneous coronary explosion. If x is the age of a rider of the Stupendous Hurlcoaster, what is the range of possible values of x ?

The end values of the range are obviously 12 and 60. But are 12 and 60 included in the range themselves, or not? If you read carefully, you'll see that only those under 12 or over 60 are barred from riding the Hurlcoaster. If you're 12 or 60, you're perfectly legal. The range of possible values of x is therefore given by $12 \le x \le 60$. Noticing the difference between "greater than" and "greater than or equal to" is crucial to many range questions.

You can manipulate ranges in a couple of ways. You can add and subtract ranges, as long as their inequality signs point the same way. You can also multiply or divide across a range to produce new information, as long as you obey that basic rule of inequalities—flip the sign if you multiply or divide by a negative number.

DRILL

> If the range of possible values for x is given by $-5 < x < 8$, find the range of possible values for each of the following:
>
> 1. $-x$: _____
> 2. $4x$: _____
> 3. $x + 6$: _____
> 4. $(2 - x)$: _____
> 5. $\dfrac{x}{2}$: _____

Adding Ranges

Occasionally, a question on the Math Subject Tests will require you to add, subtract, or multiply ranges. Take a look at this example:

> If $3 < a < 10$ and $-6 < b < 3$, what is the range of
> possible values of $a + b$?

Here, the range of $(a + b)$ will be the sum of the range of a and the range of b. The easy way to do this is to list out the four ways you can combine the endpoints of the two ranges. To do this, take the smallest a and add it to the smallest b. Then, add the smallest a to the biggest b. Then add the biggest a to the smallest b. Finally, take the biggest a and add it to the biggest b. The biggest and smallest results you get will be the endpoints of the range of $(a + b)$. Watch!

$$3 + -6 = -3$$

$$3 + 3 = 6$$

$$10 + -6 = 4$$

$$10 + 3 = 13$$

The smallest number you found is -3, and the biggest is 13, so the range of possible values looks like the following:

$$-3 < a + b < 13$$

Subtracting Ranges

To subtract one range from another, combine the endpoints just as you did when adding ranges, but in this case, subtract the four combinations of endpoints. Make sure you're subtracting in the order the question asks you to. Let's look at this example.

> If $-4 < a < 5$ and $2 < b < 12$, then what is the
> range of possible values of $a - b$?

This time, take the smallest a and subtract the smallest b. Then, find the smallest a minus the biggest b, and so on.

$$-4 - 2 = -6$$

$$-4 - 12 = -16$$

$$5 - 2 = 3$$

$$5 - 12 = -7$$

So the range you're looking for is:

$$-16 < a - b < 3$$

Multiplying Ranges

To multiply ranges, follow the same steps, but multiply the endpoints. Let's try one.

> If $-3 < f < 4$ and $-7 < g < 2$, then what is the range of possible values of fg ?

These are the four possible products of the bounds of f and g.

$$(-3)(-7) = 21 \qquad\qquad (-3)(2) = -6$$

$$(4)(-7) = -28 \qquad\qquad (4)(2) = 8$$

The greatest of these values is 21 and the least is -28. So the range of possible values of fg is:

$$-28 < fg < 21$$

And that's all there is to dealing with ranges.

DRILL

Try the following range questions. The answers to these drills can be found in Chapter 12.

1. If $-2 \leq a \leq 7$ and $3 \leq b \leq 9$, then what is the range of possible values of $b - a$?

2. If $2 \leq x \leq 11$ and $6 \geq y \geq -4$, then what is the range of possible values of $x + y$?

3. If $-3 \leq n \leq 8$, then what is the range of possible values of n^2 ?

4. If $0 < x < 5$ and $-9 < y < -3$, then what is the range of possible values of $x - y$?

5. If $-3 \leq r \leq 10$ and $-10 \leq s \leq 3$, then what is the range of possible values of $r + s$?

6. If $-6 < c < 0$ and $13 < d < 21$, then what is the range of possible values of cd ?

7. If $|3 - x| \leq 4$, then what is the range of possible values of x ?

8. If $|2a + 7| \geq 13$, then what is the range of possible values of a ?

Abso–what??
Trouble with absolute value? Pay special attention to the explanations of questions 7 and 8 from this drill.

DIRECT AND INDIRECT VARIATION

Direct and indirect variation are specific relationships between quantities. Quantities that vary directly are said to be in *proportion* or *proportional*. Quantities that vary indirectly are said to be *inversely proportional*.

Direct Variation

If x and y are in direct variation, that can be said in several ways: x and y are in proportion; x and y change proportionally; or x varies directly as y. All of these descriptions come down to the same thing: x and y increase and decrease together. Specifically, they mean that the quantity $\frac{x}{y}$ will always have the same numerical value. That's all there is to it. Take a look at a question based on this idea.

> ### A Great Way to Remember
> To remember direct variation, think "direct means divide." So in order to solve, you set up a proportion with a fraction on each side of the equation. Just solve for the one number you don't know. There are two formulas associated with direct variation that may be familiar to you. They are: $\frac{y_1}{x_1} = \frac{y_2}{x_2}$ or $y = kx$, where k is a constant.

---

17. If n varies directly as m, and n is 3 when m is 24, then what is the value of n when m is 11 ?

    (A) 1.375
    (B) 1.775
    (C) 1.95
    (D) 2.0
    (E) 2.125

Here's How to Crack It

To solve the problem, use the definition of direct variation: $\frac{n}{m}$ must always have the same numerical value. Set up a proportion.

$$\frac{3}{24} = \frac{n}{11}$$

Solve by cross-multiplying and isolating n.

$$24n = 33$$

$$n = 33 \div 24$$

$$n = 1.375$$

And that's all there is to it. The correct answer is (A). All direct variation questions can be answered this way.

Opposites Attract

A great way to remember indirect or inverse variation is that direct and indirect are opposites. What's the opposite of division? Multiplication! So set up an inverse variation as two multiplication problems on either side of an equation. There are two formulas associated with indirect variation that may be familiar to you. They are: $x_1 y_1 = x_2 y_2$ or $y = \dfrac{k}{x}$, where k is a constant.

Indirect Variation

If x and y are in inverse variation, this can be said in several ways as well: x and y are in inverse proportion; x and y are inversely proportional; or x varies indirectly as y. All of these descriptions come down to the same thing: x increases when y decreases, and decreases when y increases. Specifically, they mean that the quantity xy will always have the same numerical value.

Take a look at this question based on inverse variation:

15. If a varies inversely as b, and $a = 3$ when $b = 5$, then what is the value of a when $b = 7$?

   (A)   2.14
   (B)   2.76
   (C)   3.28
   (D)   4.2
   (E)   11.67

Here's How to Crack It

To answer the question, use the definition of inverse variation. That is, the quantity ab must always have the same value. Therefore, you can set up this simple equation.

$$3 \times 5 = a \times 7$$
$$7a = 15$$
$$a = 15 \div 7$$
$$a = 2.142857$$

So the correct answer is (A). All inverse variation questions on the Math Subject Tests can be handled this way.

DRILL

Try these practice exercises using the definitions of direct and inverse variation. The answers to these drills can be found in Chapter 12.

15. If a varies inversely as b, and $a = 3$ when $b = 5$, then what is the value of a when $b = x$?

   (A) $\dfrac{3}{x}$

   (B) $\dfrac{5}{x}$

   (C) $\dfrac{15}{x}$

   (D) $3x$

   (E) $3x^2$

18. If n varies directly as m, and $n = 5$ when $m = 4$, then what is the value of n when $m = 5$?

   (A) 4.0
   (B) 4.75
   (C) 5.5
   (D) 6.25
   (E) 7.75

24. If p varies directly as q, and $p = 3$ when $q = 10$, then what is the value of p when $q = 1$?

   (A) 0.3
   (B) 0.43
   (C) 0.5
   (D) 4.3
   (E) 4.33

26. If y varies directly as x^2, and $y = 24$ when $x = 3.7$, what is the value of y when $x = 8.3$?

   (A) 170.67
   (B) 120.77
   (C) 83.23
   (D) 64.00
   (E) 53.83

WORK AND TRAVEL QUESTIONS

Word problems dealing with work and travel tend to cause a lot of careless mistakes, because the relationships among distance, time, and speed—or among work-rate, work, and time—sometimes confuse test takers. When working with questions about travel, just remember this:

$$\text{distance} = \text{rate} \times \text{time}$$

When working with questions about work being done, remember this:

$$\text{work done} = \text{rate of work} \times \text{time}$$

Look familiar?

If these two formulas seem the same, it's because they are. After all, what is work done if not the distance from the start of work to the end? Don't worry about learning too many equations; generally speaking, the few you'll need are more useful than their wording indicates.

DRILL

Answer the following practice questions using these formulas. The answers to these drills can be found in Chapter 12.

11. A factory contains a series of water tanks, all of the same size. If Pump 1 can fill 12 of these tanks in a 12-hour shift, and Pump 2 can fill 11 tanks in the same time, then how many tanks can the two pumps fill, working together, in 1 hour?

    (A) 0.13
    (B) 0.35
    (C) 1.92
    (D) 2.88
    (E) 3.33

12. A projectile travels 227 feet in one second. If there are 5,280 feet in 1 mile, then which of the following best approximates the projectile's speed in miles per hour?

    (A) 155
    (B) 170
    (C) 194
    (D) 252
    (E) 333

18. A train travels from Langston to Hughesville and back in 5.5 hours. If the two towns are 200 miles apart, what is the average speed of the train in miles per hour?

(A) 36.36
(B) 72.73
(C) 109.09
(D) 110.10
(E) 120.21

25. Jules can make m muffins in s minutes. Alice can make n muffins in t minutes. Which of the following gives the number of muffins that Jules and Alice can make together in 30 minutes?

(A) $\dfrac{m+n}{30st}$

(B) $\dfrac{30(m+n)}{st}$

(C) $30(mt+ns)$

(D) $\dfrac{30(mt+ns)}{st}$

(E) $\dfrac{mt+ns}{30st}$

Average Speed

The "average speed" question is a specialized breed of travel question. Here's what a basic "average speed" question might look like.

15. Roberto travels from his home to the beach, driving at 30 miles per hour. He returns along the same route at 50 miles per hour. If the distance from Roberto's house to the beach is 10 miles, then what is Roberto's average speed for the round-trip in miles per hour?

(A) 32.5
(B) 37.5
(C) 40.0
(D) 42.5
(E) 45.0

Don't Be Joe!
Remember, Joe takes the easy way out. He thinks that if you need the average of two averages, you should just average them. No! But knowing what Joe would do helps you. Now you know you can eliminate (C), because it's what Joe would pick.

The easy mistake to make on this question is to simply choose answer choice (C), the average of the two speeds. Average speed isn't found by averaging speeds, however. Instead, you have to use this formula:

$$\text{average speed} = \frac{\text{total distance}}{\text{total time}}$$

The total distance is easy to figure out—10 miles each way is a total of 20 miles. Total time is a little trickier. For that, you have to use the "distance = rate × time" formula. Here, it's useful to rearrange the eqution to read as follows:

$$\text{time} = \frac{\text{distance}}{\text{rate}}$$

Look Familiar?

This formula may look familiar to you. That's because it's taken from our average pie. Another way to work with average speed questions is to use the average pie where the total is the total distance and the number of things is the time. So it would look like this:

On the way to the beach, Roberto traveled 10 miles at 30 mph, which took 0.333 hours, according to the formula. On the way home, he traveled 10 miles at 50 mph, which took 0.2 hours. That makes 20 miles in a total of .533 hours. Plug those numbers into the average-speed formula, and you get an average speed of 37.5 mph. The answer is (B).

Here's a general tip for "average speed" questions: On any round-trip in which the traveler moves at one speed heading out and another speed returning, the traveler's average speed will be a little lower than the average of the two speeds.

DRILL

Try these "average speed" questions. The answers to these drills can be found in Chapter 12.

19. Alexandra jogs from her house to the lake at 12 miles per hour and jogs back by the same route at 9 miles per hour. If the path from her house to the lake is 6 miles long, what is her average speed in miles per hour for the round-trip?

(A) 11.3
(B) 11.0
(C) 10.5
(D) 10.3
(E) 10.1

24. A truck travels 50 miles from Town S to Town T in 50 minutes, and then immediately drives 40 miles from Town T to Town U in 40 minutes. What is the truck's average speed in miles per hour, from Town S to Town U ?

(A) 1
(B) 10
(C) 45
(D) 60
(E) 90

33. Ben travels a certain distance at 25 miles per hour and returns across the same distance at 50 miles per hour. What is his average speed in miles per hour for the round-trip?

(A) 37.5
(B) 33.3
(C) 32.0
(D) 29.5
(E) It cannot be determined from the information given.

SIMULTANEOUS EQUATIONS

It's possible to have a set of equations that can't be solved individually but can be solved in combination. A good example of such a set of equations would be:

$$4x + 2y = 18$$

$$x + y = 5$$

You can't solve either equation by itself. But you can if you put them together. It's called simultaneous equations. All you do is stack them and then add or subtract them to find what you're looking for. Often, what you're looking for is another equation. For example, the question that contains the two equations you were given wants to know what the value of $10x + 6y$ is. Do you need to know x or y? No! You just need to know $10x + 6y$. Let's try adding the two equations:

$$\begin{array}{r} 4x + 2y = 18 \\ +\ x +\ \ y = 5 \\ \hline 5x + 3y = 23 \end{array}$$

Did adding help? It did! Even though we didn't get what they were asking for, we did get half of what they were asking for. So just multiply the entire equation by 2 and you have your answer: 46.

That Nasty Phrase "In Terms Of"
Remember how we had you cross off the phrase "in terms of" when you plugged in because it doesn't help you at all? Well, solving x "in terms of" y for simultaneous equations doesn't help either. It takes too much time and there is too much room for error to solve in terms of one variable and then put that whole thing into the other equation. And much of the time, that's unnecessary because we don't care what the values of the individual variables are!

Here's another example of a system of simultaneous equations as they might appear on a Math Subject Test question. Try it.

Add It Up

Do you notice how adding brings you close to what the question is asking for?

7. If x and y are real numbers such that $3x + 4y = 10$ and $2x - 4y = 5$, then what is the value of x ?

$$\begin{array}{r} 3x + 4y = 10 \\ +\ 2x - 4y = 5 \\ \hline 5x = 15 \\ x = 3 \end{array}$$

In the question above, instead of solving to find a third equation, you need to find one of the variables. Your job doesn't change: Stack 'em; then add or subtract. This will be the case with every simultaneous equations question. Every once in a while you may want to multiply or divide one equation by a number before you add or subtract.

Try another one. Solve it yourself before checking the explanation.

8. If $12a - 3b = 131$ and $5a - 10b = 61$, then what is the value of $a + b$?

Avoid Subtraction Mistakes

If adding doesn't work and you want to try subtracting, wait! Multiply one of the equations by –1 and add instead. That way you ensure that you don't make any calculation errors along the way.

This time adding didn't work, did it? Let's go through and see what subtraction does:

$$\begin{array}{r} 12a - 3b = 131 \\ -1(5a - 10b) = 61 \\ \hline 12a - 3b = 131 \\ -5a + 10b = -61 \\ \hline 7a + 7b = 70 \\ a + b = 10 \end{array}$$

A little practice will enable you to see quickly whether adding or subtracting will be more helpful. Sometimes it may be necessary to multiply one of the equations by a convenient factor to make terms that will cancel out properly. For example:

6. If $4n - 8m = 6$, and $-5n + 4m = 3$, then $n =$

$$4n - 8m = 6$$
$$-5n + 4m = 3$$

Here, it quickly becomes apparent that neither adding nor subtracting will combine these two equations very usefully. However, things look a little brighter when the second equation is multiplied by 2.

$$4n - 8m = 6$$
$$-10n + 8m = 6$$
$$2(-5n + 4m = 3) \qquad \overline{-6n \quad\;\; = 12}$$
$$n \quad\;\; = -2$$

Occasionally, a simultaneous equation can be solved only by *multiplying* all of the pieces together. This will generally be the case only when the equations themselves involve multiplication alone, not the kind of addition and subtraction that the previous equations contained. Take a look at this example:

$$ab = 3 \qquad\qquad bc = \frac{5}{9} \qquad\qquad ac = 15$$

34. If the above statements are true, what is one possible value of *abc* ?

    (A)   5.0
    (B)   8.33
    (C)   9.28
    (D)   18.54
    (E)   25.0

Here's How to Crack It

This is a tough one. No single one of the three small equations can be solved by itself. In fact, no two of them together can be solved. It takes all three to solve the system, and here's how it's done:

$$ab \times bc \times ac = 3 \times \frac{5}{9} \times 15$$

$$aabbcc = 25$$

$$a^2 b^2 c^2 = 25$$

Once you've multiplied all three equations together, all you have to do is take the square roots of both sides, and you've got a value for *abc*.

$$a^2 b^2 c^2 = 25$$

$$abc = 5, -5$$

And so (A) is the correct answer.

# of Equations = # of Variables

We've been talking about two equations, two variables. But ETS doesn't stop there. A good rule of thumb is, if the number of equations is equal to the number of variables, you can solve the equations. So count 'em and don't get discouraged! They're always easier than they look!

Where's the Trap?

Remember that a number 34 is a difficult question. What do you notice about choice (E)?

DRILL

Try answering the following practice questions by solving equations simultaneously. The answers to these drills can be found in Chapter 12.

26. If $a + 3b = 6$, and $4a - 3b = 14$, $a =$

    (A) −4
    (B) 2
    (C) 4
    (D) 10
    (E) 20

31. If $2x - 7y = 12$ and $-8x + 3y = 2$, which of the following is the value of $x - y$?

    (A) 12.0
    (B) 8.0
    (C) 5.5
    (D) 1.0
    (E) 0.8

$$ab = \frac{1}{8}, bc = 6, ac = 3$$

34. If all of the above statements are true, what is one possible value of abc ?

    (A) 3.75
    (B) 2.25
    (C) 2.0
    (D) 1.5
    (E) 0.25

37. If $xyz = 4$ and $y^2z = 5$, what is the value of $\dfrac{x}{y}$?

    (A) 20.0
    (B) 10.0
    (C) 1.25
    (D) 1.0
    (E) 0.8

FOIL

A binomial is an algebraic expression that has two terms (pieces connected by addition or subtraction). FOIL is how to multiply two binomials together.

The letters of FOIL stand for:

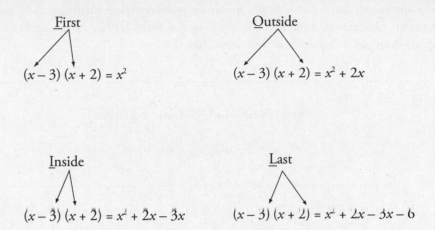

First

$(x - 3)(x + 2) = x^2$

Outside

$(x - 3)(x + 2) = x^2 + 2x$

Inside

$(x - 3)(x + 2) = x^2 + 2x - 3x$

Last

$(x - 3)(x + 2) = x^2 + 2x - 3x - 6$

Suppose you wanted to do the following multiplication:

$$(x + 5)(x - 2)$$

You would multiply the two *first* terms together, $(x)(x) = x^2$.
And then the *outside* terms, $(x)(-2) = -2x$.
And then the *inside* terms, $(5)(x) = 5x$.
And finally the two *last* terms, $(5)(-2) = -10$.

String the four products together and simplify them to produce an answer.

$$x^2 - 2x + 5x - 10$$

$$x^2 + 3x - 10$$

And that's the product of $(x + 5)$ and $(x - 2)$.

DRILL

Practice using FOIL on the following binomial multiplications. The answers to these drills can be found in Chapter 12.

1. $(x - 2)(x + 11) =$

2. $(b + 5)(b + 7) =$

3. $(x - 3)(x - 9) =$

4. $(2x - 5)(x + 1) =$

5. $(n2 + 5)(n - 3) =$

6. $(3a + 5)(2a - 7) =$

7. $(x - 3)(x - 6) =$

8. $(c - 2)(c + 9) =$

9. $(d + 5)(d - 1) =$

FACTORING QUADRATICS

An expression like $x^2 + 3x + 10$ is a quadratic polynomial. A quadratic is an expression that fits into the general form $ax^2 + bx + c$, with a, b, and c as constants. An equation in general quadratic form looks like this:

General Form of a Quadratic Equation

$$ax^2 + bx + c = 0$$

Often, the best way to solve a quadratic equation is to factor it into two binomials—basically FOIL in reverse. Let's take a look at the quadratic you worked with in the previous section, and the binomials that are its factors.

$$x^2 + 3x - 10 = (x + 5)(x - 2)$$

Notice that the coefficient of the quadratic's middle term (3) is the sum of the constants in the binomials (5 and –2), and that the third term of the quadratic (–10) is the product of those constants. That relationship between a quadratic expression and its factors will always be true. To factor a quadratic, look for a pair of constants whose sum equals the coefficient of the middle term, and whose product equals the last term of the quadratic. Suppose you had to solve this equation:

$$x^2 - 6x + 8 = 0$$

Your first step would be to factor the quadratic polynomial. That means looking for a pair of numbers that add up to –6 and multiply to 8. Because their sum is negative but their product is positive, you know that the numbers are both negative. And as always, there's only one pair of numbers that fits the bill—in this case, –2 and –4.

$$x^2 - 6x + 8 = 0$$

$$(x - 2)(x - 4) = 0$$

Since zero multiplied by anything is equal to zero, this equation will be true if $(x - 2) = 0$ or if $(x - 4) = 0$. Therefore,

$$x = \{2, 4\}$$

Two and four are therefore called the zeros of the equation. They are also known as the roots or solutions of the equation.

Once a quadratic is factored, it's easy to solve for x. The product of the binomials can be zero only if one of the binomials is equal to zero—and there are only two values of x that will make one of the binomials equal to zero (2 and 4). The equation is solved.

DRILL

Solve the following equations by factoring the quadratic polynomials. Write down all of the roots of each equation (values of the variable that make the equations true). The answers to these drills can be found in Chapter 12.

1. $a^2 - 3a + 2 = 0$
2. $d^2 + 8d + 7 = 0$
3. $x^2 + 4x - 21 = 0$
4. $3x^2 + 9x - 30 = 0$
5. $2x^2 + 40x + 198 = 0$

6. $p^2 + 10p = 39$
7. $c^2 + 9c + 20 = 0$
8. $s^2 + 4s - 12 = 0$
9. $x^2 - 3x - 4 = 0$
10. $n^4 - 3n^2 - 10 = 0$

Special Quadratic Identities

There are a few quadratic expressions that you should be able to factor at a glance. Because they are useful mathematically, and above all, because ETS likes to put them on the Math Subject Tests, you should memorize the following identities:

$$(x + y)^2 = x^2 + 2xy + y^2$$

$$(x - y)^2 = x^2 - 2xy + y^2$$

$$(x + y)(x - y) = x^2 - y^2$$

Here are some examples of these quadratic identities in action.

1. $n^2 + 10n + 25 = (n + 5)(n + 5) = (n + 5)^2$
2. $r^2 - 16 = (r + 4)(r - 4)$
3. $n^2 - 4n + 4 = (n - 2)(n - 2) = (n - 2)^2$

But knowing the quadratic identities will do more for you than just allow you to factor some expressions quickly. ETS writes questions based specifically on these identities. Such questions are easy to solve if you remember these equations and use them, and quite tricky (or even impossible) if you don't. Here's an example.

---

36. If $a + b = 7$, and $a^2 + b^2 = 37$, then what is the value of ab ?

    (A)   6
    (B) 12
    (C) 15
    (D) 22
    (E) 30

Here's How to Crack It

Algebraically, this is a tough problem to crack. You can't divide $a^2 + b^2$ by $a + b$ and get anything useful. In fact, most of the usual algebraic approaches to questions like these don't work here. Even plugging the answer choices back into the question (PITA) isn't very helpful. What you can do is recognize that the question is giving you all of the pieces you need to build the quadratic identity: $(x + y)^2 = x^2 + 2xy + y^2$. To solve the problem, just rearrange the identity a little and Plug In the values given by the question.

$$(a + b)^2 = a^2 + b^2 + 2ab$$

$$(7)^2 = 37 + 2ab$$

$$49 = 37 + 2ab$$

$$12 = 2ab$$

$$6 = ab$$

And presto, the answer appears. It's not easy to figure out what a or b is specifically—and you don't need to. Just find the value asked for in the question. If you remember the quadratic identities, solving the problem is easy.

DRILL

Try solving the following questions using the quadratic identities, and take note of the clues that tell you when the identities will be useful. The answers to these drills can be found in Chapter 12.

17. If $n - m = -3$ and $n^2 - m^2 = 24$, then which of the following is the sum of n and m ?

(A) –8
(B) –6
(C) –4
(D) 6
(E) 8

19. If $x + y = 3$ and $x^2 + y^2 = 8$, then $xy =$

(A) 0.25
(B) 0.5
(C) 1.5
(D) 2.0
(E) 2.25

24. If the sum of two nonzero integers is 9 and the sum of their squares is 36, then what is the product of the two integers?

(A) 9.0
(B) 13.5
(C) 18.0
(D) 22.5
(E) 45.0

Pencil It In
Don't forget to put pencil to paper on these and other algebra questions with lots of steps. Seeing your work will help you better understand the questions and solutions and avoid careless mistakes.

THE QUADRATIC FORMULA

Unfortunately, not all quadratic equations can be factored by the reverse-FOIL method. The reverse-FOIL method is practical only when the roots of the equation are integers. Sometimes, however, the roots of a quadratic equation will be non-integer decimal numbers, and sometimes a quadratic equation will have no real roots at all. Consider the following quadratic equation:

$$x^2 - 7x + 8 = 0$$

There are no integers that add up to –7 and multiply to 8. This quadratic cannot be factored in the usual way. To solve this equation, it's necessary to use the quadratic formula—a formula that produces the root or roots of any equation in the general quadratic form $ax^2 + bx + c = 0$.

**In Case You
Were Worried...**
On Math Level 1, the quadratic formula is necessary only on difficult questions. You may be able to skip over tough quadratic equation questions and avoid having to use the quadratic formula altogether.

The a, b, and c in the formula refer to the coefficients of an expression in the form $ax^2 + bx + c$. For the equation $x^2 - 7x + 8 = 0$, $a = 1$, $b = -7$, and $c = 8$. Plug these values into the quadratic formula and you get the roots of the equation.

$$x = \frac{-(-7) + \sqrt{(-7)^2 - 4(1)(8)}}{2(1)} \qquad x = \frac{-(-7) - \sqrt{(-7)^2 - 4(1)(8)}}{2(1)}$$

$$x = \frac{7 + \sqrt{49 - 32}}{2} \qquad\qquad x = \frac{7 - \sqrt{49 - 32}}{2}$$

$$x = \frac{7 + \sqrt{17}}{2} \qquad\qquad\qquad x = \frac{7 - \sqrt{17}}{2}$$

$$x = 5.56 \qquad\qquad\qquad\qquad x = 1.44$$

So the equation $x^2 - 7x + 8 = 0$ has two real roots, 5.56 and 1.44.

It's possible to tell quickly, without going all the way through the quadratic formula, how many roots an equation has. The part of the quadratic formula under the radical, $b^2 - 4ac$, is called the *discriminant*. The value of the discriminant gives you the following information about a quadratic equation:

- If $b^2 - 4ac > 0$, then the equation has two distinct real roots.
- If $b^2 - 4ac = 0$, then the equation has one distinct real root and is a perfect square. Actually, it has two identical real roots, which ETS will call a "double root."
- If $b^2 - 4ac < 0$, then the equation has no real roots. Both of its roots are imaginary.

DRILL

In the following exercises, use the discriminant to find out how many roots each equation has and whether the roots are real or imaginary. For equations with real roots, find the exact value of those roots using the quadratic formula. The answers to these drills can be found in Chapter 12.

1. $x^2 - 7x + 5 = 0$
2. $3a^2 - 3a + 7 = 0$
3. $s^2 - 6s + 4 = 0$
4. $x^2 - 2 = 0$
5. $n^2 + 5n + 6.25 = 0$

GRAPHING CALCULATOR TO THE RESCUE

Perhaps the easiest way to find the roots of a hard-to-factor quadratic is to graph it on your calculator and see where the quadratic intersects the x-axis. Your calculator will most likely have several functions that can help you find the answer(s) like "zeros," "intersect," "trace," and/or "table." Consult your calculator's manual and use whatever method you're most comfortable with.

Summary

○ Plugging In is a great way to sidestep the land-mines that ETS tries to set for you.

○ You can Plug In whenever
- you see variables, percents, or fractions (without an original amount) in the answers
- you're tempted to write and then solve an algebraic equation
- you see the phrase "in terms of" in the question
- there are unknown quantities or variables in the question

○ Plug In the answer choices when you have numbers in the answers but don't know where to start or you are still tempted to write an algebraic equation. Don't forget to start with choice (C)!

○ Inequalities get solved just like equations, but when you multiply or divide by a negative number, flip the sign.

○ When combining ranges, remember to write out all four possibilities.

○ Absolute value questions often have two answers. Write out and solve both equations created by the absolute value.

○ Direct and indirect variation questions ask for the relationships between numbers:
- Direct: as x goes up, y goes up. Direct means divide. So you'll have an equation with two fractions.
- Indirect: as x goes up, y goes down. Indirect (also known as inverse) means multiply. So you'll have an equation with two quantities being multiplied.

○ Work and travel questions often require either the rate equation: distance = rate × time (or work done = rate of work × time), or the average pie, which can be used to find average speed.

o   Simultaneous equation questions don't require solving one variable in terms of another. Just stack 'em and add or subtract to find what you need. Remember that you can multiply or divide before or after you add or subtract to get to what you want.

o   The general form for a quadratic equation is $ax^2 + bx + c = 0$. To find the factors, just reverse FOIL the equation. There are three special quadratics that you should keep an eye out for to save time and brainpower. They are:

   • $(x + y)^2 = x^2 + 2xy + y^2$
   • $(x - y)^2 = x^2 - 2xy + y^2$
   • $(x + y)(x - y) = x^2 - y^2$

o   If you have a quadratic equation that you can't factor, try using the quadratic formula:

$$x = \frac{-b \pm \sqrt{b^2 - 4ac}}{2a}$$

Chapter 5
Plane Geometry

ETS uses the term "plane geometry" to refer to the kind of geometry that is commonly tested on the SAT—questions about lines and angles, triangles and other polygons, and circles. Simply put, plane geometry is the study of two-dimensional figures in a plane. Don't confuse plane geometry with coordinate geometry, which involves plotting ordered pairs of numbers on a grid, referred to as the "coordinate plane."

Questions testing plane geometry appear almost exclusively on the Math Level 1 Subject Test. About 20 percent of the questions on the Math Level 1 concern plane geometry. None of the questions on the Math Level 2 will focus on plane geometry, but you'll need the tools in this chapter to answer some Math Level 2 questions about coordinate geometry, solid geometry, and trigonometry.

Definitions

Here are some geometry terms that appear on the Math Subject Tests. Make sure you're familiar with them. If the meaning of any of these vocabulary words keeps slipping your mind, add that word to your flash cards.

Line	A "line" in plane geometry is perfectly straight and extends infinitely in both directions.
Line Segment	A line segment is a section of a line—still perfectly straight, but having limited length. It has two endpoints.
Ray	A ray has one endpoint and extends infinitely in one direction.
Bisector	Any line that cuts a line segment, angle, or polygon exactly in half. It *bisects* another shape.
Midpoint	The point that divides a line segment into two equal halves.
Equidistant	Having equal distance from two different things.
Plane	A "plane" in plane geometry is a perfectly flat surface that extends infinitely in two dimensions.
Complementary Angles	Angles whose measures add up to 90 degrees.
Supplementary Angles	Angles whose measures add up to 180 degrees.
Parallel Lines	Lines that run in exactly the same direction—they are separated by a constant distance, never growing closer together or farther apart. Parallel lines never intersect.
Polygon	A flat shape formed by straight line segments, such as a rectangle or triangle.
Regular Polygon	A polygon that has all equal sides and angles. For example, equilateral triangles and squares are regular.
Quadrilateral	A four-sided polygon.
Altitude	A vertical line drawn from the polygon's base to the opposite vertex. Altitudes are always drawn perpendicular to the base.
Perimeter	The sum of the lengths of a polygon's sides.
Radius	A line segment extending from the center of a circle to a point on that circle.
Arc	A portion of a circle's edge.
Chord	A line segment connecting two distinct points on a circle.
Sector	A portion of a circle's area between two radii, like a slice of pie.

Inscribed	A shape that is *inscribed* in another shape is placed inside that shape with the tightest possible fit. For example, a circle inscribed in a square is the largest circle that can be placed inside that square. The two shapes will touch at points, but they'll never overlap.
Circumscribed	A *circumscribed* shape is drawn around another shape with the tightest fit possible. For example, a circle circumscribed around a square is the smallest circle that can be drawn around that square. The two shapes will touch at points, but they'll never overlap.
Perpendicular	Perpendicular lines are at right angles to one another.
Tangent	Something that is *tangent* to a curve touches that curve at only one point without crossing it. A shape may be "internally" or "externally" tangent to a curve, meaning that it may touch the inside or outside of the curve.

BASIC RULES OF LINES AND ANGLES

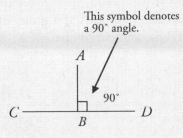

This symbol denotes a 90° angle.

A right angle has a measure of 90°. The angles formed by perpendicular lines are right angles. In the figure above, we see that $AB \perp CD$. The symbol $\perp$ means "perpendicular."

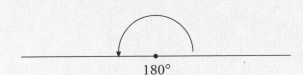

180°

Approximation

In Chapter 2, we discussed approximation, and how it can help you use POE to eliminate answer choices that are too big or too small. Unless ETS indicates that a figure is NOT drawn to scale, you can assume it is and use approximation to eliminate impossible lengths, angles, and areas (such as shaded regions). If a figure is not drawn to scale, you should redraw it according to any information ETS gives you. If, on the other hand, no figure is given at all, you'll want to make sure to draw one yourself so you can solve the problem more easily. Try to make your picture match the information given as closely as possible—you may be able to approximate and eliminate answer choices that are the wrong size.

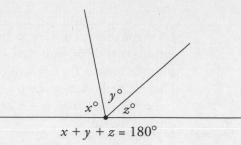

$$x + y + z = 180°$$

An angle opened up into a straight line (called a "straight angle") has a measure of 180°. If a number of angles makes up a straight line, then the measures of those angles add up to 180°.

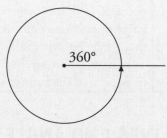

360°

Any line rotated through a full circle moves through 360°. If a group of angles makes up a full circle, then the measures of those angles add up to 360°.

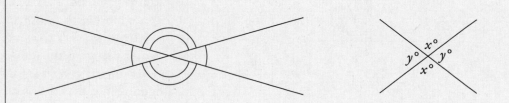

When two lines cross, opposite angles are equal (these are called "vertical angles"). Adjacent angles form straight lines and, therefore, add up to 180°.

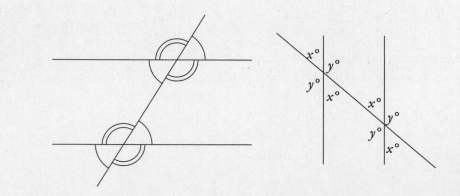

Fred's theorem: When parallel lines are crossed by a third line, two kinds of angles are formed—little angles and big angles. All of the little angles are equal, all of the big angles are equal, and any little angle plus any big angle equals 180°. Why is it called "Fred's" theorem? Well, we had to call it something and Fred is as good a name as any.

ETS will sometimes use the parallel symbol as well. For example, $AC \parallel DE$ means that AC is parallel to DE. Think of the two *l*'s in *parallel* to help you remember this.

Likewise, the symbol for perpendicular is ⊥, as in $GH \perp JK$. It's easy to remember this symbol because it looks like perpendicular lines: two lines meeting to form right angles.

What's with All the Symbols?

In geometry questions ETS sometimes will write out the geometric phrase "line segment *AB*." Sometimes, however, the test writers will use only geometric symbols or write these kinds of things in "code form." So line segment *AB* would be $\overline{AB}$.

This is just one more way ETS tries to confuse you or throw you off your game. You'll notice symbols and their explanations in sidebars throughout the book to remind you what they mean. Make sure you're familiar with them!

DRILL

In the following exercises, find each measure. The answers to these drills can be found in Chapter 12.

$f \parallel g$

$m \parallel n$

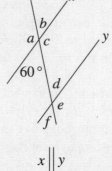

$x \parallel y$

1. x ____   a ____
    y ____   b ____
    z ____   c ____

2. x ____
    y ____

3. a ____   d ____
    b ____   e ____
    c ____   f ____

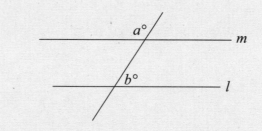

8. If line l and line m are parallel, then $a + b =$

   (A) 90°
   (B) 180°
   (C) 270°
   (D) 360°
   (E) It cannot be determined from the information given.

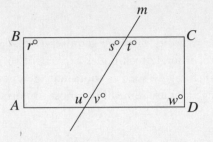

13. If line *m* intersects rectangle *ABCD* as shown, then which of the following is equal to *t* ?

(A) *v*
(B) *w*
(C) *r + s*
(D) *w − v*
(E) *r + w − s*

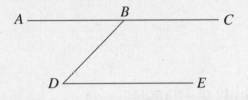

16. If $AC \parallel DE$, then which of the following is the difference between the degree measures of $\angle DBC$ and $\angle BDE$?

(A)   0°
(B)   45°
(C)   90°
(D) 180°
(E) It cannot be determined from the information given.

TRIANGLES

Triangles appear in the majority of plane geometry questions on the Math Subject Tests. What's more, triangle techniques are useful in solving questions that don't obviously relate to triangles, such as coordinate geometry and solid geometry questions. The following rules are some of the most important in plane geometry.

The Rule of 180°

For starters, the three angles of any triangle add up to 180°. This rule helps to solve a great many plane geometry questions.

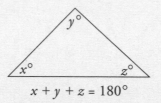

$$x + y + z = 180°$$

The Proportionality of Triangles

Opposite Side? Huh?
If you have trouble figuring out which side is opposite a certain angle in a triangle, remember this simple rule: The opposite side is the side that doesn't touch the angle you're talking about.

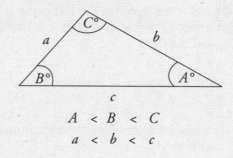

$$A < B < C$$
$$a < b < c$$

In a triangle, the smallest angle is always opposite the shortest side; the middle angle is opposite the middle side; and the largest angle is opposite the longest side. If a triangle has sides of equal length, then the opposite angles will have equal measures.

The Third Side Rule

The *Third Side Rule:* The length of any side of a triangle must be between the sum and the difference of the lengths of the other two sides.

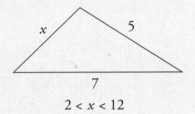

$$2 < x < 12$$

Sneaky ETS!
The Third Side Rule is commonly used to create tricky triangle questions.

Isosceles Triangles

An isosceles triangle has two equal sides and two equal angles.

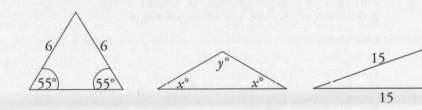

Isosceles and the Third Side
Watch out for questions that employ the Third Side Rule in isosceles triangles.

Equilateral Triangles

An equilateral triangle has three equal sides and three equal angles. Each angle has a measure of 60°.

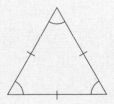

DRILL

The answers to these drills can be found in Chapter 12.

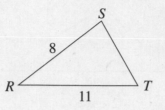

12. Which of the following expresses the possible values of p, if p is the perimeter of RST ?

   (A) $3 < p < 19$
   (B) $3 < p < 22$
   (C) $19 < p < 22$
   (D) $19 < p < 38$
   (E) $22 < p < 38$

17. An isosceles triangle has sides of lengths 5, 11, and x. How many possible values of x exist?

   (A) One
   (B) Two
   (C) Three
   (D) Four
   (E) More than four

18. The distance between points A and D is 6, and the distance between D and F is 4. Which of the following is NOT a possible value for the distance between F and A ?

   (A)   3
   (B)   4
   (C)   7
   (D)   9
   (E)   11

Right Triangles

Right triangles are, not surprisingly, triangles that contain right angles. The sides of right triangles are referred to by special names. The sides that form the right angle are called the legs of the triangle and the longest side, opposite the right angle, is called the hypotenuse. There are many techniques and rules for right triangles that won't work on just any triangle. The most important of these rules is the relationship between sides described by the Pythagorean theorem.

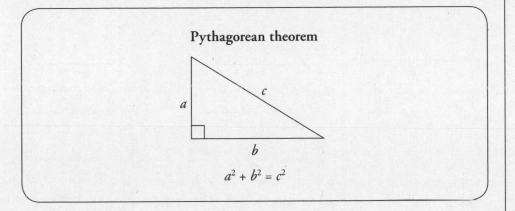

Pythagorean theorem

$$a^2 + b^2 = c^2$$

Keep in mind when you use the Pythagorean theorem that the c always represents the hypotenuse.

DRILL

In the following triangles, use the Pythagorean theorem to fill in the missing sides of the triangles shown. The answers to these drills can be found in Chapter 12.

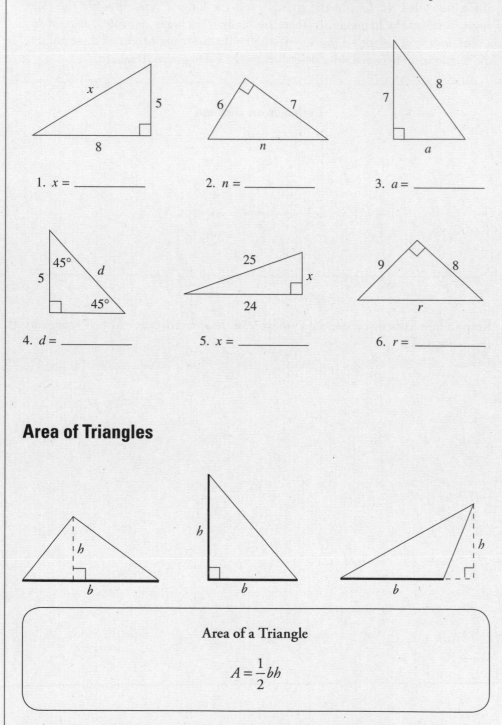

1. $x =$ _____

2. $n =$ _____

3. $a =$ _____

4. $d =$ _____

5. $x =$ _____

6. $r =$ _____

Area of Triangles

Area of a Triangle

$$A = \frac{1}{2}bh$$

Notice that the height, or altitude, of a triangle can be inside the triangle, outside the triangle, or formed by a side of the triangle. In each case, the height is always perpendicular to the base. The height of a triangle must sometimes be computed with the Pythagorean theorem.

Area of an Equilateral Triangle

The height of an equilateral triangle can be found by dividing it into two 30°-60°-90° triangles, but you can save yourself the time and trouble if you memorize the following formula:

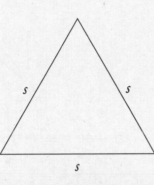

Area of an Equilateral Triangle

$$A = \frac{s^2 \sqrt{3}}{4}$$

Trigonometry and the Area of a Triangle

On the Math Level 2, a useful formula that involves trigonometry is given by the following formula:

Area of a Triangle

$$A = \frac{1}{2} ab \sin \theta$$

This formula is useful if you know the lengths of two sides of a triangle (*a* and *b*), and the measure of the angle between them (θ).

Level 2 Only

Trig Tricks
Later in this book you'll also use the basic functions of trigonometry to find the height of a triangle. This formula will come in handy for those types of questions.

Drill

Try the following practice questions about the areas of triangles. The answers to these drills can be found in Chapter 12.

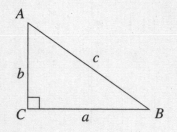

9. If the area of △ABC is equal to 3b, then a =

(A) $\dfrac{3}{4}$

(B) $\dfrac{3}{2}$

(C) 3

(D) 4

(E) 6

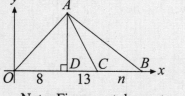

Note: Figure not drawn to scale

15. If △OAD and △ABC are of equal area, then n =

(A) 8
(B) 16
(C) 18
(D) 21
(E) 24

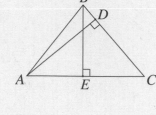

37. If AC = 12, BC = 10, and AD = 9, then BE =

(A) 7.0
(B) 7.5
(C) 8.0
(D) 8.5
(E) 9.0

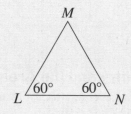

38. If △LMN has a perimeter of 24, then what is the area of △LMN ?

(A) 13.86
(B) 20.78
(C) 27.71
(D) 36.95
(E) 41.57

44. An equilateral triangle with an area of 12 has what perimeter?

(A) 12.00
(B) 13.39
(C) 15.59
(D) 15.79
(E) 18.66

46. A triangular traffic island with a flat surface is formed by the intersection of three streets. Two of the sides of the island have lengths of 6.4 meters and 10.8 meters. If the measure of the angle between these two sides is 55°, what is the area, in square meters, of the triangular surface of the island?

(A) 8.85
(B) 19.82
(C) 21.12
(D) 28.31
(E) 34.56

SPECIAL RIGHT TRIANGLES

Pythagorean Triplets

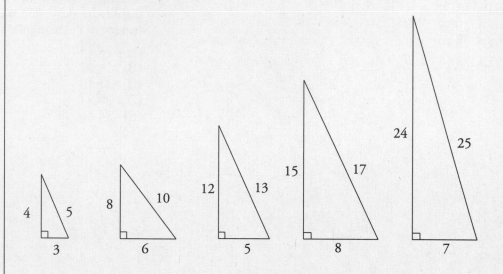

Triplet Families
Can you figure out the original triplet that a 25-60-65 sided triangle and a 30-40-50 sided triangle came from? The first is a multiple of a 5-12-13 right triangle, and the second is a multiple of a 3-4-5 right triangle. This means that a 5-12-13 triangle is similar to a 25-60-65 triangle. The same is true of a 3-4-5 and a 30-40-50. A little foreshadowing of what we'll discuss in a page or two.

There are only a few right triangles whose sides all have integer lengths. These special triangles are called "Pythagorean triplets," but that's not important. What is important is that ETS puts these triangles on the test a lot. Memorize them and keep an eye out for them.

If a right triangle has two sides that fit the proportions of a Pythagorean triplet, then you can automatically fill in the third side. The multiples of these basic proportions will also be Pythagorean triplets. That means that 25-60-65 and 30-40-50 are also proportions of right triangles.

DRILL

Use the proportions of the Pythagorean triplets to complete the triangles below. The answers to these drills can be found in Chapter 12.

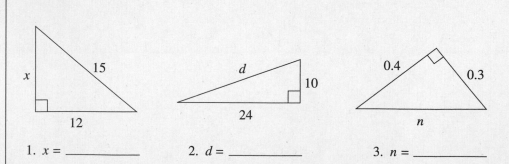

1. $x =$ _____   2. $d =$ _____   3. $n =$ _____

We've shown you some right triangles whose sides are in definite proportions. Now let's look at some specific right triangles whose angles also create sides that are in definite proportions.

The 45°-45°-90° Triangle

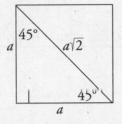

If you cut a square along its diagonal, you end up with two 45°-45°-90° triangles. Notice that this is an isosceles right triangle. The relation of the sides to the hypotenuse will always be the same.

The ratio of the sides of a 45°-45°-90° will always be $a : a : a\sqrt{2}$, where a is the length of one leg. The legs will be equal and the hypotenuse will always be equal to the length of a leg times $\sqrt{2}$. You can use this ratio for questions that ask for the length of either the leg or the hypotenuse. If the question gives you the length of the hypotenuse, just divide by $\sqrt{2}$ to find the length of each leg.

Remember that you can use the Pythagorean theorem on most right triangle problems. However, if you recognize that a triangle is a 45°-45°-90°, this is a great shortcut to use to find the lengths.

DRILL

Use the proportions of the 45°-45°-90° triangle to complete the dimensions of the following triangles. The answers to these drills can be found in Chapter 12.

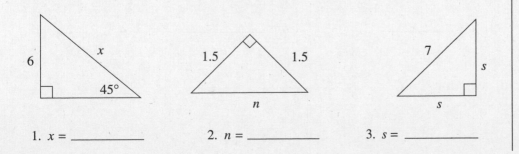

1. $x =$ _____   2. $n =$ _____   3. $s =$ _____

The 30°-60°-90° Triangle

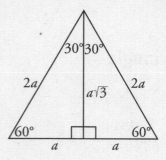

What's ETS Up To?
Remember that often questions that appear difficult at first just have more steps to them. So when ETS gives you a square or an equilateral triangle, see if it's useful to cut the shape and use the formulas we've given you.

The altitude (height) of an equilateral triangle cuts it into two 30°-60°-90° triangles. As with 45°-45°-90° triangles, all right triangles with angles of 30°, 60°, and 90° have sides in a definite proportion. In a 30°-60°-90° triangle, the hypotenuse is twice as long as the shorter leg. The length of the longer leg is equal to the length of the shorter leg times $\sqrt{3}$. So the ratio of the sides is $a : a\sqrt{3} : 2a$, where a is the length of the shorter leg of the triangle. If you are given the length of the longer leg, what can you do? That's right, just divide the leg and the hypotenuse by $\sqrt{3}$.

DRILL

Use the proportions of the 30°-60°-90° triangles to complete the dimensions of the following triangles. The answers to these drills can be found in Chapter 12.

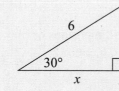

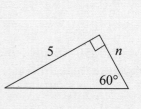

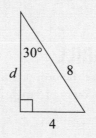

1. $x =$ _____

2. $n =$ _____

3. $d =$ _____

Drill

Use all of your right-triangle techniques to answer the following questions. The answers to these drills can be found in Chapter 12.

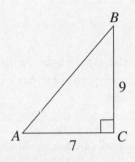

7. The perimeter of triangle *ABC* has how many possible values?

   (A) One
   (B) Two
   (C) Three
   (D) Four
   (E) Infinitely many

13. A right triangle with a side of length 6 and a side of length 8 also has a side of length *x*. What is *x* ?

   (A) 7
   (B) 10
   (C) 12
   (D) 14
   (E) It cannot be determined from the information given.

16. A straight 32-foot ladder is leaned against a vertical wall so that it forms a 30° angle with the wall. To what height in feet does the ladder reach?

   (A) 9.24
   (B) 16.00
   (C) 27.71
   (D) 43.71
   (E) 54.43

19. An isosceles right triangle has a perimeter of 23.9. What is the area of this triangle?

   (A) 16.9
   (B) 24.5
   (C) 25.0
   (D) 33.8
   (E) 49.0

Similar Triangles

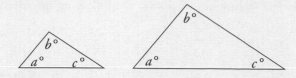

Triangles are said to be "similar" when they have the same angle measures. Basically, similar triangles have exactly the same shape, although they may be different sizes. Their sides, therefore, are in the same proportion.

> Corresponding sides and heights of similar triangles are proportional.

Proportionality

Here's a quick reminder: Not only are all 30°-60°-90° triangles similar to each other, but so are all 45°-45°-90° triangles. Also, the Pythagorean triplets that we mentioned are similar to their multiples.

For example, two 30°-60°-90° triangles of different sizes would be similar. If the short side of one triangle were twice as long as the short side of the other, then you could expect all of the larger triangle's dimensions to be twice the smaller triangle's dimensions. Similar triangles don't have to be right triangles, however. Sides of triangles will be related proportionally whenever they have identical angle measures.

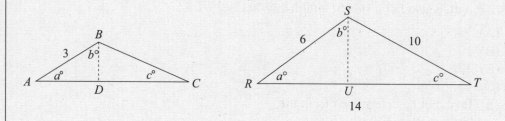

Similar Symbols

A similarity question can say "Triangle *ABC* is similar to Triangle *DEF*," or it can say that △*ABC* ~ △*DEF*. These are just two ways of saying the same thing.

In the figure above, both triangles have angles measuring *a*, *b*, and *c*. Because they have the same angles, you know they're similar triangles. Side *RS* of the large triangle and side *AB* of the smaller triangle are corresponding sides; each is the short side of its triangle. You can use the lengths of those two sides to figure out the proportion between the triangles. The length of *AB* is 3 and the length of *RS* is 6. So, *RS* is twice as long as *AB*. You can expect every side of *RST* to be twice as long as the corresponding side of *ABC*. That makes *BC* = 5 and *AC* = 7. Also, the height of triangle *RST* will be twice as long as the height of triangle *ABC*.

More Similarity

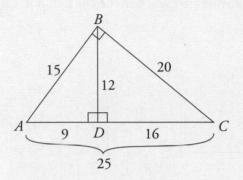

Whenever a right triangle is divided in two by a height drawn from the right angle, the result is three similar triangles of different sizes. The sides of the three triangles will be proportional. Let's separate the triangles so you can see them more clearly.

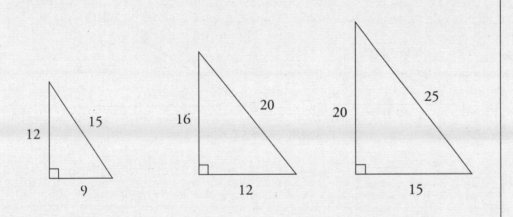

DRILL

Use the proportionality of similar triangles to complete the dimensions of the triangles below. The answers to these drills can be found in Chapter 12.

1.

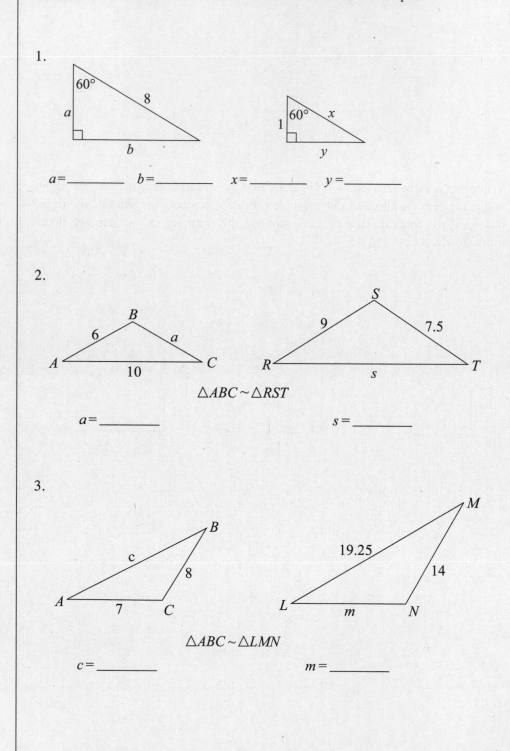

$a=$ _____ $b=$ _____ $x=$ _____ $y=$ _____

2.

$\triangle ABC \sim \triangle RST$

$a=$ _____ $s=$ _____

3.

$\triangle ABC \sim \triangle LMN$

$c=$ _____ $m=$ _____

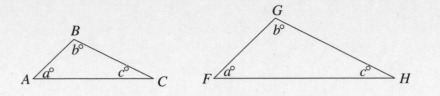

37. *FG* is twice as long as *AB*. If the area of triangle *FGH* is 0.5, what is the area of triangle *ABC* ?

(A) 0.13
(B) 0.25
(C) 0.50
(D) 1.00
(E) 2.00

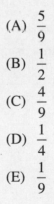

BC ∥ *DE*

40. If the length of *DB* is half of the length of *AD* and *BC* ∥ *DE*, then the area of triangle *ADE* is what fraction of the area of triangle *ABC* ?

(A) $\dfrac{5}{9}$

(B) $\dfrac{1}{2}$

(C) $\dfrac{4}{9}$

(D) $\dfrac{1}{4}$

(E) $\dfrac{1}{9}$

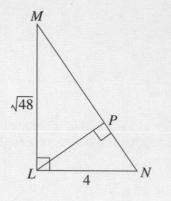

45. What is the area of $\triangle LPN$?

    (A)   3.46
    (B)   6.93
    (C)   8.00
    (D) 11.31
    (E) 13.86

QUADRILATERALS

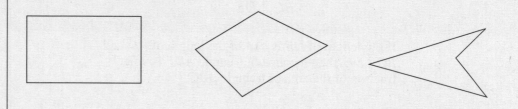

A quadrilateral is any shape formed by four intersecting lines in a plane. The internal angle measures of a quadrilateral always add up to 360°.

Parallelograms

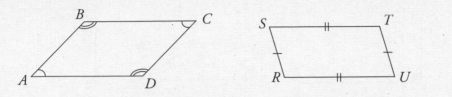

A parallelogram is a quadrilateral whose opposite sides are parallel. Rectangles are parallelograms, but a parallelogram does not need to have right angles. Note, however, that since the sides are parallel, Fred's theorem applies to the angles of a parallelogram. Parallelograms have the following characteristics:

- Opposite angles in a parallelogram are equal.
- Adjacent angles in a parallelogram are supplementary; they add up to 180°, because of Fred's theorem.
- Opposite sides in a parallelogram are of equal length.
- The diagonals of a parallelogram bisect each other.

The area of a parallelogram is given by this formula:

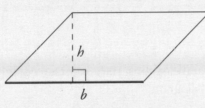

> ### Area of a Parallelogram
>
> $$A = bh$$

Connect the Dots
Notice that the area of a parallelogram is twice the area of a triangle. So you can always figure out one formula if you forget the other!

If you know two adjacent sides of a parallelogram (a and b) and the angle between them (θ), you can use a formula involving trigonometry to find the area as well.

Level 2 Only

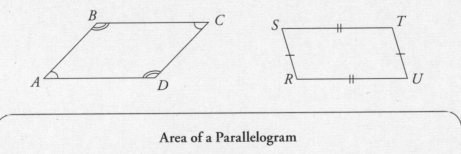

> ### Area of a Parallelogram
>
> $$A = ab \sin \theta$$

Height? There's No Height!
If you're having trouble finding the height in a parallelogram involving area, you can often use Pythagorean theorem or one of the special right triangles.

Rectangles

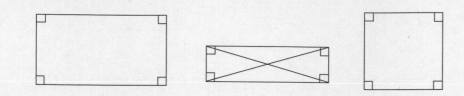

A rectangle is just a parallelogram with four right angles. Rectangles have all the properties of parallelograms. In addition,

- each of the four interior angles measures 90°
- the diagonals of a rectangle are of equal length

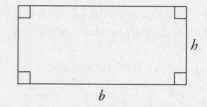

Since all rectangles are parallelograms, the area of a rectangle is given by the same formula as that of a parallelogram.

Area of a Rectangle

$$A = bh$$

Squares

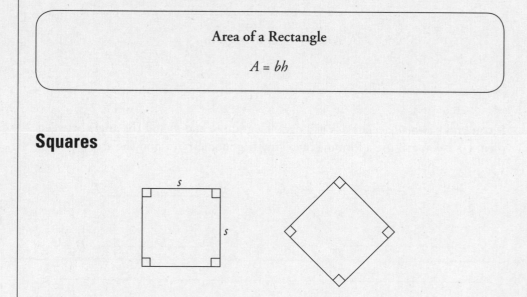

A square is a rectangle with four sides of equal length. (If you are asked to draw a rectangle, drawing a square is a legitimate response.)

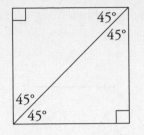

A diagonal in a square divides the square into two 45°-45°-90° triangles. The area of a square is given by either one of these formulas:

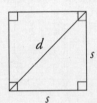

What's with All This Memorization?!
Notice that the area of a square, s^2, is just the base times the height, which is the formula for area of a parallelogram and area of a rectangle. Because the base and height of a square are the same, we give you a shortcut formula, but it's really no different from the others. So, no need to memorize it. You can always figure it out!

Area of a Square

$$A = s^2$$

or

$$A = \frac{d^2}{2}$$

The second, less-known formula for the area of a square can be used to shortcut questions that would otherwise take many more steps and require you to use a 45°-45°-90° triangle.

Trapezoids

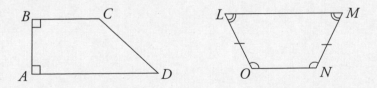

A trapezoid is a quadrilateral whose top and bottom are parallel but differ in length.

The area of a trapezoid is given by the following formula:

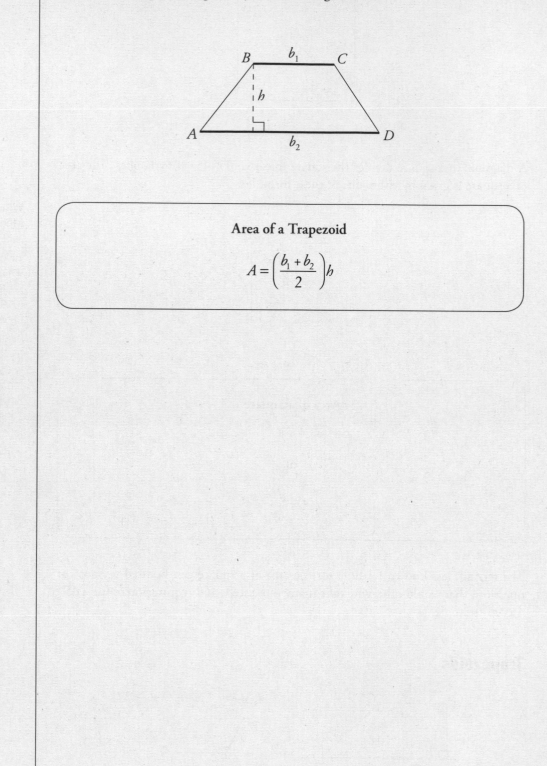

Area of a Trapezoid

$$A = \left(\frac{b_1 + b_2}{2}\right)h$$

Drill

Try the following practice questions using quadrilateral formulas. The answers to these drills can be found in Chapter 12.

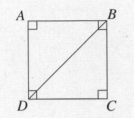

22. If $AB = BC$ and $DB = 5$, then the area of $ABCD =$

(A) 12.50
(B) 14.43
(C) 17.68
(D) 35.36
(E) 43.30

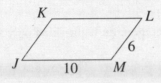

34. If the measure of $\angle KJM$ is 60°, what is the area of parallelogram $JKLM$?

(A) 18.34
(B) 25.98
(C) 34.64
(D) 51.96
(E) 60.00

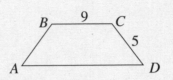

40. The bases of trapezoid $ABCD$ differ in length by 6, and the perimeter of the trapezoid is 34. What is the area of $ABCD$?

(A) 45.0
(B) 48.0
(C) 54.0
(D) 60.0
(E) 62.5

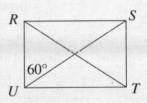

45. If the area of rectangle $RSTU$ is 62.35, then $RT + SU =$

(A) 18.8
(B) 24.0
(C) 32.0
(D) 36.0
(E) 40.8

OTHER POLYGONS

The Math Subject Tests may occasionally require you to deal with polygons other than triangles and quadrilaterals. Here are the names of the other polygons you're likely to see:

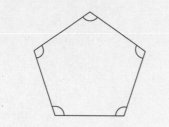

pentagon: a five-sided polygon

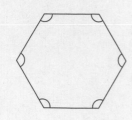

hexagon: a six-sided polygon

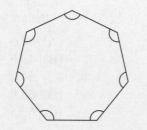

heptagon: a seven-sided polygon

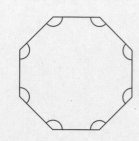

octagon: an eight-sided polygon

All of the polygons pictured above are *regular* polygons. That means that their sides and angles are all of the same size.

You know that the internal angles of a triangle add up to 180° and that the internal angles of a quadrilateral add up to 360°. But what about the angles of a hexagon or an octagon? You can compute the sum of a polygon's internal angles using this formula:

> **Sum of the Angles of an *n*-sided Polygon**
>
> Sum of Angles = $(n - 2) \times 180°$

Using this formula, you can figure out that the angles of a hexagon (a 6-sided figure) would have a sum of (4 × 180) degrees. That's 720°. If you know that the figure is a regular hexagon, then you can even figure out the measure of each angle: 720° ÷ 6 = 120°.

Just Make Triangles!

This formula may seem random and now you're stressing about all the memorizing you're going to have to do. But in reality, you don't have to know the formula. Now you're saying "What?! If we don't have to know it, why are we memorizing it?!" There are almost always ways around knowing formulas. It's great if you can memorize this, but if you can't, then count the triangles! Start at one vertex of the polygon you're looking at and create triangles by drawing a line from that same vertex to every other vertex in the figure, like this:

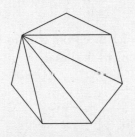

Now just count the triangles. For our picture, there are 5 triangles. You already know that there are 180° in a triangle. So there must be 5 × 180°, or 900°, in the polygon. Notice that 5 is 7 − 2 and 180 is just the number of degrees in a triangle. Funny, you just created the formula for the sum of the angles in a polygon!

CIRCLES

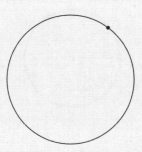

A circle is defined as the set of all the points located at a certain distance from a given center point. A point that is said to be on a circle is a point on the edge of the circle, not contained within the circle.

The *radius* is the distance from the center to the edge of the circle.

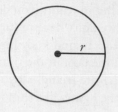

The *diameter* of a circle is the distance from edge to edge through the circle's center. The diameter is twice as long as the radius.

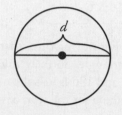

The *circumference* of a circle is the distance around the circle—essentially, the circle's perimeter. The circumference is given by the following formula:

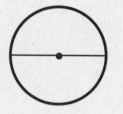

Circumference of a Circle

$C = \pi d$ **or** $C = 2\pi r$

The *area* of a circle is given by the following formula:

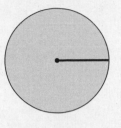

Area of a Circle

$$A = \pi r^2$$

DRILL

Use formulas to complete the dimensions of the following circles. The answers to these drills can be found in Chapter 12.

Radius = 4   Area − 20   Circumference = 8

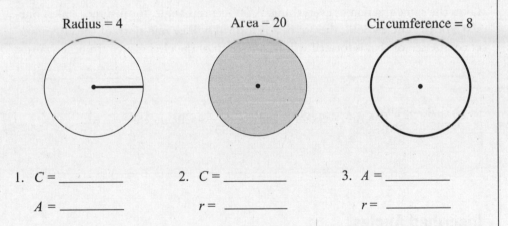

1. C = _____   2. C = _____   3. A = _____

    A = _____   r = _____   r = _____

A Slice of Pie

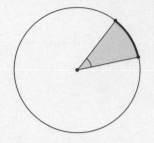

The portion of a circle's area between two radii is called a sector. The portion of the circle's circumference that falls between the radii is called an arc. Between any two points on a circle's edge, there are two arcs, a major arc and a minor arc. The minor arc is the shorter of the two, and it's usually the one ETS is concerned about.

The angle between two radii is called a central angle. The degree measure of a central angle is equal to the degree measure of the arc that it cuts out of the circle's circumference. In other words, the minor arc formed by a 40° central angle is a 40° arc.

To put it simply, the piece of a circle defined by a central angle (like a slice of pie) takes the same fraction of everything. A 60° central angle, for instance, takes one-sixth of the circle's 360°; the arc that is formed will be one-sixth of the circumference; the sector that is formed will be one-sixth of the circle's area. In other words:

$$\frac{\text{degree}}{360} \bullet \text{Area} = \text{Sector} \quad \text{and} \quad \frac{\text{degree}}{360} \bullet \text{Circumference} = \text{Arc}$$

Inscribed Angles

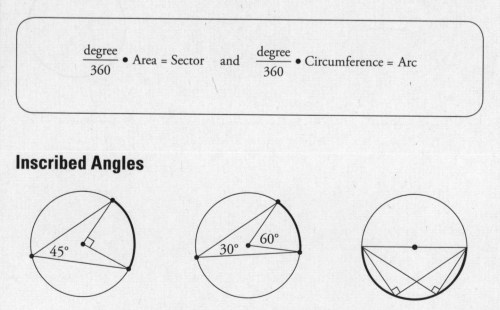

Same Segments
All angles inscribed in the same segment of a circle (or identical circles) are equal.

An angle formed by two chords (lines drawn from any point on the circle to any other point on the circle) is called an inscribed angle. While a central angle with a certain degree measure intercepts an arc of the same degree measure, an inscribed angle intercepts an arc with twice the degree measure of the angle. For example, a 30° central angle intercepts a 30° arc, while a 30° inscribed angle intercepts a 60° arc.

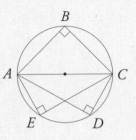

Any time you draw two lines, one from each endpoint of the diameter, to the same point on the semicircle, the lines will meet at a right angle. In other words, any angle inscribed in a semicircle is a right angle.

Tangent Lines

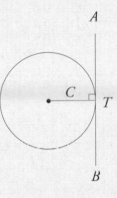

A *tangent line* to a circle is a line that touches the circle at only one point. A tangent line is always perpendicular to the radius touching the same point.

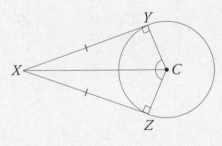

From any point outside a circle, there are two separate tangent lines to that circle. The distances to the two points of tangency are equal, and the radii to the points of tangency make equal angles with the line connecting the external point to the circle's center.

Drill

Try the following practice questions using the rules and techniques for circles. The answers to these drills can be found in Chapter 12.

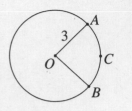

Note: Figure not drawn to scale

12. In the circle with center O, if the length of minor arc ACB is 4.71, which of the following best approximates the measure of $\angle AOB$?

(A) 60.0°
(B) 72.0°
(C) 86.4°
(D) 90.0°
(E) 98.6°

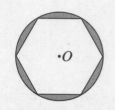

31. A regular hexagon is inscribed in the circle with center O. If the circle has a radius of 4, what is the area of the shaded region?

(A) 8.3
(B) 8.7
(C) 9.0
(D) 9.4
(E) 10.2

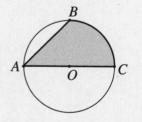

29. If the circle with center O has a radius of 5 and the measure of $\angle BAC$ is 45°, then what is the area of the shaded region?

(A) 32.13
(B) 31.52
(C) 26.70
(D) 25.41
(E) 24.26

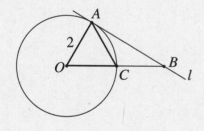

43. Line l is tangent to the circle with center O at A, and $OA = AC$. What is the length of AB ?

(A) 1.73
(B) 2.83
(C) 3.46
(D) 4.74
(E) 5.20

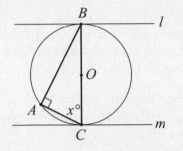

Note: Figure not drawn to scale.

45. The right angle CAB is inscribed in the circle with center O and diameter BC. Lines l and m are tangent to the circle at B and C, respectively. Which of the following must be true?

    I. $AB < BC$
    II. $x = 60$
    III. l and m meet when extended to the right.

(A) I only
(B) III only
(C) I and II only
(D) II and III only
(E) I, II, and III

Summary

o Plane geometry appears on the Level 1 Math Subject Test, but it's a useful knowledge base for those taking the Level 2 Test as well.

o Some rules about lines and angles:
   - A 90° angle is formed by two lines perpendicular to each other.
   - There are 180° in a line.
   - When two straight lines intersect, the angles created opposite each other are equal. The adjacent angles (two angles beside each other along the same straight line) have a sum of 180°.

o Fred's theorem states that when parallel lines are crossed by a third line, big angles and small angles are created. All the big angles are equal, all the small angles are equal, and a big plus a small equals 180°.

o Triangles form the largest set of plane geometry questions on the test.
   - The sum of the angles in a triangle is 180°.
   - The longest side of a triangle is across from the largest angle. The smallest side of a triangle is across from the smallest angle. Equal sides are across from equal angles.
   - Isosceles triangles have at least two equal sides and two equal angles. Equilateral triangles have three equal sides and three equal angles.
   - The third side rule states that the length of any side of a triangle must be between the sum and the difference of the other two sides.
   - The area of a triangle is $A = \dfrac{1}{2}bh$. The height must be perpendicular to the base.

o Right triangles are triangles with one 90° angle. The Pythagorean theorem states that, in a right triangle, $a^2 + b^2 = c^2$, where c is the hypotenuse of the triangle and a and b are the two legs.

o   Special right triangles are helpful in simplifying the math. They often provide an easier route to the correct solution than using the Pythagorean theorem, so look closely for opportunities to use them. The following is a list of special right triangles:

- There are some Pythagorean triplets that are helpful to have in your back pocket. They are 3-4-5, 5-12-13, 7-24-25, and any multiples of these as well.
- The sides of a 45°-45°-90° triangle have a very specific ratio: $x : x : x\sqrt{2}$, where x is the length of each leg.
- The sides of a 30°-60°-90° triangle have a very specific ratio: $x : x\sqrt{3} : 2x$, where x is the length of the shorter leg.

o   Similar triangles have the same angle measures. The corresponding sides and heights of similar triangles are proportional.

o   Quadrilaterals are four-sided figures. The sum of the angles in a quadrilateral is 360°.

- Parallelograms have two sets of equal, parallel lines. The area of a parallelogram is $A = bh$, where the base is perpendicular to the height.
- Rectangles are parallelograms with four right angles.
- Squares are rectangles with four equal sides.
- Trapezoids are four-sided figures whose top and bottom are parallel but different in length. The area of a trapezoid is $A = \left(\dfrac{b_1 + b_2}{2}\right)h$, where b_1 is one base and b_2 is the other.

o   The sum of the angles of an n-sided polygon is $(n-2) \times 180°$.

o   Here are some things to remember about a circle:

- A circle contains a total of 360°.
- The radius is the distance from the center of the circle to any point on the circle.
- The diameter is a straight line drawn from one point on a circle through the center to another. Its length is twice the radius.

- The circumference of the circle is the distance around the circle. You can think of it as the perimeter of the circle. Its formula is $C = \pi d$. You may also know it as $C = 2\pi r$.
- The formula for area of a circle is $A = \pi r^2$.
- A sector is a slice of pie of the circle. The part of the circumference that the sector contains is called an arc and is in the same proportion to the circumference as the angle of the sector is to 360°.
- A central angle is an angle whose vertex is the center of the circle. An inscribed angle has its vertex on the circle and its two endpoints on the circle. Its angle is half of what the central angle is to those same two endpoints.
- Any angle inscribed in a semicircle is a right angle.
- A line tangent to the circle touches the circle in only one place and is always perpendicular to the radius drawn to the point of tangency.

○ Some information for Level 2 test takers:
- The area of a triangle, using trigonometry, is $A = \dfrac{1}{2}\,ab\,\sin\theta$.
- The area of a parallelogram, using trigonometry, is $A = ab\,\sin\theta$.

Chapter 6
Solid Geometry

Questions about solid geometry frequently test plane geometry techniques. They're difficult mostly because the added third dimension makes them harder to visualize. You're likely to run into three or four solid geometry questions on either one of the Math Subject Tests, however, so it's important to practice. If you're not the artistic type and have trouble drawing cubes, cylinders, and so on, it's worthwhile to practice sketching the shapes in the following pages. The ability to make your own drawing is often helpful.

PRISMS

Prisms are three-dimensional figures that have two parallel bases that are polygons. Cubes and rectangular solids are examples of prisms that ETS often asks about. In general, the volume of a prism is given by the following formula:

> **Volume of a Prism**
>
> $V = Bh$

Area and Volume
In general the volume of a shape involves the area of the base, often referred to as B, and the height, or h, of the solid.

In this formula, B represents the area of either base of the prism (the top or the bottom), and h represents the height of the prism (perpendicular to the base). The formulas for the volume of a rectangular solid, a cube, and a cylinder all come from this basic formula.

RECTANGULAR SOLID

A rectangular solid is simply a box; ETS also sometimes calls it a rectangular prism. It has three distinct dimensions: *length*, *width*, and *height*. The volume of a rectangular solid (the amount of space it contains) is given by this formula:

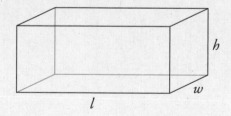

> **Volume of a Rectangular Solid**
>
> $V = lwh$

The surface area (SA) of a rectangular solid is the sum of the areas of all of its faces. A rectangular solid's surface area is given by the formula on the next page.

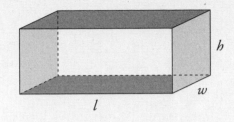

The volume and surface area of a solid make up the most basic information you can have about that solid (volume is tested more often than surface area). You may also be asked about *lengths* within a rectangular solid—edges and diagonals. The dimensions of the solid give the lengths of its edges, and the diagonal of any *face* of a rectangular solid can be found using the Pythagorean theorem. There's one more length you may be asked about—the long diagonal (or space diagonal) that passes from corner to corner through the center of the box. The length of the long diagonal is given by this formula:

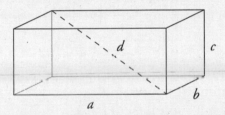

This is the Pythagorean theorem with a third dimension added, and it works just the same way. This formula will work in any rectangular box. The long diagonal is the longest straight line that can be drawn inside any rectangular solid.

CUBES

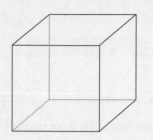

A cube is a rectangular solid that has the same length in all three dimensions. All six of its faces are squares. This simplifies the formulas for volume, surface area, and the long diagonal.

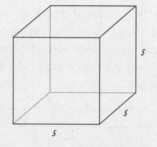

Volume of a Cube

$$V = s^3$$

Surface Area of a Cube

$$SA = 6s^2$$

Face Diagonal of a Cube

$$f = s\sqrt{2}$$

Long Diagonal of a Cube

$$d = s\sqrt{3}$$

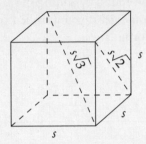

CYLINDERS

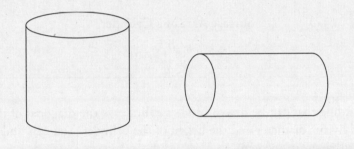

A cylinder is like a prism but with a circular base. It has two important dimensions—radius and height. Remember that volume is the area of the base times the height. In this case, the base is a circle. The area of a circle is πr^2. So the volume of a cylinder is $\pi r^2 h$.

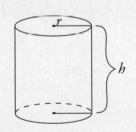

> **Volume of a Cylinder**
>
> $$V = \pi r^2 h$$

The surface area of a cylinder is found by adding the areas of the two circular bases to the area of the rectangle you'd get if you unrolled the side of the cylinder. That boils down to the following formula:

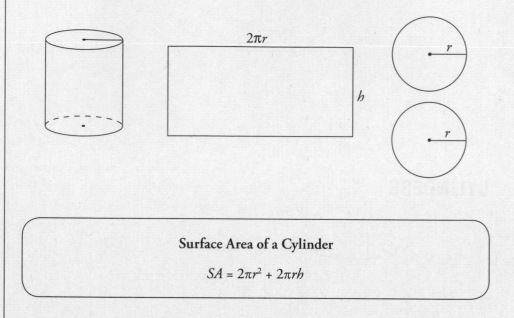

Surface Area of a Cylinder

$$SA = 2\pi r^2 + 2\pi rh$$

The longest line that can be drawn inside a cylinder is the diagonal of the rectangle formed by the diameter and the height of the cylinder. You can find its length with the Pythagorean theorem.

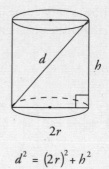

$$d^2 = \left(2r\right)^2 + h^2$$

CONES

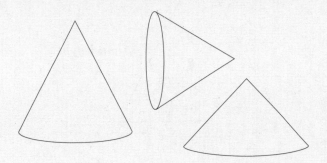

If you take a cylinder and shrink one of its circular bases down to a point, then you have a cone. A cone has three significant dimensions which form a right triangle—its radius, its height, and its *slant height,* which is the straight-line distance from the tip of the cone to a point on the edge of its base. The formulas for the volume and surface area of a cone are given in the information box at the beginning of both of the Math Subject Tests. The formula for the volume of a cone is pretty straightforward:

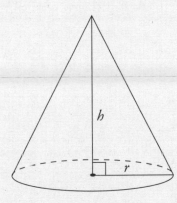

Volume of a Cone

$$V = \frac{1}{3}\pi r^2 h$$

Connect the Dots
Notice that the volume of a cone is just one-third of the volume of a circular cylinder. Make memorizing easy!

But you have to be careful computing *surface area* for a cone using the formula provided by ETS. The formula at the beginning of the Math Subject Tests is for the *lateral area* of a cone—the area of the sloping sides—not the complete surface area. It doesn't include the circular base. Here's a more useful equation for the surface area of a cone.

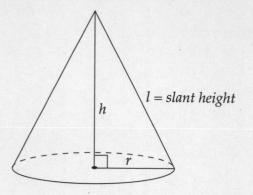

l = slant height

Surface Area of a Cone

$$SA = \pi rl + \pi r^2$$

If you want to calculate only the lateral area of a cone, just use the first half of the above formula—leave the πr^2 off.

SPHERES

A sphere is simply a hollow ball. It can be defined as all of the points in space at a fixed distance from a central point. The one important measure in a sphere is its radius. The formulas for the volume and surface area of a sphere are given to you at the very beginning of both Math Subject Tests. That means that you don't need to have them memorized, but here they are anyway:

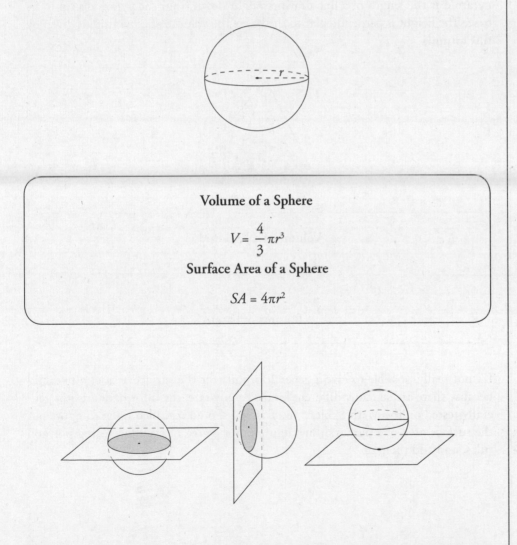

Volume of a Sphere

$$V = \frac{4}{3}\pi r^3$$

Surface Area of a Sphere

$$SA = 4\pi r^2$$

The intersection of a plane and a sphere always forms a circle unless the plane is *tangent* to the sphere, in which case the plane and sphere touch at only one point.

PYRAMIDS

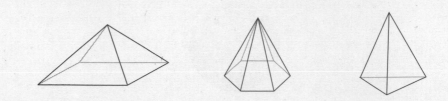

A pyramid is a little like a cone, except that its base is a polygon instead of a circle. Pyramids don't show up often on the Math Subject Tests. When you do run into a pyramid, it will almost always have a rectangular base. Pyramids can be pretty complicated solids, but for the purposes of the Math Subject Tests, a pyramid has just two important measures—the area of its base and its height. The height of a pyramid is the length of a line drawn straight down from the pyramid's tip to its base. The height is perpendicular to the base. The volume of a pyramid is given by this formula.

Connect the Dots
Notice that the volume of a pyramid is just one-third of the volume of a prism. Make memorizing easy!

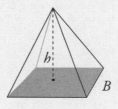

Volume of a Pyramid

$$V = \frac{1}{3}Bh$$

(B = area of base)

It's not really possible to give a general formula for the surface area of a pyramid because there are so many different kinds. At any rate, the information is not generally tested on the Math Subject Tests. If you should be called upon to figure out the surface area of a pyramid, just figure out the area of each face using polygon rules, and add them up.

TRICKS OF THE TRADE

Here are some of the most common solid geometry question types you're likely to encounter on the Math Subject Tests. They occur much more often on the Math Level 2 Subject Test than on the Math Level 1 Subject Test, but they can appear on either test.

Triangles in Rectangular Solids

Many questions about rectangular solids are actually testing triangle rules. Such questions generally ask for the lengths of the diagonals of a box's faces, the long diagonal of a box, or other lengths. These questions are usually solved using the Pythagorean theorem and the Super Pythagorean theorem that finds a box's long diagonal (see the section on Rectangular Solids)

DRILL

Here are some practice questions using triangle rules in rectangular solids. The answers to these drills can be found in Chapter 12.

32. What is the length of the longest line that can be drawn in a cube of volume 27 ?

    (A) 3.0
    (B) 4.2
    (C) 4.9
    (D) 5.2
    (E) 9.0

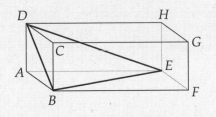

36. In the rectangular solid shown, if $AB = 4$, $BC = 3$, and $BF = 12$, what is the perimeter of triangle *EDB* ?

    (A) 27.33
    (B) 28.40
    (C) 29.20
    (D) 29.50
    (E) 30.37

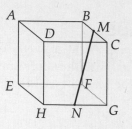

39. In the cube above, *M* is the midpoint of *BC*, and *N* is the midpoint of *GH*. If the cube has a volume of 1, what is the length of *MN* ?

    (A) 1.23
    (B) 1.36
    (C) 1.41
    (D) 1.73
    (E) 1.89

Volume Questions

Many solid geometry questions test your understanding of the relationship between a solid's volume and its other dimensions—sometimes including the solid's surface area. To solve these questions, just plug the numbers you're given into the solid's volume formula.

Drill

Try the following practice questions. The answers to these drills can be found in Chapter 12.

17. The volume and surface area of a cube are equal. What is the length of an edge of this cube?

    (A) 1
    (B) 2
    (C) 4
    (D) 6
    (E) 9

24. A rectangular solid has a volume of 30, and its edges have integer lengths. What is the greatest possible surface area of this solid?

    (A) 62
    (B) 82
    (C) 86
    (D) 94
    (E) 122

28. The water in Allegra's swimming pool has a depth of 7 feet. If the area of the pentagonal base of the pool is 150 square feet, then what is the volume, in cubic feet, of the water in her pool?

    (A)   57
    (B)   50
    (C) 1,050
    (D) 5,250
    (E) It cannot be determined from the information given.

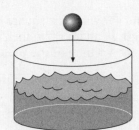

43. A sphere of radius 1 is totally submerged in a cylindrical tank of radius 4, as shown. The water level in the tank rises a distance of h. What is the value of h ?

    (A) 0.072
    (B) 0.083
    (C) 0.096
    (D) 0.108
    (E) 0.123

17. A cube has a surface area of $6x$. What is the volume of the cube?

    (A) $x^{\frac{2}{3}}$

    (B) $x^{\frac{3}{2}}$

    (C) $6x^2$

    (D) $36x^2$

    (E) x^3

36. A sphere has a radius of r. If this radius is increased by b, then the surface area of the sphere is increased by what amount?

    (A) b^2
    (B) $4\pi b^2$
    (C) $8\pi rb + 4\pi b^2$
    (D) $8\pi rb + 2rb + b^2$
    (E) $4\pi r^2 b^2$

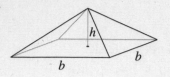

40. If the pyramid shown has a square base with edges of length b, and $b = 2h$, then which of the following is the volume of the pyramid?

(A) $\dfrac{h^3}{3}$

(B) $\dfrac{4h^3}{3}$

(C) $4h^3$

(D) $8h^2 - h$

(E) $\dfrac{8h^3 - 4h}{3}$

Inscribed Solids

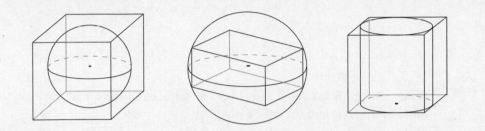

Some questions on the Math Subject Tests will be based on spheres inscribed in cubes or cubes inscribed in spheres (these are the most popular inscribed shapes). Occasionally you may also see a rectangular solid inscribed in a sphere, or a cylinder inscribed in a rectangular box, etc. The trick to these questions is always figuring out how to get from the dimensions of one of the solids to the dimensions of the other.

Following are a few basic tips that can speed up your work on inscribed solids questions.

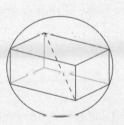

- When a cube or rectangular solid is inscribed in a sphere, the long diagonal of that solid is equal to the diameter of the sphere.

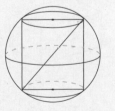

- When a cylinder is inscribed in a sphere, the sphere's diameter is equal to the diagonal of the rectangle formed by the cylinder's heights and diameter.

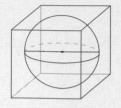

- When a sphere is inscribed in a cube, the diameter of the sphere is equal to the length of the cube's edge.

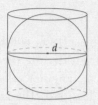

- If a sphere is inscribed in a cylinder, both solids have the same diameter.

Most inscribed solids questions fall into one of the preceding categories. If you run into a situation not covered by these tips, just look for the way to get from the dimensions of the inner shape to those of the external shape, or vice versa.

DRILL

Here are some practice inscribed solids questions. The answers to these drills can be found in Chapter 12.

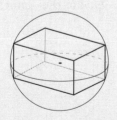

32. A rectangular solid is inscribed in a sphere as shown. If the dimensions of the solid are 3, 4, and 6, then what is the radius of the sphere?

(A) 2.49
(B) 3.91
(C) 4.16
(D) 5.62
(E) 7.81

35. A cylinder is inscribed in a cube with an edge of length 2. What volume of space is enclosed by the cube but not by the cylinder?

(A) 1.41
(B) 1.56
(C) 1.72
(D) 3.81
(E) 4.86

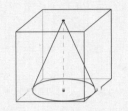

38. A cone is inscribed in a cube of volume 1 in such a way that its base is inscribed in one face of the cube. What is the volume of the cone?

(A) 0.21
(B) 0.26
(C) 0.33
(D) 0.42
(E) 0.67

Solids Produced by Rotation

Three types of solids can be produced by the rotation of simple two-dimensional shapes—spheres, cylinders, and cones. Questions about solids produced by rotation are generally fairly simple; they usually test your ability to visualize the solid generated by the rotation of a flat shape. Sometimes, rotated solids questions begin with a shape in the coordinate plane—that is, rotated around one of the axes or some other line. Practice will help you figure out the dimensions of the solid from the dimensions of the original flat shape.

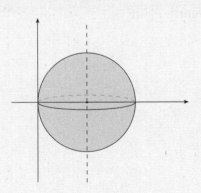

A sphere is produced when a circle is rotated around its diameter. This is an easy situation to work with, as the sphere and the original circle will have the same radius. Find the radius of the circle, and you can figure out anything you want to about the sphere.

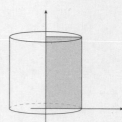

A cylinder is formed by the rotation of a rectangle around a central line *or* one edge.

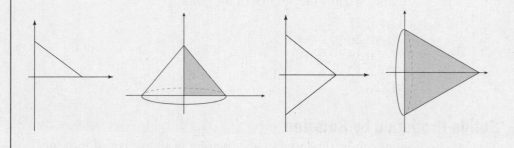

A cone is formed by rotating a right triangle around one of its legs (think of it as spinning the triangle) or by rotating an isosceles triangle around its axis of symmetry. Another way of thinking about it is if you spun the triangle in the first figure above around the *y*-axis (so you're rotating around the leg that's sitting on the *y*-axis) you would get the second figure. Likewise, if you spun the third figure above around the *x*-axis (so you're rotating around the axis of symmetry), you would end up with the fourth figure.

DRILL

Try these rotated solids questions for practice. The answers to these drills can be found in Chapter 12.

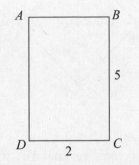

34. What is the volume of the solid generated by rotating rectangle *ABCD* around *AD* ?

    (A) 15.7
    (B) 31.4
    (C) 62.8
    (D) 72.0
    (E) 80.0

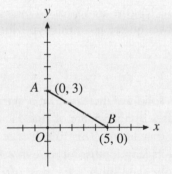

39. If the triangle created by *OAB* is rotated around the *x*-axis, what is the volume of the generated solid?

    (A) 15.70
    (B) 33.33
    (C) 40.00
    (D) 47.12
    (E) 78.54

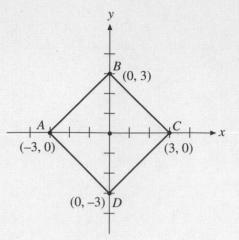

46. What is the volume generated by rotating square *ABCD* around the *y*-axis?

(A) 24.84
(B) 28.27
(C) 42.66
(D) 56.55
(E) 84.82

Changing Dimensions

Some solid geometry questions will ask you to figure out what happens to the volume of a solid if all of its lengths are increased by a certain factor or if its area doubles, and so on. To answer questions of this type, just remember a basic rule.

> When the lengths of a solid are increased by a certain factor, the surface area of the solid increases by the square of that factor, and the volume increases by the cube of that factor. This rule is true only when the solid's shape doesn't change—its length must increase in *every* dimension, not just one. For that reason, cubes and spheres are most often used for this type of question because their shapes are constant.

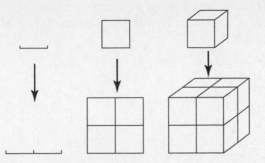

In the illustration above, a length is doubled, which means that the corresponding area is 4 times as great, and the volume is 8 times as great. If the length had been tripled, the area would have increased by a factor of 9, and the volume by a factor of 27.

DRILL

Try these practice questions. The answers to these drills can be found in Chapter 12.

13. If the radius of sphere A is one-third as long as the radius of sphere B, then the volume of sphere A is what fraction of the volume of sphere B ?

(A) $\dfrac{1}{3}$

(B) $\dfrac{1}{4}$

(C) $\dfrac{1}{9}$

(D) $\dfrac{1}{12}$

(E) $\dfrac{1}{27}$

18. A rectangular solid with length l, width w, and height h has a volume of 24. What is the volume of a rectangular solid with length $\dfrac{l}{2}$, width $\dfrac{w}{2}$, and height $\dfrac{h}{2}$?

(A) 18
(B) 12
(C) 6
(D) 3
(E) 2

21. If the surface area of a cube is increased by a factor of 2.25, then its volume is increased by what factor?

(A) 1.72
(B) 3.38
(C) 4.50
(D) 5.06
(E) 5.64

Summary

o   Solid geometry questions are often plane geometry questions in disguise.

o   For the purposes of the SAT Math 1 & 2 Subject Tests, prisms are 3-dimensional figures with two parallel, identical bases. The bases can be any shape from plane geometry.

o   The volume of a prism is the area of the base, often referred to as B, times the height, h.

o   Let's talk rectangular prisms:
   •   The formula for the volume of a rectangular prism is $V = lwh$.
   •   The formula for the surface area of a rectangular solid is $SA = 2lw + 2wh + 2lh$. Think about painting the outside of the figure. Find the area of each side.
   •   The Super Pythagorean theorem, which is helpful in solving questions about the diagonal of a rectangular prism, is $a^2 + b^2 + c^2 = d^2$.

o   Let's talk cubes. Remember that a cube is just a rectangular prism whose length, width, and height are equal. If you forget a formula, just use the rectangular prism formula!
   •   The volume of a cube is $V = s^3$.
   •   The surface area of a rectangular solid is $SA = 6s^2$.

o   Let's talk cylinders. A cylinder is a prism whose bases are circles.
   •   The volume of a cylinder is $V = \pi r^2 h$.
   •   The surface area of a rectangular solid is $SA = 2\pi r^2 + 2\pi rh$. If you forget this, remember that you're just painting the outside. So you'll need the area of two circles and the area of the other piece, which, when rolled out (like a roll of paper towels), is a rectangle whose sides are the circumference of the circle and the height.

- A cone is similar to a cylinder except that one of its bases is merely a point.

    - The formula for the volume of a cone is $V = \frac{1}{3}\neq r^2 h$, where the height must be perpendicular to the base.
    - The formula for the surface area of a cone is $SA = \pi r l + \pi r^2$, where l is the slant height.

- A sphere is a hollow ball.

    - The formula for the volume of a sphere is $V = \frac{4}{3}\neq r^3$.

    - The formula for the surface area of a cone is $SA = 4\pi r^2$.

- Pyramids are like cones, but the base is a plane geometry shape. The formula for the volume of a pyramid is $V = \frac{1}{3}Bh$.

- Inscribed figures always have a line or curve that connects the inner figure to the outer figure.

- Questions about solids produced by rotation usually test your ability to visualize the solid created by the rotation of a flat shape.

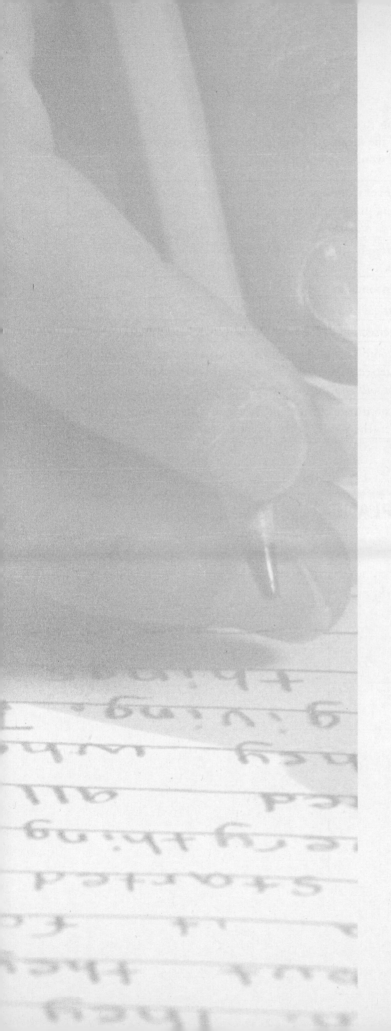

Chapter 7
Coordinate
Geometry

About 12 percent of the questions on each Math Subject Test will concern graphs on the coordinate plane. Most coordinate geometry questions on the Math Level 1 Subject Test are about lines, slopes, and distances. On the Math Level 2 Subject Test, you're more likely to see hyperbolas, ellipses, and more complicated curves. Simple circles and parabolas can appear on either test. The techniques in this chapter will prepare you for all major coordinate geometry question types.

DEFINITIONS

Here are some geometry terms that appear on the Math Subject Tests. Make sure you're familiar with them. If the meaning of any of these vocabulary words keeps slipping your mind, add that word to your flash cards.

Coordinate Plane	A system of two perpendicular axes used to describe the position of a point using a pair of coordinates—also called the *rectangular coordinate system*, or the *Cartesian plane*.
Slope	For a straight line, the ratio of vertical change to horizontal change.
x-axis	The horizontal axis of the coordinate plane.
y-axis	The vertical axis of the coordinate plane.
Origin	The intersection of the x- and y-axes, with coordinates (0, 0).
x-intercept	The x-coordinate of the point at which a line or other function intersects the x-axis. These values are also known as *zeros, roots,* or *solutions*. At the x-intercept, y = 0.
y-intercept	The y-coordinate of the point at which a line or other function intersects the y-axis. At the y-intercept, x = 0.

THE COORDINATE PLANE

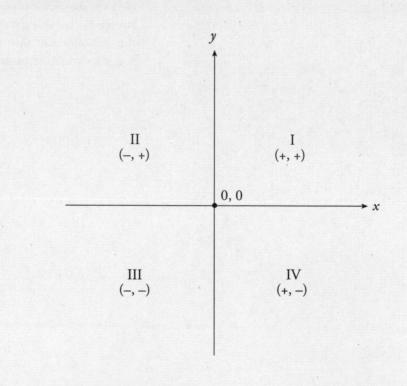

The plane is divided into four regions by two perpendicular axes called the *x*- and *y*-axes. These axes are like rulers that measure horizontal distances (the *x*-axis) and vertical distances (the *y*-axis). Okay, now follow along with the picture. Each axis has a positive direction and a negative direction; up and right are positive, down and left are negative. The four regions created by the axes are known as *quadrants*. The quadrants are numbered from I to IV, starting on the upper right and moving counterclockwise.

The location of every point on the coordinate plane can be expressed by a pair of *coordinates* that show the point's position with relation to the axes. The *x*-coordinate is always given first, followed by the *y*-coordinate: (2, 3), for example. This is called a coordinate pair—it is read as "two *right*, three *up*." These coordinates reflect the distance on each axis from the *origin*, or intersection of the axes.

The Coordinate Plane
The coordinate plane is a perfectly flat surface that extends an infinite distance in two dimensions. Oh, and it doesn't exist. It's just an abstract idea, a way of seeing mathematical relationships visually.

DRILL

On the coordinate plane below, match each coordinate pair to the corresponding point on the graph and identify the quadrant in which the point is located. The answers to these drills can be found in Chapter 12.

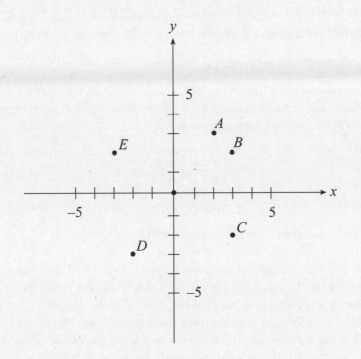

1. (–3, 2) Point _____, quadrant _____
2. (2, 3) Point _____, quadrant _____
3. (3, –2) Point _____, quadrant _____
4. (–2, –3) Point _____, quadrant _____
5. (3, 2) Point _____, quadrant _____

THE EQUATION OF A LINE

Most of the coordinate geometry questions on the Math Level 1 Subject Test will deal with the equations and graphs of lines. Lines will also be tested on the Math Level 2 Subject Test, but will generally be outnumbered on the Math Level 2 Subject Test by more complicated functions.

The equation of a line can show up on the test in two forms. The more common form is called the slope-intercept formula, and it is shown here:

> **Slope-Intercept Form of the Equation of a Line**
>
> $$y = mx + b$$

You may have seen this before. In this form, m and b are constants; m is the slope and b is the y-intercept. An equation in this form might look like: $y = \frac{2}{3}x - 4$. So $m = \frac{2}{3}$ and $b = -4$.

Let's talk a little about the y-intercept. This is the y-coordinate of the point at which the line intersects the y-axis. So, the slope-intercept formula of a line gives you the slope of the line and a specific point on the line, the y-intercept. The line $y = \frac{2}{3}x - 4$ therefore has a slope of $\frac{2}{3}$ and contains the point $(0, -4)$.

If you see an equation of a line in any other form, just convert what ETS gives you into slope-intercept form by solving for y. Here's how you'd convert the equation $y + 2 = 3(x - 1)$ to the slope-intercept form.

$$y + 2 = 3(x - 1)$$
$$y + 2 = 3x - 3$$
$$y = 3x - 5$$

The line therefore contains the point $(0, -5)$ and has a slope of 3.

Notice that the x-coordinate of the y-intercept is always 0. That's because at any point on the y-axis, the x-coordinate will be 0. So, whenever you're given the equation of a line in any form, you can find the y-intercept by making $x = 0$ and then solving for the value of y. In the same way, you can find the x-intercept by making $y = 0$ and solving for the value of x. The x- and y-intercepts are often the easiest points on a line to find. If you need to identify the graph of a linear equation, and the slope of the line isn't enough to narrow your choices down to one, finding the x- and y-intercepts will help.

To graph a line, simply plug a couple of x-values into the equation of the line, and plot the coordinates that result. The y-intercept is generally the easiest point to plot. Often, the y-intercept and the slope are enough to graph a line accurately enough or to identify the graph of a line.

DRILL

Try the following practice questions. The answers to these drills can be found in Chapter 12.

7. If a line of slope 0.6 contains the point $(3, 1)$, then it must also contain which of the following points?

   (A) $(-2, -2)$
   (B) $(-1, -4)$
   (C) $(0, 0)$
   (D) $(2, -1)$
   (E) $(3, 4)$

10. The line $y - 1 = 5(x - 1)$ contains the point $(0, n)$. What is the value of n ?

    (A) $\ \ 0$
    (B) -1
    (C) -2
    (D) -3
    (E) -4

11. What is the slope of the line whose equation is $2y - 13 = -6x - 5$?

    (A) -5
    (B) -3
    (C) -2
    (D) $\ \ 0$
    (E) $\ \ 3$

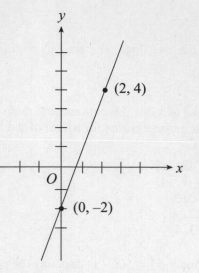

19. If the line $y = mx + b$ is graphed above, then which of the following statements is true?

(A) $m < b$

(B) $m = b$

(C) $2m = 3b$

(D) $2m + 3b = 0$

(E) $m = \dfrac{2b}{3}$

Let's Talk About Slope

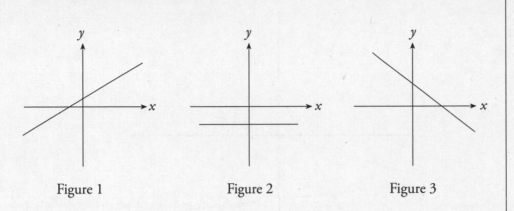

Figure 1   Figure 2   Figure 3

Often, slope is all you need to match the equation of a line to its graph. To begin with, it's easy to distinguish positive slopes from negative slopes. A line with a positive slope is shown in Figure 1 above; it goes uphill from left to right. A line with zero slope is shown in Figure 2; it's horizontal, and neither rises nor falls. A line with a negative slope is shown in Figure 3; it goes downhill from left to right.

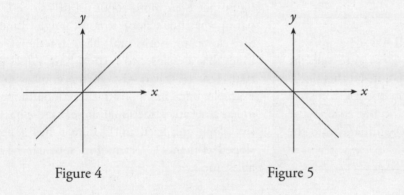

Figure 4   Figure 5

A line with a slope of 1 rises at a 45° angle, as shown in Figure 4. A line with a slope of −1 falls at a 45° angle, as shown in Figure 5.

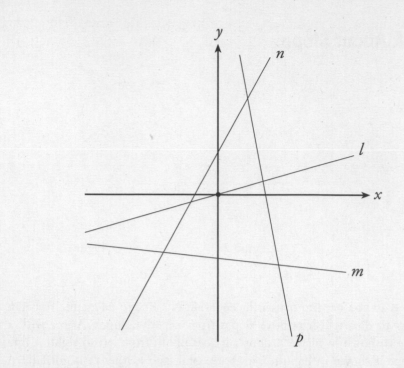

Because a line with a slope of 1 or −1 forms a 45° angle with either axis, you can figure out even more about a line's slope by comparing that line's slope to a 45° angle. Lines that are closer to horizontal have fractional slopes. Lines that are closer to vertical have slopes greater than 1 or less than −1. On the graph above, for example, line *l* has a positive fractional slope. Line *m* has a negative fractional slope. Line *n* has a positive slope greater than 1. Line *p* has a negative slope less than −1. Estimating slope can be a valuable time-saver.

You Have Two Points, You Have It All!

Using the slope formula, you can figure out the slope of any line given only two points on that line—which means that you can figure out the complete equation of the line. Just find the line's slope and plug the slope and one point's coordinates into the point-slope equation of a line.

Remember that the equation of a line gives you the slope without requiring calculation. But what if you're only given the coordinates of a couple of points on a line? Since the slope of a line is rise (change in *y*) over run (change in *x*), the coordinates of two points on a line provide you with enough information to figure out a line's slope. All you need is the following formula:

Slope Formula

$$m = \frac{y_2 - y_1}{x_2 - x_1}$$

Slopes can also help you determine the relationship between lines in a coordinate plane.

- The slopes of parallel lines are identical.
- The slopes of perpendicular lines are opposite reciprocals.

That means that if line l has a slope of 2, then any line parallel to l will also have a slope of 2. Any line perpendicular to l will have a slope of $-\frac{1}{2}$.

Flip It!
Opposite reciprocal means
flip the number over and
reverse the sign.

DRILL
The answers to these drills can be found in Chapter 12.

4. What is the slope of the line that passes through the origin and the point $(-3, 2)$?

   (A) −1.50
   (B) −0.75
   (C) −0.67
   (D) 1.00
   (E) 1.50

17. Lines l and m are perpendicular lines that intersect at the origin. If line l passes through the point $(2, -1)$, then line m must pass through which of the following points?

   (A) $(0, 2)$
   (B) $(1, 3)$
   (C) $(2, 1)$
   (D) $(3, 6)$
   (E) $(4, 0)$

23. Which of the following could be the graph of
$2(y + 1) = -6(x - 2)$?

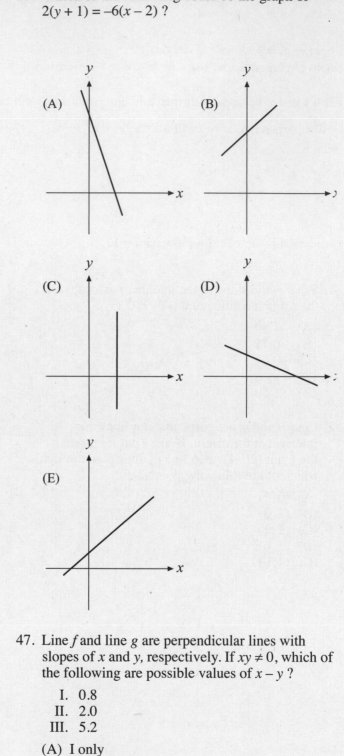

(A)

(B)

(C)

(D)

(E)

47. Line f and line g are perpendicular lines with slopes of x and y, respectively. If $xy \neq 0$, which of the following are possible values of $x - y$?

   I. 0.8
  II. 2.0
 III. 5.2

(A) I only
(B) I and II only
(C) I and III only
(D) II and III only
(E) I, II, and III

Line Segments

A line by definition goes on forever—it has infinite length. Coordinate geometry questions may also ask about line *segments,* however. Any coordinate geometry question asking for the distance between two points is a line segment question. Any question that draws or describes a rectangle, triangle, or other polygon in the coordinate plane may also involve line segment formulas. The most commonly requested line segment formula gives the length of a line segment.

Let's look at a line segment:

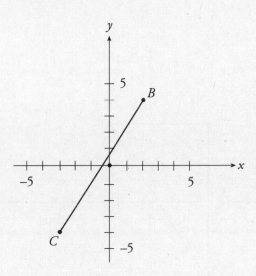

If you want to find the length of $\overline{BC}$, turn it into a triangle:

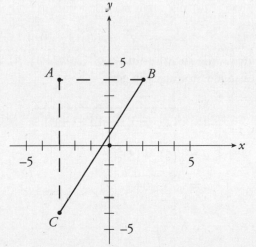

We've added in point A to illustrate the point. You know how to find the hypotenuse of a triangle, right? Pythagorean theorem! It's easy to find the distance from A to B, just count across. The distance is 5. The distance between A and C is 8. Using the Pythagorean theorem, we can fill in $5^2 + 8^2 = 89$. So the length of $\overline{BC}$ is $\sqrt{89}$. If you ever forget the distance formula, remember: All you have to do is make a triangle. After all, that's how the distance formula was created in the first place!

$$\boxed{\begin{array}{c} \textbf{The Distance Formula} \\[4pt] \text{For the two points } (x_1, y_1) \text{ and } (x_2, y_2), \\[6pt] d = \sqrt{(x_2 - x_1)^2 + (y_2 - y_1)^2} \end{array}}$$

How Did We Get There?
Look carefully at the distance formula. Notice anything familiar? If you square both sides, it's just the Pythagorean theorem!

Now let's take a look at the same triangle we were working with and use the distance formula.

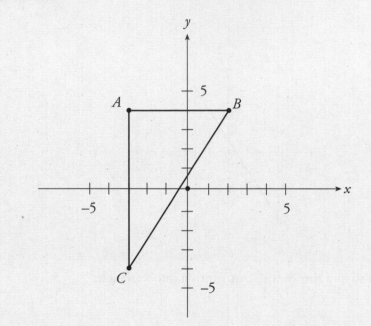

The coordinates of B are $(2, 4)$. The coordinates of C are $(-3, -4)$. If you plug these coordinates into the distance formula, you get

$$d = \sqrt{(2 - (-3))^2 + (4 - (-4))^2}$$
$$d = \sqrt{(5)^2 + (8)^2}$$
$$d = \sqrt{25 + 64}$$
$$d = \sqrt{89}$$
$$d = 9.434$$

Notice that you would get the same answer by counting the vertical distance between B and C (8) and the horizontal distance between B and C (5), and using the Pythagorean theorem to find the diagonal distance.

The other important line segment formula is used to find the coordinates of the middle point of a line segment with endpoints (x_1, y_1) and (x_2, y_2).

> **Coordinates of the Midpoint of a Line Segment**
>
> For the two points (x_1, y_1) and (x_2, y_2),
>
> $$M = \left(\frac{x_1 + x_2}{2}, \frac{y_1 + y_2}{2} \right)$$

Another Way to Think About It
The midpoint formula finds the average of the x-coordinates and the average of the y-coordinates.

The midpoint and distance formulas used together can answer any line segment question.

DRILL

The answers to these drills can be found in Chapter 12.

12. What is the distance between the origin and the point $(-5, 9)$?

   (A)   5.9
   (B)   6.7
   (C)   8.1
   (D)   10.3
   (E)   11.4

19. Point A has coordinates $(-4, 3)$, and the midpoint of AB is the point $(1, -1)$. What are the coordinates of B ?

   (A) $(-3, 4)$
   (B) $(-4, 5)$
   (C) $(4, -5)$
   (D) $(5, -4)$
   (E) $(6, -5)$

27. Which of the following points is farthest from the point $(2, 2)$?

   (A) $(8, 8)$
   (B) $(-6, 2)$
   (C) $(4, -6)$
   (D) $(-5, -3)$
   (E) $(9, 4)$

LINEAR INEQUALITIES

A linear inequality looks just like a linear equation, except that an inequality sign replaces the equal sign. They are graphed just as lines are graphed, except that the "greater than" or "less than" is represented by shading above or below the line. If the inequality is a "greater than or equal to" or "less than or equal to," then the line itself is included and is drawn as a solid line. If the inequality is a "greater than" or "less than," then the line itself is not included; the line is drawn as a dotted line, and only the shaded region is included in the inequality. Take a look at some examples.

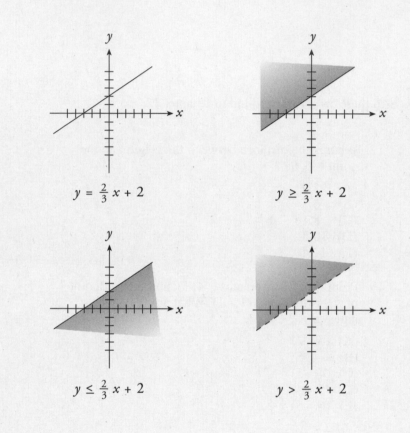

$$y = \tfrac{2}{3}x + 2 \qquad\qquad y \geq \tfrac{2}{3}x + 2$$

$$y \leq \tfrac{2}{3}x + 2 \qquad\qquad y > \tfrac{2}{3}x + 2$$

GENERAL EQUATIONS

While lines are the focus of most coordinate geometry questions, you may also be required to work with the graphs of other shapes in the coordinate plane. In the next few pages, you'll find the general forms of the equations of a number of shapes, and listings of the special information each equation contains.

When ETS asks a coordinate geometry question about nonlinear shapes, the questions are generally very simple. It will be very useful to you to remember the basic equations in this chapter and the shapes of their graphs. Questions on this material generally test your understanding of the information contained in the standard forms of these equations.

The Parabola

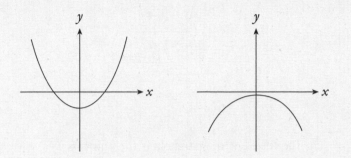

A parabola takes the form of a single curve opening either upward or downward, becoming increasingly steep as you move away from the center of the curve. Parabolas are the graphs of *quadratic* functions, which were discussed in Chapter 4. The equation of a parabola can come in two forms. Here is the one that will make you happiest on SAT Math.

> **Standard Form of the Equation of a Parabola**
>
> $$y = a(x - h)^2 + k$$

In this formula, *a, h,* and *k* are constants. The following information can be gotten from the equation of a parabola in standard form:

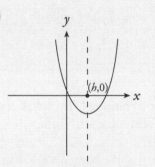

The axis of symmetry of the parabola is the line $x = h$.

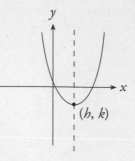

The vertex of the parabola is the point (h, k).

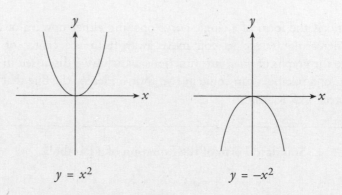

$y = x^2$ $y = -x^2$

If a is positive, the parabola opens upward. If a is negative, the parabola opens downward.

Déjà Vu?

This equation may look familiar. It turns out that quadratic equations are equations of parabolas. It's all connected.

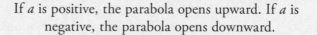

General Form of the Equation of a Parabola

$$y = ax^2 + bx + c$$

In this formula, a, b, and c are constants. The following information can be gotten from the equation of a parabola in general form:

- The axis of symmetry of the parabola is the line $x = -\dfrac{b}{2a}$.

- The x-coordinate of the parabola's vertex is $-\dfrac{b}{2a}$. The y-coordinate of the vertex is whatever you get when you plug $-\dfrac{b}{2a}$ into the equation as x.

- The y-intercept of the parabola is the point $(0, c)$.
- If a is positive, the parabola opens upward. If a is negative, the parabola opens downward.

Since a parabola is simply the graph of a quadratic equation, the quadratic formula can be used to find the roots (*x*-intercepts or zeros), if any, of the parabola. The discriminant, or $b^2 - 4ac$, can be used to determine how many distinct real roots the quadratic has, which is the number of *x*-intercepts the parabola has. For example, if the discriminant is 0, you know that the parabola has one root, which means that the graph is tangent to the *x*-axis at the vertex of the parabola. If the discriminant is positive, the graph intercepts the *x*-axis at two points. If the discriminant is negative, the parabola does not cross the *x*-axis.

DRILL

The answers to these drills can be found in Chapter 12.

34. What is the minimum value of $f(x)$ if
$f(x) = x^2 - 6x + 8$?

    (A) –3
    (B) –2
    (C) –1
    (D) 0
    (E) 2

37. What are the coordinates of the vertex of the

    parabola defined by the equation $y = \dfrac{1}{2}x^2 + x + \dfrac{5}{2}$?

    (A) (–2, 4)
    (B) (–1, 2)
    (C) (1, 2)
    (D) (2, 4)
    (E) (2, –4)

38. At which of the following *x*-values does the
parabola defined by $y = (x - 3)^2 - 4$ cross the
x-axis?

    (A) –3
    (B) 3
    (C) 4
    (D) 5
    (E) 9

The Circle

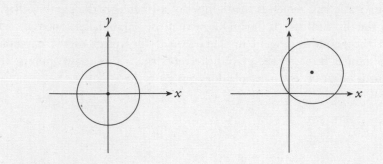

The circle is that round shape you know and love. It's also probably ETS's favorite nonlinear shape in the coordinate plane, particularly on the Math Level 1 Subject Test. Below is the formula for a circle.

Standard Form of the Equation of a Circle

$$(x - h)^2 + (y - k)^2 = r^2$$

In this formula, *h*, *k*, and *r* are constants. The following information can be learned from the equation of a circle in standard form:

- The center of the circle is the point (h, k).
- The length of the circle's radius is *r*.

And that's all there is to know about a circle. Once you know its radius and the position of its center, you can sketch the circle yourself or identify its graph easily. It's also a simple matter to estimate the radius and center coordinates of a circle whose graph is given, and make a good guess at the equation of that circle. One last note: If the circle's center is the origin, then $(h, k) = (0, 0)$. This greatly simplifies the equation of the circle.

Equation of a Circle with Center at Origin

$$x^2 + y^2 = r^2$$

DRILL

The answers to these drills can be found in Chapter 12.

30. Which of the following points does NOT lie on the circle whose equation is $(x - 2)^2 + (y - 4)^2 = 9$?

   (A) $(-1, 4)$
   (B) $(-1, -1)$
   (C) $(2, 1)$
   (D) $(2, 7)$
   (E) $(5, 4)$

34. Points S and T lie on the circle with equation $x^2 + y^2 = 16$. If S and T have identical y-coordinates but distinct x-coordinates, then which of the following is the distance between S and T ?

   (A) 4.0
   (B) 5.6
   (C) 8.0
   (D) 11.3
   (E) It cannot be determined from the information given.

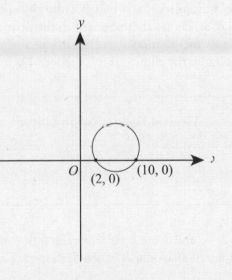

50. Which of the following equations could represent the circle shown in the figure above?

   (A) $x^2 + y^2 - 14x - 8y + 40 = 0$
   (B) $x^2 + y^2 - 14x + 8y + 40 = 0$
   (C) $x^2 + y^2 - 12x - 6y + 20 = 0$
   (D) $x^2 + y^2 - 10x + 8y + 16 = 0$
   (E) $x^2 + y^2 + 4x - 6y - 12 = 0$

The Ellipse

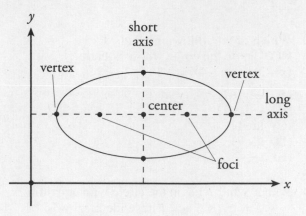

The equation of an ellipse looks similar to the equation of a circle, but an ellipse is actually a much more complex shape. You don't need to worry about the ellipse if you're taking the Math Level 1 Subject Test; it appears exclusively on the Math Level 2 Subject Test.

An ellipse has a center like a circle, but since it's squashed a little flatter than a circle; it has no constant radius. Instead, an ellipse has two *vertices* (the plural of *vertex*) at the ends of its long axis, and two *foci* (the plural of *focus*), points within the ellipse. The foci of an ellipse are important to the definition of an ellipse. The distances from the two foci to a point on the ellipse always add up to the same number for every point on the ellipse. This is the formula for an ellipse:

General Equation of an Ellipse

$$\frac{(x-h)^2}{a^2} + \frac{(y-k)^2}{b^2} = 1$$

In this formula, *a*, *b*, *h*, and *k* are constants. The following information can be learned from the equation of an ellipse in standard form:

> The center of an ellipse is the point (*h*, *k*).
> The width of the ellipse is 2*a*, and the height is 2*b*.

An ellipse can be longer either horizontally or vertically. If the constant under the $(x - h)^2$ term is larger than the constant under the $(y - k)^2$ term, then the major axis of the ellipse is horizontal. If the constant under the $(y - k)^2$ term is bigger, then the major axis is vertical. Like that of a circle, the equation for an ellipse becomes simpler when it's centered at the origin, and (*h*, *k*) = (0, 0).

The few ellipses that show up on the Math Level 2 Subject Test are usually in this simplified form; they are centered at the origin.

DRILL

The answers to these drills can be found in Chapter 12.

15. How long is the major axis of the ellipse with a formula of $\frac{x^2}{16} + \frac{y^2}{25} = 1$?
    (A) 1
    (B) 4
    (C) 5
    (D) 8
    (E) 10

40. Which of the following points is the center of the ellipse whose formula is $\frac{(x+5)^2}{9} + \frac{(y-3)^2}{4} = 1$?

    (A) $\left(\frac{25}{9}, -\frac{9}{4}\right)$

    (B) $\left(-\frac{5}{9}, \frac{3}{4}\right)$

    (C) $(-5, 3)$

    (D) $(25, -9)$

    (E) $(9, 16)$

The Hyperbola

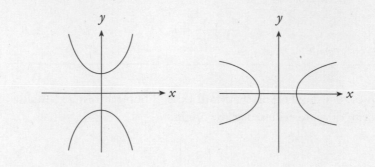

A hyperbola is basically an oval turned inside out. Like the ellipse, the hyperbola only shows up on the Math Level 2 Subject Test, and it doesn't show up frequently. The equation of a hyperbola differs from the equation of an ellipse only by a sign.

General Equation of a Hyperbola

$$\frac{(x-h)^2}{a^2} - \frac{(y-k)^2}{b^2} = 1$$

In this formula, *a, b, h,* and *k* are constants. The following information can be learned from the equation of a hyperbola in standard form:

The hyperbola's center is the point (*h, k*).

Like an ellipse, a hyperbola can be oriented either horizontally or vertically. If the *y*-term is negative, like in the equations above, then the curves open out to the right and left. If the *x*-term is negative—that is, the *x, h,* and *a* switch places with the *y, k,* and *b*—then the curves open up and down. Like that of an ellipse, a hyperbola's equation becomes simpler when it is centered at the origin, and (*h, k*) = (0, 0).

Equation of a Hyperbola with Center at Origin

$$\frac{x^2}{a^2} - \frac{y^2}{b^2} = 1$$

The few hyperbolas that show up on the Math Level 2 Subject Test are usually in this simplified form; they are centered at the origin.

DRILL

Try this hyperbola question. The answer can be found in Chapter 12.

38. The hyperbola $\dfrac{(x+4)^2}{9} - \dfrac{(y+5)^2}{4} = 1$ has its center at which of the following points?

(A) $(-9, -4)$
(B) $(-4, -5)$
(C) $(4, 5)$
(D) $(9, -4)$
(E) $(16, 25)$

TRIAXIAL COORDINATES: THINKING 3-D

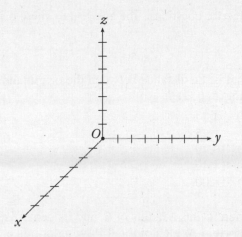

On the Math Level 2 (or the difficult third of the Math Level 1), you may run into a twist on the coordinate plane—a coordinate *space*. A third dimension can be added to the coordinate plane by introducing a third axis (often referred to as the *z*-axis) that passes through the origin at right angles to both the *x*-axis and the *y*-axis. While the *x*- and *y*-axes define the location of a point in a plane, the *x*-, *y*-, and *z*-axes define the location of a point in a three-dimensional space.

Such a system of three axes is called a *three-dimensional coordinate system*, a *triaxial coordinate system,* or a *coordinate space*. Sometimes it's not called anything at all; ETS will simply show you a diagram of a three-dimensional graph, or a set of triple coordinates, and expect you to understand what you're seeing. The coordinates of a point in three dimensions are given in this form: (x, y, z). The point $(3, 4, 5)$ is located 3 units along the *x*-axis, 4 units along the *y*-axis, and 5 units along the *z*-axis. Always check the labels on the axes if you're given a diagram, because there's no firm convention about which axis is pictured in which position.

Connect the Dots
This formula is equivalent
to the Super Pythagorean
theorem: $a^2 + b^2 + c^2 = d^2$.

If you are given two points in 3-D, (x_1, y_1, z_1) and (x_2, y_2, z_2), then the distance, d, between them is given by the following formula:

> ### Distance in a Three-Dimensional Space
>
> $$d = \sqrt{(x_2 - x_1)^2 + (y_2 - y_1)^2 + (z_2 - z_1)^2}$$

Most of the three-dimensional coordinate questions on the Math Subject Tests require you to calculate a distance between two points in a 3-D coordinate system. Just use the formula.

DRILL

Try the following practice questions. The answers to these drills can be found in Chapter 12.

29. What is the distance between the origin and the point $(5, 6, 7)$?

    (A) 4.24
    (B) 7.25
    (C) 10.49
    (D) 14.49
    (E) 18.00

34. Sphere O has a radius of 6, and its center is at the origin. Which of the following points is NOT inside the sphere?

    (A) $(-3, 5, 1)$
    (B) $(-4, -4, 3)$
    (C) $(5, -2, 2)$
    (D) $(4, 1, -4)$
    (E) $(2, -4, -3)$

Summary

o   The coordinate plane is created by the perpendicular intersection of the x- and y-axis. This intersection creates four quadrants.

o   The slope-intercept form of the equation of a line is $y = mx + b$. The slope of the line is m and the y-intercept is b.

o   To find the slope of a line, take two points on the line and put them in the formula $m = \dfrac{y_2 - y_1}{x_2 - x_1}$.

o   The distance formula comes from the Pythagorean theorem. It is $d = \sqrt{\left(x_2 - x_1\right)^2 + \left(y_2 - y_1\right)^2}$.

o   To find the coordinates of the midpoint of a line, take the average of the endpoints. The formula is $M = \left(\dfrac{x_1 + x_2}{2}, \dfrac{y_1 + y_2}{2}\right)$.

o   The general form of the equation of a parabola is $y = a\,(x - h)^2 + k$, where (h, k) is the vertex of the parabola. The general form of a parabola is a quadratic equation: $y = ax^2 + bx + c$. Use the general form to find the axis of symmetry, the vertex, and whether the parabola opens up or down.

o   The general form of the equation of a circle is $(x - h)^2 + (y - k)^2 = r^2$, where (h, k) is the center of the circle.

o   The general form of the equation of an ellipse is $\dfrac{(x - h)^2}{a^2} + \dfrac{(y - k)^2}{b^2} = 1$, where (h, k) is the center of the ellipse.

- The general form of the equation of a hyperbola is $\dfrac{(x-h)^2}{a^2} - \dfrac{(y-k)^2}{b^2} = 1$, where (h, k) is the center of the hyperbola.

- The 3-D coordinate plane has 3 axes, x, y, and z. The formula for the distance of a line in three-dimensional space is

$$d = \sqrt{(x_2 - x_1)^2 + (y_2 - y_1)^2 + (z_2 - z_1)^2}.$$

Chapter 8
Trigonometry

The rules of trigonometry tested on the Math Level 1 Subject Test are much more limited than those tested on the Math Level 2 Subject Test. Trigonometry on the Math Level 1 Subject Test is confined to right triangles and the most basic relationships between the sine, cosine, and tangent functions. If you're taking the Math Level 1, that's the only material from this chapter you need to know. If you plan to take the Math Level 2, then this entire chapter is your domain; rule it wisely.

DEFINITIONS

Here are some trigonometric terms that appear on the Math Subject Tests. Make sure you're familiar with them. If the meaning of any of these vocabulary words keeps slipping your mind, add that word to your flash cards.

Acute Angle	An angle whose measure in degrees is between 0 and 90, exclusive.
Obtuse Angle	An angle whose measure in degrees is between 90 and 180, exclusive.
Theta	The symbol θ (pronounced thay-tuh) is a variable, just like x and y, used to represent the measure of an angle in trigonometry.
arc–	Prefix added to trigonometric functions, meaning *inverse*.

THE BASIC FUNCTIONS

The basis of trigonometry is the relationship between the parts of a right triangle. When you know the measure of one of the acute angles in a right triangle, you know all the angles in that triangle. For example, if you know that a right triangle contains a 20° angle, then you know all three angles—the right triangle must have a 90° angle, and because there are 180° in a triangle, the third angle must measure 70°. You don't know the lengths in the triangle, but you know its shape and its proportions.

A right triangle that contains a 20° angle can have only one shape, though it can be any size. The same is true for a right triangle containing any other acute angle. That's the fundamental idea of trigonometry. Once you know the measure of an acute angle in a right triangle, you know that triangle's proportions.

Similar **Right Triangles**
Remember that similar triangles have the same angles. So, any right triangle that contains a 20° angle will be similar to all other right triangles with a 20° angle.

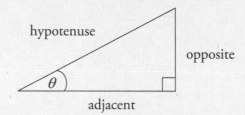

The three basic functions in trigonometry—the sine, cosine, and tangent—are ways of expressing proportions in a right triangle (that's the ratio of one side to another). They may sound familiar to you. Or maybe you've heard of a little phrase called SOHCAHTOA?

Let's break it down.

$$\boxed{\begin{array}{c} \text{SOHCAHTOA} \\[1em] s\text{in} = \dfrac{opposite}{hypotenuse} \qquad c\text{os} = \dfrac{adjacent}{hypotenuse} \qquad t\text{an} = \dfrac{opposite}{adjacent} \end{array}}$$

Sine

The sine of an angle is the ratio of the opposite side to the hypotenuse. The sine function of an angle θ is abbreviated sin θ.

Cosine

The cosine of an angle is the ratio of the adjacent side to the hypotenuse. The cosine function of an angle θ is abbreviated cos θ.

Tangent

The tangent of an angle is the ratio of the opposite side to the adjacent side. The tangent function of an angle θ is abbreviated tan θ.

These three functions form the basis of everything else in trigonometry. All of the more complicated functions and rules in trigonometry can be derived from the information contained in SOHCAHTOA.

It's All About Proportions

A trigonometric function of any angle comes from the proportions of a right triangle containing that angle. For any given angle, there is only one possible set of proportions.

What Your Calculator Can Do for You

Tables of sine, cosine, and tangent values are programmed into your calculator—that's what the "sin," "cos," and "tan" keys do.

- If you press one of the three trigonometric function keys and then enter an angle measure, your calculator will give you the function (sine, cosine, or tangent) of that angle. Just make sure that your calculator is in degree mode. This operation is written:

  sin 30° = 0.5   cos 30° = 0.866   tan 30° = 0.577

- Your calculator can also take a trig function value and tell you what angle would produce that value. Press the "2nd" key, then press "sin," "cos," or "tan," then enter the decimal or fraction you're given, and your calculator will give you the measure of that angle. This is called taking an inverse function, and it's written:

  $\sin^{-1}(0.5) = 30°$ $\cos^{-1}(0.866) = 30°$ $\tan^{-1}(0.577) = 30°$

  OR

  arcsin (0.5) = 30°   arccos (0.866) = 30°   arctan (0.577) = 30°

The expressions "$\sin^{-1}(0.5)$" and "arcsin (0.5)" have the same meaning. Both mean "the angle whose sine is 0.5." While ordinary trig functions take angle measures and output ratios, inverse trig functions take ratios and produce the corresponding angle measures; they work in reverse.

Check Your Calculator

For some scientific calculators, you need to enter things in reverse order. To find sin 30°, for example, you would type "30" first and then hit "sin." To find $\sin^{-1}(0.5)$, you would type "0.5" first and then hit "2nd" and "sin."

Finding Trig Functions in Right Triangles

On the Math Level 1 Subject Test, the three basic trigonometric functions always occur in right triangles—particularly the Pythagorean triplets from Chapter 5.

DRILL

Use the definitions of the sine, cosine, and tangent to fill in the requested quantities in the following triangles. The answers to these drills can be found in Chapter 12.

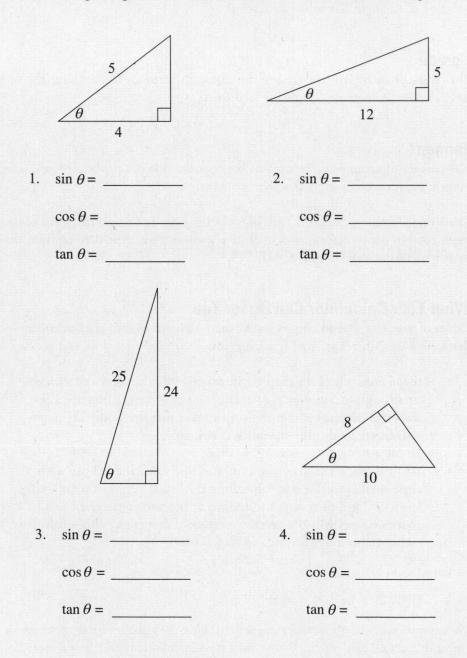

1. $\sin \theta =$ _____

    $\cos \theta =$ _____

    $\tan \theta =$ _____

2. $\sin \theta =$ _____

    $\cos \theta =$ _____

    $\tan \theta =$ _____

3. $\sin \theta =$ _____

    $\cos \theta =$ _____

    $\tan \theta =$ _____

4. $\sin \theta =$ _____

    $\cos \theta =$ _____

    $\tan \theta =$ _____

Completing Triangles

The preceding examples have all involved figuring out the values of trigonometric functions from lengths in a right triangle. Slightly more difficult trigonometry questions may require you to go the other way and figure out lengths or measures of angles using trigonometry. For example:

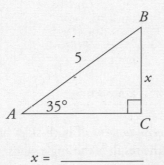

$$x = \underline{\hspace{3cm}}$$

Because we're dealing with the hypotenuse and the side that is opposite the angle, the best definition to use is sine.

$$\sin = \frac{opposite}{hypotenuse}$$

$$\sin 35° = \frac{x}{5}$$

$$5(\sin 35°) = x$$

$$5(0.5736) = x$$

$$2.8679 = x$$

$\overline{BC}$ of $\triangle ABC$ therefore has a length of 2.87.

You can use a similar technique to find the measure of an unknown angle in a right triangle. For example:

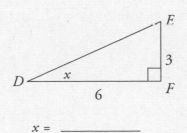

$$x = \underline{\hspace{3cm}}$$

Check Your Mode

For Math Level 1, your calculator should always be in degree mode. For Math Level 2, it may sometimes need to be in radian mode (more on that later).

The Unknown

In triangle ABC, you know only two quantities—the length of AB and the measure of $\angle A$. This question, unlike previous examples, doesn't give you enough information to use the Pythagorean theorem. What you need is an equation that relates the information you have (AB and $\angle A$) to the information you don't have (x). Use the SOHCAHTOA definitions to set up an equation. Solve that equation, and you find the value of the unknown.

In triangle *DEF*, you know $\overline{EF}$ and $\overline{DF}$. $\overline{EF}$ is the side that is opposite the angle we're looking for, and $\overline{DF}$ is the side that is adjacent to that same angle. So the best definition to use is tangent.

$$\tan = \frac{opposite}{adjacent}$$

$$\tan x = \frac{EF}{FD}$$

$$\tan x = \frac{3}{6}$$

$$\tan x = 0.5$$

Let Your Calculator Help
To take the inverse tangent of the right side of this equation, press the "2nd" key, press the "tan" key, and then type in 0.5.

To solve for *x*, take the *inverse tangent* of both sides of the equation. On the left side, that just gives you *x*. The result is the angle whose tangent is 0.5.

$$\tan^{-1}(\tan x) = \tan^{-1}(0.5)$$

$$x = 26.57°$$

The measure of $\angle D$ is therefore 26.57°.

DRILL

Use the techniques you've just reviewed to complete the following triangles. The answers to these drills can be found in Chapter 12.

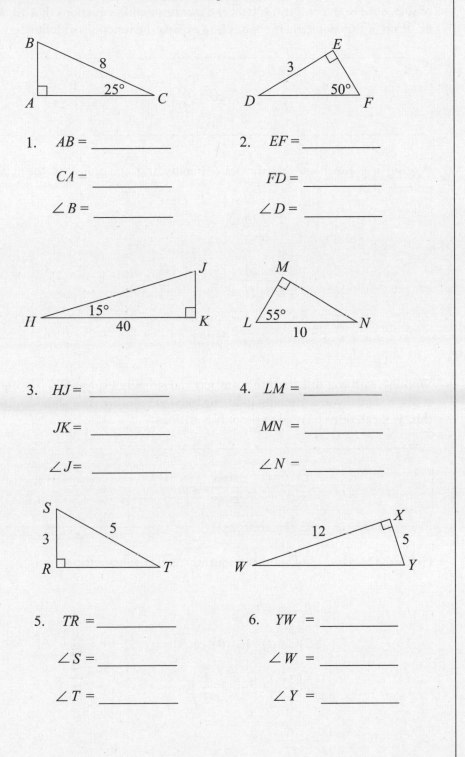

1. $AB =$ _____

   $CA =$ _____

   $\angle B =$ _____

2. $EF =$ _____

   $FD =$ _____

   $\angle D =$ _____

3. $HJ =$ _____

   $JK =$ _____

   $\angle J =$ _____

4. $LM =$ _____

   $MN =$ _____

   $\angle N =$ _____

5. $TR =$ _____

   $\angle S =$ _____

   $\angle T =$ _____

6. $YW =$ _____

   $\angle W =$ _____

   $\angle Y =$ _____

TRIGONOMETRIC IDENTITIES

Some Math Subject Test questions will ask you to do algebra with trigonometric functions. These questions usually involve using the SOHCAHTOA definitions of sine, cosine, and tangent. Often, the way to simplify equations that are mostly made up of trigonometric functions is to express the functions as follows:

$$\sin = \frac{O}{H} \qquad \cos = \frac{A}{H} \qquad \tan = \frac{O}{A}$$

Writing trig functions this way can simplify trig equations, as the following example shows:

$$\frac{\sin x}{\cos x} =$$

$$\frac{O}{H} \div \frac{A}{H} =$$

$$\frac{O}{A} = \tan x$$

Working with trig functions this way lets you simplify expressions. The equation above is actually a commonly used *trigonometric identity*. You should memorize this, as it can often be used to simplify equations.

$$\frac{\sin x}{\cos x} = \tan x$$

Here's the breakdown of another frequently used trigonometric identity:

$$\sin^2 \theta + \cos^2 \theta =$$

$$(\sin\theta)(\sin\theta) + (\cos\theta)(\cos\theta) =$$

$$\left(\frac{O}{H}\right)\left(\frac{O}{H}\right) + \left(\frac{A}{H}\right)\left(\frac{A}{H}\right) =$$

$$\frac{O^2}{H^2} + \frac{A^2}{H^2} =$$

$$\frac{O^2 + A^2}{H^2} = 1$$

That last step may seem a little baffling, but it's really simple. This equation is based on a right triangle, in which O and A are legs of the triangle, and H is the hypotenuse. Consequently you know that $O^2 + A^2 = H^2$. That's just the Pythagorean theorem. That's what lets you do the last step, in which $\frac{O^2 + A^2}{H^2} = 1$. This completes the second commonly used identity that you should memorize.

$$\sin^2 \theta + \cos^2 \theta = 1$$

In addition to memorizing these two identities, you should practice working algebraically with trig functions in general. Some questions may require you to use the SOHCAHTOA definitions of the trig functions; others may require you to use the two identities you've just reviewed. Take a look at these examples:

---

35. If $\sin x = 0.707$, then what is the value of $(\sin x) \bullet (\cos x) \bullet (\tan x)$?

    (A) 1.0
    (B) 0.707
    (C) 0.5
    (D) 0.4
    (E) 0.207

Here's How to Crack It
This is a tricky question. To solve it, simplify that complicated trigonometric expression. Writing in the SOHCAHTOA definitions works just fine, but in this case it's even faster to use one of those identities.

$$(\sin x) \bullet (\cos x) \bullet (\tan x) =$$
$$(\sin x) \bullet (\cos x) \bullet \left(\frac{\sin x}{\cos x} \right) =$$
$$(\sin x) \bullet (\sin x) =$$
$$\sin^2 x =$$

Now it's a simpler matter to answer the question. If $\sin x = 0.707$, then $\sin^2 x = 0.5$. The answer is (C).

Take a look at this one:

---○---

36. If $\sin a = 0.4$, and $1 - \cos^2 a = x$, then what is the value of x ?

(A) 0.8
(B) 0.6
(C) 0.44
(D) 0.24
(E) 0.16

Here's How to Crack It

Here again, the trick to the question is simplifying the complicated trig expression. Since $\sin^2 \theta + \cos^2 \theta = 1$, you can rearrange any of those terms to rephrase it. Using the second trig identity, you can quickly take these steps:

$$1 - \cos^2 a = x$$
$$\sin^2 a = x$$
$$(0.4)^2 = x$$
$$x = 0.16$$

And that's the answer. (E) is correct.

---○---

Using the SOHCAHTOA definitions and the two trigonometric identities reviewed in this section, simplify trigonometric expressions to answer the following sample questions.

DRILL

Try the following practice questions. The answers to these drills can be found in Chapter 12.

25. $(1 - \sin x)(1 + \sin x) =$

    (A) $\cos x$
    (B) $\sin x$
    (C) $\tan x$
    (D) $\cos^2 x$
    (E) $\sin^2 x$

31. $\dfrac{\tan x \cos x}{\sin x} =$

    (A) $\dfrac{1}{\tan x}$

    (B) $\dfrac{1}{\cos x}$

    (C) 1

    (D) $\cos^2 x$

    (E) $\tan x$

39. $\dfrac{1}{\cos x} - (\sin x)(\tan x) =$

    (A) $\cos x$
    (B) $\sin x$
    (C) $\tan x$
    (D) $\cos^2 x$
    (E) $\sin^7 x$

42. $\dfrac{\tan x - \sin x \cos x}{\tan x} =$

    (A) $1 - \cos x$
    (B) $1 - \sin x$
    (C) $\tan x + 1$
    (D) $\cos^2 x$
    (E) $\sin^2 x$

The Other Trig Functions

On the Math Level 2 Subject Test, you may run into the *other* three trigonometric functions—the cosecant, secant, and cotangent. These functions are abbreviated $\csc\theta$, $\sec\theta$, and $\cot\theta$, respectively, and they are simply the reciprocals of the three basic trigonometric functions you've already reviewed.

Here's how they relate:

$$\csc\theta = \frac{1}{\sin\theta} \qquad \sec\theta = \frac{1}{\cos\theta} \qquad \cot\theta = \frac{1}{\tan\theta} = \frac{\cos\theta}{\sin\theta}$$

You can also express these functions in terms of the sides of a right triangle—just by flipping over the SOHCAHTOA definitions of the three basic functions.

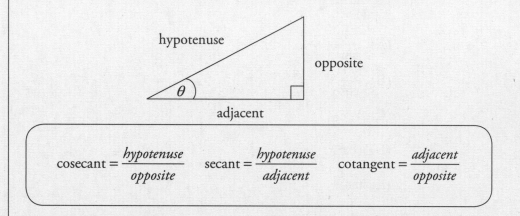

$$\text{cosecant} = \frac{hypotenuse}{opposite} \qquad \text{secant} = \frac{hypotenuse}{adjacent} \qquad \text{cotangent} = \frac{adjacent}{opposite}$$

These three functions generally show up in algebra-style questions, which require you to simplify complex expressions containing trig functions. The goal is usually to get an expression into the simplest form possible, one that contains no fractions. Such questions are like algebra-style questions involving the three basic trig functions; the only difference is that the addition of three more functions increases the number of possible forms an expression can take. For example:

$$(\cos x)(\cot x) + (\sin^2 x \csc x) =$$

$$(\cos x)(\frac{\cos x}{\sin x}) + (\sin^2 x)(\frac{1}{\sin x}) =$$

$$\frac{\cos^2 x}{\sin x} + \frac{\sin^2 x}{\sin x} =$$

$$\frac{\cos^2 x + \sin^2 x}{\sin x} =$$

$$\frac{1}{\sin x} =$$

$$\csc x$$

The entire expression $(\cos x)(\cot x) + (\sin^2 x \csc x)$ is therefore equivalent to a single trig function, the cosecant of x. That's generally the way algebraic trigonometry questions work on the Math Level 2 Subject Test.

DRILL

Simplify each of these expressions to a single trigonometric function. Keep an eye out for the trigonometric identities reviewed on pages 186–188; they'll still come in handy. The answers to these drills can be found in Chapter 12.

Level 2 Only

19. $\sec^2 x - 1 =$

    (A) $\sin x \cos x$
    (B) $\sec^2 x$
    (C) $\cos^2 x$
    (D) $\sin^2 x$
    (E) $\tan^2 x$

23. $\dfrac{1}{\sin x \cot x} =$

    (A) $\cos x$
    (B) $\sin x$
    (C) $\tan x$
    (D) $\sec x$
    (E) $\csc x$

24. $\sin x + (\cos x)(\cot x) =$

    (A) $\csc x$
    (B) $\sec x$
    (C) $\cot x$
    (D) $\tan x$
    (E) $\sin x$

GRAPHING TRIGONOMETRIC FUNCTIONS

There are two common ways to represent trigonometric functions graphically—on the *unit circle*, or on the coordinate plane (you'll get a good look at both methods in the coming pages). Both of these graphing approaches are ways of showing the repetitive nature of trigonometric functions. All of the trig functions (sine, cosine, and the rest) are called *periodic* functions. That simply means that they cycle repeatedly through the same values.

The Unit Circle

What Goes Around Comes Around

If you picked a certain angle and its sine, cosine, and tangent, and then slowly changed the measure of that angle, you'd see the sine, cosine, and tangent change as well. But after a while, you would have increased the angle by 360°—in other words, you would come full circle, back to the angle you started with, going counterclockwise. The new angle, equivalent to the old one, would have the same sine, cosine, and tangent as the original. As you continued to increase the angle's measure, the sine, cosine, and tangent would cycle through the same values all over again. All trigonometric functions repeat themselves every 360°. The tangent and cotangent functions actually repeat every 180°.

Thus, angles of 0° and 360° are mathematically equivalent. So are angles of 40° and 400°, or 360° and 720°. Any two angle measures separated by 360° are equivalent. For example, to find equivalent angles to 40°, you just keep adding 360°. Likewise, you can go around the unit circle *clockwise* by *subtracting* multiples of 360°. Some angles equivalent to 40° would thus be 40° − 360° = −320°, −680°, −1040°, and so on. In the next few sections, you'll see how that's reflected in the graphs of trigonometric functions.

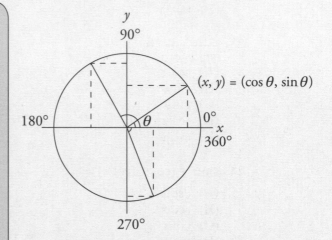

This is the unit circle. It looks a little like the coordinate plane; in fact, it *is* the coordinate plane, or at least a piece of it. The circle is called the *unit circle* because it has a radius of 1 (a single unit). This is convenient because it makes trigonometric values easy to figure out. The radius touching any point on the unit circle is the hypotenuse of a right triangle. The length of the horizontal leg of the triangle is the cosine (which is therefore the *x*-coordinate) and the length of the vertical leg is the sine (which is the *y*-coordinate). It works out this way because sine = opposite ÷ hypotenuse, and cosine = adjacent ÷ hypotenuse; and here the hypotenuse is 1, so the sine is simply the length of the opposite side, and the cosine simply the length of the adjacent side.

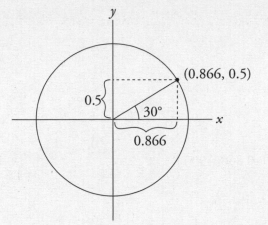

Suppose you wanted to show the sine and cosine of a 30° angle. That angle would appear on the unit circle as a radius drawn at a 30° angle to the positive *x*-axis (above). The *x*-coordinate of the point where the radius intercepts the circle is 0.866, which is the value of cos 30°. The *y*-coordinate of that point is 0.5, which is the value of sin 30°.

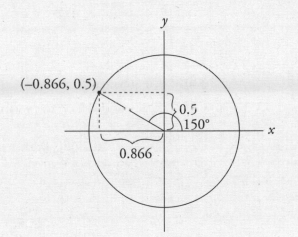

Now take a look at the sine and cosine of a 150° angle. As you can see, it looks just like the 30° angle, flipped over the *y*-axis. Its *y*-value is the same— sin 150° = 0.5—but its *x*-value is now *negative*. The cosine of 150° is −0.866.

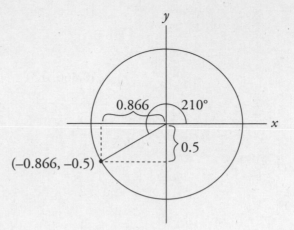

Here, you see the sine and cosine of a 210° angle. Once again, this looks just like the 30° angle, but this time flipped over the *x*- and *y*-axes. The sine of 210° is −0.5; the cosine of 210° is −0.866.

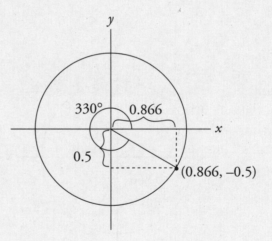

This is the sine and cosine of a 330° angle. Like the previous angles, the 330° angle has a sine and cosine equivalent in magnitude to those of the 30° angle. In the case of the 330° angle, the sine is negative and the cosine positive. So, sin 330° = −0.5 and cos 330° = 0.866. Notice that a 330° angle is equivalent to an angle of −30°.

Following these angles around the unit circle gives us some useful information about the sine and cosine functions.

- Sine is positive between 0° and 180° and negative between 180° and 360°. At 0°, 180°, and 360°, sine is zero. At 90°, sine is 1. At 270°, sine is –1.
- Cosine is positive between 0° and 90° and between 270° and 360°. (You could also say that cosine is positive between –90° and 90°.) Cosine is negative between 90° and 270°. At 90° and 270°, cosine is zero. At 0° and 360°, cosine is 1. At 180°, cosine is –1.

When these angles are sketched on the unit circle, sine is positive in quadrants I and II, and cosine is positive in quadrants I and IV. There's another important piece of information you can get from the unit circle. The biggest value that can be produced by a sine or cosine function is 1. The smallest value that can be produced by a sine or cosine function is –1.

Following the tangent function around the unit circle also yields useful information.

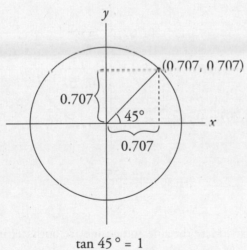

tan 45° = 1

The sine of 45° is $\frac{\sqrt{2}}{2}$, or 0.707, and the cosine of 45° is also $\frac{\sqrt{2}}{2}$, or 0.707. Since the tangent is the ratio of the sine to the cosine, that means that the tangent of 45° is 1.

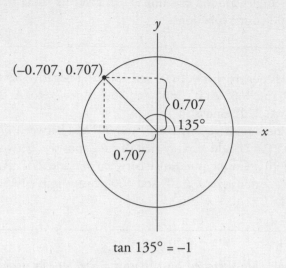

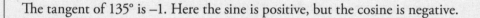

tan 135° = −1

The tangent of 135° is −1. Here the sine is positive, but the cosine is negative.

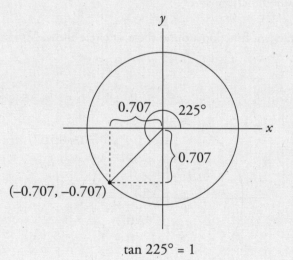

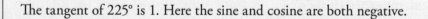

tan 225° = 1

The tangent of 225° is 1. Here the sine and cosine are both negative.

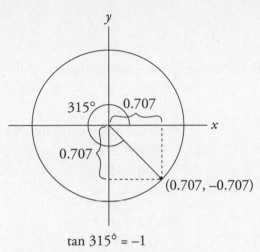

$$\tan 315° = -1$$

The tangent of 315° is –1. Here the sine is negative, and the cosine is positive.

This is the pattern that the tangent function always follows. It's positive in quadrants I and III and negative in quadrants II and IV.

- Tangent is positive between 0° and 90° and between 180° and 270°.
- Tangent is negative between 90° and 180° and between 270° and 360°.

The unit circle is extremely useful for identifying equivalent angles (like 270° and –90°), and also for seeing other correspondences between angles, like the similarity between the 45° angle and the 135° angle, which are mirror images of one another on the unit circle.

A good way to remember where sine, cosine, and tangent are positive is to write the words of the phrase All Students Take Calculus in quadrants I, II, III, and IV, respectively, on the coordinate plane. The first letter of each word (A S T C) tells you which functions are positive in that quadrant. So All three functions are positive in quadrant I, the Sine function is positive in quadrant II, the Tangent function is positive in quadrant III, and the Cosine function is positive in quadrant IV.

Drill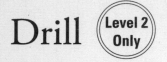

Make simple sketches of the unit circle to answer the following questions about angle equivalencies. The answers to these drills can be found in Chapter 12.

18. If sin 135° = sin x, then x could equal

(A) −225°
(B) −45°
(C) 225°
(D) 315°
(E) 360°

21. If cos 60° = cos n, then n could be

(A) 30°
(B) 120°
(C) 240°
(D) 300°
(E) 360°

26. If sin 30° = cos t, then t could be

(A) −30°
(B) 60°
(C) 90°
(D) 120°
(E) 240°

30. If tan 45° = tan x, then which of the following could be x ?

(A) −45°
(B) 135°
(C) 225°
(D) 315°
(E) 360°

36. If 0° ≤ θ ≤ 360° and (sin θ)(cos θ) < 0, which of the following gives the possible values of θ ?

(A) 0° ≤ θ ≤ 180°
(B) 0° ≤ θ ≤ 180° or 270° ≤ θ ≤ 360°
(C) 0° < θ < 90° or 180° < θ < 270°
(D) 90° < θ < 180° or 270° < θ < 360°
(E) 0° < θ < 180° or 270° < θ < 360°

Degrees and Radians

On the Math Level 2 Subject Test, you may run into an alternate means of measuring angles. This alternate system measures angles in *radians* rather than degrees. One degree is defined as $\frac{1}{360}$ of a full circle. One radian, on the other hand, is the measure of an angle that intercepts an arc exactly as long as the circle's radius. Since the circumference of a circle is 2π times the radius, the circumference is about 6.28 times as long as the radius, and there are about 6.28 radians in a full circle.

Because a number like 6.28 isn't easy to work with, angle measurements in radians are usually given in multiples or fractions of π. For example, there are exactly 2π radians in a full circle. There are π radians in a semicircle. There are $\frac{\pi}{2}$ radians in a right angle. Because 2π radians and 360° both describe a full circle, you can relate degrees and radians with the following proportion:

$$\frac{\text{degrees}}{360} = \frac{\text{radians}}{2\pi}$$

To convert degrees to radians, just plug the number of degrees into the proportion and solve for radians. The same technique works in reverse for converting radians to degrees. The figures on the next page show what the unit circle looks like in radians, compared to the unit circle in degrees.

Level 2
Only

Radians

Degrees

DRILL

By referring to these unit circles and using the proportion given on page 199, fill in the following chart of radian–degree equivalencies. The answers to these drills can be found in Chapter 12.

Level 2
Only

The Shift
A scientific or graphing calculator can calculate trigonometric functions of angles entered in radians, as well. However, it is necessary to shift the calculator from degree mode into radian mode. Consult your calculator's operating manual and make sure you know how to do this.

Degrees	Radians
30°	
45°	
	$\dfrac{\pi}{3}$
	$\dfrac{\pi}{2}$
120°	
	$\dfrac{3\pi}{4}$
150°	
	π
	$\dfrac{5\pi}{4}$
240°	
	$\dfrac{3\pi}{2}$
300°	
315°	
330°	$\dfrac{11\pi}{6}$
	2π

Trigonometric Graphs on the Coordinate Plane

In a unit-circle diagram, the *x*-axis and *y*-axis represent the horizontal and vertical components of an angle, just as they do on the coordinate plane. The angle itself is represented by the angle between a certain radius and the positive *x*-axis. Any trigonometric function can be represented on a unit-circle diagram.

Periodic Repetitions
Trigonometric functions are called *periodic functions*. The *period* of a function is the distance a function travels before it repeats. A periodic function will repeat the same pattern of values forever. As you can see from the graph, the period of the sine function is 2π radians, or 360°.

When a single trigonometric function is graphed, however, the axes take on different meanings. The *x*-axis represents the value of the angle; this axis is usually marked in radians. The *y*-axis represents a specific trigonometric function of that angle. For example, here is the coordinate plane graph of the *sine* function.

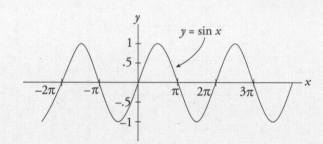

Compare this graph to the unit circle on page 200. A quick comparison will show you that both graphs present the same information. At an angle of zero, the sine is zero; at a quarter circle ($\frac{\pi}{2}$ radians, or 90°), the sine is 1; and so on.

Here is the graph of the *cosine* function.

Make Things Easier
Because the sine and cosine curves have the same shape and size, you can focus on memorizing the facts for just one of them.

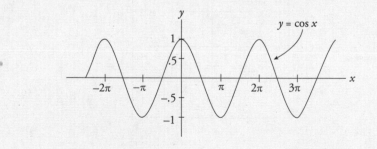

Notice that the cosine curve is identical to the sine curve, only shifted to the left by $\frac{\pi}{2}$ radians, or 90°. The cosine function also has a period of 2π radians.

Finally, here is the graph of the *tangent* function.

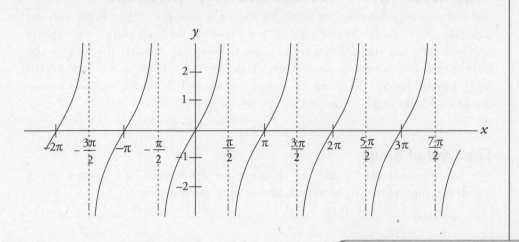

This function, obviously, is very different from the others. First, the tangent function has no upper or lower limit, unlike the sine and cosine functions, which produce values no higher than 1 or lower than –1. Second, the tangent function has *asymptotes*. These are values on the *x*-axis at which the tangent function does not exist; they are represented by vertical dotted lines. Finally, the tangent function has a period of π radians.

It's important to be able to recognize the graphs of the three basic trigonometric functions. You'll find more information about these functions and their graphs in the following chapter on functions.

The Undefined Tangent

It's easy to see why the tangent function's graph has asymptotes, if you recall the definition of the tangent.

$$\tan \theta = \frac{\sin \theta}{\cos \theta}$$

A fraction is undefined whenever its denominator equals zero. At any value where the cosine function equals zero, therefore, the tangent function is undefined—it doesn't exist. As you can see by comparing the cosine and tangent graphs, the tangent has an asymptote wherever the cosine function equals zero.

TRIGONOMETRY IN NON-RIGHT TRIANGLES

The rules of trigonometry are based on the right triangle, as you've seen in the preceding sections. Right triangles are *not*, however, the only places you can use trigonometric functions. There are a couple of powerful rules relating angles and lengths that you can use in *any* triangle. These are rules that only come up on the Math Level 2 Subject Test, and there are only two basic laws you need to know—the Law of Sines and the Law of Cosines.

The Law of Sines

The Law of Sines can be used to complete the dimensions of a triangle about which you have partial information. This is what the law says:

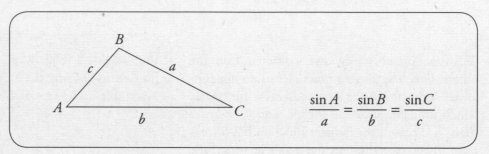

Let's take a look at an example.

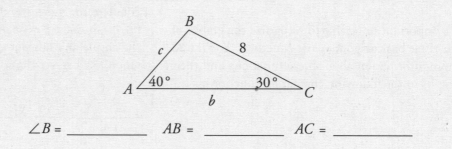

$$\angle B = \underline{\hspace{2cm}} \qquad AB = \underline{\hspace{2cm}} \qquad AC = \underline{\hspace{2cm}}$$

In this triangle, you know only two angles and one side. Immediately, you can fill in the third angle, knowing that there are 180° in a triangle. Then, you can fill in the missing sides using the Law of Sines. Write out the proportions of the Law of Sines, filling in the values you know.

$$\frac{\sin 40°}{8} = \frac{\sin 110°}{b} = \frac{\sin 30°}{c}$$

$$\frac{0.643}{8} = \frac{0.940}{b} = \frac{0.5}{c}$$

$$0.0803 = \frac{0.940}{b} = \frac{0.5}{c}$$

Please Explain
In English, this law means that the sine of each angle in a triangle is related to the length of the opposite side by a constant proportion. Once you figure out the proportion relating the sine of one angle to the opposite side, you know the proportion for every angle.

We Know, We Know
Yes, 0.643 ÷ 8 rounds to 0.0804, but if you keep the value of sin 40° in your calculator and divide by 8, you'll get 0.0803.

At this point, you can set up two individual proportions and solve them individually for b and c, respectively.

$$0.0803 = \frac{0.940}{b}$$
$$b = \frac{0.940}{0.0803}$$
$$b = 11.70$$

$$0.0803 = \frac{0.5}{c}$$
$$c = \frac{0.5}{0.0803}$$
$$c = 6.23$$

The length of AB is therefore 6.23, and the length of AC is 11.70. Now you know every dimension of triangle ABC.

> The Law of Sines can be used in any triangle if you know
>
> - two sides and one of their opposite angles (this gives you two different possible triangles)
> - two angles and any side

The Law of Cosines

When you don't have the information necessary to use the Law of Sines, you may be able to use the Law of Cosines instead. The Law of Cosines is another way of using trigonometric functions to complete partial information about a triangle's dimensions.

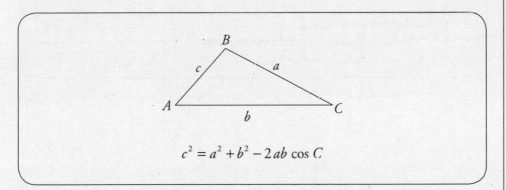

$$c^2 = a^2 + b^2 - 2ab \cos C$$

The Law of Cosines is a way of completing the dimensions of any triangle. You'll notice that it looks a bit like the Pythagorean theorem. That's basically what it is, with a term added to the end to compensate for non-right angles. If you use the Law of Cosines on a right triangle, the "$2ab \cos C$" term becomes zero, and the law becomes the Pythagorean theorem. The Law of Cosines can be used to fill in unknown dimensions of a triangle when you know any three of the quantities in the formula.

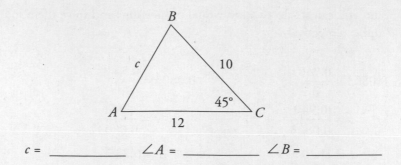

$c =$ _____ $\angle A =$ _____ $\angle B =$ _____

In this triangle, you know only two sides and an angle—the angle between the known sides. That is, you know a, b, and C. In order to find the length of the third side, c, just fill the values you know into the Law of Cosines, and solve.

$$c^2 = a^2 + b^2 - 2ab \cos C$$
$$c^2 = (10)^2 + (12)^2 - 2(10)(12) \cos 45°$$
$$c^2 = 100 + 144 - 240(0.707)$$
$$c^2 = 74.3$$
$$c = 8.62$$

The length of AB is therefore 8.62. Now that you know the lengths of all three sides, just use the Law of Sines to find the values of the unknown angles, or re-arrange the Law of Cosines to put the other unknown angles in the C position, and solve to find the measures of the unknown angles.

> The Law of Cosines can be used in any triangle if you know
>
> - all three sides
> - two sides and the angle between them

DRILL

In the following practice exercises, use the Law of Sines and the Law of Cosines to complete the dimensions of these non-right triangles. The answers to these drills can be found in Chapter 12.

Level 2
Only

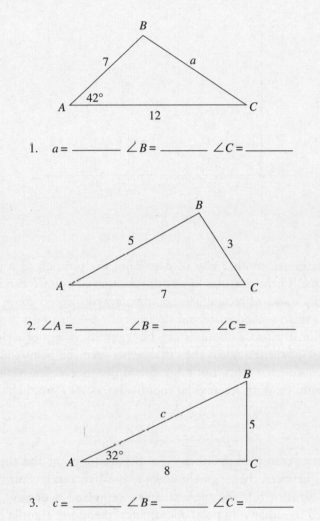

1. $a =$ _____ $\angle B =$ _____ $\angle C =$ _____

2. $\angle A =$ _____ $\angle B =$ _____ $\angle C =$ _____

3. $c =$ _____ $\angle B =$ _____ $\angle C =$ _____

POLAR COORDINATES

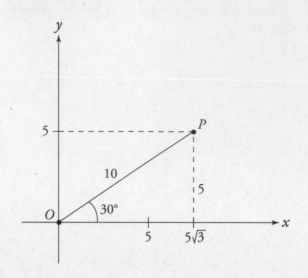

Polar coordinates are another way of describing the position of a point in the coordinate plane. In the previous figure, the position of point P can be described in two ways. In standard rectangular coordinates, you would count across from the origin to get an x-coordinate and up from the origin to get a y-coordinate. (Remember: These x and y distances can be regarded as legs of a right triangle. The hypotenuse of the triangle is the distance between the point and the origin.) Rectangular coordinates consist of a horizontal distance and a vertical distance, and take the form (x, y). In rectangular coordinates, point P would be described as $\left(5\sqrt{3}, 5\right)$.

Polar coordinates consist of the distance, r, between a point and the origin, and the angle, θ, between that segment and the positive x-axis. Polar coordinates thus take the form (r, θ). The angle θ can be expressed in degrees, but is more often expressed in radians. In polar coordinates, therefore, P could be described as $(10, 30°)$ or $\left(10, \dfrac{\pi}{6}\right)$.

As you saw in the unit circle, there's more than one way to express any angle. For any angle, there is an infinite number of equivalent angles that can be produced by adding or subtracting $360°$ (or 2π, if you're working in radians) any number of times.

Therefore, there is an infinite number of equivalent polar coordinates for any point. Point P, at (10, 30°), can also be expressed as (10, 390°), or $\left(10, \dfrac{13\pi}{6}\right)$. You can continually produce equivalent expressions by adding or subtracting 360° (or 2π).

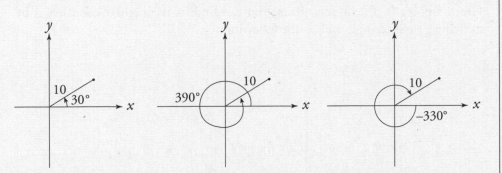

There's still another way to produce equivalent polar coordinates. The distance from the origin—the r in (r, θ)—can be negative. This means that once you've found the angle at which the hypotenuse must extend, a negative distance extends in the *opposite* direction, 180° away from the angle. Therefore, you can also create equivalent coordinates by increasing or decreasing the angle by 180° and flipping the sign on the distance. The point $P(10, 30°)$ or $\left(10, \dfrac{\pi}{6}\right)$ could also be expressed as (–10, 210°) or $\left(-10, \dfrac{7\pi}{6}\right)$. Other equivalent coordinates can be generated by pairing equivalent angles with these negative distances.

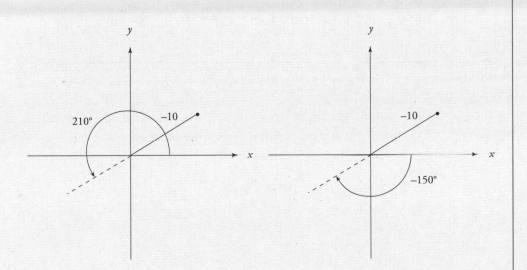

Converting Coordinates

Converting rectangular coordinates to polar coordinates and vice versa is simple. You just use the trigonometry techniques reviewed in this chapter.

Given a point (r, θ) in polar form, you can find its rectangular coordinates by drawing a right triangle such as the following:

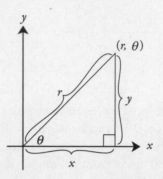

From this picture, using SOHCAHTOA and the Pythagorean theorem, you can see the following relationships:

$$\cos \theta = \frac{x}{r}; \quad \sin \theta = \frac{y}{r}; \quad \tan \theta = \frac{y}{x}; \quad x^2 + y^2 = r^2; \quad \theta = \tan^{-1}\left(\frac{y}{x}\right)$$

DRILL

Try the following practice questions about polar coordinates. The answers to these drills can be found in Chapter 12.

39. Which of the following rectangular

    coordinate pairs is equivalent to the polar

    coordinates $\left(6, \dfrac{\pi}{3}\right)$?

    (A) (0.5, 1.7)
    (B) (2.6, 5.2)
    (C) (3.0, 5.2)
    (D) (4.2, 4.8)
    (E) (5.2, 15.6)

42. The point $\left(7, \dfrac{3\pi}{4}\right)$ in polar coordinates is how far

    from the x-axis?

    (A) 3.67
    (B) 4.95
    (C) 5.25
    (D) 6.68
    (E) 16.71

$$A = \left(6, \frac{\pi}{3}\right) \qquad B = \left(6, \frac{5\pi}{3}\right) \qquad C = (3, 2\pi)$$

45. The points A, B, and C in polar coordinates define which of the following?

    (A) A point
    (B) A line
    (C) A plane
    (D) A three-dimensional space
    (E) None of these

Summary

○ For the purposes of the Level 1 Subject Test, trigonometry questions will deal only with basic trig.

○ Memorize SOHCAHTOA. It's your best friend. $sin = \dfrac{opp}{hyp}$, $cos = \dfrac{adj}{hyp}$, and $tan = \dfrac{opp}{adj}$. Tan is also equal to $\dfrac{sin}{cos}$. ETS will test these with trigonometric identity questions.

○ You can use the inverse of a function on your calculator to find the angle when you know the value of the corresponding trigonometric function.

○ The unit circle is a circle on the coordinate plane with a radius of 1. You can use Pythagorean theorem, SOHCAHTOA, and the fact that if you draw a line from the origin to any point on the circle and create a triangle, the hypotenuse will always be 1.

○ For the Level 2 Subject Test only, it is important to know the following:

   • The reciprocals of the trig functions are cosecant, secant, and cotangent. Their relation to the trig functions are: $\csc\theta = \dfrac{1}{\sin\theta}$, $\sec\theta = \dfrac{1}{\cos\theta}$, and $\cot\theta = \dfrac{1}{\tan\theta}$.

   • Radians are just another way to measure angles. The relationship between degrees and radians is: $\dfrac{degrees}{360} = \dfrac{radians}{2\neq}$.

   • Use **All Students Take Calculus** to remember which trig functions are positive in each quadrant.

- The graphs of trigonometric functions are periodic functions. Know what each graph looks like.
- For non-right triangles, there are two important laws. In a triangle with sides a, b, and c and corresponding angles A, B, and C, the Law of Sines says that $\dfrac{\sin A}{a} = \dfrac{\sin B}{b} = \dfrac{\sin C}{c}$; and the Law of Cosines says that $c^2 = a^2 + b^2 - 2ab \cos C$.
- Polar coordinates use the distance, r, between a point and the origin, and the angle θ, which can be written in degrees or radians. A point in polar coordinates would be (r, θ).
- When converting coordinates between rectangular and polar, use either SOHCAHTOA and the Pythagorean theorem, or the following relationships: $\cos\theta = \dfrac{x}{r}$; $\sin\theta = \dfrac{y}{r}$; $\tan\theta = \dfrac{y}{x}$; $x^2 + y^2 = r^2$; and $\theta = \tan^{-1}\left(\dfrac{y}{x}\right)$.

Chapter 9
Functions

ETS will test you on two types of functions. One type is what they call "algebraic functions." They use a funny symbol to represent a series of algebraic operations. Here are a couple of examples:

$$¥x = (x + 3)^2 - x^2 \qquad \|a\| = |7a - 12|$$

These are generally testing your basic math skills, everything from vocabulary to PEMDAS. Functions sometimes do show up in this form on the Math Subject Tests—especially the Math Level 1—but you're likely to encounter more functions in mathematical notation, like this:

$$f(x) = (x + 3)^2 - x^2 \qquad f(a) = |7a - 12|$$

Functions in $f(x)$ notation should be treated just like functions with funny symbols. When dealing with functions in the $f(x)$ form, however, you can expect to need a few other rules as well—rules relating to the properties of functions and their graphs. This chapter will take you through what you need to know.

Definitions

Here are some terms concerning algebraic functions that appear on the Math Subject Tests. Make sure you're familiar with them. If the meaning of any of these vocabulary words keeps slipping your mind, add that word to your flash cards.

Domain	The set of values that may be put into a function.
Range	The set of values that can be produced by a function.
Even Function	A function for which $f(x) = f(-x)$—even functions are symmetrical across the y-axis.
Odd Function	A function for which $-f(x) = f(-x)$—odd functions have origin symmetry, which means that they are the same when reflected across the origin.
Root	Values in a function's domain at which the function equals zero—a root is also called a *zero, solution,* or *x-intercept* of a function.
Degree	The sum of the exponents in an algebraic term—the degree of a polynomial is the highest degree of any term in the polynomial.
Asymptote	A line that the graph of a function approaches but never reaches.
Period	In periodic functions, the distance traveled by the function before it repeats itself.
Frequency	The number of times a graph repeats itself in a given distance; the reciprocal of the function's period.
Amplitude	In a periodic function, the distance that the graph rises above a central value.
Nonnegative	The values of a function that are greater than or equal to zero.

$&#*@! FUNCTIONS

These are the functions with the funny symbols. ETS will try to frighten you with weird characters, but as long as you can follow the directions and Plug In, you'll have little trouble with these questions.

---

13. If $\lozenge a \lozenge = a^2 - 5a + 4$, then $\lozenge 6 \lozenge =$

    (A) 6
    (B) 8
    (C) 10
    (D) 12
    (E) 14

Here's How to Crack It

Answer this question by plugging 6 into the definition of the function everywhere a is found.

$$(6)^2 - 5(6) + 4 =$$

$$36 - 30 + 4 =$$

$$10$$

The answer is (C).

———○———

Don't be confused if a question requires you to plug something strange into a function. Just follow the instructions, and the answer will become clear.

———○———

17. If $\&y = y^2 - 6$, then which of the following equals $\&(y + 6)$?

(A) y^2
(B) $y^2 - 36$
(C) $2y - 36$
(D) $y^2 + 12y + 30$
(E) $y^2 + 12y + 42$

Here's How to Crack It

To find the answer, just Plug In a number. Let's pick $y = 2$.

That means we want to find the value of $\&(2 + 6)$, which is $\&8$. Plugging 8 into the definition gives us

$$(8)^2 - 6 = 58$$

Now just Plug In 2 for y in the answer choices to see which one becomes 58, your target number. (D) is the correct answer.

———○———

DRILL

Practice your techniques on the following function questions. The answers to these drills can be found in Chapter 12.

34. If $[x] = -\left|x^3\right|$, then $[4] - [3] =$
    (A) −91
    (B) −37
    (C)   1
    (D) 37
    (E) 91

35. If $¥c$ is defined as $5(c - 2)^2$, then $¥5 + ¥6 =$
    (A) ¥7
    (B) ¥8
    (C) ¥9
    (D) ¥10
    (E) ¥11

$$§a = \begin{cases} a \text{ if } a \text{ is even} \\ -a \text{ if } a \text{ is odd} \end{cases}$$

36. $§1 + §2 + §3 \ldots §100 + §101 =$
    (A) −151
    (B) −51
    (C)   0
    (D)   50
    (E)   51

FUNCTIONS WITHOUT WEIRD SYMBOLS

On many questions, ETS will also give you functions with letters like f and g, that look like the ones you've probably studied in school. A function is a type of relation between two sets of numbers called the domain and range of the function. Specifically, a function is a relation in which every element in the domain corresponds to only one element in the range; for every x in the function, there is only one possible $f(x)$ (or y, on a graph).

The most basic function questions test only your understanding of functions and the algebra required to work with them. Here are some examples of basic functions.

$$f(x) = \left| x^2 - 16 \right| \qquad g(x) = \frac{1}{4}(x-2)^3$$

$$t(a) = a(a-6) + 8 \qquad p(q) = \frac{3-q}{q}$$

The best way to think of function is that it's like a machine. It spits out a different result depending on what you put into it. As long as you follow the directions of the machine, it will spit out the right response for you. The test may bring up a couple of phrases: independent variable and dependent variable. The *independent variable* is what you put into the machine. You could put anything in; it doesn't rely on anything, so it's *independent*. The *dependent variable* is what your machine spits out. What it is depends on what's put into the machine. That's why it's the *dependent variable*. On a graph, the independent variable is on the x-axis and the dependent variable is on the y-axis.

When questions ask you to work with algebraic functions, you'll be required to do one of two things: plug numbers into a function and get a numerical answer, or plug variables into a function and get an algebraic answer. For example, given the function $g(x) = (x + 2)^2$, you could run into two types of questions:

---

3. If $g(x) = (x + 2)^2$, what is the value of $g(4)$?

(A) 8
(B) 12
(C) 16
(D) 36
(E) 64

Here's How to Crack It
Answering this question is a simple matter of plugging 4 into the function, and simplifying $(4 + 2)^2$ to get 36.

Here, on the other hand, is an algebraic version of the same question:

f(x) = y
Sometimes it helps to think of f(x) as being equal to y. Both are the result you get when you put a number into the equation.

The Rare Occasion
There are a few unusual function types that you should be prepared for. It is possible, for example, for elements in the domain to consist of more than one value, like this:

$$f(a,b) = \frac{a^2 + b^2}{ab}$$

$$g(x,y) = (x+2)^2 - (y-2)^2$$

In each of these functions, an element in the domain is a pair of values. Functions of this kind are fairly rare on the Math Subject Tests, but you may run into one. Although they're unusual, they're not difficult. Simply treat them like ordinary functions—to calculate the value of $f(3,4)$, for example, simply take the values 3 and 4 and plug them into the definition of the function in the positions of a and b, respectively (you get $\frac{25}{12}$).

18. If $g(x) = (x + 2)^2$, what is the value of $g(x + 2)$?

   (A) $x^2 + 4$
   (B) $x^2 + 6$
   (C) $x^2 + 4x + 4$
   (D) $x^2 + 4x + 6$
   (E) $x^2 + 8x + 16$

Here's How to Crack It

To solve this question, just Plug In a number for x. Let's pick $x = 3$, and plug that into $g(x + 2)$. You need to find $g(3 + 2) = g(5)$, which is $(5 + 2)^2 = 49$, our target number. Now, plug $x = 3$ into the answer choices, to see which one turns into 49. (E) is the correct answer.

You may also have to work with a *split function*—sometimes called a *piecewise function*. A split function is one that has different definitions, depending on some condition that is part of the function. Here are a couple of examples of split functions:

$$y(x) = \begin{cases} x^2, & x > 0 \\ 1, & x = 0 \\ -x^2, & x < 0 \end{cases} \qquad f(x) = \begin{cases} 5x, \text{ if } x \text{ is odd} \\ 4x, \text{ if } x \text{ is even} \end{cases}$$

Functions of this type are fairly self-explanatory. It's just necessary to check the conditions of the function before plugging values in to make sure you're using the right function definition.

Drill

Practice working with functions in the following questions. The answers to these drills can be found in Chapter 12.

14. If $f(x) = x^2 - x^3$, then $f(-1) =$

    (A) –2
    (B) –1
    (C) 0
    (D) 1
    (E) 2

17. If $f(z) = \sqrt{z^2 + 8z}$, then how much does $f(z)$ increase as z goes from 7 to 8 ?

    (A) 0.64
    (B) 1.07
    (C) 2.96
    (D) 3.84
    (E) 5.75

26. If $g(t) = t^3 + t^2 - 9t - 9$, then $g(3) =$

    (A) –9
    (B) 0
    (C) 9
    (D) 27
    (E) 81

29. If $f(x,y) = \dfrac{xy}{x+y}$, which of the following is equal to $f(3, -6)$?

    (A) –48
    (B) –6
    (C) 3
    (D) 6
    (E) 18

30. If $h(x) = x^2 + x - 2$, and $h(n) = 10$, then n could be which of the following?

    (A) –4
    (B) –3
    (C) –1
    (D) 1
    (E) 2

33. The function f is given by $f(x) = x \bullet [x]$, where $[x]$ is defined to be the greatest factor of x that does not equal x. What is $f(75)$?

    (A) 25
    (B) 225
    (C) 625
    (D) 1,125
    (E) 1,875

$$g(x) = \begin{cases} 2|x| & \text{if } x \leq 0 \\ -|x| & \text{if } x > 0 \end{cases}$$

34. What is the value of $g(-y)$ if $y = 3$?

    (A) –6.0
    (B) –3.0
    (C) –1.5
    (D) 1.5
    (E) 6.0

COMPOUND FUNCTIONS

A compound function is a combination of two or more functions, in sequence. It's essentially a function of a function—you take the output of the first function and put it into the second function. For example:

$$f(x) = x^2 + 10x + 3 \qquad\qquad g(x) = \frac{1}{\sqrt{x+22}}$$

$$g(f(x)) = \frac{1}{\sqrt{x^2 + 10x + 25}}$$

The expression $g(f(x))$ is a compound function made up of the functions $f(x)$ and $g(x)$. As with any algebraic expression with parentheses, you start with the inner-most part. To find $g(f(x))$ for any x, calculate the value of $f(x)$, and plug that value into $g(x)$. The result is $g(f(x))$. Like questions based on simple algebraic functions, compound-function questions come in two flavors—questions that require you to plug numbers into compound functions and do the arithmetic, and questions that require you to plug terms with variables into compound functions and find an algebraic answer. For example:

$$f(x) = x^2 + 10x + 3$$

$$g(x) = \frac{1}{\sqrt{x+22}}$$

34. What is the value of $g(f(-4))$?

　　(A) 0.15
　　(B) 1.00
　　(C) 2.75
　　(D) 3.00
　　(E) 6.56

Here's How to Crack It

To find the value of $g(f(-4))$, just plug -4 into $f(x)$; you should find that $f(-4) = -21$. Then, plug -21 into $g(x)$. You should find that $g(-21) = 1$. The correct answer is (B).

The more complicated type of compound-function question asks you to find the algebraic expression of a compound function. Essentially, that means you'll be combining the definitions of two functions. Try an example.

$$f(x) = x^2 + 10x + 3$$

$$g(x) = \frac{1}{\sqrt{x+22}}$$

36. Which of the following is $g(f(x))$?

(A) $\dfrac{1}{x-5}$

(B) $\dfrac{1}{x+5}$

(C) $\sqrt{x^2 + 10x + 3}$

(D) $\dfrac{1}{x^2 + 10x + 3}$

(E) $\dfrac{1}{(x+5)^2}$

Here's How to Crack It

Instead of doing lots of messy algebra, just pick an easy number to Plug In for x. Let's try $x = 3$. So you're looking for $g(f(3))$. Work from the inside out, $f(3) = 42$, so $g(f(3)) = g(42)$. When you plug 42 into g, you get $\dfrac{1}{8}$, the target number. Plugging $x = 3$ into the answer choices, you find that answer choice (B) hits that target.

Drill

Practice working with compound functions in the following questions. The answers to these drills can be found in Chapter 12.

17. If $f(x) = 3x$ and $g(x) = x + 4$, what is the difference between $f(g(x))$ and $g(f(x))$?

    (A) 0
    (B) 2
    (C) 4
    (D) 8
    (E) 12

24. If $f(x) = |x| - 5$ and $g(x) = x^3 - 5$, what is $f(g(-2))$?

    (A) –18
    (B) –5
    (C) 0
    (D) 3
    (E) 8

25. If $f(x) = 5 + 3x$ and $f(g(x)) = 17$, then $g(x) =$

    (A) 3
    (B) 4
    (C) 56
    (D) 3 + 5x
    (E) 5 + 3x

$$f(x) = x^2 + 10x + 25$$
$$g(x) = \sqrt{x} + 4$$

32. Which of the following is $g(f(x))$?

    (A) $x - 1$
    (B) $x + 1$
    (C) $x + 7$
    (D) $x + 9$
    (E) $x^2 - 2x - 1$

$$f(x) = \sqrt{x}$$
$$g(x) = x^3 - 2$$

36. What is the positive difference between $f(g(3))$ and $g(f(3))$?

    (A) 0.7
    (B) 0.9
    (C) 1.8
    (D) 3.4
    (E) 6.8

INVERSE FUNCTIONS

Inverse functions are opposites—functions that undo each other. Here's a simple example.

$$f(x) = 5x \qquad\qquad f^{-1}(x) = \frac{x}{5}$$

Here, the function $f(x)$ multiplies x by 5. Its inverse, symbolized by $f^{-1}(x)$, divides x by 5. Any number put through one of these functions and then the other would come back to where it started. Here's a slightly more complex pair of inverse functions:

$$f(x) = 5x + 2 \qquad\qquad f^{-1}(x) = \frac{x-2}{5}$$

Here, the function $f(x)$ multiplies x by 5 and then adds 2. The inverse function $f^{-1}(x)$ does the opposite steps in reverse order, subtracting 2 and then dividing by 5. Let's add one more step:

$$f(x) = \frac{5x+2}{4} \qquad\qquad f^{-1}(x) = \frac{4x-2}{5}$$

Now, the function $f(x)$ multiplies x by 5, adds 2, and then divides by 4. The inverse function $f^{-1}(x)$ once again does the reverse; it multiplies by 4, subtracts 2, and then divides by 5. An inverse function always works this way; it does the opposite of each operation in the original function, in reverse order.

The typical inverse-function question gives you the definition of a function and asks you to identify the function's inverse.

Remember the Machine?

Okay, so now we have two machines. We drop a number into one, and it spits out a number. If we drop that number into the second machine, the second machine spits out our original number. The two machines negate each other.

$f(g(x)) = x$

Compound functions and inverse functions are often used together in questions on the Math Subject Tests. It's characteristic of inverse functions that they have opposite effects—they undo each other. For that reason, whenever you see the statement $f(g(x)) = x$, you know that the functions $f(x)$ and $g(x)$ are inverse functions. When a value x is put through one function and then the other, it returns to its original value. That means that whatever changes $f(x)$ makes are undone by $g(x)$. The statement $f(g(x)) = x$ means that $g(x) = f^{-1}(x)$.

---

40. If $f(x) = \dfrac{x}{4} + 3$ and $f(g(x)) = x$, which of the following is $g(x)$?

    (A) $x - \dfrac{3}{4}$

    (B) $x - 12$

    (C) $4x - 3$

    (D) $4x - 12$

    (E) $4(x + 12)$

Here's How to Crack It

In this question, the statement $f(g(x)) = x$ tells you that $f(x)$ and $g(x)$ are inverse functions. Finding $g(x)$, then, amounts to finding the inverse of $f(x)$. You could do this by picking out the function that does the opposite of the operations in $f(x)$, in reverse order; but there's an easier way. By definition, inverse functions undo each other. In practice, this means that if you plug an easy number into $f(x)$ and get a result, the inverse function will be the function that turns that result back into your original number.

For example, given the function $f(x)$, you might decide to Plug In 8, a number that makes the math easy.

$$f(x) = \frac{x}{4} + 3$$

$$f(8) = \frac{8}{4} + 3$$

$$f(8) = 2 + 3$$

$$f(8) = 5$$

You find that $f(x)$ turns 8 into 5. The inverse function $g(x)$ will be the one that does the reverse—that is, turns 5 into 8. To find $g(x)$, plug 5 into each of the answer choices. The answer choice that gives you 8 will be the correct answer. In this case, the correct answer is (D).

Invert x and y

If it doesn't look like Plugging In will help you, another great way to find the inverse of a function is to switch x and y, or $f(x)$. So if the original function is $f(x) = 3x - 4$, move it all around. First replace $f(x)$ with y so you can see it all more easily. Now you have $y = 3x - 4$. Switch x and y: $x = 3y - 4$. Now solve for y; $x + 4 = 3y$; and $\frac{x + 4}{3} = y$. As a final touch, replace y with $f^{-1}(x)$: $f^{-1}(x) = \frac{x + 4}{3}$. And you now have the inverse of $f(x) = 3x - 4$.

DRILL

Practice your inverse-function techniques on these questions. The answers to these drills can be found in Chapter 12.

22. If $f(x) = \dfrac{4x-5}{2}$ and $f(g(x)) = x$, then $g(x) =$

    (A) $2x + \dfrac{5}{4}$

    (B) $\dfrac{2x+5}{4}$

    (C) $x + \dfrac{5}{2}$

    (D) $\dfrac{x}{4} + \dfrac{2}{5}$

    (E) $\dfrac{5x+2}{4}$

33. If $f(x) = 4x^2 - 12x + 9$ for $x \geq 0$, what is $f^{-1}(9)$?

    (A) 1
    (B) 3
    (C) 5
    (D) 12
    (E) 16

35. If $f(3) = 9$, then $f^{-1}(4) =$

    (A) –2
    (B) 0
    (C) 2
    (D) 16
    (E) It cannot be determined from the information given.

DOMAIN AND RANGE

Some function questions will ask you to make statements about the domain and range of functions. With a few simple rules, it's easy to figure out what limits there are on the domain or range of a function.

Domain

Domain

An easy way to think about it is that the domain is all the possible values of *x*.

The domain of a function is the set of values that may be put into a function without violating any laws of math. When you're dealing with a function in the $f(x)$ form, the domain includes all of the allowable values of *x*. Sometimes a function question will limit the function's domain in some way, like the following:

> For all integers n, $f(n) = (n - 2)\pi$. What is the value of $f(7)$?

In this function, the independent variable *n* is limited; *n* can be only an integer. The domains of most functions, however, are not obviously limited. Generally, you can put whatever number you want into a function; the domain of many functions is all real numbers. Only certain functions have domains that are mathematically limited. To figure out the limits of a function's domain, you need to use a few basic rules. Here are the laws that can limit a function's domain.

Mathematical Impossibilities for Domain:

- **A fraction having a denominator of zero:** Any values that would make the bottom of a fraction equal to zero must be excluded from the domain of that function.
- **The square root of a negative number:** Any values that would make a number under a square root sign negative must be excluded from the domain of that function.
- **Any even-numbered root of a negative number:** This refers to $\sqrt[4]{}$, $\sqrt[6]{}$, etc. No value in the domain can make the function include an even-numbered root of a negative number.

Whenever a function contains a fraction, a square root, or another even-numbered root, it's possible that the function will have a limited domain. Look for any values that would make denominators zero, or even-numbered roots negative. Those values must be eliminated from the domain. Take a look at these examples.

$$f(x) = \frac{x+5}{x}$$

In this function, there is a variable in the denominator of a fraction. This denominator must not equal zero, so the domain of $f(x)$ is $\{x \neq 0\}$.

$$g(x) = \frac{x}{x+5}$$

Once again, this function has a variable in the denominator of a fraction. In this case, the value of x that would make the denominator equal zero is –5. Therefore, the domain of $g(x)$ is $\{x \neq -5\}$.

$$t(a) = 4\sqrt{a}$$

This function has a variable under a square root sign. The quantity under a square root sign must not be negative, so the domain of $t(a)$ is $\{a \geq 0\}$.

$$s(a) = 3 \cdot \sqrt{10 - a}$$

Here again, you have a function with a variable under a square root. This time, the values that would make the expression negative are values greater than 10; all of these values must be eliminated from the function's domain. The domain of $s(a)$ is therefore $\{a \leq 10\}$.

A function can involve both fractions and square roots. Always pay careful attention to any part of a function that could place some limitation on the function's domain. It's also possible to run into a function where it's not easy to see what values violate the denominator rule or the square root rule. Generally, factoring is the easiest way to make these relationships clearer. For example:

$$f(x) = \frac{1}{x^3 + 2x^2 - 8x}$$

Here, you've got variables in the denominator. You know this is something to watch out for, but it's not obvious what values might make the denominator equal zero. To make it clearer, factor the denominator.

$$f(x) = \frac{1}{x(x^2 + 2x - 8)}$$

$$f(x) = \frac{1}{x(x+4)(x-2)}$$

Now, things are much clearer. Whenever quantities are being multiplied, the entire product will equal zero if any one piece equals zero. Any value that makes the denominator equal zero must be eliminated from the function's domain. In this case, the values 0, –4, and 2 all make the denominator zero. The domain of $f(x)$ is $\{x \neq -4, 0, 2\}$. Take a look at one more example.

$$g(x) = \sqrt{x^2 + 4x - 5}$$

Once again, you've got an obvious warning sign—variables under a radical. Any values of x that make the expression under the radical negative must be eliminated from the domain. But what values are those? Are there any? To make it clear, factor the expression.

$$g(x) = \sqrt{(x+5)(x-1)}$$

The product of two expressions can be negative only when one of the expressions is negative and the other positive. If both expressions are positive, their product is positive. If both expressions are negative, their product is still positive. So the domain of $g(x)$ must contain only values that make $(x + 5)$ and $(x - 1)$ both negative or both nonnegative. With a little experimentation, you'll find that both expressions are negative when $x < -5$, and both expressions are nonnegative when $x \geq 1$. The domain of $g(x)$ is therefore $\{x \leq -5\}$ or $\{x \geq 1\}$.

Domain Notation

The domain of a function is generally described using the variable x. A function $f(x)$ whose domain includes only values greater than 0 and less than 24, could be described in the following ways:

The domain of $f(x)$ is $\{0 < x < 24\}$.
The domain of f is the set $\{x: 0 < x < 24\}$.

A function in the form $f(x)$ can be referred to either as $f(x)$ or simply as f.

Range

The range of a function is the set of possible values that can be produced by the function. When you're dealing with a function in the $f(x)$ form, the range consists of all the allowable values of $f(x)$. The range of a function, like the domain, is limited by a few laws of mathematics. Several of these laws are the same laws that limit the domain. Here are the major rules that limit a function's range.

Range
An easy way to think about it is that the range is all possible values of y. In the case of functions, the range is all the possible values of $f(x)$.

- An even exponent produces only nonnegative numbers. Any term raised to an even exponent must be positive or zero.
- The square root of a quantity represents only the positive root. Like even powers, a square root can't be negative. The same is true for other even-numbered roots ($\sqrt[4]{}$, $\sqrt[6]{}$, etc.).
- Absolute values produce only nonnegative values.

These three operations—even exponents, even roots, and absolute values—can produce only nonnegative values. Consider these three functions.

$$f(x) = x^4 \qquad\qquad f(x) = \sqrt{x} \qquad\qquad f(x) = |x|$$

These functions all have the same range, $\{ f(x) \geq 0 \}$. These are the three major mathematical operations that often limit the ranges of functions. They can operate in unusual ways. The fact that a term in a function must be nonnegative can affect the entire function in different ways. Take a look at the following examples.

$$f(x) = -x^4 \qquad\qquad f(x) = -\sqrt{x} \qquad\qquad f(x) = -|x|$$

Each of these functions once again contains a nonnegative operation, but in each case the sign is now flipped by a negative sign. The range of each function is now $\{f(x) \leq 0\}$. In addition to being flipped by negative signs, ranges can also be slid upward or downward by addition and subtraction. Take a look at these examples.

$$f(x) = x^4 - 5 \qquad\qquad f(x) = \sqrt{x} - 5 \qquad\qquad f(x) = |x| - 5$$

Each of these functions contains a nonnegative operation that is then decreased by 5. The range of each function is consequently also decreased by 5, becoming $\{f(x) \geq -5\}$. Notice the pattern: A nonnegative operation has a range of $\{f(x) \geq 0\}$. When the sign of the nonnegative operation is flipped, the sign of the range also flips. When a quantity is added to the operation, the same quantity is added to the range. These changes can also be made in combination.

$$g(x) = \frac{-x^2 + 6}{2}$$

In this function, the sign of the nonnegative operation is flipped, 6 is added, and the whole thing is divided by 2. As a result, the range of $g(x)$ is $\{g(x) \leq 3\}$. The range of x^2, which is $\{y: y \geq 0\}$, has its sign flipped, is increased by 6, and is then divided by 2.

Range Notation

Ranges can be represented in several ways. If the function $f(x)$ can produce values between -10 and 10, then a description of its range could look like any of the following:

- The range of $f(x)$ is given by $\{f: -10 < f(x) < 10\}$.
- The range of $f(x)$ is $\{-10 < f(x) < 10\}$.
- The range of $f(x)$ is the set $\{y: -10 < y < 10\}$.

Why Do I See *y*?
Because a function's range is represented on the *y*-axis when the function is graphed, the range is sometimes described using the variable *y*, even when *y* doesn't appear in the function.

Solving a Range Question

Now that you've learned about ranges, let's try out a question. Take a look at the following example.

---

25. If $f(x) = \left| -x^2 - 8 \right|$ for all real numbers x, then which of the following sets is the range of f?

(A) $\{y: y \geq -8\}$
(B) $\{y: y > 0\}$
(C) $\{y: y \geq 0\}$
(D) $\{y: y \leq 8\}$
(E) $\{y: y \geq 8\}$

Plugging In on Range Questions

Because all questions on the Math Subject Tests are multiple choice, you can always Plug In and use POE on range questions. It may take a little longer but it gives you a chance to score another point. So, if you're confused by the process of finding the range, or not sure what steps to take on a particular range question, Plug In!

Let's take another look at question 25 on this page. If you Plugged In $x = 3$, you would find that $f(3) = 17$. From that info you could eliminate (D). If you Plugged In 0, you'd see that $f(0) = 8$. If you Plugged In numbers less than 0, you'd see that $f(x)$ never gets smaller than 8. The answer is (E). You still get to the right answer!

Here's How to Crack It

Start out with what you know about the equation. Since the result of absolute value is a nonnegative number, you can eliminate (A) right away. Is there a maximum number that an absolute value creates? No. So you can also eliminate (D). Now look at x^2. We know that there's no maximum that x^2 can be, but there is a minimum. The smallest x^2 can be is 0. If $x^2 = 0$, then the result inside the absolute value sign would be −8. This means that, when $x = 0$, $f(x) = 8$. So the answer is (E). Now you may be thinking, but what about that negative sign? Well, a negative minus a negative makes a number more negative and it's in absolute value so it would get more positive. The smallest number that machine can produce is 8.

FUNCTIONS WITHIN INTERVALS: DOMAIN MEETS RANGE

A question that introduces a function will sometimes ask about that function only within a certain interval. This interval is a set of values for the variable in the x position.

For example:

Remember?
Don't forget that x represents the independent variable!

If $f(x) = 4x - 5$ for $[0, 10]$, then which of the following sets represents the range of f?
If $f(x) = 4x - 5$ for $0 \leq x \leq 10$, what is the range of f?

These two questions present the same information and ask the same question. The second version simply uses a different notation to describe the interval, or domain, in which $f(x)$ is being looked at.

The example given above also demonstrates the most common form of a function-interval question, in which you're given a domain for the function and asked for the range. Whenever the function has no exponents, finding the range is easy. Just plug the upper and lower extremes of the domain into the function. The results will be the upper and lower bounds of the range. In the example above, the function's range is the set $\{y: -5 \leq y \leq 35\}$.

The interval that you are given means that, for that particular question, you have a different set of values for the function's domain.

Be Careful
You have to be alert when domains or ranges are given in this notation, because it's easy to mistake intervals in this form for coordinate pairs. Tricky!

DRILL

Practice your domain and range techniques on the following questions. The answers to these drills can be found in Chapter 12.

24. If $f(x) = \dfrac{1}{x^3 - x^2 - 6x}$, then which of the following sets is the domain of f?

(A) $\{x: x \neq -2, 0, 3\}$
(B) $\{x: x \neq 0\}$
(C) $\{x: x > -2\}$
(D) $\{x: x > 0\}$
(E) $\{x: x > 3\}$

27. If $g(x) = \sqrt{x^2 - 4x - 12}$, then the domain of g is given by which of the following?

(A) $\{x: x \geq -2\}$
(B) $\{x: x \neq 3, 4\}$
(C) $\{x: -2 \leq x \leq 6\}$
(D) $\{x: -2 < x < 6\}$
(E) $\{x: x \leq -2 \text{ or } x \geq 6\}$

30. If $t(a) = \dfrac{a^2 + 5}{3}$, then which of the following sets is the range of t?

    (A) $\{y: y \neq 0\}$
    (B) $\{y: y \geq 0\}$
    (C) $\{y: y \geq 0.60\}$
    (D) $\{y: y \geq 1.67\}$
    (E) $\{y: y \geq 2.24\}$

34. If $f(x) = 4x + 3$ for $-1 \leq x \leq 4$, then which of the following gives the range of f?

    (A) $\{y: -4 \leq y \leq 7\}$
    (B) $\{y: -4 \leq y \leq 19\}$
    (C) $\{y: -1 \leq y \leq 7\}$
    (D) $\{y: -1 \leq y \leq 19\}$
    (E) $\{y: 1 \leq y \leq 19\}$

GRAPHING FUNCTIONS

All of the function techniques covered in this chapter so far have dealt with the algebra involved in doing functions. Most of the function questions on each Math Subject Test will be algebra questions like the ones you've seen so far. However, there's another class of function questions that appears on the Math Subject Tests—graphical questions.

Graphical function questions require you to relate an algebraic function to the graph of that function in some way. Here are some of the tasks you might be required to do on a graphical function question:

- Match a function's graph with the function's domain or range.
- Match the graph of a function with the function's algebraic definition.
- Decide whether statements about a function are true or false, based on its graph.

None of these tasks is very difficult, as long as you're prepared for them. The next few pages will tell you everything you need to know.

Identifying Graphs of Functions

The most useful tool for identifying the graph of a function is the *vertical-line test*. Remember: A function is a relation of a domain and a range, in which each value in the domain matches up with only one value in the range. Simply put, there's only one $f(x)$, or y, for each x. Graphically, that means that any vertical line drawn through the x-axis can intersect a function only once. If you can intersect a graph more than once with a vertical line, it isn't a function. Here's the vertical-line test in action.

> ### Looking at a Graph
> When a function $f(x)$ is graphed, the x-axis represents the values of x. The y-axis represents the values of $f(x)$. When you look at the coordinates (x, y) of any point on the function's graph, x represents a value in the function's domain (the input of the function), and y represents the function of that value (the output of the function).

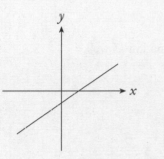

This is a function, because no vertical line can intersect it more than once. All straight lines are functions, with only one exception. A vertical line is not a function, because another vertical line would intersect it at an infinite number of points.

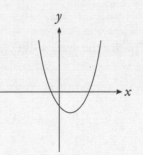

This is also a function. Any parabola that opens up or down is a function.

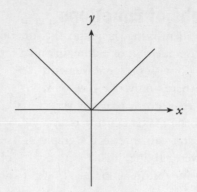

This is the graph of $y = |x|$, and it's a function as well.

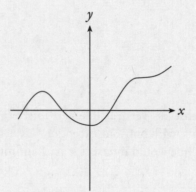

This complicated curve also passes the vertical-line test for functions.

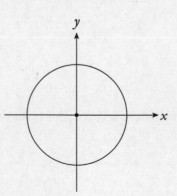

This is not a function; there are many places where a vertical line can intersect a circle twice.

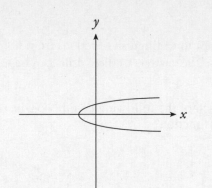

This isn't a function either. Although this graph is parabolic in shape, it fails the vertical-line test.

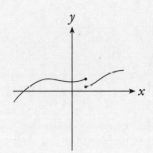

Nope. It's close, but there's one point where a vertical line can intersect this graph twice—it can't be a function.

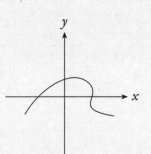

This curve is also not a function. It's possible to cross this curve more than once with one vertical line.

DRILL

Use the vertical-line test to distinguish functions from nonfunctions in the following practice questions. The answers to these drills can be found in Chapter 12.

9. Which of the following could NOT be the graph of a function?

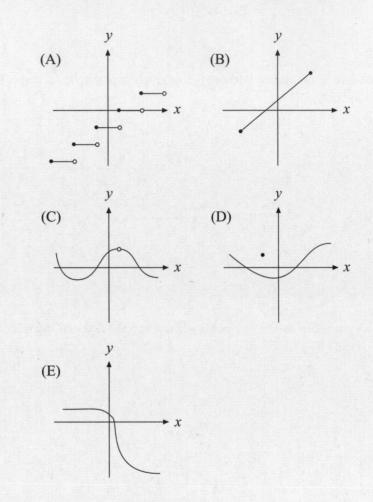

15. Which of the following could NOT be the graph of a function?

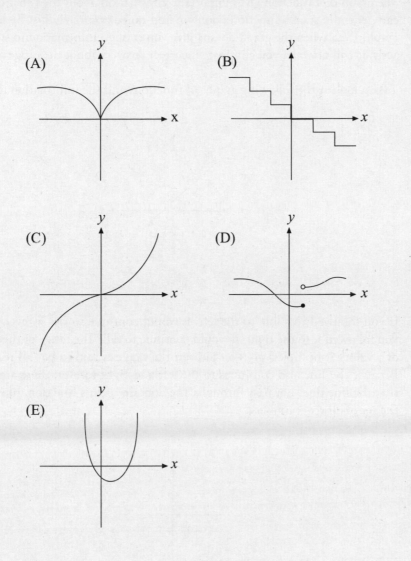

(A)

(B)

(C)

(D)

(E)

RANGE AND DOMAIN IN GRAPHS

The graph of a function gives important information about the function itself. You can generally state a function's domain and range accurately just by looking at its graph. Even when the graph doesn't give you enough information to state them exactly, it will often let you eliminate incorrect answers about the range and domain.

Take a look at the following graphs of functions and the information they provide:

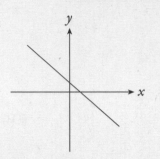

If you followed this line to the left, it would continue to rise forever. Likewise, if you followed it to the right, it would continue to fall. The range of this line (the set of *y*-values it occupies) goes on forever; the range is said to be "all real numbers." Because the line also continues to the left and right forever, there are no *x*-values that the line does not pass through. The domain of this function, like its range, is the set of all real numbers.

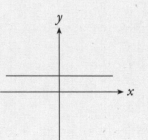

The same thing is true of all linear functions (whose graphs are straight lines); their ranges and domains include all real numbers. There's only one exception. A horizontal line extends forever to the left and right (through all *x*-values) but has only one *y*-value. Its domain is therefore all real numbers, while its range contains only one value.

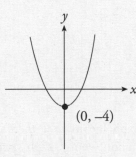

(0, −4)

The domain of this function is the set of all real numbers, because parabolas continue widening forever. Its range, however, is limited. The parabola extends upward forever, but never descends lower along the *y*-axis than $y = -4$. The range of this function is therefore $\{y: y \geq -4\}$.

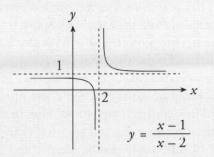

$$y = \frac{x-1}{x-2}$$

This function has two asymptotes. Asymptotes are lines that the function approaches but never reaches. They mark values in the domain or range at which the function does not exist or is undefined. The asymptotes on this graph mean that it's impossible for *x* to equal 2, and it's impossible for *y* to equal 1. The domain of $f(x)$ is therefore $\{x: x \neq 2\}$, and the range is $\{y: y \neq 1\}$.

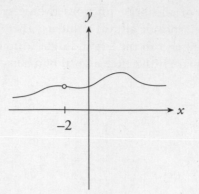

The hole in this function's graph means that there's an *x*-value missing at that point. The domain of any function whose graph sports a little hole like this one must exclude the corresponding *x*-value. The domain of this function, for example, would simply be {*x*: *x* ≠ –2}.

To estimate range and domain based on a function's graph, just use common sense and remember these rules:

- If something about a function's shape will prevent it from continuing forever up and down, then that function has a limited range.
- If the function has a horizontal asymptote at a certain *y*-value, then that value is excluded from the function's range.
- If anything about a function's shape will prevent it from continuing forever to the left and right, then that function has a limited domain.
- If a function has a vertical asymptote or hole at a certain *x*-value, then that value is excluded from the function's domain.
- If you are asked to identify an asymptote, Plug In very large positive and negative numbers for *x* or *y* and see what values the other variable approaches. Try 1, 1,000, –1, –1,000, etc.
- Sometimes you can Plug In the answers (PITA) and see which values of *x* or *y* don't make sense in the equation.
- Graphing the function on your calculator may be the easiest approach.

Drill

Test your understanding of range and domain with the following practice questions. The answers to these drills can be found in Chapter 12.

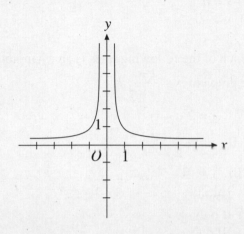

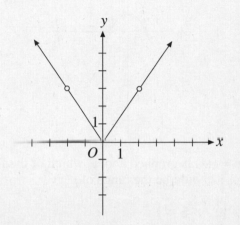

17. If the graph of $y = f(x)$ is shown above, which of the following could be the domain of f?

    (A) $\{x : x \neq 0\}$
    (B) $\{x : x > 0\}$
    (C) $\{x : x \geq 0\}$
    (D) $\{x : x > 1\}$
    (E) $\{x : x \geq 1\}$

24. Which of the following could be the domain of the function graphed above?

    (A) $\{x : x \neq 2\}$
    (B) $\{x : -2 < x < 2\}$
    (C) $\{x : x < -2 \text{ or } x > 2\}$
    (D) $\{x : |x| \neq 2\}$
    (E) $\{x : |x| > 2\}$

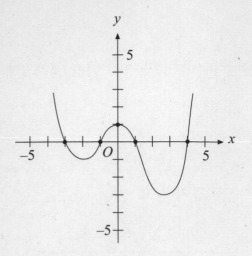

28. If $y = g(x)$ is graphed above, which of the following sets could be the range of $g(x)$?

(A) $\{y : y \leq -1\}$

(B) $\{y : y \geq -1\}$

(C) $\{y : y \geq -3\}$

(D) $\{y : -3 \leq y \leq -1\}$

(E) $\{y : y \leq -3 \text{ or } y \geq -1\}$

37. Which of the following lines is an asymptote of the graph of $y = 3e^{-2x} + 5$?

(A) $x = 0$

(B) $x = -2$

(C) $y = 5$

(D) $y = 0$

(E) $y = -6$

48. Which of the following lines is an asymptote of the graph of $y = \dfrac{1 - x}{x - 2}$?

   I. $x = 2$

   II. $y = -\dfrac{1}{2}$

   III. $y = -1$

(A) I only

(B) II only

(C) III only

(D) I and II only

(E) I and III only

ROOTS OF FUNCTIONS IN GRAPHS

The roots of a function are the values that make the function equal to zero. Hence, the roots are also called zeros or solutions of the function. To find the roots of a function $f(x)$ algebraically, you simply set $f(x)$ equal to zero and solve for x. The values of x that you find are the roots of the function.

Graphically, the roots of a function are the values of x at which the graph crosses the x-axis, that is, the x-intercepts. That makes them easy to spot on a graph. If you are asked to match a function to its graph, it's often helpful to find the roots of the function using algebra; then it's a simple matter to compare the function's roots to the x-intercepts on the graph. Take a look at this function:

$$f(x) = x^3 + 3x^2 - 4x$$

If you factor it to find its roots, you get:

$$f(x) = x(x + 4)(x - 1)$$

The roots of $f(x)$ are therefore $x = -4$, 0, and 1. You can expect the graph of $y = f(x)$ to cross the x-axis at those three x-values.

DRILL

Try the following practice questions by working with the roots of functions. The answers to these drills can be found in Chapter 12.

16. Which of the following is a zero of
    $f(x) = 2x^2 - 7x + 5$?

    (A) 1.09
    (B) 1.33
    (C) 1.75
    (D) 2.50
    (E) 2.75

19. The function $g(x) = x^3 + x^2 - 6x$ has how many distinct roots?

    (A) 1
    (B) 2
    (C) 3
    (D) 4
    (E) It cannot be determined from the information given.

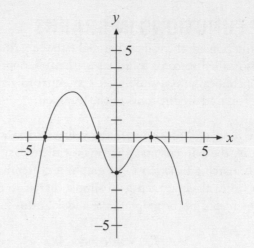

25. If the graph of $y = f(x)$ is shown above, which of the following sets represents all the roots of $f(x)$?

(A) $\{x = -2, 0, 2\}$

(B) $\{x = -4, -1, 0\}$

(C) $\{x = -1, 2\}$

(D) $\{x = -4, -1, 2\}$

(E) $\{x = -4, -1\}$

SYMMETRY IN FUNCTIONS

Symmetry Across the y-Axis (Even Functions)

When a function contains exponents and fractions *and* you're given an interval, you'll have to take the question in two steps. First, Plug In the upper and lower limits of the domain of the function. Then use the range techniques from the previous section to see whether there are other limits on the function's range. If the paper were folded along the y-axis, the left and right halves of the graph would meet perfectly. Functions with symmetry across the y-axis are sometimes called even functions. This is because functions with only even exponents have this kind of symmetry, even though they are not the only even functions. Look at the graph of $y = \cos x$ on the next page.

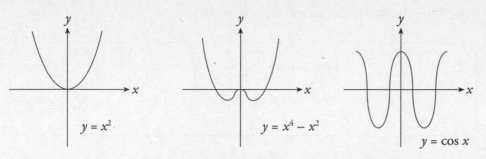

Even Functions

This is the algebraic definition of symmetry across the *y*-axis:

A function is symmetrical across the *y*-axis when

$$f(-x) = f(x)$$

This means that the negative and positive versions of any *x*-value produce the same *y*-value.

Origin Symmetry (Odd Functions)

A function has origin symmetry when one half of the graph is identical to the other half and reflected across the point (0, 0). Functions with origin symmetry are sometimes called odd functions, because functions with only odd exponents (as well as some other functions) have this kind of symmetry.

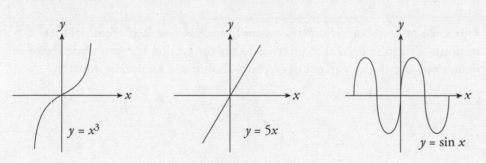

Odd Functions

This is the algebraic definition of origin symmetry:

A function has origin symmetry when

$$f(-x) = -f(x)$$

This means that the negative and positive versions of any x-value produce opposite y-values.

Symmetry Across the x-Axis

Some equations will produce graphs that are symmetrical across the x-axis. These equations can't be functions, however, because each x-value would then have to have two corresponding y-values. A graph that is symmetrical across the x-axis automatically fails the vertical-line test.

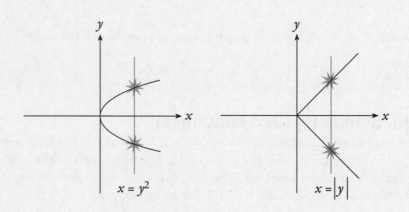

Questions asking about symmetry generally test basic comprehension of these definitions. It's also important to understand the connection between these algebraic definitions and the appearance of graphs with different kinds of symmetry.

DRILL

Try these practice questions. The answers to these drills can be found in Chapter 12.

6. Which of the following graphs is symmetrical with respect to the x-axis?

(A)

(B)

(C)

(D)

(E)

17. If an even function is one for which $f(x)$ and $f(-x)$ are equal, then which of the following is an even function?

(A) $g(x) = 5x + 2$

(B) $g(x) = x$

(C) $g(x) = \dfrac{x}{2}$

(D) $g(x) = x^3$

(E) $g(x) = -|x|$

Periodic Functions

A *periodic function* is a function that repeats a pattern of range values forever.
Always look for a pattern when you're dealing with a periodic function.

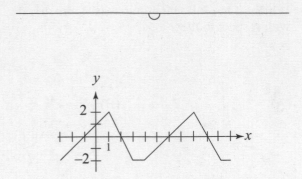

40. Two cycles of periodic function *f* are shown in the
    graph of *y* = *f*(*x*) above. What is the value of *f*(89) ?

    (A) −2
    (B) −1
    (C)   0
    (D)   1
    (E)   2

Here's How to Crack It

In this question, we need to find the period of the function, that is, how often
it repeats its range values. Find the pattern. From peak to peak, it goes from
x = 1 to *x* = 8. This means that the function repeats itself every 7 units (the
period is 7). Where does 89 fall in this pattern? Well, you want to take away multiples of 7 from 89, to find out an equivalent range value on the graph above. So,
f(89) = *f*(82) = *f*(75)…and so on. Since 89 ÷ 7 = 12 remainder 5, this means that
f(89) = *f*(5). From the graph, *f*(5) = −1, and the answer is (B).

Movement of a Function

When giving you a function question, ETS may decide to fool around with the variable. Sometimes you'll be asked how this affects the graph of the function. For example, ETS may show you $f(x)$ and ask you about the graph of $|f(x)|$. You can either Plug In points or know the following rules.

In relation to $f(x)$:

- $f(x) + c$ is shifted upward c units in the plane
- $f(x) - c$ is shifted downward c units in the plane
- $f(x + c)$ is shifted to the left c units in the plane
- $f(x - c)$ is shifted to the right c units in the plane
- $-f(x)$ is flipped upside down over the x-axis
- $f(-x)$ is flipped left-right over the y-axis
- $|f(x)|$ is the result of flipping upward all of the parts of the graph that appear below the x-axis

Of course, you may have to combine these rules. If so, Plugging In some points may be the easiest way to go.

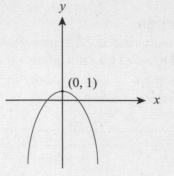

(0, 1)

Mirror, Mirror on the Axis

A function that seems to have a mirror image reflected in the *y*-axis is symmetrical across the *y*-axis.

45. The graph of $y = f(x)$ is shown above. Which of the following is the graph of $y = -f(x + 1)$?

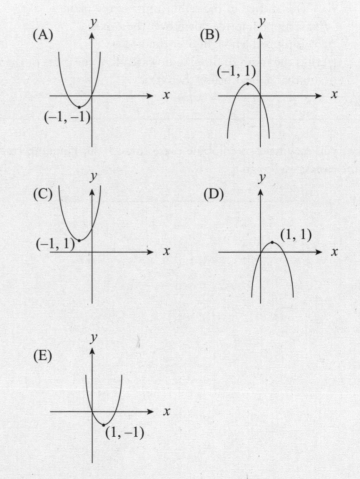

(A)

(-1, -1)

(B)

(-1, 1)

(C)

(-1, 1)

(D)

(1, 1)

(E)

(1, -1)

Here's How to Crack It

To figure out what happens to the graph of $f(x)$, just use the rules on page 251. The $x + 1$ inside the parentheses shifts the graph one unit to the left. If this were the final answer, the vertex would be at (–1, 1). Now you have to take care of the negative sign outside the function. It reflects the entire function across the *x*-axis, so the vertex gets reflected to (–1, –1) and the parabola opens upward. If you reflected first and then shifted to the left, you'd get the same result. The answer is (A).

DEGREES OF FUNCTIONS

The degree of a polynomial is the highest degree of any term in the polynomial. The degree also determines at most how many distinct roots the polynomial will have. For example, the function $p(x) = x^3 - 4x^2 + 7x - 12$ is a third-degree function. This means that $p(x)$ has at most three distinct roots. These roots can be distinct or identical. A sixth-degree function can have at most 6 distinct roots. It can actually have anywhere from 0 to 6 distinct roots. Let's take a look at two sixth-degree functions:

$$f(x) = x^6$$
$$g(x) = (x - 1)(x - 2)(x - 3)(x - 4)(x - 5)(x - 6)$$

The function $f(x)$ has six roots, but they're all the same: $f(x) = 0$ when $x = 0$, which makes the function equal $0 \cdot 0 \cdot 0 \cdot 0 \cdot 0 \cdot 0$. Basically, the function has six roots of zero—it has only one *distinct* root. The function $g(x)$ has six distinct roots: $g(x) = 0$ when $x = 1, 2, 3, 4, 5,$ or 6. Another example is that a function might have four roots of 2, a root of 3, and a root of 4, for a total of three distinct roots. The equation of this function would look like

$$f(x) = (x - 2)^4(x - 3)(x - 4)$$

This is still a sixth-degree function, and it has six roots. That's the algebraic meaning of the degree of a function: It equals the maximum number of roots that the function has.

The degree of a function tells you a great deal about the shape of the function's graph. Take a look at the graphs on the following pages.

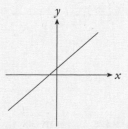

This is the graph of a first-degree function. All first-degree functions are linear functions, whose graphs are straight lines. A first-degree function has no extreme values—that is, it has no point which is higher or lower than all of the others.

Getting the Third (or Fourth or Fifth…) Degree
The degree of a term in a polynomial is the sum of the exponents of the variables in that term. So if the term in a polynomial is $3xy^2$, the degree of that term is 3.

Math Vocab
Remember that *distinct* means *different*.

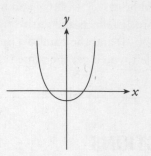

A second-degree function is usually a parabola. The function graphed above must be at least a second-degree function. A second-degree function has one extreme value, a maximum or minimum. This function's extreme value is a minimum.

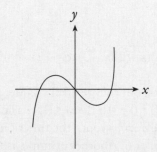

A third-degree function can have as many as two local extreme values. The function graphed above, which has a local maximum and a local minimum, must be at least a third-degree function. A "local" maximum (or minimum) means the values of the function are bigger (or smaller) than all of the surrounding values, but that the function may be bigger (or smaller) at some distant values of x.

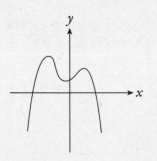

A fourth-degree function can have as many as three local extreme values. The function above has three extreme values, two local maxima and a local minimum between them. It must be at least a fourth-degree function.

By now, you should see the pattern. A fourth-degree function can have a maximum of three extreme values in its graph; a fifth-degree function can have a maximum of four extreme values in its graph. This pattern goes on forever. An nth-degree function has a maximum of n distinct roots and a maximum of ($n - 1$) extreme values in its graph. These two rules are the basis of a number of Math Level 2 questions. Take a look at the following practice questions.

DRILL

The answers to these drills can be found in Chapter 12.

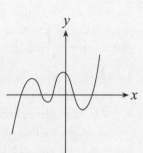

31. If the graph above is a portion of the graph of
    $y = f(x)$, then which of the following could be $f(x)$?

    (A) $ax + b$
    (B) $ax^2 + bx + c$
    (C) $ax^3 + bx^2 + cx + d$
    (D) $ax^4 + bx^3 + cx^2 + dx + e$
    (E) $ax^5 + bx^4 + cx^3 + dx^2 + ex + f$

35. If $g(x)$ is a fourth-degree function, then which of
    the following could be the definition of $g(x)$?

    (A) $g(x) = (x - 3)(x + 5)$
    (B) $g(x) = x(x + 1)^2$
    (C) $g(x) = (x - 6)(x + 1)(x - 5)$
    (D) $g(x) = x(x + 8)(x - 1)^2$
    (E) $g(x) = (x - 2)^3(x + 4)(x - 3)$

Reviewing Functions Further

It's impossible to cover every aspect of functions that may turn up on the Math Subject Tests; this is one of the most varied question categories on the tests. To be thoroughly prepared for function questions on the Math Subject Tests—particularly on the Math Level 2—you should read this chapter carefully and then take a cruise through your precalculus textbook.

Summary

o Algebraic functions are the functions with weird symbols. They tell you what to do. Just follow the directions of the function.

o Mathematical functions relate two sets of numbers: the domain and the range. Think of it like a machine. You put in one number, and the machine spits out another number.

o A compound function is a combination of two or more functions. It's like having two machines. You put your number in one machine, and you take the result from that and put it into the second machine.

o Inverse functions are opposites. Here are a couple of specifics:
   • An example of what inverse functions do is the following: If you put 5 into your first machine and get 12, then you put 12 into the inverse of that machine, you'll get 5.
   • Inverse functions will be symbolized either by $f^{-1}(x)$, or $f(g(x)) = x$.
   • Inverse function questions can be solved, either by Plugging In or by replacing $f(x)$ with y, switching x and y in the equation and solving.

o Domain is all the possible values of x in a given function. These are the numbers you put into the function. They are independent.

o Range is all the possible values of y (or $f(x)$) in a given function. These are the numbers you get out of the function. They are dependent.

o In order to figure out if a graph is a function, use the vertical line test. The line will touch only one point on the graph if the graph is a function.

○ When answering domain and range questions with graphs, take a look to see what values x can't be and what values y can't be.

○ The roots of a function will make the function equal to 0 when you substitute them for the independent variable. Graphically, a function crosses the x-axis at its root values.

○ There are a few types of symmetry discussed in this chapter. An easy way to think about symmetry is this: If you physically folded your paper along the line of symmetry and all the points on both sides touched, the graph would be symmetrical along that line.
  • A function is symmetrical across the y-axis when $f(-x) = f(x)$. This is called an even function.
  • A function has origin symmetry when $f(-x) = -f(x)$. This is called an odd function.
  • A graph that is symmetrical across the x-axis isn't a function, because it fails the vertical line test.

○ You may see questions that ask about the movement of a function. If the number is outside the parentheses of the function, the graph shifts along the y-axis. If it is inside the parentheses, the graph shifts along the x-axis.

○ The following is only for people taking the Level 2 Subject Test:
  • A periodic function is a function that repeats a pattern of range values forever.
  • The degree of a term is the sum of the exponents in that term.

Chapter 10
Statistics and Sets

Math Subject Test questions about statistics and sets deal with the arrangements and combinations of large groups, probability, overlapping groups, and statistical measures like mean, median, and mode. On each Math Subject Test, only about one question in 20 will involve statistics and sets, so spend time on this chapter only after you've mastered the more essential material in earlier chapters.

DEFINITIONS

Here are some terms dealing with sets and statistics that appear on the Math Subject Tests. Make sure you're familiar with them. If the meaning of any of these vocabulary words keeps slipping your mind, add that word to your flash cards.

Mean	An average—also called an arithmetic mean.
Median	The middle value in a list of numbers when the numbers are arranged in order. When there is an even number of values in the list, the median is the average of the two middle values.
Mode	The value that occurs most often in a list.
Range	The result when you subtract the smallest value from the largest value in a list.
Standard Deviation	A measure of the variation of the values in a list.
Combination	A grouping of distinct objects in which order is not important.
Permutation	An arrangement of distinct objects in a definite order.

WORKING WITH STATISTICS

The science of statistics is all about working with large groups of numbers and trying to see patterns and trends in those numbers. To look at those numbers in different ways, statisticians use a variety of mathematical tools. And, just to keep you guessing, ETS tests your knowledge of several of these tools. The three most commonly tested statistical measures are the mean, the median, and the mode.

Mean

The mean (or "arithmetic mean") of a set is simply its average value—the sum of all its elements divided by the number of elements. To calculate averages on the Math Subject Tests, use the average wheel we discussed in Chapter 3.

Median

The median is the middle value of a set. To find a set median, you must first put all of its elements in order. If the set has an odd number of elements, then there will be one value in the exact middle, which is the median value. If the set has an even number of elements, then there will be two middle values; the median value is the average of these two middle values.

Mode

The mode of a set is simply the value that occurs most often in that list.

Many statistics questions require you to work with all three of these measures. The calculations involved are usually not very difficult. However, the real challenge of these questions is simply understanding these terms and knowing how to use them. Similarly, there are two more statistical terms that you may be required to know for certain questions—range and standard deviation.

Range

The range of a set is the positive difference between the set's highest and lowest values. You can also think of the range as the distance on the number line from the lowest to the highest value in the set. Remember that distances are always positive.

Level 2 Only

Stem-and-Leaf Plots and Boxplots

ETS may ask you about a stem-and-leaf plot or a boxplot once in a while. The good news is that the questions are usually pretty simple if you understand the basic concepts.

Suppose that a class earned these quiz scores: 65, 70, 70, 78, 80, 81, 84, 86, 89, 89, 93, 93, 93, 98, 100.

A stem-and-leaf plot would show the data like this:

```
 6 | 5
 7 | 0  0  8
 8 | 0  1  4  6  9  9
 9 | 3  3  3  8
10 | 0
```

The tens digits are listed vertically, and then each ones digit is listed horizontally. For example, the row that reads "7| 0 0 8" means "70, 70, 78". This forms a sort of bar graph, but we have actual numbers instead of bars.

A boxplot shows the data broken into quartiles. Using our fifteen quiz scores, this would be the boxplot:

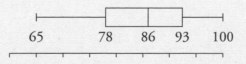

Each part of the boxplot represents 25% of the data. Here, 78 is the *first quartile,* or Q_1, 86 is the median (sometimes called the *second quartile,* or Q_2), and 93 is the *third quartile,* or Q_3. The only other thing you need to know is that the *interquartile range* is the range of the middle 50%: $Q_3 - Q_1$, or the width of the box. In this example, that's $93 - 78 = 35$.

Standard Deviation

The standard deviation of a set is a measure of the set's variation from its mean. A set composed of 10 identical values (having a range of 0) could have the same mean as a set with widely scattered values. The first list would have a much smaller standard deviation than the second.

Standard deviation comes up very infrequently on the Math Level 2. Computing a standard deviation is a long, annoying process that you will not be asked to endure. (Aren't you glad?) Just remember that the standard deviation is a measure of how far the typical value in a set is from the set's average. The bigger the standard deviation, the more widely dispersed the values are. The smaller the standard deviation, the more closely grouped the values in a set are around the mean. On some questions, you need to know how many standard deviations above or below the mean a certain value is. On other questions, drawing a rough sketch of the data will be enough.

Level 2 Only

How Far From the SD?
Some questions may ask you to figure out how many deviations above or below the mean a number is. In order to figure that out, find the difference between the mean and the number you're dealing with. Then divide it by the standard deviation.

DRILL

Try the following practice questions using these statistical definitions. The answers to these drills can be found in Chapter 12.

25. List *M* contains ten elements whose sum is zero. Which of the following statements must be true?

   I. The mean of the elements in *M* is zero.
   II. The median of the elements in *M* is zero.
   III. The mode of the elements in *M* is zero.

   (A) None
   (B) I only
   (C) I and II only
   (D) II and III only
   (E) I, II, and III

42. The subjects in a research study are divided into Group *A* and Group *B*. Both groups are given the same test. The mean score in Group *A* is greater than that in Group *B*, but the standard deviation of scores in Group *A* is less than that in Group *B*. Which of the following must be true?

(A) The range of scores in Group *A* is equal to the range of scores in Group *B*.

(B) The median score in Group *A* is greater than the median score in Group *B*.

(C) The scores are more closely grouped about the mean in Group *A* than in Group *B*.

(D) The highest score in Group *A* is greater than the highest score in Group *B*.

(E) The number of subjects in Group *A* is less than the number of subjects in Group *B*.

Level 2 Only

PROBABILITY

Probability is a mathematical expression of the likelihood of an event. The basis of probability is simple. The likelihood of any event is discussed in terms of all of the possible outcomes. To express the probability of a given event, *x*, you would count the number of possible outcomes, count the number of outcomes that give you what you want, and arrange them in a fraction, like this:

$$\text{Probability of } x = \frac{\text{number of outcomes that are } x}{\text{total number of possible outcomes}}$$

Every probability is a fraction. The largest a probability can be is 1. A probability of 1 indicates total certainty. The smallest a probability can be is 0, meaning that it's something that cannot happen. Most probabilities you'll be asked to find on the Math Subject Tests are fractions between 0 and 1. Figuring out the probability of any single event is usually simple. When you flip a coin, there are only two possible outcomes, heads and tails. The probability of getting heads is therefore 1 out of 2, or $\frac{1}{2}$. When you roll a die, there are six possible outcomes, 1 through 6; the odds of getting a 6 is therefore $\frac{1}{6}$. The odds of getting an even result when rolling a die are $\frac{1}{2}$ since there are three even results in six possible outcomes. Here's a typical example of a simple probability question.

Not!
You can find the probability that something WILL NOT happen by subtracting the probability that it WILL happen from 1. For example, if the weatherperson tells you that there is a 0.3 probability of rain today, then there must be a 0.7 probability that it won't rain, because $1 - 0.3 = 0.7$.

11. A bag contains 7 blue marbles and 14 marbles that are not blue. If one marble is drawn at random from the bag, what is the probability that the marble is blue?

(A) $\dfrac{1}{7}$

(B) $\dfrac{1}{3}$

(C) $\dfrac{1}{2}$

(D) $\dfrac{2}{3}$

(E) $\dfrac{3}{7}$

Here's How to Crack It

Here, there are 21 marbles in the bag, 7 of which are blue. The probability that a marble chosen at random would be blue is therefore $\dfrac{7}{21}$, or $\dfrac{1}{3}$. The correct answer is (B).

Probability of Multiple Events

Some advanced probability questions require you to calculate the probability of more than one event. Here's a typical example:

23. If a fair coin is flipped three times, what is the probability that the result will be tails exactly twice?

(A) $\dfrac{1}{8}$

(B) $\dfrac{1}{5}$

(C) $\dfrac{3}{8}$

(D) $\dfrac{5}{8}$

(E) $\dfrac{2}{3}$

Here's How to Crack It

When the number of possibilities involved is small enough, the easiest and safest way to do a probability question like this is to write out all of the possibilities and count the ones that give you what you want. Here are all the possible outcomes of flipping a coin three times.

heads, heads, heads	tails, tails, tails
heads, heads, tails	tails, tails, heads
heads, tails, heads	tails, heads, tails
heads, tails, tails	tails, heads, heads

As you can see by counting, only three of the eight possible outcomes produce tails exactly twice. The chance of getting exactly two tails is therefore $\frac{3}{8}$. The correct answer is (C).

Sometimes, however, you'll be asked to calculate probabilities for multiple events when there are too many outcomes to write out easily. Consider, for example, this variation on an earlier question.

41. A bag contains 7 blue marbles and 14 marbles that are not blue. What is the probability that the first three marbles drawn at random from this bag will be blue?

(A) $\frac{1}{3}$

(B) $\frac{1}{9}$

(C) $\frac{1}{21}$

(D) $\frac{1}{38}$

(E) $\frac{1}{46}$

Here's How to Crack It

Three random drawings from a bag of 21 objects produce a huge number of possible outcomes. It's not practical to write them all out. To calculate the likelihood of three events combined, you need to take advantage of a basic rule of probability.

The probability of multiple events occurring together is the product of the probabilities of the events occurring individually.

In order to calculate the probability of a series of events, calculate the odds of each event happening separately and multiply them together. This is especially important in processes like drawings, because each event affects the odds of following events. This is how you'd calculate the probability of those three marble drawings.

The first drawing is just like the simple question you did earlier; there are 7 blue marbles out of 21 total—a probability of $\frac{1}{3}$.

For the second drawing, the numbers are different. There are now 6 blue marbles out of a total of 20, making the probability of drawing another blue marble $\frac{6}{20}$, or $\frac{3}{10}$.

For the third drawing, there are now 5 blue marbles remaining out of a total of 19. The odds of getting a blue marble this time are $\frac{5}{19}$.

To calculate the odds of getting blue marbles on the first three random drawings, just multiply these numbers together.

$$\frac{1}{3} \times \frac{3}{10} \times \frac{5}{19} = \frac{1}{38}$$

The odds of getting three blue marbles is therefore $\frac{1}{38}$, and the answer is (D). This can also be expressed as a decimal, as 0.026. ETS often asks for answers in decimal form on the Math Subject Tests, just to make sure you haven't forgotten how to push the little buttons on your calculator. Just bear with them.

Drill

Try the following practice questions about probability. The answers to these drills can be found in Chapter 12.

13. If the probability that it will rain is $\frac{5}{12}$, then what is the probability that it will NOT rain?

    (A) $\frac{7}{12}$

    (B) $\frac{5}{7}$

    (C) $\frac{12}{7}$

    (D) $\frac{12}{5}$

    (E) It cannot be determined from the information given.

16. In an experiment, it is found that the probability that a released bee will land on a painted target is $\frac{2}{5}$. It is also found that when a bee lands on the target, the probability that the bee will attempt to sting the target is $\frac{1}{3}$. In this experiment, what is the probability that a released bee will land on the target and attempt to sting it?

    (A) $\frac{2}{15}$

    (B) $\frac{1}{5}$

    (C) $\frac{2}{5}$

    (D) $\frac{1}{3}$

    (E) $\frac{6}{5}$

Day	Daily Cookie Production	Number Burned
Monday	256	34
Tuesday	232	39
Wednesday	253	41

20. The chart above shows the cookie production at MunchCo for three days. What is the probability that a cookie made on one of these three days will be burned?

    (A) $\frac{1}{26}$

    (B) $\frac{2}{13}$

    (C) $\frac{1}{7}$

    (D) $\frac{3}{13}$

    (E) It cannot be determined from the information given.

24. If two six-sided dice are rolled, each having faces numbered 1 to 6, what is the probability that the product of the two numbers rolled will be odd?

    (A) $\frac{1}{6}$

    (B) $\frac{1}{4}$

    (C) $\frac{1}{3}$

    (D) $\frac{1}{2}$

    (E) $\frac{7}{12}$

44. In a basketball-shooting contest, if the probability that Heather will make a basket on any given attempt is $\frac{4}{5}$, then what is the probability that she will make at least one basket in three attempts?

(A) $\frac{12}{125}$

(B) $\frac{64}{125}$

(C) $\frac{124}{125}$

(D) 1

(E) $\frac{12}{5}$

PERMUTATIONS, COMBINATIONS, AND FACTORIALS

Questions about permutations, combinations, and factorials are fairly rare on the Math Subject Tests and more common on the Math Level 2 than on the Math Level 1. As is the case with many of the odds and ends of precalculus, questions about permutations and combinations are rarely mathematically difficult; they just test your understanding of the concepts and ability to work with them. Both permutations and combinations are simply ways of counting groups of numbers.

Simple Permutations

A permutation is an arrangement of objects of a definite order. The simplest sort of permutation question might ask you how many different arrangements are possible for 6 different chairs in a row, or how many different 4-letter arrangements of the letters in the word FUEL are possible. Both of these simple questions can be answered with the same technique.

Just draw a row of boxes corresponding to the positions you have to fill. In the case of the chairs, there are six positions, one for each chair. You would make a sketch like the following:

Then, in each box, write the number of objects available to put into that box. Keep in mind that objects put into previous boxes are no longer available. For the chair-arranging example, there would be 6 chairs available for the first box; only 5 left for the second box; 4 for the third, and so on until only one chair remained to be put into the last position. Finally, just multiply the numbers in the boxes together, and the product will be the number of possible arrangements, or permutations.

There are 720 possible permutations of a group of 6 chairs. This number can also be written as "6!"—that's not a display of enthusiasm—the exclamation point means *factorial*. The number is read "six factorial," and it means $6 \cdot 5 \cdot 4 \cdot 3 \cdot 2 \cdot 1$, which equals 720. A factorial is simply the product of a series of integers counting down to 1 from the specified number. For example, the number 70! means $70 \cdot 69 \cdot 68 \ldots 3 \cdot 2 \cdot 1$.

The number of possible arrangements of any group with n members is simply $n!$. In this way, the number of possible arrangements of the letters in FUEL is 4!,

On a TI-83, you can calculate a factorial by hitting the MATH key and then scrolling over to PRB. Most scientific calculators have a factorial feature, but not all of them do.

because there are 4 letters in the group. That means 4 • 3 • 2 • 1 arrangements, or 24. If you sketched 4 boxes for the 4 letter positions and filled in the appropriate numbers, that's exactly what you'd get.

Advanced Permutations

Permutations get a little trickier when you work with smaller arrangements. For example, what if you were asked how many 2-letter arrangements could be made from the letters in FUEL? It's just a modification of the original counting procedure. Sketch 2 boxes for the 2 positions. Then fill in the number of letters available for each position. As before, there are 4 letters available for the first space, and 3 for the second. The only difference is that you're done after two spaces.

$$\boxed{4}\ \boxed{3} = 12$$

As you did before, multiply the numbers in the boxes together to get the total number of arrangements. You should find that there are 12 possible 2-letter arrangements from the letters in FUEL.

That's all there is to permutations. The box-counting procedure is the safest way to approach them. Just sketch the number of positions available, and fill in the number of objects available for each position, from first to last—then multiply those numbers together.

On to Combinations

Combinations differ from permutations in just one way. In combinations, order doesn't matter. A permutation question might ask you to form different numbers from a set of digits. Order would certainly matter in that case, because 135 is very different from 513. Similarly, a question about seating arrangements would be a permutation question, because the word "arrangements" tells you that order is important. So questions that ask about "schedules" or "orderings" require you to calculate the number of *permutations*.

Which One to Use?

Combination and permutation questions can be very similar in appearance. Always ask yourself carefully whether sequence is important in a certain question before you proceed.

Combination questions, on the other hand, deal with groupings in which order isn't important. Combination questions often deal with the selection of committees. Josh, Lisa, Andy isn't any different from Andy, Lisa, Josh, as far as committees go. In the same way, a question about the number of different 3-topping pizzas you could make from a 10-topping list would be a combination question, because the order in which the toppings are put on is irrelevant. Questions that refer to "teams" or "pairs" are therefore asking about the number of possible *combinations*.

Calculating Combinations

Calculating combinations is surprisingly easy. All you have to do is throw out duplicate answers that count as separate permutations, but not as separate combinations. For example, let's make a full-fledged combination question out of that pizza example.

---

pepperoni   sausage
meatballs   anchovies
green peppers   onion
mushrooms   garlic
tomato   broccoli

36. If a pizza must have 3 toppings chosen from the list above, and no topping may be used more than once on a given pizza, how many different kinds of pizza can be made?

(A) 720
(B) 360
(C) 120
(D)   90
(E)   30

Here's How to Crack It

To calculate the number of possible combinations, start by figuring out the number of possible *permutations*.

$$\boxed{10}\ \boxed{9}\ \boxed{8} = 720$$

That tells you that there are 720 possible 3-topping permutations that can be made from a list of 10 toppings. You're not done yet, though. Because this is a list of permutations, it contains many arrangements that duplicate the same group of elements in different orders. For example, those 720 permutations would include these:

pepperoni, mushrooms, onion   mushrooms, onion, pepperoni
pepperoni, onion, mushrooms   onion, pepperoni, mushrooms
mushrooms, pepperoni, onion   onion, mushrooms, pepperoni

All six of these listings are different permutations of the same group. In fact, for every 3-topping combination, there will be 6 different permutations. You've got to divide 720 by 6 to get the true number of combinations, which is 120. The correct answer is (C).

So, how do you know what number to divide permutations by to get combinations? It's simple. For the 3-position question above, we divided by 6, which is 3!. That's all there is to it. To calculate a number of possible combinations, calculate the possible permutations first, and divide that number by the number of positions, factorial. Take a look at one more:

---

29. How many different 4-person teams can be made from a roster of 9 players?

(A) 3,024
(B) 1,512
(C) 378
(D) 254
(E) 126

Here's How to Crack It

This is definitely a combination question. Start by sketching 4 boxes for the 4 team positions.

Then fill in the number of possible contestants for each position, and multiply them together. This gives you the number of possible *permutations*.

$$\boxed{9}\ \boxed{8}\ \boxed{7}\ \boxed{6} = 3,024$$

Finally, divide this number by 4! for the 4 positions you're working with. This gets rid of different permutations of identical groups. You divide 3,024 by 24 and get the number of possible combinations, 126. The correct answer is (E).

Factorials

On the Math Level 2, ETS occasionally asks you to calculate a factorial itself. If you try to do a factorial question in your head, you're likely to fall into one of ETS's traps. Use your calculator and be careful.

Level 2 Only

18. $\dfrac{5!}{6!-5!} =$

(A) $\dfrac{1}{6!}$

(B) $\dfrac{1}{6}$

(C) $\dfrac{1}{5}$

(D) 5

(E) $\dfrac{5!}{6}$

For this question, just use your calculator. $5! = 120$ and $6! = 720$, so you have $\dfrac{120}{600} = \dfrac{1}{5}$. The answer is (C). It's supposed to be easy, but don't try to simplify this in your head. Joe Bloggs might choose any of the answer choices here.

Factoring the Factorial
Sometimes numbers will be too bulky for your calculator, or you'll realize there's a faster way. You can factor factorials. Let's take another look at question 18. Notice that the denominator is $6! - 5!$. $6!$ is the same as $6 \cdot 5!$, which means you can factor $5!$ out of the denominator and you're left with $5!(6 - 1)$. Now you can cancel and you end up with $\dfrac{1}{5}$.

DRILL

Try the following practice questions about permutations, combinations, and factorials. The answers to these drills can be found in Chapter 12.

27. How many different 4-student committees can be chosen from a panel of 12 students?

    (A)   236
    (B)   495
    (C)   1,980
    (D) 11,880
    (E) 20,736

31. $\dfrac{x!(x+1)!}{(x-1)!} =$

    (A) $x!(x+2)!$
    (B) $(x^2-1)!$
    (C) $x(x-2)!$
    (D) $x!(x-1)$
    (E) $x(x+1)!$

32. In how many different orders may 6 books be placed on a shelf?

    (A)   36
    (B)   216
    (C)   480
    (D)   720
    (E) 46,656

45. How many 7-person committees consisting of 4 females and 3 males may be assembled from a pool of 17 females and 12 males?

    (A)   523,600
    (B) 1,560,780
    (C) 1.26×10^7
    (D) 7.54×10^7
    (E) 7.87×10^9

GROUP QUESTIONS

Group questions are a very specific type of counting problem. They don't come up frequently on the Math Subject Tests, but when they do come up, they're easy pickings if you're prepared for them. If you're not, they can be a bit confusing. Here's a sample group question.

---

34. At Bedlam Music School, 64 students are enrolled in the gospel choir, and 37 students are enrolled in the handbell choir. Fifteen students are enrolled in neither group. If there are 100 students at Bedlam, how many students are enrolled in both the gospel choir and the handbell choir?

    (A) 12
    (B) 16
    (C) 18
    (D) 21
    (E) 27

Here's How to Crack It

As you can see, part of the difficulty of such problems lies in reading them—they're confusing. The other trick lies in the actual counting. If there are students in both the gospel choir and the handbell choir, then when you count the members of both groups, you're counting some kids twice—the kids who are in both groups. To find out how many students are in both groups, just use the group problem formula.

Group Problem Formula

Total = Group 1 + Group 2 + Neither – Both

For question 34, this formula gives you 64 + 37 + 15 – Both = 100. Solve this, and you get Both = 16. The correct answer is (B).

The group problem formula will work for any group question with two groups. Just Plug In the information you know, and solve for the piece that's missing.

DRILL

Use the group formula on the following practice questions. The answers to these drills can be found in Chapter 12.

25. At Buford Prep School, 253 students are enrolled in French, and 112 students are enrolled in Latin. 23 students are enrolled in both Latin and French. If there are 530 students at Buford Prep School, how many students are enrolled in neither French nor Latin?

    (A) 188
    (B) 342
    (C) 388
    (D) 484
    (E) 507

28. On the Leapwell gymnastics team, 14 gymnasts compete on the balance beam, 12 compete on the uneven bars, and 9 compete on both the balance beam and the uneven bars. If 37 gymnasts compete on neither the balance beam nor the uneven bars, how many gymnasts are on the Leapwell team?

    (A) 45
    (B) 51
    (C) 54
    (D) 63
    (E) 72

42. In a European tour group, $\frac{1}{3}$ of the tourists speak Spanish, $\frac{2}{5}$ of the tourists speak French, and $\frac{1}{2}$ of the tourists speak neither language. What fraction of the tourists in the tour group speak both Spanish and French?

    (A) $\frac{2}{15}$

    (B) $\frac{7}{30}$

    (C) $\frac{1}{3}$

    (D) $\frac{1}{2}$

    (E) $\frac{14}{15}$

Summary

o Statistics is about working with large groups of numbers and looking for patterns and trends in those numbers
   - The mean is the average value of a set.
   - The median is the middle value of a set when the values of the set are in chronological order.
   - The mode is the value that occurs the most in a set.

o Probability is the number of ways to get what you want divided by the total number of possible outcomes.

o The probability of multiple events occurring can be calculated either by writing them all out or by multiplying the individual probabilities together.

o Permutations and combinations are more common on the Level 2 test, but do appear on the Level 1 test.
   - A permutation is the number of ways you can arrange objects in a definite order.
   - A combination is the number of ways you can group objects. Order doesn't matter. With the same set of objects, the combination will be smaller than the permutation.

o Group questions require one formula:
   Total − Group 1 + Group 2 + Neither − Both.

o Here are some Level 2–only concepts:
   - Standard deviation is a measure of a set's variation from its mean. It comes up very infrequently on the Level 2, but it does pop up.
   - The range of a set in statistics is the difference between the set's highest and lowest values.
   - A factorial is found when multiplying the numbers between 1 and the number you're looking for. $4! = 4 \times 3 \times 2 \times 1$. Use your calculator on these questions.

Chapter 11
Miscellaneous

The techniques and rules covered in this chapter are relatively rare on the Math Subject Tests. They occur only on the Math Level 2 or the difficult third of the Math Level 1; if you're not supposed to be tackling those questions, don't waste your time on this chapter. If you will take the Math Level 2, or will take the Math Level 1 very aggressively, then it's a good idea to learn the rules in this chapter—but remember, the material in the preceding chapters is still more important.

LOGARITHMS

Exponents can also be written in the form of logarithms. For example, $\log_2 8$ represents the exponent that turns 2 into 8. In this case, the "base" of the logarithm is 2. It's easy to make a logarithmic expression look like a normal exponential expression. Here you can say $\log_2 8 = x$, where x is the unknown exponent that turns 2 into 8. Then you can rewrite the equation as $2^x = 8$. Notice that, in this equation, 2 is the base of the exponent, just as it was the base of the logarithm. Logarithms can be rearranged into exponential form using the following definition:

> **Definition of a Logarithm**
>
> $$\log_b n = x \Leftrightarrow b^x = n$$

A logarithm that has no written base is assumed to be a base-10 logarithm. Base-10 logarithms are called "common logarithms," and are so frequently used that the base is often left off. Therefore, the expression "log 1,000" means $\log_{10} 1{,}000$. Most calculations involving logarithms are done in base-10 logs. When you punch a number into your calculator and hit the "log" button, the calculator assumes you're using a base-10 log. There will be times when you're dealing with other bases. A nifty formula allows you to use your calculator to evaluate logs with other bases.

> **Change of Base Formula**
>
> $$\log_B A = \frac{\log A}{\log B}$$

For example, $\log_7 54$ can be entered into your calculator as $\log(54)/\log(7)$, which gives you 2.0499.

A Nifty Trick!
So you know how any number to the first power is that same number? For example, $4^1 = 4$. Well, that means that $\log_4 4 = 1$. Any log that has the same base as number is going to equal 1. So any time you see that, no work is necessary. Pretty cool, huh?

DRILL

Test your understanding of the definition of a logarithm with the following exercises. The answers to these drills can be found in Chapter 12.

1. $\log_2 32 = $ _____

2. $\log_3 x = 4$: $x = $ _____

3. $\log 1000 = $ _____

4. $\log_b 64 = 3$: $b = $ _____

5. $x^{\log_x y} = $ _____

6. $\log_7 1 = $ _____

7. $\log_x x = $ _____

8. $\log_x x^{12} = $ _____

9. $\log 37 = $ _____

10. $\log 5 = $ _____

For the Math Level 1 Subject Test, that's about all you need to know about logarithms. As long as you can convert them from logarithmic form to exponential form, you should be able to handle any logarithm question you run into. For the Math Level 2 Subject Test, however, you will need to work with logarithms in more complicated ways.

Logarithmic Rules

There are three properties of logarithms that are often useful on the Math Level 2 Subject Test. These properties are very similar to the rules for working with exponents—which isn't surprising, because logarithms and exponents are the same thing. The first two properties deal with the logarithms of products and quotients.

The Product Rule

$$\log_b (xy) = \log_b x + \log_b y$$

The Quotient Rule

$$\log_b \left(\frac{x}{y}\right) = \log_b x - \log_b y$$

These rules are just another way of saying that when you multiply terms, you add exponents, and when you divide terms, you subtract exponents. Be sure to remember that when you use them, the logarithms in these cases all have the same base.

The third property of logarithms deals with the logarithms of terms raised to powers.

The Power Rule

$$\log_b (x^r) = r \log_b x$$

This means that whenever you take the logarithm of a term with an exponent, you can pull the exponent out and make it a coefficient.

$$\log (7^2) = 2 \log 7 = 2(0.8451) = 1.6902$$

$$\log_3 (x^5) = 5 \log_3 x$$

These logarithm rules are often used in reverse to simplify a string of logarithms into a single logarithm. Just as the product and quotient rules can be used to expand a single logarithm into several logarithms, the same rules can be used to consolidate several logarithms that are being added or subtracted into a single logarithm. In the same way, the power rule can be used backward to pull a coefficient into a logarithm, as an exponent. Take a look at how these rules can be used to simplify a string of logarithms with the same base.

$$\log 8 + 2 \log 5 - \log 2 =$$
$$\log 8 + \log 5^2 - \log 2 = \quad \textit{(Power Rule)}$$
$$\log 8 + \log 25 - \log 2 =$$
$$\log (8 \times 25) - \log 2 = \quad \textit{(Product Rule)}$$
$$\log 200 - \log 2 =$$
$$\log \left(\frac{200}{2}\right) = \quad \textit{(Quotient Rule)}$$
$$\log 100 = 2$$

DRILL

In the following exercises, use the Product, Quotient, and Power rules of logarithms to simplify each logarithmic expression into a single logarithm with a coefficient of 1. The answers to these drills can be found in Chapter 12.

1. $\log 5 + 2 \log 6 - \log 9 =$
2. $2 \log_5 12 - \log_5 8 - 2 \log_5 3 =$
3. $4 \log 6 - 4 \log 2 - 3 \log 3 =$
4. $\log_4 320 - \log_4 20 =$
5. $2 \log 5 + \log 3 =$

Logarithms in Exponential Equations

Logarithms can be used to solve many equations that would be very difficult or even impossible to solve any other way. The trick to using logarithms in solving equations is to convert all of the exponential expressions in the equation to base-10 logarithms, or common logarithms. Common logarithms are the numbers programmed into your calculator's logarithm function. Once you express exponential equations in term of common logarithms, you can run the equation through your calculator and get real numbers.

When using logarithms to solve equations, be sure to remember the meaning of the different numbers in a logarithm. Logarithms can be converted into exponential form using the definition of a logarithm provided at the beginning of this section.

Level 2
Only

Let's take a look at the kinds of tough exponential equations that can be solved using logarithms:

39. If $5^x = 2^{700}$, then what is the value of x ?

This deceptively simple equation is practically impossible to solve using conventional algebra. Two to the 700th power is mind-bogglingly huge; there's no way to calculate that number. There's also no way to get x out of that awkward exponent position. This is where logarithms come in. Take the logarithm of each side of the equation.

$$\log 5^x = \log 2^{700}$$

Now use the Power Rule of logarithms to pull the exponents out.

$$x \log 5 = 700 \log 2$$

Then isolate x.

$$x = 700 \times \frac{\log 2}{\log 5}$$

Now use your calculator to get decimal values for log 2 and log 5, and plug them into the equation.

$$x = 700 \times \frac{.3010}{.6990}$$

$$x = 700 \times .4307$$

$$x = 301.47$$

And *voilà*, a numerical value for x. This is the usual way in which logarithms will prove useful on the Math Subject Tests (especially the Math Level 2). Solving tough exponent equations will usually involve taking the common log of both sides of the equation, and using the Power Rule to bring exponents down. Another method can be used to find the values of logarithms with bases other than 10, even though logarithms with other bases aren't programmed into your calculator. For example:

25. What is the value of x if $\log_3 32 = x$?

You can't do this one in your head. The logarithm is asking, "What exponent turns 3 into 32?" Obviously, it's not an integer. You know that the answer will be between 3 and 4, because $3^3 = 27$ and $3^4 = 81$. That might be enough information to eliminate an answer choice or two, but it probably won't be enough to pick one answer choice. Here's how to get an exact answer:

$$x = \log_3 32$$

$$x = \frac{\log 32}{\log 3} \text{ (Change of Base Formula)}$$

$$x = \frac{1.5051}{0.4771}$$

$$x = 3.1546$$

And there's the exact value of x.

DRILL

In the following examples, use the techniques you've just seen to solve these exponential and logarithmic equations. The answers to these drills can be found in Chapter 12.

1. If $2^4 = 3^x$, then $x =$
2. $\log_5 18 =$
3. If $10^n = 137$, then $n =$
4. $\log_{12} 6 =$
5. If $4^x = 5$, then $4^{x+2} =$
6. $\log_2 50 =$
7. If $3^x = 7$, then $3^{x+1} =$
8. If $\log_3 12 = \log_4 x$, then $x =$

Natural Logarithms

On the Math Level 2 Subject Test, you may run into a special kind of logarithm called a natural logarithm. Natural logarithms are logs with a base of e, a constant that is approximately equal to 2.718.

The constant e is a little like π. It's a decimal number that goes on forever without repeating itself, and, like π, it's a basic feature of the universe. Just as π is the ratio of a circle's circumference to its diameter, no matter what, e is a basic feature of growth and decay in economics, physics, and even in biology.

The role of e in the mathematics of growth and decay is a little complicated. Don't worry about that, because you don't need to know very much about e for the Math Level 2. Just memorize a few rules and you're ready to go.

Natural logarithms are so useful in math and science that there's a special notation for expressing them. The expression ln x (which is read as "ell-enn x") means the log of x to the base e, or $\log_e x$. That means that there are three different ways to express a natural logarithm.

> **Definitions of a Natural Logarithm**
>
> $$\ln n = x \iff \log_e n = x \iff e^x = n$$

You can use the definitions of a natural logarithm to solve equations that contain an e^x term. Since e equals $2.718281828\ldots$, there's no easy way to raise it to a specific power. By rearranging the equation into a natural logarithm in "$\ln x$" form, you can make your calculator do the hard work for you. Here's a simple example:

19. If $e^x = 6$, then $x =$

   (A) 0.45
   (B) 0.56
   (C) 1.18
   (D) 1.79
   (E) 2.56

Here's How to Crack It

The equation in the question, $e^x = 6$, can be converted directly into a logarithmic equation using the definition of a logarithm. It would then be written as $\log_e 6 = x$, or $\ln 6 = x$. To find the value of x, just hit the "LN" key on your calculator and punch in 6. You'll find that $x = 1.791759$. The correct answer is (D).

For the Math Level 2 Subject Test, you may also have to know the shapes of some basic graphs associated with natural logs.

Calculator Tip
On some scientific calculators, you'll punch in 6 first, and then hit the "ln x" key

Here they are:

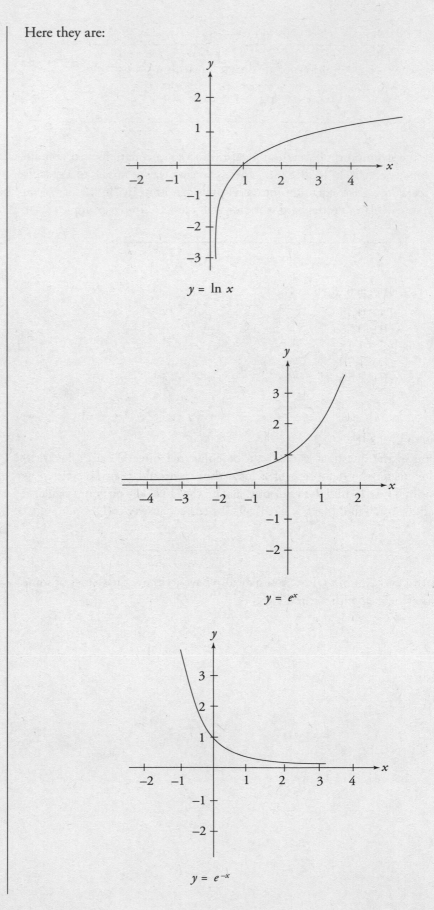

$y = \ln x$

$y = e^x$

$y = e^{-x}$

Finally, some questions may require you to estimate the value of e to answer a question. Just remember that $e \approx 2.718$. If you forget the value of e, you can always get your calculator to give it to you. Just hit the "2nd" key followed by the "LN" key, and punch in 1. The result will be e to the first power, which is just plain e.

DRILL

The answers to these drills can be found in Chapter 12.

18. If $e^z = 8$, then $z =$

   (A) 1.74
   (B) 2.08
   (C) 2.35
   (D) 2.94
   (E) 3.04

23. If set $M = \{\pi, e, 3\}$, then which of the following shows the elements in set M in descending order?

   (A) $\{\pi, e, 3\}$
   (B) $\{e, 3, \pi\}$
   (C) $\{\pi, 3, e\}$
   (D) $\{3, \pi, e\}$
   (E) $\{3, e, \pi\}$

38. If $6e^{\frac{n}{3}} = 5$, then what is the value of n ?

   (A) −0.55
   (B) −0.18
   (C)   0.26
   (D)   0.64
   (E)   1.19

VISUAL PERCEPTION

Some questions on the Math Subject Tests ironically do not appear to test mathematical skills in any conventional sense of the phrase. One type of non-mathematical question on the test is the visual perception question, which asks you to visualize (that is, draw) a picture of a situation described in two or three dimensions.

The only technique for such questions is to draw your best representation of the situation described and use that as a guide in eliminating answers. You don't have to be a great artist, but a simple diagram will go a long way.

24. Which of the following equations describes the set of points equidistant from the lines described by the equations $y = 2x + 7$ and $y = 2x + 1$?

   (A) $y = 4x + 8$
   (B) $y = 4x + 6$
   (C) $y = 2x + 8$
   (D) $y = 2x + 6$
   (E) $y = 2x + 4$

This is asked in words because if there were a picture, it would be too easy. So make it easier by drawing a picture.

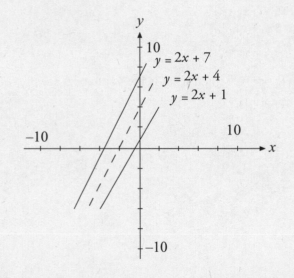

If you draw points halfway between the two lines, you get another line. It's parallel to the other two (so its slope is 2, eliminate A and B), and it's halfway between the two, so its y-intercept is halfway between 7 and 1. That's a y-intercept of 4, so E is the answer.

DRILL

Try the following practice questions about visual perception. The answers to these drills can be found in Chapter 12.

27. Lines l, m, n, and o are all distinct lines which lie in the same plane. If line l is perpendicular to line m, line m is parallel to line o, and line o is perpendicular to line n, which of the following must be true?

    I. Line l is parallel to line n.
   II. Line n is perpendicular to line l.
  III. Line n is parallel to line m.

(A) I only
(B) II only
(C) III only
(D) I and III only
(E) I, II, and III

42. Which of the following could be the number of circles created by the intersection of a sphere and a cube?

    I. 5
   II. 6
  III. 7

(A) I only
(B) II only
(C) III only
(D) I and II only
(E) I and III only

ARITHMETIC AND GEOMETRIC SEQUENCES

The average Math Subject Test has one question dealing with arithmetic or geometric sequences. They're very easy once you know how they work, so read the next few paragraphs and fear not.

Arithmetic Sequences

The big-forehead people at ETS define an arithmetic sequence as "one in which the difference between successive terms is constant." Real human beings just say that an arithmetic sequence is what you get when you pick a starting value and add the same number again and again.

Here are some sample arithmetic sequences.

$$\{a_n\} = 1, 7, 13, 19, 25, 31,\dots$$
$$\{b_n\} = 3, 13, 23, 33, 43, 53,\dots$$
$$\{c_n\} = 12, 7, 2, -3, -8, -13,\dots$$

It's not hard to figure out what difference separates any two terms in a sequence. To continue a sequence, you would just continue adding that difference. The larger letter in each case is the name of the sequence (these are sequences a, b, and c). The subscript, n, represents the number of the term in the sequence. The expression a_4, for example, represents the fourth term in the a sequence, which is 19. The expression b_7 means the seventh term in the b sequence, which would be 63.

The typical arithmetic sequence question asks you to figure out the difference between any two successive terms in the sequence, and then calculate the value of a term much farther along. There's just one trick to that—to calculate the value of a_{26}, for example, start by figuring out the difference between any two consecutive terms. You'll find that the terms in the a sequence increase at intervals of 6. Now here's the trick: To get to the 26th term in the sequence, you'll start with a_1, which is 1, and increase it by 6 twenty-five times. The term $a_{26} = 1 + (25 \times 6)$, or 151. It's like climbing stairs in a building; to get to the fifth floor, you climb 4 flights. To get to the 12th floor, you climb 11 flights, and so on. In the same way, it takes 11 steps to get to the 12th term in a sequence from the first term. To get to the nth term in a sequence, take $(n - 1)$ steps from the first term.

Here's another example—to figure out the value of c_{17}, start with 12 and add -5 sixteen times. The value of $c_{17} = 12 + (16 \times -5)$, or -68. That's all there is to calculating values in arithmetic sequences.

Here's the algebraic definition of the nth term of an arithmetic sequence, if the starting value is a_1 and the difference between any two successive terms is d.

> **The nth Term of an Arithmetic Sequence**
>
> $$a_n = a_1 + (n - 1)d$$

Finding the Sum of an Arithmetic Sequence

You might be asked to figure out the sum of the first 37 terms of an arithmetic sequence, or the first 48 terms, and so on. To figure out the sum of a chunk of an arithmetic sequence, take the average of the first and last terms in that chunk, and multiply by the number of terms you're adding up. For example,

$$\{a_n\} = 5, 11, 17, 23, 29, 35,\dots$$

What is the sum of the first 40 terms of a_n ?

The first term of a_n is 5. The fortieth term is 239. The sum of these terms will be the average of these two terms, 122, multiplied by the number of terms, 40. The product of 122 and 40 is 4,880. That's the sum of the first 40 terms of the sequence. Here's the algebraic definition of the sum of the first n terms of an arithmetic sequence, where the difference between any two successive terms is d.

Sum of the First n Terms of an Arithmetic Sequence

$$\text{sum} = n\left(\frac{a_1 + a_n}{2}\right)$$

Summations

A *summation* (or *series*) is a list of numbers to be added together. First, plug the number below the sigma (Σ) into the formula and get a result. Then do this for every integer up to the number above the sigma. Finally, add up all of your results to get your final answer.

Level 2 Only

43. $\displaystyle\sum_{k=1}^{8} 2k + 1 =$

(A) 20
(B) 36
(C) 40
(D) 72
(E) 80

Here's How to Crack It

Here, plug $k = 1$ into the formula to get $2(1) + 1 = 3$. Now, repeat for $k = 2$, $k = 3$, etc., up to and including $k = 8$. You end up with $3 + 5 + \dots + 17$. You could also use the formula for the sum of the first n terms of an arithmetic sequence, and you'd get $8\left(\dfrac{3+17}{2}\right)$, which is 80. The answer is (E).

Level 2
Only

Geometric Sequences

A geometric sequence is formed by taking a starting value and multiplying it by the same factor again and again. While any two successive terms in an arithmetic sequence are separated by a constant difference, any two successive terms in a geometric sequence are separated by a constant factor. Here are some sample geometric sequences.

$$\{a_n\} = 2, 6, 18, 54, 162, 486,\ldots$$
$$\{b_n\} = 8, 4, 2, 1, 0.5, 0.25,\ldots$$
$$\{c_n\} = 3, 15, 75, 375, 1{,}875,\ldots$$

Just like arithmetic sequence questions, geometric sequence questions most often test your ability to calculate the value of a term farther along in the sequence. As with arithmetic sequences, the trick to geometric sequences is that it takes 19 steps to get to the 20th term, 36 steps to get to the 37th term, and so on.

To find the value of a_{10}, for example, start with the basic information about the sequence. Its starting value is 2, and each term increases by a factor of 3. To get to the tenth term, start with 2 and multiply it by 3 nine times—that is, multiply 2 by 3^9. You get 39,366, which is the value of a_{10}. As you can see, geometric sequences tend to grow much faster than arithmetic sequences do.

Here's the algebraic definition of the nth term in a geometric sequence, where the first term is a_1 and the factor separating any two successive terms is r.

> **The nth Term of a Geometric Sequence**
>
> $$a_n = a_1 r^{n-1}$$

Level 2
Only

The Sum of a Geometric Sequence

You may also be asked to find the sum of part of a geometric sequence. This is a bit tougher than calculating the sum of an arithmetic sequence. To add the first n terms of a geometric sequence, use this formula. Once again, the first term in the sequence is a_1, and the factor separating any two successive terms is r.

> **Sum of the First n Terms of a Geometric Sequence**
>
> $$\text{sum} = \frac{a_1\left(1 - r^n\right)}{1 - r}$$

This is not a formula that is called upon very often, but it's good to know it if you're taking the Math Level 2.

The Sum of an Infinite Geometric Sequence

Every now and then, a question will ask you to figure out the sum of an infinite geometric sequence—that's right, add up an infinite number of terms. There's a trick to this as well. Whenever the factor between any two terms is greater than 1, the sequence keeps growing and growing. The sum of such a sequence is infinitely large—it never stops increasing, and its sum cannot be calculated.

> The sum of an infinite geometric series can be calculated only when the constant factor is between −1 and 1.

When the constant factor of a geometric sequence is less than 1, the terms in the sequence continually decrease, and there exists some value that the sum of the sequence will never exceed. For example:

$$\{a_n\} = 1, 0.5, 0.25, 0.125, 0.0625,\dots$$

The sequence a_n above will never be greater than 2. The more of its terms you add together, the closer the sum gets to 2. If you add all of its terms, all the way out to infinity, you get exactly 2. Here's the formula you use to figure that out. Once again, a_1 is the first term in the sequence, and r the factor between each two terms. Remember that r must be between −1 and 1.

> **Sum of an Infinite Geometric Sequence**
>
> $$\text{sum} = \frac{a_1}{1 - r} \qquad \text{for } -1 < r < 1$$

In most cases, though, you can simply use approximation to eliminate ridiculously large or small answer choices. The five formulas in the boxes are all you'll ever need to work with arithmetic and geometric sequences on the Math Subject Tests.

DRILL

Try the following practice questions about arithmetic and geometric sequences. The answers to these drills can be found in Chapter 12.

14. In an arithmetic sequence, the second term is 4 and the sixth term is 32. What is the fifth term in the sequence?

    (A) 8
    (B) 15
    (C) 16
    (D) 24
    (E) 25

19. In the arithmetic sequence a_n, $a_1 = 2$ and $a_7 = 16$. What is the value of a_{33}?

    (A) 72.00
    (B) 74.33
    (C) 74.67
    (D) 75.14
    (E) 76.67

26. If the second term of a geometric sequence is 4, and the fourth term of the sequence is 25, then what is the ninth term in the sequence?

    (A) 804.43
    (B) 976.56
    (C) 1864.35
    (D) 2441.41
    (E) 6103.52

34. $3 + 1 + \dfrac{1}{3} + \dfrac{1}{9} + \dfrac{1}{27} + \dfrac{1}{81} \ldots =$

    (A) 4.17
    (B) 4.33
    (C) 4.50
    (D) 5.00
    (E) ∞

LIMITS

A limit is the value a function approaches as its independent variable approaches a given constant. That may be confusing to read, but the idea is really fairly simple. A limit can be written in different ways, as the following examples show:

$$\lim_{x \to 2} \frac{2x^2 + x - 10}{x - 2} =$$

What is the limit of $\dfrac{2x^2 + x - 10}{x - 2}$ as x approaches 2?

If $f(x) = \dfrac{2x^2 + x - 10}{x - 2}$, then what value does $f(x)$ approach as x approaches 2?

These three questions are equivalent. The first of the three is in limit notation and is read exactly like the question, "What is the limit of $\dfrac{2x^2 + x - 10}{x - 2}$ as x approaches 2?"

Finding a limit is very simple. Just take the value that x approaches and plug it into the expression. The value you get is the limit. It's so simple that you just know there's got to be a hitch—and there is. The limits that appear on the Math Subject Tests share a common problem—tricky denominators. The question introduced above is no exception. Let's take a look at it again.

$$\lim_{x \to 2} \frac{2x^2 + x - 10}{x - 2} =$$

You can find the value of this limit just by plugging 2 into the expression as x. But there's a hitch. When $x = 2$, the fraction's denominator is undefined, and it seems that the limit does not exist. The same solution always applies to such questions. You need to factor the top and bottom of the fraction and see whether there's anything that will make the denominator cancel out and stop being such a nuisance. Let's see how this expression factors out.

$$\lim_{x \to 2} \frac{2x^2 + x - 10}{x - 2} = \lim_{x \to 2} \frac{(x - 2)(2x + 5)}{x - 2} =$$

Now, you can cancel out that pesky $(x - 2)$.

$$\lim_{x \to 2} (2x + 5) =$$

Now the expression is no longer undefined when you Plug In 2. It simply comes out to 2(2) + 5, or 9. The limit of $\dfrac{2x^2 + x - 10}{x - 2}$ as x approaches 2 is 9.

That's all there is to limit questions. Just factor the top and bottom of the expression as much as possible, and try to get the problematic terms to cancel out so that the limit is no longer undefined. When it's no longer undefined, just Plug In the constant value to find the limit.

One more dirty trick—you might run into a limit problem in which it's impossible to cancel out the term that makes the expression undefined. Take a look at this example:

$$\lim_{x \to -3} \frac{3x^2 + 3x - 36}{x^2 - 9}$$

Because the constant that x approaches, –3, makes the limit undefined, you've got to factor the expression and try to cancel out the problematic part of the denominator.

$$\lim_{x \to -3} \frac{3x^2 + 3x - 36}{x^2 - 9}$$

$$\lim_{x \to -3} \frac{3(x - 3)(x + 4)}{(x - 3)(x + 3)}$$

$$\lim_{x \to -3} \frac{3(x + 4)}{(x + 3)}$$

The expression can be factored, and you can even cancel out a term in the denominator. When the dust clears, however, you find that the denominator of the fraction still approaches zero, and that the limit remains undefined. When this happens, it's said that the limit does not exist, and that would be the correct answer.

DRILL

Try the following practice questions involving limits. The answers to these drills can be found in Chapter 12.

30. What value does the expression $\dfrac{4x^2 - x - 5}{16x^2 - 25}$

    approach as x approaches 1.25 ?

    (A) 0
    (B) 0.225
    (C) 0.625
    (D) 1.275
    (E) 2.250

38. $\displaystyle\lim_{x \to 3} \dfrac{x^2 + x - 12}{2x^2 - 6x} =$

    (A) 1.17
    (B) 2.25
    (C) 3.33
    (D) 6.67
    (E) The limit does not exist.

40. $\displaystyle\lim_{x \to -3} \dfrac{x^3 + 4x^2 - 21x}{x^2 + 10x + 21} =$

    (A) –3.00
    (B) 2.46
    (C) 7.50
    (D) 10.33
    (E) The limit does not exist.

VECTORS

A vector is a visual representation of something that has both direction and magnitude. A vector can represent a force, a velocity, a distance traveled, or any of a variety of physical quantities. On the Math Subject Tests, vectors usually represent travel.

A vector arrow's orientation indicates the direction of travel. Its length represents the distance traveled (this is the magnitude of the vector). Sometimes, test questions will deal with vectors without telling you what they represent.

Basically, there are only two things you have to do with vectors on the Math Subject Tests—compute their lengths, and add or subtract them. Computing their lengths is generally done on the coordinate plane, where it's just a matter of using the Pythagorean theorem. Adding and subtracting vectors is also pretty simple. Here's how it's done.

Adding Vectors

Suppose you wanted to add these two vectors together:

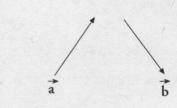

To add them, redraw the second vector so that its tail stands on the tip of the first vector. Then draw the resulting vector, closing the triangle (make sure that the resulting vector's direction is in agreement with the vectors you added). This is what the addition of vectors **a** and **b** looks like.

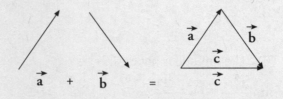

Vector **c** is the sum of vectors **a** and **b**.

If ETS gives you a figure and asks you to add two vectors, they need to be connected tip-to-tail. If necessary, move one of the vectors, and then try using the Law of Cosines.

Subtracting Vectors

To subtract vectors, you'll use the same technique you used to add them, with one extra step. First, reverse the sign of the vector that's being subtracted. You do this by simply moving the arrowhead to the other end of the vector. Then add the two vectors as you usually would. Here's an example of subtraction using the two vectors you just added. First, reverse the sign of the subtracted vector:

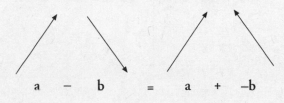

$$\mathbf{a} \quad - \quad \mathbf{b} \quad = \quad \mathbf{a} \quad + \quad \mathbf{-b}$$

And then, add them up:

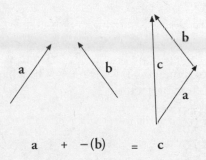

$$\mathbf{a} \quad + \quad \mathbf{-(b)} \quad = \quad \mathbf{c}$$

Vector **c** is the vector produced by subtracting vector **b** from vector **a**.

You can add or subtract two vectors by adding or subtracting their x and y components. For example, if vector **u** has components (1, 3) and vector **v** has components (−1, 5), then the resulting vector **u** + **v** would have components (1 + (−1), 3 + 5) = (0, 8).

Tip to Tail
Remember, you're always going to connect vectors tip to tail.

DRILL

The answers to these drills can be found in Chapter 12.

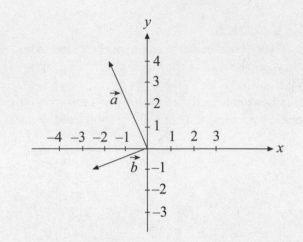

36. If $\vec{c} = \vec{a} + \vec{b}$, then what is the magnitude of $\vec{c}$?

    (A) 2
    (B) 3
    (C) 4
    (D) 5
    (E) 6

41. Vector **a** has components (8, 15), and vector **b** has components (3, 3). If **c** = **a** − **b**, what is the magnitude of vector **c** ?

    (A) 10.5
    (B) 13.0
    (C) 15.6
    (D) 16.5
    (E) 21.1

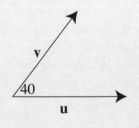

44. If, in the figure above, the magnitude of vector **u** is 9 and the magnitude of vector **v** is 7, what is the magnitude of vector (**u** + **v**) ?

    (A)   5.79
    (B)   7.00
    (C) 11.40
    (D) 12.26
    (E) 15.05

LOGIC

Every now and then, as you proceed innocently through a Math Subject Test, you will come upon a question asked in simple English that seems to have nothing at all to do with math. This is a logic question. Here's a typical example.

―――――――○――――――――

24. If every precious stone is harder than glass, which of the following statements must also be true?

    (A) Glass can be a precious stone.
    (B) Every stone harder than glass is a precious stone.
    (C) No stone is exactly as hard as glass.
    (D) Some stones softer than glass are precious stones.
    (E) Every stone softer than glass is not a precious stone.

Here's How to Crack It

This is madness. There's no math here at all. However, there is a rule here for you to work with. The rule states that given one statement, there's only one other statement that is logically necessary, the contrapositive. This is what the contrapositive states:

―――――――――――――――――――――――――――――――――――――――
The Contrapositive

Given the statement $A \rightarrow B$, you also know $\sim B \rightarrow \sim A$.
―――――――――――――――――――――――――――――――――――――――

In English, that means that the statement "If A, then B" also tells you that "If not B, then not A." To find the contrapositive of any statement, switch the order of the first and second parts of the original statement, and negate their meaning. But you can't be sure of anything else. For example, "If not A" doesn't necessarily mean "then not B." And "if B" doesn't necessarily mean "then A." This is how you'd find the contrapositive of the statement, "Every precious stone is harder than glass." Start by making sure that you clearly see what the two parts of the original statement are.

stone is precious $\rightarrow$ stone harder than glass

Then switch the order of the statement's parts, and negate their meanings:

stone not harder than glass $\rightarrow$ stone is not precious

This is the contrapositive. Once you've found it, just check the answer choices for a statement with an equivalent meaning. In this case, answer choice (E) is equivalent to the contrapositive. Joe Bloggs answers will typically say things like "Every stone that is harder than glass is precious" or "Every stone that is not precious is softer than glass."

Almost all logic questions test your understanding of the contrapositive. There are just a couple of other points that might come up in logic questions.

- If you see the statement "Some *A* are *B*," then you also know that "Some *B* are *A*." For example, "Some teachers are pretty cool people" also means that "Some pretty cool people are teachers."
- To disprove the claim, "*X* might be true," or "*X* is possible," you must show that *X* is never, ever true, in any case, anywhere.
- To disprove the claim, "*X* is true," you only need to show that there's one exception, somewhere, sometime.

In other words, a statement that something *may* be true is very hard to disprove; you've got to demonstrate conclusively that there's no way it could be true. On the other hand, a statement that something is *definitely* true is easy to disprove; all you have to do is find one exception. If you remember the three bullet points above and the contrapositive, you'll be prepared for any logic question on the Math Subject Tests.

DRILL

Exercise your powers of logic on these practice questions. The answers to these drills can be found in Chapter 12.

28. At Legion High School in a certain year, no sophomore received failing grades. Which of the following statements must be true?

(A) There were failures in classes other than the sophomore class.
(B) Sophomores had better study skills than other students that year.
(C) No student at Legion High School received failing grades that year.
(D) Any student who received failing grades was not a sophomore.
(E) There were more passing grades in the sophomore class than in other classes.

33. "If one commits arson, a building burns." Which of the following is a contradiction to this statement?

(A) Many people would refuse to commit arson.
(B) A building did not burn, and yet arson was committed.
(C) Some buildings are more difficult to burn than others.
(D) A building burned, although no arson was committed.
(E) Arson is a serious crime.

35. In a necklace of diamonds and rubies, some stones are not genuine. If every stone that is not genuine is a ruby, which of the following statements must be true?

(A) There are more diamonds than rubies in the necklace.
(B) The necklace contains no genuine rubies.
(C) No diamonds in the necklace are not genuine.
(D) Diamonds are of greater value than rubies.
(E) The necklace contains no genuine diamonds.

IMAGINARY NUMBERS

Almost all math on the Math Subject Tests is confined to real numbers. Only a few questions deal with the square roots of negative numbers—imaginary numbers. For the sake of simplicity, imaginary numbers are expressed in terms of i. The quantity i is equal to the square root of -1. It's used to simplify the square roots of negative numbers. On the Math Level 1 Subject Test, ETS will remind you of this in the question by saying "If $i = \sqrt{-1}$" or "If $i^2 = 1$." On the Math Level 2 Subject Test, they won't bother. For example, here's how i can be used to simplify square roots of negative numbers.

$$\sqrt{-25} = \sqrt{25}\sqrt{-1} = 5\sqrt{-1} = 5i$$
$$\sqrt{-48} = \sqrt{48}\sqrt{-1} = \sqrt{16}\sqrt{3}\sqrt{-1} = 4i\sqrt{3}$$
$$\sqrt{-7} = \sqrt{7}\sqrt{-1} = i\sqrt{7}$$

There are three basic kinds of questions on the Math Subject Tests that require you to work with imaginary numbers.

Computing Powers of i

You may run into a question that asks you to find the value of i^{34}, or something equally outrageous. This may seem difficult or impossible at first, but, as usual, there's a trick to it. The powers of i repeat in a cycle of 4 values, over and over.

$$i^1 = i \qquad i^5 = i$$
$$i^2 = -1 \qquad i^6 = -1$$
$$i^3 = -i \qquad i^7 = -i$$
$$i^4 = 1 \qquad i^8 = 1$$

And so on. These are the only four values that can be produced by raising i to an integer power. To find the value of i^{34}, either write out the cycle of four values up to the 34th power, which would take less than a minute, or, more simply, divide 34 by 4. You find that 34 contains eight cycles of 4, with a remainder of 2. The eight cycles of 4 just bring you back to where you started. It's the remainder that's important. The remainder of 2 means that the value of i^{34} is equal to the value of i^2, or -1. In order to raise i to any power, just divide the exponent by 4 and use the remainder as your exponent.

Doing Algebra with i

Algebra that includes complex numbers is no different from ordinary algebra. You just need to remember that i raised to an exponent changes in value, which can have some odd effects in algebra.

An ETS Trick

As you can see, i sometimes has a way of dropping out of algebraic expressions. ETS likes this trick, so keep an eye out for it.

Here's an example.

$$(x - 3i)(2x + 6i) =$$
$$2x^2 - 6ix + 6ix + 18i^2 =$$
$$2x^2 - 18i^2 =$$
$$2x^2 - 18(-1) =$$
$$2x^2 + 18$$

Level 2 Only

The Complex Plane

A complex number is a specific kind of imaginary number—specifically, the sum of a real number and an imaginary number, such as $5 + 3i$. A complex number is one that takes the form $a + bi$, where a and b are real numbers and i is the imaginary unit, the square root of -1. On the Math Level 2 Subject Test, the principal importance of complex numbers is that they can be represented on the complex plane. This is what the complex plane looks like.

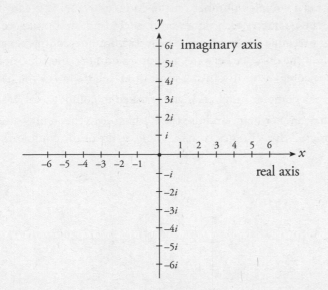

Notice that the complex plane looks just like the ordinary coordinate plane, but the axes have different meanings. On the complex plane, the *x*-axis is referred to as the real axis. The *y*-axis is referred to as the imaginary axis. Each unit on the *x*-axis equals 1—a real unit. Each unit on the imaginary axis equals *i*—the imaginary unit. Any complex number in the form $a + bi$, such as $5 + 3i$, can be plotted on the complex plane almost like a coordinate pair. Just plot *a*, the real component of the complex number, on the *x*-axis; and *bi*, the imaginary component, on the *y*-axis.

Here are several complex numbers plotted on the complex plane.

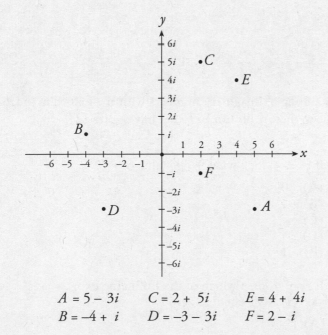

$A = 5 - 3i$ $C = 2 + 5i$ $E = 4 + 4i$

$B = -4 + i$ $D = -3 - 3i$ $F = 2 - i$

Once you've plotted a complex number on the complex plane, you can use all of the usual coordinate-geometry techniques on it, including the Pythagorean theorem and even right-triangle trigonometry. The most common complex-plane question asks you to find the distance between a complex number and the origin, using the Pythagorean theorem. This distance is most often referred to as the magnitude or absolute value of a complex number. If you're asked to compute $|4 + 3i|$, just plot the number on the complex plane and use the Pythagorean theorem to find its distance from the origin. This distance is the absolute value of the complex number.

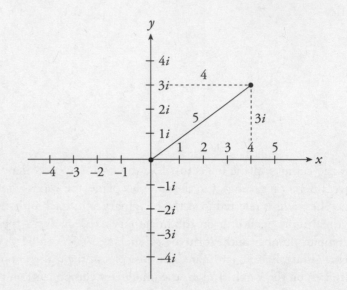

The Pythagorean theorem will quickly show you that $|4 + 3i| = 5$.

DRILL

Test your understanding of imaginary numbers with the following practice questions. The answers to these drills can be found in Chapter 12.

25. If $i^2 = -1$, then what is the value of i^{51} ?

    (A) 0
    (B) −1
    (C) −i
    (D) i
    (E) 1

36. If $i^2 = -1$, then which of the following expressions is NOT equal to zero?

    (A) $i^0 - i^{12}$
    (B) $i + i^3$
    (C) $i^4 + i^{10}$
    (D) $i^{11} - i^9$
    (E) $i^8 - i^{12}$

40. $\dfrac{(2+4i)(2-4i)}{5} =$

(A) 2.2
(B) 4.0
(C) 4.6
(D) 5.0
(E) 8.4

43. $\left|5 - 12i\right| =$

(A) $7i$
(B) 7
(C) 8
(D) 13
(E) $13i$

POLYNOMIAL DIVISION

Most of the factoring questions on the Math Subject Tests are very traditional, using only the tools reviewed in Chapter 4. You will rarely need anything more advanced than the reverse FOIL technique for quadratics. On the Math Level 2 Subject Test, however, you may run into a question that requires you to factor a polynomial of a higher degree than a quadratic. You could use polynomial division, a messy algebraic process. But since there are variables in the answer choices of these questions, it's much easier to Plug In. See the following for typical questions of this type.

21. If $x^3 + x^2 - 7x + 20 = (x + 4) \bullet f(x)$, where $f(x)$ is a polynomial in x, then $f(x) =$

(A) $x + 20$
(B) $x^2 + 5$
(C) $x^2 - 2x$
(D) $x^2 - 3x + 5$
(E) $x^2 - 7x + 20$

Here's How to Crack It

To figure out $f(x)$, you must divide $x^3 + x^2 - 7x + 20$ by $x + 4$. That's polynomial division. Polynomial division is actually just like ordinary division. You set it up like this:

$$x + 4 \overline{)x^3 + x^2 - 7x + 20}$$

Now, just Plug In a number for x. Let's pick $x = 2$. Now, we're just dividing 18 by 6, which gives us 3, with no remainder. So our target answer is 3. Plug In 2 for x in the answers to see which one equals 3. It's (D).

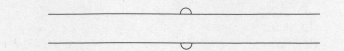

30. What is the remainder when $x^4 - 5x^2 + 12x + 18$ is divided by $(x + 1)$?

    (A) $x^2 - 1$
    (B) $x - 6$
    (C) 6
    (D) 3
    (E) 2

Here's How to Crack It

Once again, just Plug In $x = 2$. Now the question is asking for the remainder when 38 is divided by 3. The remainder is 2, our target answer. So the answer is (E). That's all there is to polynomial division. As we mentioned in Chapter 4, don't Plug In 0 or 1. When you Plug In on polynomial division questions that ask for a remainder, you'll find that bigger numbers, such as 10, are better. If you Plug In and something weird happens, Plug In a different number.

DRILL

Try your talents on these practice questions. The answers to these drills can be found in Chapter 12.

21. If $x^4 - 5x^3 - 2x^2 + 24x = g(x) \bullet (x + 2)$, then which of the following is $g(x)$?

    (A) $x + 12$
    (B) $x^2 + 3x - 18$
    (C) $x^3 - 7x^2 + 12x$
    (D) $x^3 + 10x^2 + 6x$
    (E) $x^4 - 3x^3 + 2x^2 - 6$

27. What is the remainder when $x^3 + 2x^2 - 27x + 40$ is divided by $(x - 3)$?

    (A) 4
    (B) 16
    (C) $2x + 2$
    (D) $x^2 - 5$
    (E) $x^2 + 5x - 12$

WHAT IS THE MATRIX?

If you've never seen matrices before, don't worry; there's a good chance that you won't even see one on your Math Level 2. But don't say we didn't warn you.

> The determinant of the 2×2 matrix $\begin{bmatrix} a & b \\ c & d \end{bmatrix}$ is $ad - bc$.

The determinant of a matrix is sometimes indicated by plain vertical bars around the elements, like a big absolute value symbol. The folks at ETS may simply write

$\begin{vmatrix} a & b \\ c & d \end{vmatrix}$ if they want you to find the determinant of the matrix above.

> The determinant of the 3×3 matrix
>
> $\begin{bmatrix} a & b & c \\ d & e & f \\ g & h & i \end{bmatrix}$ is $aei + bfg + cdh - bdi - afh - ceg$.

A Clue
A good way to remember the determinant of a 2×2 matrix is that you multiply the diagonals and subtract.

If you take the first two columns of the matrix and recopy them to the right of the original matrix, the parts of the formula form diagonal lines of three elements, with the positive parts going from the upper left to the bottom right, and the negative parts going from the upper right down to the bottom left, like this:

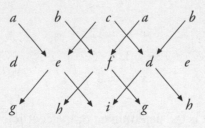

A What by What?
When you're looking at a particular matrix, for example, a 3×2 matrix, remember that this describes the matrix as row by column. So there are 3 rows and 2 columns.

Right now you may be feeling a bit like Alice, tumbling down the rabbit hole. Just remember a few other facts about matrices:

- You can only multiply matrices if the first matrix has the same number of columns as the second matrix has rows. And when you multiply an $m \times n$ matrix by an $n \times p$ matrix, you get an $m \times p$ matrix.
- When you are shown simultaneous equations, the coefficient matrix refers to the matrix formed by the coefficients of the variables (which are on the left side of the equals signs).

DRILL

If you feel ready for the matrix, try these examples. The answers to these drills can be found in Chapter 12.

30. If matrix X has dimension 3×2, matrix Y has dimension 2×5, and $XY = Z$, then matrix Z must have dimension

    (A) 2×2
    (B) 2×5
    (C) 3×2
    (D) 3×5
    (E) 6×10

40. If $A = \begin{bmatrix} 1 & 2 \\ -1 & 0 \end{bmatrix}$, then what is the determinant of A ?

    (A) -2
    (B) -1
    (C) 0
    (D) 1
    (E) 2

Use Technology!
A graphing calculator can find the determinant of a 3×3 matrix a lot faster than you can. Check your owner's manual for advice.

45. If $\begin{bmatrix} 0 & 1 & 3 \\ -1 & 1 & 2 \\ -2 & 1 & 2 \end{bmatrix} = X$, then $|X| =$

    (A) -2
    (B) 0
    (C) 1
    (D) 2
    (E) 3

$$2x + 3y - z = 12$$
$$x - 3y + 2z = -5$$
$$x + z = 3$$

46. What is the determinant of the coefficient matrix of the system of equations shown above?

    (A) -6
    (B) 0
    (C) 2
    (D) 3
    (E) 10

Summary

o   A logarithm is just another way to write exponents, so make sure you're up to speed on your exponent rules.

o   The concepts in this chapter pop up rarely on the SAT Math Subject Tests but are still worth knowing if you want a top score.
   • An arithmetic sequence is created by adding the same number to the previous member in the sequence.
   • The nth term of an arithmetic sequence can be found with the formula
     $a_n = a_1 + (n - 1)d$.
   • The sum of the first n terms of an arithmetic sequence can be found with the formula
     $n\left(\dfrac{a_1 + a_n}{2}\right)$.

o   The only thing you need to know for logic questions is the contrapositive. If the initial statement is "If A, then B," then the contrapositive states "If not B, then not A."

o   There are three types of questions that ETS will ask about imaginary numbers:
   • ETS will ask questions that use the definition of i, which is $\sqrt{-1}$.
   • The powers of i create a pattern: i, -1, $-i$, 1. It then repeats. So find the closest multiple of 4 to the power in your question and just count forward or back until you get to your number.

o   You may have to use FOIL on a question with imaginary numbers. Treat it like a regular quadratic, and then simplify i as your last step.

o   Here are some Level 2–only concepts:
   • A summation is a list of numbers to be added together. You'll recognize it because of the sigma (Σ). Put the number below the sigma into the equation given. Find the result of that and every following integer up to the number above the sigma. Then add your results.

- A geometric sequence is created by taking an initial value and multiplying it by the same number again and again.
- The nth term of a geometric sequence can be found with this formula: $a_n = a_1 r^{n-1}$.
- The sum of the first n terms of a geometric sequence can be found with this formula: $\dfrac{a_1\left(1-r^n\right)}{1-r}$.

- The sum of an infinite geometric sequence is $\dfrac{a_1}{1-r}$. This can be found only if $-1 < r < 1$. If r is bigger than 1, there is no sum, because the sequence never converges.
- A limit is the value a function approaches as its independent variable approaches a given constant.
- A vector contains direction and magnitude and is represented by a line with an arrow. When adding or subtracting vectors, make sure you're connecting tip to tail. When subtracting vectors, add the opposite vector instead.
- A complex number is made up of a real number and an imaginary number. The complex plane is a coordinate plane in which the y-axis is imaginary numbers and the x-axis is real numbers.
- The best and fastest way to conquer a polynomial division question is to Plug In.
- Matrix questions appear in the form of determinant questions. They pop up rarely, but make sure you know your determinant formulas or how to work with matrices on your calculator.

Chapter 12
Drills: Answers
and Explanations

Chapter 3: Arithmetic

Prime factors, p. 23

Question	Explanation
1	$64 = 2 \times 2 \times 2 \times 2 \times 2 \times 2$
2	$70 = 2 \times 5 \times 7$
3	$18 = 2 \times 3 \times 3$
4	$98 = 2 \times 7 \times 7$
5	$68 = 2 \times 2 \times 17$
6	$51 = 3 \times 17$

Factors, p. 24

Question	Answer	Explanation
3	B	21 can also be written as 3×7, and 18 as $2 \times 3 \times 3$. The smallest number that contains both is $2 \times 3 \times 3 \times 7$, or 126.
7	E	53 is a prime number; its largest prime factor is 53. None of the other answers contains so large a prime factor. (A) is (2)(5)(17), so its greatest prime factor is 17. (B) is (3)(3)(13), so its greatest prime factor is 13. (C) is (2)(2)(2)(11), so its greatest prime factor is 11. (D) is (2)(31), so its greatest prime factor is 31.
9	C	The smallest integer divisible by 10 and 32 is 160, and the smallest integer divisible by 6 and 20 is 60. The difference between them is 100. Remember to factor each time as shown in number 3, above.

Even and odd, positive and negative, pp. 26–27

Question	Answer	Explanation
15	A	Let's start with I. We know from our rules that an odd number times an odd number is an odd number. So I has to be true. Use POE to eliminate (B). Now let's skip down to III for a moment. We know from I that odd times odd equals odd. We also know that odd plus odd is even. And an even times an even is even. So III will be an even number. Since III isn't true, eliminate (D) and (E). Let's look at II. Remember that the question asks which of the following *must* be an odd *integer*. Since an odd integer divided by an odd integer isn't always an integer, you can eliminate (C). If you ever forget a rule, you can always try a couple of numbers.
18	D	The statement $cd < 0$ means that one of the numbers is positive and one negative; that's the only way to get a negative product. Try your own numbers to eliminate answer choices. If you try $c = 1$ and $d = -3$, only (A) and (D) are true. Switch them and try $c = -3$ and $d = 1$, and only (D) remains true.
20	C	Use your rules. Choice (A) would be an even times an odd, which is even. Choice (B) would be an odd times an even (even result), plus an even, squared, which would remain even. Choice (C) would be even minus one, which results in an odd number. Choice (D) would be an odd plus an even, which is odd, and (E) would be an odd divided by an even, which may not be an integer. So we're down to (C) and (D). Since y is negative, it is possible that (D) would yield a negative number. The answer must be (C). Again, you can always try out sample numbers to prove the rules.

PEMDAS and your calculator, p. 28

Question	Answer
1	5
2	35
3	12
4	35
5	0

Word-problem translation, p. 31

Question	Answer
1	$6.5 = \dfrac{x}{100} \cdot 260$; $x = 2.5$
2	$20 = \dfrac{n}{100} \cdot 180$; $n = 11$
3	$\dfrac{30}{100} \cdot \dfrac{40}{100} \cdot 25 = x$; $x = 3$
4	$x = \sqrt{\dfrac{1}{3} \cdot 48}$; $x = 4$
5	$\sqrt{y} = \dfrac{1}{8} \cdot y$; $y = \dfrac{1}{64} y^2$; $\dfrac{1}{y} = \dfrac{1}{64}$; $y = 64$

Percent change, p. 32

Question	Answer	Explanation
2	B	You already know that the difference is going to be 25. Set up your formula: $\dfrac{25}{150} \cdot 100 = 16.67$. So, adding 25 gallons to 150 gallons is a 16.67% increase.
5	B	The decrease from 5 to 4 is a 20% decrease, and the increase from 4 to 5 is a 25% increase. So the difference is 5%.
12	C	Using the formula $12 = (150 \div x)100$, you get $x = 1{,}250$, so 1,250 must have been the original amount. $1{,}250 + 150 = 1{,}400$. Be careful to read "after the deposit" in the question.

Repeated percent change, p. 37

Question	Answer	Explanation
35	D	Using the formula, you get $1{,}000(1.05^{12}) = 1{,}795.856$.
40	E	For this question, you need to compute 100 annual increases of 8%, so you must multiply the starting amount, 120,000, by 1.08^{100}, which gives you 263,971,350.8—which can also be written as 2.6×10^8. If you weren't sure, multiply the answers in your calculator to check your work.
43	C	This question is a little trickier. For each annual decrease of 4%, you must multiply by 0.96. The easiest way to solve the question is to start with 2,000 and keep multiplying until the result is less than 1,000—just count the number of decreases it takes. The seventeenth annual decrease makes it less than 1,000, so the sixteenth is the last one that is not less than 1,000—and $1995 + 16 = 2011$. You can also use logs, which we'll get to in a little while.

Averages, pp. 38–39

Question	Explanation
1	There were 9 people at dinner.
2	All told, 4,500 apples were picked.
3	The average height of a chess club member is 5.5 feet.

Multiple-average questions, p. 41

Question	Answer	Explanation
33	D	Nineteen donations averaging $485 total $9,215. Twenty donations averaging $500 total $10,000. The difference is $785.
35	A	The *Tribune* received 80 letters in the first 20 days and 70 for the last 10 days. That's a total of 150 in 30 days, or $150 \div 30 = 5$ letters per day on average.
36	A	One day in five out of a year is 73 days. At 12 a day, that's 876 umbrellas sold on rainy days. The rest of the year (292 days) is clear. At 3 umbrellas a day, that's another 876 umbrellas. A total of 1,752 umbrellas in 365 days makes a daily average of 4.8 umbrellas.

Exponents, p. 47

Question	Answer	Explanation
1		$b = 3$ (1 root)
2		$x = 11, -11$ (2 roots)
3		$n = 2$ (1 root)
4		$c = \sqrt{10}, -\sqrt{10}$ (2 roots)
5		$x = 3, -3$ (2 roots)
6		$x = -2$ (1 root)
7		$d = 3, -3$ (2 roots)
8		$n =$ any real number; everything to the 0 power is 1.
1	C	Remember that the top is the exponent and the bottom is the root. So in your calculator, put in 4^(3/2). This is the same as cubing 4 and then taking the square root of your result (or taking the square root of 4 and then cubing that result). Any way you slice it, the answer is 8.
2	D	Remember your rules. A negative exponent means flip it. And a fractional exponent means the top is the exponent and the bottom is the root. You may have ended up with $\dfrac{1}{\left(\sqrt[4]{x}\right)^3}$, which isn't wrong. It just happens to not be in the answers. The only correct answer is $\dfrac{1}{\left(\sqrt[4]{x^3}\right)}$.
3	A	Flip and square it: $\left(\dfrac{3}{2}\right)^2 = 2.25$. Don't forget your parentheses in your calculator.
4	E	Flip and take the third root.
5	A	In your calculator it goes, either as is (with parentheses) or if you need to take more steps, just remember that the numerator is the exponent and the denominator is the root. Or notice that $\sqrt[3]{25}$ must be less than $\sqrt{25}$ and use POE.
6	D	What's anything raised to the zero power? That's right, 1.

Chapter 4: Algebra

Solving equations, pp. 54–55

Question	Answer	Explanation
1	$x = \{5, -5\}$	If you're having trouble, think of peeling away the layers of the left side until you get to just x. So you're going to multiply by 17, then add 7, then divide by 3, then take the square root of both sides. Remember: When you take the square root of both sides, you'll end up with two answers: positive and negative.
2	$n = \{0, 5\}$	This is tricky. You most likely found that the answer is 5. Remember: You can divide both sides by n only if n isn't 0. So you also have to consider that n could be 0. In this case, it can.
3	$a = 0.75$	Peel away those layers.
4	$s = 12$	*Keep peeling.*
5	$x = 0.875$	Make sure you didn't cancel the 5's. You can cancel only when numbers are being multiplied or divided, not added or subtracted. Did you get $\frac{7}{8}$? Same thing!
6	$m = 9$ or $m = -14$	Because the left side of the equation is inside absolute value signs, you know it can be either positive or negative. So set up two equations! In the first equation, set $2m + 5$ equal to 23. In the second equation, set $2m + 5$ equal to -23. Then solve each equation for m. These are your two possible values for m.
7	$r = 27$ or $r = -13$	Set this problem up just like question 6, above. The value inside the absolute value signs can be either positive or negative, so write an equation for each scenario. Solve each equation to come up with the two possible values for r.

Factoring and distributing, pp. 56–57

Question	Answer	Explanation
3	D	This equation can be rearranged to look like: $50x(11 + 29) = 4,000$. This is done simply by factoring out 50 and x. Once you've done that, you can add 11 and 29 to produce $50x(40) = 2,000x = 4,000$. Therefore, $x = 2$.
17	E	Here, distributing makes your math easier. Distributing $-3b$ into the expression $(a + 2)$ on top of the fraction gives you $\dfrac{-3ab - 6b + 6b}{-ab}$, which simplifies to $\dfrac{-3ab}{-ab}$, which equals 3.
36	B	The trap in this question is to try to cancel similar terms on the top and bottom—but that's not possible, because these terms are being added together, and you can cancel only in multiplication. Instead, factor out x^2 on top of the fraction. That gives you $\dfrac{x^2\left(x^3 + x^2 + x + 1\right)}{x^3 + x^2 + x + 1}$. The whole mess in parentheses cancels out (now that it's being multiplied), and the answer is x^2.

Plugging In, p. 61

Question	Answer	Explanation
5	E	Let's make $p = 20$, $t = 10$, and $n = 3$. That's 3 items for $20.00 each with 10% tax. Each item would then cost $22.00, and three could cost $66.00. Only answer choice (E) equals $66.00.
8	C	Let's make $x = 5$, $a = 2$, $b = 3$. That means Vehicle A travels at 5 mph for 5 hours, or 25 miles. Vehicle B travels at 7 mph for 8 hours, or 56 miles. That's a difference of 31 miles. Only (C) equals 31.
17	C	Let's make $n = 3$, then $5 - 3 = 2$ and $3 - 5 = -2$. These numbers have the same absolute value, so the difference between them is zero.
20	B	Let's Plug In $a = 10$, $b = 1$, $m = 4$. That means that Company A builds 10 skateboards a week and 40 skateboards in 4 weeks. Company B builds 7 skateboards in a week (1 per day), or 28 in 4 weeks. That's a difference of 12 between the two companies. Only (B) equals 12 when you Plug In $a = 10$, $b = 1$, $m = 4$.
23	E	Plug In $a = 4$ and $b = 2$. Okay, all three fail. Let's try some different-sized numbers like $a = 10$ and $b = 2$. Now I works; eliminate (B) and (D). Let's try to make $a + b$ small; Plug In $a = 4$ and $b = -4$. Now II and III work; eliminate (A) and (C).
30	A	Plug In $x = 2$ and $y = 3$. Oh well—they all work! Try $x = -3$ and $y = -2$. Now II fails; eliminate (C), (D), and (E). III also fails; eliminate (B).

Plugging In The Answers (PITA), p. 64

Question	Answer	Explanation
11	D	The answer choices represent Michael's hats. Start with answer (C): If Michael has 12 hats, then Matt has 6 hats and Aaron has 2. That adds up to 20, not 24—you need more hats, so move on to the next bigger answer, (D). Michael now has 14 hats, meaning Matt has 7 and Aaron has 3. That adds up to 24, so you're done.
17	D	There's a little shortcut you can take if you remember the average pie. Since the total is 3,200 and you have two parts, you know that the average will be 1,600. This means that the difference will be 800. Work through the answer choices, starting with (C). A ratio of 2:5 has 7 parts. Divide 3,200 by 7. Each part would be 457.14— It doesn't work out with whole numbers, so it can't be right. Then move on to (D), a ratio of 3:5 has 8 parts, each of which would be 400. That means the shipment is divided into shares of 1,200 and 2,000. Their difference is 800, and their average is 1,600, which is what we're looking for!
27	D	Start with (C); if the largest of the three integers is 5, then the total of the other two integers would have to be 15 − 5 or 10. No two numbers less than 5 have a sum of 10, so eliminate (A), (B), and (C). If you Plug In (D), 9 is the largest number. For the product of all three integers to be 45, the product of the other two integers must be 5. So these two integers can only be 5 and 1. Now we find the sum of all three numbers. 9 + 5 + 1 = 15, so (D) is the correct answer.

Inequalities, p. 65

Question	Answer
1	$n \geq 3$
2	$r < 7$
3	$x \geq -\dfrac{1}{2}$
4	$x < \dfrac{1}{8}$
5	$t \leq 3$
6	$n \leq 4$
7	$p > \dfrac{1}{5}$
8	$s \geq 1$
9	$x \geq -7$
10	$s \geq \dfrac{2}{5}$

Working with ranges, p. 66

Question	Answer
1	$-8 < -x < 5$
2	$-20 < 4x < 32$
3	$1 < (x + 6) < 14$
4	$7 > (2 - x) > -6$
5	$-2.5 < \dfrac{x}{2} < 4$

Working with ranges, p. 68

Question	Answer
1	$-4 \leq b - a \leq 11$
2	$-2 \leq x + y \leq 17$
3	$0 \leq n^2 \leq 64$
4	$3 < x - y < 14$
5	$-13 \leq r + s \leq 13$
6	$-126 < cd < 0$
7	$-1 \leq x \leq 7$ Because the absolute value is less than 4, whatever's inside the absolute value must be between -4 and 4. Therefore, $-4 \leq 3 - x \leq 4$. Start solving this by subtracting 3 from all three sides: $-7 \leq -x \leq 1$. Then divide through by -1 (remember to flip the direction of the inequality signs because you're dividing by a negative number): $7 \geq x \geq -1$.
8	$a \leq -10$ or $a \geq 3$ Because the absolute value is greater than 13, the stuff inside the absolute value must be either less than -13 or greater than 13. Therefore, you have two inequalities: $2a + 7 \leq -13$ or $2a + 7 \geq 13$. Solve each inequality separately.

Direct and inverse variation, p. 71

Question	Answer	Explanation
15	C	There are variables in the answers, so Plug In! Quantities in inverse variation always have the same product. That means that $ab = 3 \bullet 5$, or 15, always. Plug In a number for x, such as 10. Now set up your proportion: $3 \bullet 5 = a \bullet 10$. So $10a = 15$, and $a = 2.5$. Plug $x = 10$ into the answers and find the answer choice that gives you 2.5. Only (C) does.
18	D	Remember your formulas. Direct means divide. Quantities in direct variation always have the same proportion. In this case, that means that $\frac{n}{m} = \frac{5}{4}$. When $m = 5$, solve the equation $\frac{5}{4} = \frac{n}{5}$. Multiply both sides by 5 and you'll find that $n = 6.25$.
24	A	Direct variation means the proportion is constant, so that $\frac{p}{q} = \frac{3}{10}$. To find the value of p when $q = 1$, solve the equation $\frac{3}{10} = \frac{p}{1}$; p must be 0.3.
26	B	Remember that direct means divide. Set up your proportion: $\frac{24}{3.8^2} = \frac{y}{8.3^2}$. If you simplify this, you get 120.77, which is (B). Be careful. If you answered (E), you forgot that the direct variation was between y and x^2, not y and x.

Work and travel questions, pp. 72–73

Question	Answer	Explanation
11	C	The important thing to remember here is that when two things or people work together, their work rates are added up. Pump 1 can fill 12 tanks in 12 hours, and Pump 2 can fill 11 tanks in 12 hours. That means that together, they could fill 23 tanks in 12 hours. To find the work they would do in 1 hour, just divide 23 by 12. You get 1.91666....
12	A	To translate feet per second to miles per hour, take it one step at a time. First, find the feet per hour by multiplying 227 feet per second by the number of seconds in an hour (3,600). You find that the projectile travels at a speed of 817,200 feet per hour. Then divide by 5,280 to find out how many miles that is. You get 154.772.
18	B	The train travels a total of 400 miles (round-trip) in 5.5 hours. Now that you know distance and time, plug them into the formula and solve to find the rate. $400 = r \times 5.5$, so $r = 72.73$.
25	D	Plug In! Say Jules can make 3 muffins in 5 minutes ($m = 3$, $s = 5$). Say Alice can make 4 muffins in 6 minutes ($n = 4$, $t = 6$). That means that Jules can make 18 muffins in 30 minutes, and Alice can make 20 muffins in 30 minutes. Together, they make 38 muffins in 30 minutes. That's your target number. Take the numbers you plugged in to the answers and find the one that gives you 38. Answer choice (D) does the trick.

Average speed, pp. 74–75

Question	Answer	Explanation
19	D	Find the total distance and total time. The round-trip distance is 12 miles. It takes $\frac{1}{2}$ hour to jog 6 miles at 12 mph, and $\frac{2}{3}$ hour to jog back at 9 mph, for a total of $1\frac{1}{6}$ hours. Do the division, and you get 10.2857 mph.
24	D	This one is easier than it looks. Fifty miles in 50 minutes is a mile a minute, or 60 mph. Forty miles in 40 minutes is also 60 mph. The whole trip is made at one speed, 60 mph.
33	B	Plug In an easy number for the unknown distance, like 50 miles. It takes 2 hours to travel 50 miles at 25 mph, and 1 hour to return across 50 miles at 50 mph. That's a total distance of 100 miles in 3 hours, for an average speed of $33\frac{1}{3}$ mph. (A) and (E) are Joe Bloggs answers.

Simultaneous equations, p. 78

Question	Answer	Explanation
26	C	Here, you want to make all of the b terms cancel out. Add the two equations, and you get $5a = 20$, so $a = 4$.
31	D	Here, you need to get x and y terms with the same coefficient. If you subtract the second equation from the first, you get $10x - 10y = 10$, so $x - y = 1$.
34	D	The question is solvable as the example on the previous page was, by multiplication. Multiplying all three equations together gives you $a^2b^2c^2 = 2.25$. Don't pick (B)! Take the positive square root of both sides, and you get $abc = 1.5$.
37	E	Here, you need to get rid of the z term and cancel out a y. The way to do it is to divide the first equation by the second one, $\dfrac{xyz}{y^2z} = \dfrac{4}{5}$. The z and a y cancel out, and you're left with $\dfrac{x}{y} = \dfrac{4}{5}$, or 0.8. Even though there are more variables than equations, ETS questions almost always have a trick to let you solve them the easy way.

FOIL, p. 79

Question	Answer
1	$x^2 + 9x - 22$
2	$b^2 + 12b + 35$
3	$x^2 - 12x + 27$
4	$2x^2 - 3x - 5$
5	$n^3 - 3n^2 + 5n - 15$
6	$6a^2 - 11a - 35$
7	$x^2 - 9x + 18$
8	$c^2 + 7c - 18$
9	$d^2 + 4d - 5$

Factoring quadratics, p. 81

Question	Answer
1	$a = \{1, 2\}$ Factor to $(a - 1)(a - 2) = 0$.
2	$d = \{-7, -1\}$ Factor to $(d + 7)(d + 1) = 0$.
3	$x = \{-7, 3\}$ Factor to $(x + 7)(x - 3) = 0$.
4	$x = \{-5, 2\}$ Factor to $3(x^2 + 3x - 10) = 3(x + 5)(x - 2) = 0$.
5	$x = \{-11, -9\}$ Factor to $2(x^2 + 20x + 99) = 2(x + 11)(x + 9) = 0$.
6	$p = \{-13, 3\}$ Factor to $(p + 13)(p - 3) = 0$. Subtract 39 from both sides first.
7	$c = \{-5, -4\}$ Factor to $(c + 5)(c + 4) = 0$.
8	$s = \{-6, 2\}$ Factor to $(s + 6)(s - 2) = 0$.
9	$x = \{-1, 4\}$ Factor to $(x + 1)(x - 4) = 0$.
10	Factor the expression $(n^2 - 5)(n^2 + 2) = 0$. So $n^2 = 5$ or -2. But n^2 is never negative, so $n = \pm\sqrt{5}$.

Special quadratic identities, p. 83

Question	Answer	Explanation
17	A	Remember that $n^2 - m^2 = (n - m)(n + m)$. So fill in what you know and solve for what you don't: $24 = (-3)(n + m)$. You don't need to find each variable individually.
19	B	Remember that $(x + y)^2 = x^2 + 2xy + y^2$. Again you have all the parts except for what the question is asking for: $3^2 = 8 + 2xy$. So $2xy = 1$ and $xy = 0.5$.
24	D	Translate into math. You know that $x + y = 9$ and $x^2 + y^2 = 36$. It's asking for xy. The pieces that the question gives you relate to $(x + y)^2 = x^2 + 2xy + y^2$. So, $9^2 = 36 + 2xy$; $2xy = 45$; and $xy = 22.5$. Notice that (E) is a partial answer.

The quadratic formula, p. 85

Question	Answer
1	2 distinct real roots; $x = \{0.81, 6.19\}$
2	no real roots (2 imaginary roots)
3	2 distinct real roots; $s = \{0.76, 5.24\}$
4	2 distinct real roots; $x = \{-1.41, 1.41\}$
5	1 real root; $n = -2.5$ (2 identical real roots, that is, a "double root")

Chapter 5: Plane Geometry

Basic rules of lines and angles, pp. 94–95

Question	Answer	Explanation
1		$x = 50°$; $y = 130°$; $z = 130°$; $a = 50°$; $b = 130°$; $c = 50°$
2		$x = 105°$; $y = 75°$
3		$a = 120°$; $b = 60°$; $c = 120°$; $d = 60°$; $e = 120°$; $f = 60°$
8	B	When parallel lines are crossed by a third line, any small angle plus any big angle equals 180°.
13	E	Plug In! Remember that where the line intersects the parallel sides of the rectangle, any small angle plus any big angle is 180°. Plug In, for example, 80° for the smaller angles s and v, and 100° for the larger angles, t and u. The angles r and w must measure 90° each. Once you've plugged in these values you'll quickly see that only (E) must be equivalent to angle t.
16	E	Fred's theorem tells you that the sum of $\angle DBC$ and $\angle BDE$ is 180°. You don't, however, know anything about the *difference* between them. Plugging In various numbers should soon convince you that the difference cannot be determined. Remember Joe Bloggs though, and steer away from such enticing or easy-way-out answers as the question numbers get higher.

Third side rule, p. 98

Question	Answer	Explanation
12	E	The length of the unknown side, ST, must be between the sum and difference of the other two lengths—that is, between 3 and 19. Add the sides and that makes the *perimeter* anywhere between 22 and 38. Notice that (A) answers the wrong question.
17	A	Since the triangle is isosceles, the unknown side must be either 5 or 11. But a 5-5-11 triangle violates the Third Side Rule—it's not possible. That leaves only 11 as a possible value of the missing side.
18	E	This is just another application of the Third Side Rule. The third distance must be between 2 and 10. Only (E) violates the rule.

The Pythagorean theorem, p. 100

Question	Answer
1	$x = \sqrt{89}$, or 9.4334
2	$n = \sqrt{85}$, or 9.2195
3	$a = \sqrt{15}$, or 3.8730
4	$d = \sqrt{50} = 5\sqrt{2}$, or 7.0710
5	$x = 7$
6	$r = \sqrt{145}$, or 12.0416

Area of triangles, pp. 102–103

Question	Answer	Explanation
9	E	Write out the formula for the area of a triangle, using the lengths the question has given: $\frac{1}{2}ab$. You know that the area is $3b$. So, $\frac{1}{2}ab = 3b$. Now, solve for a. $\frac{1}{2}a = 3$ and $a = 6$.
15	A	Both triangles have the same height, and if their areas are equal, they must have the same base as well. Since triangle OAD has a base of 8, triangle ABC must also have a base of 8.
37	B	Notice that the area of ABC can be computed two different ways; with $\overline{AC}$ as the base or with $\overline{BC}$ as the base. Either way, the base and height must multiply to the same number, because a triangle can have only one area. That means that 12 times $\overline{BE}$ must equal 9 times 10: $12\overline{BE} = 90$, and $\overline{BE} = 7.5$.
38	C	If the perimeter of an equilateral triangle is 24, then each side has a length of 8. Plug that into the formula for the area of an equilateral triangle, and you get 27.71.
44	D	Just set the formula for the area of an equilateral triangle equal to 12, and solve for s. You get 5.26. The perimeter is $3s$, or 15.79. (A) is a Joe Bloggs answer, because he sees a number in the answers that reminds him of the question and he is tempted to pick familiar numbers.
46	D	You're given two sides of a triangle and the angle between them, and you're supposed to find the area. Use the formula $A = \frac{1}{2}ab\sin\theta$. In this case, $A = \frac{1}{2}(6.4)(10.8)(\sin 55°) = 28.31$. (E) is a Joe Bloggs answer $(A = \frac{1}{2}bh)$.

Pythagorean triplets, p. 104

Question	Answer
1	$x = 9$
2	$d = 26$
3	$n = 0.5$

The 45°-45°-90° triangle, p. 105

Question	Answer
1	$x = 6\sqrt{2}$, or 8.485
2	$n = 1.5\sqrt{2}$, or 2.121
3	$s\sqrt{2} = 7$, so $s = \dfrac{7}{\sqrt{2}}$. This is equivalent to $s = \dfrac{7\sqrt{2}}{2}$, or 4.950

The 30°-60°-90° triangle, p. 106

Question	Answer
1	$x = 3\sqrt{3}$, or 5.196
2	$n = \dfrac{5}{\sqrt{3}}$, or 2.887
3	$d = 4\sqrt{3}$, or 6.928

Right triangles, p. 107

Question	Answer	Explanation
7	A	With the Pythagorean Theorem, you could compute the missing length of the longest side. There's only one possible perimeter. Notice that you don't even have to know what it is in order to answer the question correctly. Don't waste time computing! (The hypotenuse turns out to be 11.4, in case you're curious.)
13	E	You can't use the Pythagorean theorem unless you know which side of a right triangle is the hypotenuse. Since you don't know whether 8 or the unknown side is the hypotenuse, it's impossible to know the length of the missing side.
16	C	 Draw it! You'll find that the floor, wall, and ladder form a 30°-60°-90° triangle. The ladder itself is the hypotenuse, so the hypotenuse is 32. Because the 30° angle is against the wall, the short leg is the ground. So the short leg is 16 and the other leg, or the wall, is $16\sqrt{3}$ or 27.71, which is (C).
19	B	An isosceles right triangle must be a 45°-45°-90° triangle, with sides x, x, and $x\sqrt{2}$. Since the perimeter equals 23.9, that means $2x + x\sqrt{2} = 23.9$. In order to solve, factor out an x and isolate x. This tells you that $x = 7$, and you can plug this value into the equation for the area of the triangle, or $\frac{1}{2}x^2$. The area of the triangle is 24.5.

Similar triangles, pp. 110–112

Question	Answer	Explanation
1		$a = 4$; $b = 6.92$; $x = 2$; $y = 1.73$
2		$a = 5$; $s = 15$
3		$c = 11$; $m = 12.25$
37	A	These triangles are similar because they have identical angles. If one length of triangle ABC is half of a corresponding length of triangle FGH, that means that *all* of the lengths in ABC will be half the corresponding lengths in FGH. The easiest way to solve the problem is by Plugging In a base and height for FGH that would yield an area of 0.5; a base of 1 and a height of 1 would be the easiest. Then just Plug In the corresponding dimensions of ABC, making sure that they're half of the dimensions in triangle FGH: The base is $\frac{1}{2}$ and the height is $\frac{1}{2}$. The area comes out to $\frac{1}{8}$, or 0.125, which rounds to 0.13.

40	C	This question is much like question 37, except that you have more freedom to Plug In numbers. Once again, the triangles are similar; Fred's theorem tells you that they have identical angles. Then just Plug In easy numbers. Suppose $AD = 4$; from the problem, $DB = 2$, so $AB = 6$. This shows you that the lengths of the smaller triangle are $\frac{2}{3}$ the lengths of the larger. Suppose $AE = 6$, then $AC = 9$. The area of triangle ADE is then 12, while the area of triangle ABC is 27. $\frac{12}{27}$ reduces to $\frac{4}{9}$.
45	A	Use the Pythagorean theorem to complete the dimensions of triangle LMN. It has sides of length 4, $\sqrt{48}$, and 8. If you simplify $\sqrt{48}$, you'll find it's equal to $4\sqrt{3}$. That makes the lengths 4, $4\sqrt{3}$, and 8, which should look familiar. It's a 30°-60°-90° triangle. (You could still figure it out if you didn't notice that it's a 30°-60°-90° triangle.) Since a right triangle divided by an altitude from its right angle forms three similar triangles, the little triangle LPN must also be a 30°-60°-90° triangle. If its hypotenuse has a length of 4, then its legs have lengths of 2 and $2\sqrt{3}$. Those legs are the base and height of triangle LPN. Use them to calculate the triangle's area, and you get 3.464.

Quadrilaterals, p. 117

Question	Answer	Explanation
22	A	Use the cool $\frac{d^2}{2}$ formula for the area of a square.
34	D	Drawing a height down from K gives you a 30°-60°-90° triangle with hypotenuse 6. So the height is $3\sqrt{3}$ or 5.196. Multiplying the base by the height gives you (D). For Math Level 2, you can use the nifty $A = ab \sin \theta$ formula. So $A = (6)(10)(\sin 60°)$. (E) is a Joe Bloggs answer ($10 \times 6 = 60$).
40	B	 AD is $9 + 6 = 15$. If the perimeter is 34, then $AB = 5$, making this an isosceles trapezoid. If you draw the heights down from B and C, they will each cut off a right triangle with a base of 3 (half of the 6 you're told about). These are 3-4-5 right triangles, so the height of the trapezoid is 4. Now you can either plug 9, 15, and 4 into the trapezoid area formula, or you can find the sum of the areas of the two right triangles and the rectangle between them. (A) is a Joe Bloggs answer ($9 \times 5 = 45$).

| 45 | B | Each diagonal cuts the rectangle into two 30°-60°-90° triangles, with the diagonal as hypotenuse. That makes the base and height of the rectangle the x and $x\sqrt{3}$ legs of the triangle. If $x \cdot x\sqrt{3} = 62.35$, then $x = 6.0$, and the hypotenuse of the triangle ($2x$) has a length of 12.0. The sum of the two diagonals is 24.0. |

Circles, p. 121

Question	Explanation
1	$C = 8\pi$; $A = 16\pi$
2	$C = 15.85$; $r = 2.52$ Divide the area (20), which is πr^2, by π and take the square root of the result to solve for r.
3	$A = 5.09$; $r = 1.27$

More circles, pp. 124–125

Question	Answer	Explanation
12	D	Remember that a sector of a circle takes equal portions of angle, circumference, and area. The circle's circumference is 6π or 18.85. Because $4.71 \div 18.85$ is about 1/4, the sector also takes up one-fourth of 360°, or 90°.
29	A	Draw a line from B to O to make two shapes. The shaded region is a quarter-circle plus a 45°-45°-90° triangle. The triangle has an area of $\frac{25}{2}$, or 12.5. The quarter-circle has an area of 19.63. They add up to 32.13.
31	B	As in most shaded-area problems, the trick is to subtract one shape from another to get the shaded region itself. Here, you need to subtract the hexagon's area from that of the circle. To compute the area of the hexagon, divide it into 6 equilateral triangles, each with a side of 4—use the equilateral triangle formula to find their areas. Then subtract the hexagon's area (41.57) from the circle's area (50.27) to get the answer, 8.7.
43	C	You know that both OA and OC are 2, since they're both radii. The question says that $OA = AC$, which means that AC is also 2. Because triangle OAC is equilateral, all of its angles measure 60°. The radius OA must be perpendicular to line l, making a 90° angle; that makes triangle OAC a 30°-60°-90° triangle. The length of AB is $2\sqrt{3}$, or 3.46.
45	A	Take one statement at a time. I must be true, since BC is the hypotenuse of a right triangle, and must be longer than the triangle's legs. Because point A could fall anywhere on the left half of the circumference, choice II *could* be true, but doesn't *have* to be; and III is impossible, since l and m must be parallel.

Chapter 6: Solid Geometry

Triangles in rectangular solids, pp. 139–140

Question	Answer	Explanation
32	D	Use the formula for the long diagonal of a cube. Given that the cube's edge is the cube root of 27, or 3, the formula will be $3^2 + 3^2 + 3^2 = d^2$. If you simplify this, you'll see that the cube's long diagonal must be 5.2.
36	E	Be careful here; you won't be using the Super Pythagorean theorem. The sides of this triangle are the diagonals of three of the solid's faces. *BD* is the hypotenuse of a 3-4-5 triangle, and *BE* is the hypotenuse of a 5-12-13 triangle. For *DE*, use the Pythagorean theorem with $a = 3$ and $b = 12$: $DE = \sqrt{153} = 12.37$. The sum of the three sides is $5 + 13 + 12.37 = 30.37$.
39	A	This is a long-diagonal question, with a twist. Each edge of the cube is 1, but you're actually finding the long diagonal of a quarter of the cube. Think of it as finding the long diagonal of a rectangular solid with dimensions $1 \cdot \frac{1}{2} \cdot \frac{1}{2}$. Plug those three numbers into the Super Pythagorean theorem. You could also solve this by finding the length of *CN* and then using the Pythagorean theorem on triangle *MCN*.

Volume, pp. 141–142

Question	Answer	Explanation
17	D	PITA! Quickly move through the answer choices (starting in this case with the smallest, easiest numbers), calculating the volumes and surface areas of each. The only answer choice that makes these quantities equal is (D).
24	E	This one's a pain. The only way to do it is to try out the various possibilities. The edges of the solid must be three factors which multiply to 30, such as 2, 3, and 5. That solid would have a surface area of 62. The solid could also have dimensions of 1, 5, and 6, which would give it a surface area of 82. Keep experimenting, and you find that the solid with the greatest surface area has the dimensions 1, 1, and 30, giving it a surface area of 122.
28	C	So you don't know the formula for the area of a pentagon? You don't need to. Just use the formula for the volume of a prism, $V = Bh$.
43	B	The sphere has a volume of 4.19. When submerged, it will push up a layer of water having equal volume. The volume of this layer of water is the product of the area of the circular surface (50.27) and the height to which it's lifted—it's like calculating the volume of a very flat cylinder. You get the equation $50.27h = 4.19$. Solve, and you find that $h = 0.083$.

17	B	If the cube's surface area is $6x$, then x is the area of one face. Pick an easy number, and Plug In! Suppose x is 4. That means that the length of any edge of the cube is 2, and that the cube's volume is 8. Just plug $x = 4$ into all of the answer choices, and find the one that gives you 8. (B) does the trick. (E) is the formula for the volume of a cube with edge x.
36	C	Plug In! Suppose the sphere's original radius is $r = 2$, which would give it a surface area of 50.3. If that radius is then increased by $b = 1$, the new radius is 3. The sphere would then have a surface area of 113.1. That's an increase of 62.8. Plug $r = 2$ and $b = 1$ into the answer choices; the one that gives you 62.8 is correct. That's (C).
40	B	Just Plug In any values for b and h that obey the proportion $b = 2h$. Then plug those values into the formula for the volume of a pyramid.

Inscribed solids, pp. 144–145

Question	Answer	Explanation
32	B	The long diagonal of the rectangular solid is the diameter of the sphere. Just find the length of the long diagonal and divide it in half.
35	C	Calculate the volume of each shape separately. The cube's volume is 8; the cylinder, with a radius of 1 and a height of 2, has a volume of 6.28. The difference between them is 1.72.
38	B	The cube must have the dimensions 1 by 1 by 1. That means that the cone's base has a radius of 0.5 and that the cone's height is 1. Plug these numbers into the formula for the volume of a cone, and you should get 0.26.

Rotation solids, pp. 147–149

Question	Answer	Explanation
34	C	This rotation will generate a cylinder with a radius of 2 and a height of 5. Its volume is 62.8.
39	D	This rotation will generate a cone lying on its side, with a height of 5 and a radius of 3. Its volume is 47.12.
46	D	Here's an odd one. The best way to think about this one is as two triangles, base to base, being rotated. The rotation will generate two cones placed base to base, one right-side-up and one upside-down. Each cone has a radius of 3 and a height of 3. The volume of each cone is 28.27. The volume of the two together is 56.55.

Changing dimensions, pp. 149–150

Question	Answer	Explanation
13	E	Just Plug In a value for the radius of sphere *A*, say 2. So the radius of sphere *B* is 6. Use the volume formula: *A* has volume $\frac{4}{3}\pi(2)^3 = \frac{4}{3}\pi(8)$, and *B* has volume $\frac{4}{3}\pi(6)^3 = \frac{4}{3}\pi(216)$. If you make a ratio, the $\frac{4}{3}\pi$ cancels, and you have $\frac{8}{216} = \frac{1}{27}$.
18	D	Plug In for the dimensions of the rectangular solid so that the volume is 24. So pick *l* = 3, *w* = 4, and *h* = 2. The volume of the solid which the question asks for will then be $\left(\frac{3}{2}\right)\left(\frac{4}{2}\right)\left(\frac{2}{2}\right) = 3$.
21	B	Plug In for the length of the edge of the cube—try 2. So the surface area formula gives you $6(2)^2 = 24$, and the volume of the cube is 8. Increasing this by a factor of 2.25 gives you a new surface area of 54. Setting the surface area formula equal to this gives you a length of 3 for the new, increased edge. So the new volume is 27. 27 ÷ 8 gives you 3.375 for the increase between the old and new volumes.

Chapter 7: Coordinate Geometry

The coordinate plane, p. 155

Question	Answer
1	Point *E*, quadrant II
2	Point *A*, quadrant I
3	Point *C*, quadrant IV
4	Point *D*, quadrant III
5	Point *B*, quadrant I

The equation of a line, pp. 157–158

Question	Answer	Explanation
7	A	You can plug the line's slope *m* and the given point (x, y) into the slope-intercept equation to get $1 = 0.6(3) + b$. So $b = -0.8$. So the equation is $y = 0.6x - 0.8$. To find the point that is also on this line, go to each answer choice and plug the *x*-coordinate into the formula. You'll have the right answer when the formula produces a *y*-coordinate that matches the given one.
10	E	Once again, get the line into slope-intercept form, $y = 5x - 4$. Then Plug In zero. You get a *y*-value of -4. Notice that this is the *y*-intercept (the value of *y* when $x = 0$).
11	B	Put the line into the slope-intercept formula by isolating *y*. So $y = -3x + 4$ and the slope is -3.
19	D	You can figure out the line formula $(y = mx + b)$ from the graph. The line has a *y*-intercept (*b*) of -2, and it rises 6 as it runs 2, giving it a slope (*m*) of 3. Use those values of *m* and *b* to test the statements in the answer choices.

Slope, pp. 161–162

Question	Answer	Explanation
4	C	Use the slope formula on the point (0,0) and (–3, 2): $\dfrac{2-0}{-3-0} = -\dfrac{2}{3}$.
17	D	Draw it. Remember that perpendicular lines have slopes that are negative reciprocals of each other. A line containing the origin and the point (2, –1) has a slope of $-\dfrac{1}{2}$. The perpendicular line must then have a slope of 2. Quickly move through the answer choices, determining the slope of a line passing through the given point and the origin. The one that gives a slope of 2 is correct.

| 23 | A | Once again, the slope-intercept formula is your most powerful tool. Isolate y, and you get $y = -3x + 5$. The line must then have a slope of -3 and a y-intercept of 5. Only (A) and (D) show lines with negative slope, and the line in (D) has a slope which is between -1 and 0, because it forms an angle with the x-axis that is less than 45°. |
| 47 | D | Remember that perpendicular lines have slopes that are negative reciprocals of each other. The slopes of x and y are therefore negative reciprocals—you can think of them as x and $-\frac{1}{x}$. The difference between them will therefore be the sum of a number and its reciprocal: $x - \left(-\frac{1}{x}\right) = x + \frac{1}{x}$. If $x = 1$, then the sum of x and its reciprocal is 2; if $x = 5$, then the sum of x and its reciprocal is 5.2; but no sum of a number and its reciprocal can be less than 2. A sum of 0.8 is impossible. |

Line segments, p. 165

Question	Answer	Explanation
12	D	Use the distance formula on the points $(-5, 9)$ and $(0, 0)$.
19	E	Drawing a rough sketch and approximating allows you to eliminate (A) and (B). Then, plug the points you know into the midpoint formula and PITA for the coordinates of B. The average of -4 and the x-coordinate of B is 1. The average of 3 and the y-coordinate of B is -1. That makes B the point $(6, -5)$.
27	D	You'll essentially be using the distance formula on $(2, 2)$ and the points in the answer choices. $(-5, -3)$ is the point at the greatest distance from $(2, 2)$.

General equations (parabolas), p. 169

Question	Answer	Explanation
34	C	This is a quadratic function, which always produces a parabola. If a parabola has a maximum or minimum, then that extreme value is the parabola's vertex. Just find the vertex. The x-coordinate is $-\frac{b}{2a}$, which is 3 in this case. The y-coordinate will be $f(3)$, or -1.
37	B	Use that vertex formula again. The x-coordinate is $-\frac{b}{2a}$, which is -1 in this case. That's enough to get you the right answer. (If you needed the y-coordinate as well, you'd just Plug In $x = -1$ and solve for y.)
38	D	At every point on the x-axis, $y = 0$. Plug each of the answer choices in for x, and see which one gives you $y = 0$. You could also put in 0 for y and solve for x; the solutions are 1 and 5.

General equations (circles), p. 171

Question	Answer	Explanation
30	B	Just plug each point into the equation. The one that does *not* make the equation true is not on the circle.
34	E	If S and T are the endpoints of a diameter, then the distance between them is 8. If they are very close to each other on the circle, then the distance between them approaches zero. The distance between S and T cannot be determined.
50	C	Notice that because the y's equal 0, you can cancel out the y's in all the answer choices. Plug In the points: (2, 0) works in (C), (D), and (E), but (10, 0) works in (A), (B), and (C). It must be (C).

General equations (ellipses), p. 173

Question	Answer	Explanation
15	E	Because $a = 4$ and $b = 5$, the minor axis is $2(4) = 8$ and the major axis is $2(5) = 10$.
40	C	For an ellipse in its general form, the center is (h, k), which in this case is $(-5, 3)$.

General equations (hyperbolas), p. 175

Question	Answer	Explanation
38	B	Like circles and ellipses, hyperbolas in general form have their centers at (h, k). This one is centered at $(-4, -5)$.

Triaxial coordinates, p. 176

Question	Answer	Explanation
29	C	This is once again a job for the Super Pythagorean theorem, which is simply another version of the 3-D distance formula. It's just like finding the long diagonal of a box which is 5 by 6 by 7. Set up this equation: $d^2 = 5^2 + 6^2 + 7^2$, and solve.
34	B	A point will be outside the sphere if the distance between it and the origin is greater than 6. Use the Super Pythagorean theorem to measure the distance of each point from the origin.

Chapter 8: Trigonometry

Trig functions in right triangles, p. 182

Question	Answer
1	$\sin\theta = \dfrac{3}{5} = 0.6$; $\cos\theta = \dfrac{4}{5} = 0.8$; $\tan\theta = \dfrac{3}{4} = 0.75$
2	$\sin\theta = \dfrac{5}{13} = 0.385$; $\cos\theta = \dfrac{12}{13} = 0.923$; $\tan\theta = \dfrac{5}{12} = 0.417$
3	$\sin\theta = \dfrac{24}{25} = 0.96$; $\cos\theta = \dfrac{7}{25} = 0.28$; $\tan\theta = \dfrac{24}{7} = 3.429$
4	$\sin\theta = \dfrac{6}{10} = 0.6$; $\cos\theta = \dfrac{8}{10} = 0.8$; $\tan\theta = \dfrac{6}{8} = 0.75$

Completing triangles, p. 185

Question	Answer
1	$AB = 3.38$; $CA = 7.25$; $\angle B = 65°$
2	$EF = 2.52$; $FD = 3.92$; $\angle D = 40°$
3	$HJ = 41.41$; $JK = 10.72$; $\angle J = 75°$
4	$LM = 5.74$; $MN = 8.19$; $\angle N = 35°$
5	$TR = 4.0$; $\angle S = 53.13°$; $\angle T = 36.87°$
6	$YW = 13$; $\angle W = 22.62°$; $\angle Y = 67.38°$

Trigonometric identities, p. 189

Question	Answer	Explanation
25	D	Use FOIL on these binomials, and you get $1 - \sin^2 x$. Because $\sin^2 x + \cos^2 x = 1$, you know that $1 - \sin^2 x = \cos^2 x$.
31	C	Express $\tan x$ as $\dfrac{\sin x}{\cos x}$. The cosine then cancels out on the top of the fraction, and you're left with $\dfrac{\sin x}{\sin x}$, or 1.
39	A	The term $(\sin x)(\tan x)$ can be expressed as $(\sin x)\left(\dfrac{\sin x}{\cos x}\right)$ or $\dfrac{\sin^2 x}{\cos x}$. The first and second terms can then be combined: $\dfrac{1}{\cos x} - \dfrac{\sin^2 x}{\cos x} = \dfrac{1-\sin^2 x}{\cos x}$. Because $1 - \sin^2 x = \cos^2 x$, this expression simplifies to $\cos x$.

42	E	Break the fraction into two terms, as follows: $\dfrac{\tan x}{\tan x} - \dfrac{\sin x \cos x}{\tan x}$. The first term simplifies to 1, and the second term becomes easier to work with when you express the tangent in terms of the sine and cosine: $\dfrac{\sin x \cos x}{\tan x} = \dfrac{\sin x \cos x}{\frac{\sin x}{\cos x}} = \cos^2 x$. The whole expression then equals $1 - \cos^2 x$, or $\sin^2 x$.

Other trig functions, p. 191

Question	Answer	Explanation
19	E	Express the function as a fraction: $\dfrac{1}{\cos^2 x} - 1$. You can then combine the terms by changing the form of the second term: $\dfrac{1}{\cos^2 x} - \dfrac{\cos^2 x}{\cos^2 x}$. This allows you to combine the terms, like this: $\dfrac{1 - \cos^2 x}{\cos^2 x} = \dfrac{\sin^2 x}{\cos^2 x} = \tan^2 x$.
23	D	Express the cotangent as a fraction, as follows: $\dfrac{1}{\sin x \cot x} = \dfrac{1}{\sin x \frac{\cos x}{\sin x}}$. The $\sin x$ then cancels out, leaving you with $\dfrac{1}{\cos x}$, or $\sec x$.
24	A	Express the cotangent as a fraction, and the second term can be simplified: $(\cos x)(\cot x) = \cos x \dfrac{\cos x}{\sin x} = \dfrac{\cos^2 x}{\sin x}$. Express both terms as fractions, and the terms can be combined: $\dfrac{\sin^2 x}{\sin x} + \dfrac{\cos^2 x}{\sin x} = \dfrac{\sin^2 x + \cos^2 x}{\sin x} = \dfrac{1}{\sin x}$, or $\csc x$.

Angle equivalencies, p. 198

Question	Answer	Explanation
18	A	Draw the unit circle. −225° and 135° are equivalent angle measures, because they are separated by 360°. Or just PITA, to see which value of x works in the equation.
21	D	Draw the unit circle. 300° and 60° are not equivalent angles, but they have the same cosine. It's a simple matter to check with your calculator. Or you could just PITA.
26	B	PITA and use your calculator!
30	C	PITA and use your calculator!
36	D	Plug In a value for θ, from the ranges in the answer choices. If $\theta = 60°$, then $(\sin 60°)(\cos 60°) = 0.433$, which is not less than zero. So cross off any answer choices that contain 60°—(A), (B), (C), and (E).

Degrees and radians, p. 201

Degrees	Radians
30°	$\dfrac{\pi}{6}$
45°	$\dfrac{\pi}{4}$
60°	$\dfrac{\pi}{3}$
90°	$\dfrac{\pi}{2}$
120°	$\dfrac{2\pi}{3}$
135°	$\dfrac{3\pi}{4}$
150°	$\dfrac{5\pi}{6}$
180°	π
225°	$\dfrac{5\pi}{4}$
240°	$\dfrac{4\pi}{3}$
270°	$\dfrac{3\pi}{2}$
300°	$\dfrac{5\pi}{3}$
315°	$\dfrac{7\pi}{4}$
330°	$\dfrac{11\pi}{6}$
360°	2π

Non-right triangles, p. 207

Question	Answer
1	$a = 8.26$, $\angle B = 103.4°$, $\angle C = 34.6°$ Your calculator will give you $\angle B = 76.6°$, but you need $180° - 76.6° = 103.4°$ in order to have an obtuse angle with the same distance from 90° as 76.6°.
2	$\angle A = 21.79°$, $\angle B = 120.0°$, $\angle C = 38.21°$
3	$c = 9.44$, $\angle B = 57.98°$, $\angle C = 90.02°$

Polar coordinates, p. 211

Question	Answer	Explanation
39	C	Draw it! The x-coordinate of the point is $6\cos\frac{\pi}{3}$, or 3. The y-coordinate is $6\sin\frac{\pi}{3}$, which is 5.196.
42	B	Draw it! The y-value of a point is its distance from the x-axis. The y-coordinate of this point is $7\sin\frac{3\pi}{4}$, which equals 4.949.
45	B	Draw it! In rectangular coordinates, A, B, and C have x-coordinates of 3. This means that they are placed in a straight vertical line. They define a straight line, but not a plane or space.

Chapter 9: Functions

$&#*@! functions, p. 218

Question	Answer	Explanation
34	B	Just follow instructions on this one, and you get $-64 - (-27)$, or $-64 + 27$, which is -37. (C) is a Joe Bloggs answer.
35	A	You've just got to plow through this one. The original expression ¥5 + ¥6 becomes $5(3)^2 + 5(4)^2$, which equals 125. Work through the answer choices from the top to find the one that gives you 125. (E) is a Joe Bloggs answer.
36	B	The function §a leaves even numbers alone and flips the signs of odd numbers. That means that the series §1 + §2 + §3…§100 + §101 will become $(-1) + 2 + (-3) + 4 + (-5) \ldots + 100 + (-101)$. Rather than adding up all those numbers, find the pattern: -1 and 2 add up to 1; -3 and 4 add up to 1; and so on, all the way up to -99 and 100. That means 50 pairs that add up to 1, plus the -101 left over. $50 + -101 = -51$.

Functions without weird symbols, p. 221

Question	Answer	Explanation
14	E	$f(-1) = (-1)^2 - (-1)^3 = 1 - (-1) = 1 + 1 = 2$
17	B	$f(7) = 10.247$. $f(8) = 11.314$. That's a difference of 1.067.
26	B	$g(3) = 3^3 + 3^2 - 9(3) - 9 = 0$
29	D	$f(3, -6) = \dfrac{3(-6)}{3+(-6)} = \dfrac{-18}{-3} = 6$
30	A	PITA for n, plug each answer choice into $h(x)$, and see which one spits out 10. Alternately, you could solve $10 = n^2 + n - 2$ by setting n equal to 0 and factoring; the solutions are -4 and 3.
33	E	The greatest factor of 75 not equal to 75 is 25. Therefore, $f(75) = 75 \cdot 25 = 1{,}875$.
34	E	If $y = 3$, then $g(-y) = g(-3)$. Because $-3 < 0$, $g(-3) = 2\lvert-3\rvert = 2(3) = 6$.

Compound functions, p. 224

Question	Answer	Explanation
17	D	Plug In a number for x. Try 3. $f(g(3)) = f(7) = 21$, and $g(f(3)) = g(9) = 13$, so the difference is 8.
24	E	To evaluate $f(g(-2))$, first find the value of $g(-2)$, which equals $(-2)^3 - 5$, or -13. Then put that result into $f(x)$: $f(-13) = |-13| - 5 = 13 - 5 = 8$.
25	B	Let's PITA. Plug In 3 for $g(x)$: $f(3) = 5 + 3(3) = 14$. Nope—eliminate (A). Now let's Plug In 4 for $g(x)$: $f(4) = 5 + 3(4) = 17$. Any of the other choices would leave a variable in the compound function, so (B) is the answer.
32	D	Just Plug In a nice little number, perhaps $x = 3$. You get $g(f(3)) = g(64) = 12$. Now just plug 3 into the answers for x, to see which one hits your target number, 12.
36	C	$f(g(3)) = 5$. $g(f(3)) = 3.196$. The difference between them is 1.804.

Inverse functions, p. 227

Question	Answer	Explanation
22	B	Plug a number into $f(x)$. For example, $f(2) = 1.5$. Since $g(1.5) = 2$, the correct answer is the function that turns 1.5 back into 2. (B) does the trick.
33	B	PITA, starting with (C). Take each answer choice, plug it in for x in $f(x)$, and see which one spits out 9.
35	E	The fact that $f(3) = 9$ doesn't tell you what $f(x)$ is. It's possible that $f(x) = x^2$, or that $f(x) = 3x$, or that $f(x) = 2x + 3$, and so on. Each of these functions would have a different inverse function. The definition of the inverse function cannot be determined.

Domain and range, pp. 233–234

Question	Answer	Explanation
24	A	This function factors to $f(x) = \dfrac{1}{x(x-3)(x+2)}$. Three values of x will make this fraction undefined: -2, 0, and 3. The function's domain must exclude these values.
27	E	This function factors to $g(x) = \sqrt{(x+2)(x-6)}$. The product of these binomials must be nonnegative (that means positive or zero), since a square root of a negative number is not a real number. The product will be nonnegative when both binomials are negative ($x \leq -2$) or when both are nonnegative ($x \geq 6$). The function's domain is $\{x: x \leq -2 \text{ or } x \geq 6\}$.

| 30 | D | Take this one step at a time. Because a number raised to an even power can't be negative, the range of a^2 is the set of nonnegative numbers—that is, $\{y: y \geq 0\}$. The range of $a^2 + 5$ is found by simply adding 5 to the range of a^2, $\{y: y \geq 5\}$. Finally, to find the range of $\dfrac{a^2 + 5}{3}$, divide the range of $a^2 + 5$ by 3, $\left\{y: y \geq \dfrac{5}{3}\right\}$, or $\{y: y \geq 1.67\}$. The correct answer is (D). |
| 34 | D | Because this is a linear function (without exponents), you can find its range over the given interval by Plugging In the bounds of the domain. $f(-1) = -1$, and $f(4) = 19$. Therefore the range of f is $\{y: -1 \leq y \leq 19\}$. |

Identifying graphs of functions, pp. 238–239

Question	Answer	Explanation
9	D	It's possible to intersect the graph shown in (D) twice with a vertical line, where the point duplicates an x-value on the curve.
15	B	It's possible to intersect the graph shown in (B) more than once with a vertical line, at each point where the graph becomes vertical.

Range and domain in graphs, pp. 243–244

Question	Answer	Explanation
17	A	The graph has a vertical asymptote at $x = 0$, so 0 must be excluded from the domain of f.
24	D	Only two x-values are absent from the graph, $x = 2$ and $x = -2$. The domain must exclude these values. This can be written as $\{x: x \neq -2, 2\}$ or $\{x: |x| \neq 2\}$.
28	C	The graph extends upward forever, but never goes lower than -3. Its range is therefore $\{y: y \geq -3\}$.
37	C	Plug In a big number, such as $x = 1{,}000$. It looks like y approaches 5.
48	E	Plug the numbers you are given into the equation to see what happens to the graph. In I, if $x = 2$, then $y = -\dfrac{1}{0}$, which does not exist. Therefore I is definitely an asymptote, and you should eliminate answer choices without I in them, that is, (B) and (C). Now, try Plugging In a big number for x, like $x = 1{,}000$. y heads toward -1, which means $y = -1$ is also an asymptote, and III is correct. Cross off answer choices without III in them, in other words, (A) and (D). The correct answer is (E).

Roots of functions, pp. 245–246

Question	Answer	Explanation
16	D	PITA! Plug In each choice for x into $f(x)$ to see which one spits out 0.
19	C	The function $g(x)$ can be factored as $g(x) = x(x + 3)(x - 2)$. Set this function equal to zero and solve for x. You'll find the function has three distinct roots, -3, 0, and 2.
25	D	The roots of a function are the x-values at which $f(x) = 0$. In short, the roots are the x-intercepts—in this case, -4, -1, and 2.

Symmetry in functions, p. 249

Question	Answer	Explanation
6	D	"Symmetrical with respect to the x-axis" means reflected as though the x-axis were a mirror. That is, the values of the function above the x-axis should match corresponding values below the x-axis.
17	E	An even function is one for which $f(x) = f(-x)$. This is true by definition of an absolute value. Confirm by Plugging In numbers.

Degrees of functions, p. 255

Question	Answer	Explanation
31	E	The graph shown has five visible distinct x-intercepts (zeros), so it must be at least fifth-degree. The degree of a function is determined by its greatest exponent. Only the function in answer choice (E) is at least a fifth-degree function.
35	D	Since the degree of a function is determined by its greatest exponent, all you need to do in order to find the fourth-degree function is figure out the greatest exponent in each answer choice when it's multiplied out. Remember, you don't need to do all of the algebra; just see what the greatest exponent will be. Answer choice (A) is a second-degree function, because its highest-order term is x^2. Answer choices (B) and (C) are third-degree functions, because the highest-order term in each function is x^3. Answer choice (E) is a fifth-degree function, since $x \cdot x \cdot x^3 = x^5$. Only answer choice (D) is a fourth-degree function.

Chapter 10: Statistics and Sets
Statistics, pp. 262–263

Question	Answer	Explanation
25	B	If the sum of a list's elements is zero, then the mean must also be zero. It's impossible to know what the median is; the list could be {0, 0, 0, 0, 0, 0, 0, 0, 0, 0} or {–9, 1, 1, 1, 1, 1, 1, 1, 1, 1}. Both lists add up to zero, but have different medians. The mode is not necessarily zero for the same reasons.
42	C	You can either draw a nice pair of bell curves like the ones we've made, or just Plug In some numbers. Imagine that Group A has the scores 5, 5, 5 and Group B has the scores 1, 5, 6. The mean of A is greater, and the standard deviation of B is greater (simply because the values are more spread out), but (A), (B), (D), and (E) are all false. (C) may sound vague, but go complain to ETS. Really, the stuff about the mean is just a smokescreen.

Probability, pp. 267–268

Question	Answer	Explanation
13	A	There are only two things that can happen, rain or not rain. If 5 out of 12 possible outcomes mean rain, then the other 7 of the 12 possible outcomes must mean no rain.
16	A	The probability that two events will occur together is the product of the chances that each will happen individually. The probability that these two events will happen together is $\frac{2}{5} \cdot \frac{1}{3}$ or $\frac{2}{15}$.
20	B	Out of a total of 741 cookies, 114 are burned. The probability of getting a burned cookie is therefore $\frac{114}{741}$. That reduces to $\frac{1}{6.5}$, which is equivalent to $\frac{2}{13}$.
24	B	For the product of the numbers to be odd, both numbers must be odd themselves. There's a $\frac{3}{6}$ chance of getting an odd number on each die. The odds of getting odd numbers on both dice are $\frac{3}{6} \cdot \frac{3}{6} = \frac{9}{36} = \frac{1}{4}$.

| 44 | C | This one's pretty tricky. It's difficult to compute the odds of getting "at least one basket" in three tries, since there are so many different ways to do it (basket-basket-basket, miss-miss-basket, basket-basket-miss, and so on). It's a simpler solution to calculate the odds of Heather's missing all three times. If the probability of her making a basket on any given try is $\frac{4}{5}$, then the probability of her missing is $\frac{1}{5}$. The probability of her missing three times in a row is $\frac{1}{5} \cdot \frac{1}{5} \cdot \frac{1}{5}$, or $\frac{1}{125}$. That means that Heather makes no baskets in 1 out of 125 possible outcomes. The other 124 possible outcomes must involve her making at least 1 basket. |

Permutations, combinations, and factorials, p. 274

Question	Answer	Explanation
27	B	All committee questions are combination questions, because different arrangements of the same people don't count as different committees. The number of permutations of 12 items in 4 spaces is $12 \times 11 \times 10 \times 9$, or 11,880. To find the number of combinations, divide this number by $4 \times 3 \times 2 \times 1$, or 24. You get 495.
31	E	Even if you know how to simplify this algebraically, there are a few different ways to express the right answer. You may have to waste time getting your (technically correct) answer to look like ETS's credited response. Plugging In numbers will always make your life easier. Let's Plug In $x = 3$. $\frac{(3!)(4!)}{2!} = \frac{(6)(24)}{2} = 72$. (A) gives us 720, (B) gives us 40,320, (C) gives us 3, (D) gives us 12, and (E) gives us 72. It's (E).
32	D	The number of permutations of 6 items in 6 spaces is $6 \times 5 \times 4 \times 3 \times 2 \times 1$, or 720.
45	A	Compute the number of combinations of females and males separately. The number of combinations of 17 females in 4 spaces is $\frac{17 \cdot 16 \cdot 15 \cdot 14}{4 \cdot 3 \cdot 2 \cdot 1}$, or 2,380. The number of combinations of 12 males in 3 spaces is $\frac{12 \cdot 11 \cdot 10}{3 \cdot 2 \cdot 1}$, or 220. The total number of combinations is the product of these two numbers, $220 \times 2,380$, or 523,600.

Group questions, p. 276

Question	Answer	Explanation
25	A	Remember the group problem formula: Total = Group 1 + Group 2 + Neither – Both. Then Plug In the numbers from the question, so $530 = 253 + 112 + N - 23$, and $N = 188$.
28	C	Remember the group-problem formula: Total = Group 1 + Group 2 + Neither – Both. Then Plug In the numbers from the question, so $T = 14 + 12 + 37 - 9 = 54$.
42	B	Plug In a number of tourists that you can easily take $\frac{1}{3}$, $\frac{2}{5}$, and $\frac{1}{2}$ of—like 30. If the total number of tourists is 30, then 10 speak Spanish, 12 speak French, and 15 speak neither language. Once again, plug these numbers into the group formula to get $30 = 10 + 12 + 15 - B$. This simplifies to $30 = 37 - B$, so $B = 7$. Seven tourists speak both Spanish and French. That's $\frac{7}{30}$ of the whole group.

Chapter 11: Miscellaneous

Logarithms, p. 280

Question	Answer
1	$2^5 = 32$, so $\log_2 32 = 5$
2	$3^4 = 81$, so $x = 81$
3	$10^3 = 1,000$, so $\log 1,000 = 3$
4	$4^3 = 64$, so $b = 4$
5	Exponents and logs undo each other, so $x^{\log_x y} = y$
6	$7^0 = 1$, so $\log_7 1 = 0$
7	The sidebar tells us that $\log_x x = 1$
8	x to what power is x^{12}? The 12th power, of course! $\log_x x^{12} = 12$
9	1.5682—use your calculator
10	0.6990—use your calculator

Logarithmic rules, p. 282

Question	Answer
1	$\log 20$
2	$\log_5 2$
3	$\log 3$
4	$\log_4 16 = 2$
5	$\log 75$

Logarithms in exponential equations, p. 284

Question	Explanation
1	Take the log of both sides and use the power rule. Your new equation will be $4\log 2 = x\log 3$. Now divide both sides by $\log 3$ and you get $4\dfrac{\log 2}{\log 3} = x$. Using your calculator, you get $x = 2.5237$.
2	Use the Change of Base formula: $\log_5 18 = \dfrac{\log 18}{\log 5} = 1.7959$
3	Use the definition of a logarithm to convert the equation: $n = \log 137 = 2.1367$
4	Use the Change of Base formula: $\log_{12} 6 = \dfrac{\log 6}{\log 12} = 0.7211$
5	$4^{x+2} = (4^x)(4^2) = 80$. Here's a great place to use the rule of multiplying exponents with like bases.
6	Use the Change of Base formula: $\log_2 50 = \dfrac{\log 50}{\log 2} = 5.6439$
7	$3^{x+1} = (3^x)(3^1) = 21$
8	Use the change of base formula for the left side of the equation. $\dfrac{\log 12}{\log 3} = 2.2619$. So you know that $\log_4 x = 2.2619$. Now use the definition of logs to see that $4^{2.2619} = x$, and x is about 23. Make sure not to round too early so that your answer is as close to ETS's answer as possible.

Natural logarithms, p. 287

Question	Answer	Explanation
18	B	The equation $e^z = 8$ converts into a natural logarithm: $\ln 8 = z$. To find the value of z, just type $\ln 8$ into your calculator and see what happens. You'll get 2.07944.
23	C	All you need to know to solve this one is that $\pi \approx 3.14$ and $e \approx 2.718$. Then it's easy to put the quantities in order; just remember that you're supposed to put them in descending order.
38	A	To solve this equation, start by isolating the e term: $$6e^{\frac{n}{3}} = 5$$ $$e^{\frac{n}{3}} = \frac{5}{6}$$ Then, use the definition of a logarithm to change the form of the equation: $$\ln \frac{5}{6} = \frac{n}{3}$$ $$n = 3\ln \frac{5}{6}$$ Finally, use your calculator to evaluate the logarithm: $$n = 3(-0.1823)$$ $$n = -0.5469$$

Visual perception, p. 289

Question	Answer	Explanation
27	A	 Drawing the described set of lines results in something looking like the above. As you can see, line *l* is parallel to line *n*, but neither of the other two statements is true.
42	D	Whenever a circle intersects with a face of cube and pokes through (as opposed to touching at just one point), it creates a circle. It's probably easiest to get six intersections by having the sphere intersect with all six faces of the cube. It's also possible to get five by having nearly the same picture but moving the sphere up a little so as not to intersect with the base of the cube. Seven is too complicated, though; there are only six faces of the cube, so how are there going to be seven circles?

Arithmetic and geometric sequences, p. 294

Question	Answer	Explanation
14	E	An arithmetic sequence is formed by adding a value again and again to an original term. From the second term to a sixth term is 4 steps. Going from 4 to 32 is a change of 28 in four steps, making each step an increase of 7. The fifth term must then be 7 less than the sixth term, or 25.
19	E	Going from the first to the seventh term of a sequence is 6 steps, and going from 2 to 16 is a difference of 14. That makes each step an increase of $\frac{14}{6}$, or 2.33. To find the 33rd term, plug these numbers into the formula for the nth term of an arithmetic sequence: $a_{33} = 2 + (33 - 1)\frac{7}{3} = 2 + 74\frac{2}{3} = 76.67$.
26	D	From the second term of a sequence to the fourth is two steps—that is, 4 is multiplied by the factor r twice to get to 25. That means that $4 \times r^2 = 25$. Solve for r and you'll find that $r = 2.5$. Just punch 4 into your calculator as the second term, and keep multiplying by 2.5 until you've counted up to the ninth term. *Or* figure out that the first term in the sequence is $\frac{4}{2.5}$, or 1.6. Then just plug those values into the formula for the nth term of a geometric sequence: $a_9 = 1.6 \times 2.5^8 = 2441.41$.
34	C	Because no end term is given, this is an infinite geometric sequence. It's decreasing, not increasing, so its sum is finite. Its first term is 3, and each successive term is multiplied by a factor of $\frac{1}{3}$. Plug those values into the formula for the sum of an infinite geometric sequence, $\text{sum} = \dfrac{3}{1 - \dfrac{1}{3}} = \dfrac{3}{\dfrac{2}{3}} = 4.5$. Of course, you can also approximate. If you add the first four terms on your calculator, you get 4.4444. So you can eliminate (A) and (B). All the numbers you add after this are really tiny, so you'll never reach 5.0 or an infinite size. Therefore you can eliminate (D) and (E).

Limits, p. 297

Question	Answer	Explanation
30	B	This expression factors into $\dfrac{(4x-5)(x+1)}{(4x-5)(4x+5)}$. The binomial $4x-5$ cancels out, leaving you with $\dfrac{(x+1)}{(4x+5)}$. This expression is no longer undefined when x equals 1.25, so just plug 1.25 into the expression—the result is the limit. Alternatively, plug something very close to 1.25 (say, 1.24999) into the expression and use your calculator to evaluate it. It should be very close to B.
38	A	This expression factors into $\dfrac{(x+4)(x-3)}{2x(x-3)}$. The binomial $x-3$ cancels out, leaving you with $\dfrac{x+4}{2x}$. This expression is no longer undefined when $x = 3$, so just plug $x = 3$ into the expression to obtain the limit. Alternatively, plug in a number very close to 3 (say, 2.99) into the expression and use your calculator to evaluate it. The result should be very close to A.
40	E	This expression factors into $\dfrac{x(x+7)(x-3)}{(x+7)(x+3)}$. The binomial $x+7$ factors out, leaving you with $\dfrac{x(x-3)}{(x+3)}$. Notice, however, that the expression is *still* undefined when $x = -3$. The limit remains undefined and does not exist. Alternatively, plug in a number very close to -3 (say, -2.99) and evaluate the expression. Notice that it doesn't appear to be close to any of the numbers in the answer choices. If you want to verify that it's not going anywhere, try numbers even closer to -3 (say, -2.999 or -2.9999) until you're convinced that the limit does not exist.

Vectors, p. 300

Question	Answer	Explanation
36	D	You can see from the graph that the components of $\vec{a}$ are (–2, 4), and the components of $\vec{b}$ are (–2, –1). So the components of $\vec{c}$ must be the result of adding the components, (–4, 3). If you draw this, you can see that the magnitude of $\vec{c}$ is the length of the hypotenuse of a 3:4:5 triangle.
41	B	Subtracting the components of **a** and **b**, you get (5, 12). So the magnitude of **c** is the length of the hypotenuse of a 5:12:13 triangle.
44	E	 Either move **u** so that its tip points to the tail of **v** or vice-versa; you'll get the same result either way. In any event, the angle between the vectors is now 140°. Draw in the resulting vector (we'll label it with a length of c) from tail to head, closing off the triangle. The Law of Cosines then gives us $c^2 = 9^2 + 7^2 - 2(9)(7)\cos 140°$. So $c = 15.05$. You could also approximate c, once you draw in the resulting vector.

Logic, pp. 302–303

Question	Answer	Explanation
28	D	The basic statement here is: sophomore → not failing. The contrapositive of this statement would be: failing → not sophomore. Answer choice (D) is the contrapositive.
33	B	The basic statement here is: arson → building burns. The contrapositive would be: no building burns → no arson. Answer choice (B) directly contradicts the contrapositive.
35	C	The basic statement here is: not genuine → ruby. The contrapositive would be: not ruby → genuine. Answer choice (C) paraphrases the contrapositive.

Imaginary numbers, pp. 306–307

Question	Answer	Explanation
25	C	Remember that the powers of i repeat in a cycle of four. Divide 51 by 4, and you'll find that the remainder is 3. i^{51} will be equal to i^3, which is $-i$.
36	D	Only (D) contains two values that do not cancel each other out. $i^{11} = i^3(i^8) = i^3(1) = i^3 = -i$, and $i^9 = i(i^8) = i(1) = i$. So $-i - i = -2i$, not 0.
40	B	Use FOIL on the top of the fraction, and you get $\dfrac{4-16i^2}{5}$, or $\dfrac{4+16}{5} = \dfrac{20}{5} = 4$.
43	D	Plot the point on the complex plane; it will have a real coordinate of 5 and an imaginary coordinate of –12. The Pythagorean theorem will give you the point's distance from the origin, 13.

Polynomial division, p. 308

Question	Answer	Explanation
21	C	Divide both sides by $(x + 2)$. Now Plug In $x = 2$. $g(2) = \dfrac{16}{4} = 4$, your target number. Plug In 2 for x in the answer choices, to see which one turns into 4. Only (C) works.
27	A	Plug In $x = 10$, and use your calculator. When 970 is divided by 7, you get 138.571. Well, $7 \times 138 = 966$, so the remainder is 4, your target number. (B) is wrong. (C), (D), and (E) are nowhere near 4, so only (A) can be correct. (E) is the answer without the remainder.

What is the matrix?, p. 310

Question	Answer	Explanation
30	D	In matrix multiplication, the two inner dimensions (the number of columns in the first matrix and the number of rows in the second matrix) must be equal; the resulting matrix will have as many rows as the first matrix and as many columns as the second matrix.
40	E	The determinant is $(1)(0) - (2)(-1) = 2$.
45	C	You can write the matrix next to itself; then the six parts of the formula form straight (diagonal) lines. So we get $0 + (-4) + (-3) - (-2) - 0 - (-6) = 1$. Alternatively, if you have a calculator that can do matrices, use your calculator.
46	A	Make a matrix out of the coefficients on the left-hand side of the equations $$\begin{bmatrix} 2 & 3 & -1 \\ 1 & -3 & 2 \\ 1 & 0 & 1 \end{bmatrix}$$ The determinant is $-6 + 6 + 0 - 3 - 0 - 3 = -6$. Alternatively, if you have a calculator that can do matrices, use your calculator.

Chapter 13
Mathematics Level 1
Practice Test Form A

For each of the following problems, decide which is the BEST of the choices given. If the exact numerical value is not one of the choices, select the choice that best approximates this value. Then fill in the corresponding oval on the answer sheet.

Notes: (1) A scientific or graphing calculator will be necessary for answering some (but not all) of the questions in this test. For each question, you will have to decide whether or not you should use a calculator.

(2) The only angle measure used on this test is degree measure. Make sure that your calculator is in degree mode.

(3) Figures that accompany problems on this test are intended to provide information useful in solving the problems. They are drawn as accurately as possible EXCEPT when it is stated in a specific problem that its figure is not drawn to scale. All figures lie in a plane unless otherwise indicated.

(4) Unless otherwise specified, the domain of any function f is assumed to be the set of all real numbers x for which $f(x)$ is a real number. The range of f is assumed to be the set of all real numbers $f(x)$, where x is in the domain of f.

(5) Reference information that may be useful in answering the questions on this test can be found below.

THE FOLLOWING INFORMATION IS FOR YOUR REFERENCE IN ANSWERING SOME OF THE QUESTIONS ON THIS TEST.

Volume of a right circular cone with radius r and height h:
$$V = \frac{1}{3}\pi r^2 h$$

Lateral area of a right circular cone with circumference of the base c and slant height ℓ: $S = \frac{1}{2}c\ell$

Volume of a sphere with radius r: $V = \frac{4}{3}\pi r^3$

Surface area of a sphere with radius r: $S = 4\pi r^2$

Volume of a pyramid with base area B and height h:
$$V = \frac{1}{3}Bh$$

---

1. If $3^{4x} = 81$, then $x =$

(A) $\dfrac{3}{4}$

(B) 1

(C) 3

(D) $\dfrac{9}{4}$

(E) 9

USE THIS SPACE FOR SCRATCHWORK.

GO ON TO THE NEXT PAGE

MATHEMATICS LEVEL 1 TEST FORM A—*Continued*

2. If $\dfrac{a}{b} = 0.625$, then $\dfrac{b}{a}$ is equal to which of the

following?

(A) 1.60
(B) 2.67
(C) 2.70
(D) 3.33
(E) 4.25

USE THIS SPACE FOR SCRATCHWORK.

3. If $x - 3 = 3(1 - x)$, then what is the value of x ?

(A) 0.33
(B) 0.67
(C) 1.50
(D) 1.67
(E) 2.25

4. Points $A, B, C,$ and D are arranged on a line in that order. If $AC = 13$, $BD = 14$, and $AD = 21$, then $BC =$

(A) 12
(B) 9
(C) 8
(D) 6
(E) 3

5. The distance between the points $(-3, 5)$ and $(-3, -12)$ is

(A) $\sqrt{17}$

(B) 7

(C) 9

(D) 17

(E) $\sqrt{60}$

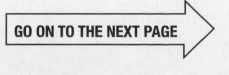
GO ON TO THE NEXT PAGE

6. At what coordinates does the graph of $3y + 5 = x - 1$ intersect the y-axis?

(A) $(0, -2)$

(B) $(0, -1)$

(C) $\left(0, \dfrac{1}{3}\right)$

(D) $(-2, 0)$

(E) $(-6, 0)$

USE THIS SPACE FOR SCRATCHWORK.

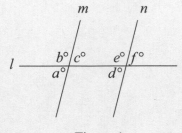

Figure 1

7. In Figure 1, if $m \| n$ and $b = 125$, then $d + f =$

(A) $50°$ (B) $55°$ (C) $110°$ (D) $130°$ (E) $180°$

8. If the cube root of the square root of a number is 2, what is the number?

(A) 16

(B) 64

(C) 128

(D) 256

(E) 1,024

9. If $7a + 2b = 11$ and $a - 2b = 5$, then what is the value of a ?

(A) −2.0

(B) −1.5

(C) −0.5

(D) 1.4

(E) 2.0

GO ON TO THE NEXT PAGE

10. If $f(x) = x^2 - 3x$, then $f(-3) =$

(A) 0
(B) 3.3
(C) 6.0
(D) 9.9
(E) 18.0

USE THIS SPACE FOR SCRATCHWORK.

11. Which of the following could be the graph of $|y| \geq 3$?

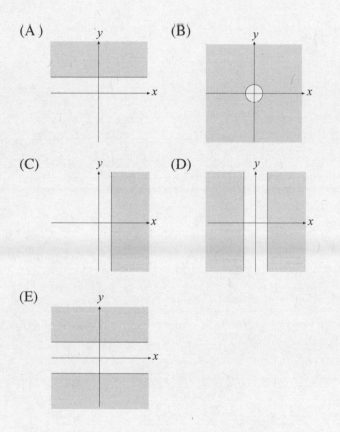

12. If m varies directly as n and $\dfrac{m}{n} = 5$, then what is the value of m when $n = 2.2$?

(A) 0.44
(B) 2.27
(C) 4.10
(D) 8.20
(E) 11.00

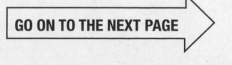

GO ON TO THE NEXT PAGE

13. What is the slope of the line given by the equation $3y - 5 = 7 - 2x$?

   (A) -2

   (B) $-\dfrac{2}{3}$

   (C) $\dfrac{3}{2}$

   (D) 2

   (E) 6

USE THIS SPACE FOR SCRATCHWORK.

14. $\dfrac{\left(n^3\right)^6 \times \left(n^4\right)^5}{n^2} =$

   (A) n^9
   (B) n^{16}
   (C) n^{19}
   (D) n^{36}
   (E) n^{40}

15. If $f(x) = 5 - 2x$ and $g(x) = x^2 + 7$, then $f(g(2)) =$

   (A) -17
   (B) -8
   (C) 8
   (D) 17
   (E) 24

16. Students in a certain research program are either engineers or doctoral candidates; some students graduate each year. In a certain year, no doctoral candidates graduate. Which of the following statements must be true?

   (A) The program then contains more engineers than doctoral candidates.
   (B) Doctoral candidates are poorer students than engineers.
   (C) More doctoral candidates will graduate in following years.
   (D) Every student graduating in that year is an engineer.
   (E) All engineers in the program graduate in that year.

GO ON TO THE NEXT PAGE

USE THIS SPACE FOR SCRATCHWORK.

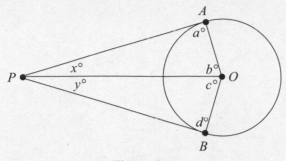

Figure 2

17. In Figure 2, if segments *PA* and *PB* are tangent to the circle with center *O* at *A* and *B*, respectively, then which of the following must be true?

    I. $PB > PO$
    II. $x = y$
    III. $x + y + b + c = a + d$

(A) I only
(B) II only
(C) I and II only
(D) II and III only
(E) I, II, and III

18. Rodney is starting a small business selling pumpkins. If he spends $200 on supplies and sells his pumpkins for $4 each, which of the following functions correctly shows the amount of money Rodney has gained or lost when he has sold *x* pumpkins?

(A) $f(x) = 800x$
(B) $f(x) = 200x + 4$
(C) $f(x) = 200x - 4$
(D) $f(x) = 4x + 200$
(E) $f(x) = 4x - 200$

19. If the perimeter of a square is 60, what is the area of the square?

(A) $15\sqrt{2}$
(B) $20\sqrt{3}$
(C)   80
(D)   150
(E)   225

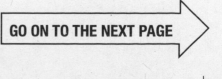

GO ON TO THE NEXT PAGE

20. If $0 < n < 1$, then all of the following must be true EXCEPT

    (A) $n^2 < n$

    (B) $n < \sqrt{n}$

    (C) $|n| < n$

    (D) $-n < n$

    (E) $n < \dfrac{1}{n}$

USE THIS SPACE FOR SCRATCHWORK.

21. Which of the following lines is perpendicular to the line $3x - 2y = 16$?

    (A) $3x - 2y = 25$
    (B) $3x + 2y = 16$
    (C) $2x - 3y = 7$
    (D) $6x + 9y = 16$
    (E) $6x - 9y = 32$

22. Where defined, $\left(\dfrac{x^2 - 4}{4}\right)\left(\dfrac{8}{2x + 4}\right) =$
    (A) 1
    (B) x
    (C) $x - 2$
    (D) $x + 2$
    (E) $2x^2 - 8$

23. The surface area of a sphere is 75 square centimeters. What is the volume of the sphere, in cubic centimeters?

    (A) 2.443
    (B) 5.968
    (C) 14.581
    (D) 18.75
    (E) 61.075

GO ON TO THE NEXT PAGE

24. If $\angle A$ and $\angle B$ are acute angles, then $\angle A$ and $\angle B$ CANNOT be

USE THIS SPACE FOR SCRATCHWORK.

(A) vertical angles
(B) complementary angles
(C) supplementary angles
(D) congruent angles
(E) adjacent angles

25. If $i^2 = -1$, then $\dfrac{(3-i)^2}{2} =$

(A) $3 - 2i$
(B) $4 - 3i$
(C) $7 + 2i$
(D) $8 - 6i$
(E) $9 + 6i$

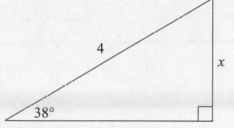

Figure 3

26. In Figure 3, what is the value of x ?

(A) 0.62
(B) 0.79
(C) 2.46
(D) 3.13
(E) 3.15

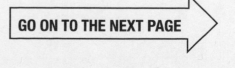

GO ON TO THE NEXT PAGE

USE THIS SPACE FOR SCRATCHWORK.

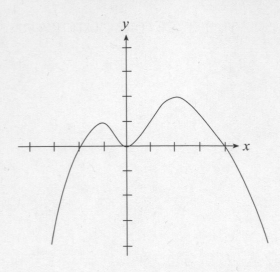

Figure 4

27. If Figure 4 shows part of the graph of $y = f(x)$, then which of the following could be the range of $f(x)$?

(A) $\{y: \ y \leq 2\}$
(B) $\{y: \ y = -2, 3\}$
(C) $\{y: \ y = 1, 2\}$
(D) $\{y: \ -2 \leq y \leq 3\}$
(E) $\{y: \ 1 \leq y \leq 2\}$

28. Joan and Grant are shopping at the deli for lunchmeat. If Joan buys 3 pounds of bologna for $2.80 per pound, and Grant buys 2 pounds of pastrami for $1.80 per pound, then what is the average (arithmetic mean) price per pound of all the lunchmeat they buy?

(A) $2.30
(B) $2.40
(C) $3.60
(D) $4.60
(E) $8.40

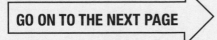
GO ON TO THE NEXT PAGE

29. If a cube and a sphere intersect at exactly eight points, then which of the following must be true?

   (A) The sphere is inscribed in the cube.
   (B) The cube is inscribed in the sphere.
   (C) The diameter of the sphere is equal in length to an edge of the cube.
   (D) The sphere and the cube have equal volumes.
   (E) The sphere and the cube have equal surface areas.

USE THIS SPACE FOR SCRATCHWORK.

30. If Set S consists of ten distinct positive integers, which of the following could be a member of S ?

   I.   The mean of the members of S
   II. The median of the members of S
   III. The mode of the members of S

   (A) None
   (B) I only
   (C) II only
   (D) I and III
   (E) II and III

31. If $f(x) = 2x^2 + 2$, then what is the value of $f(x + 4)$?

   (A) $2x^2 + 4$
   (B) $2x^2 + 6$
   (C) $2x^2 + x + 6$
   (D) $2x^2 + 16x + 32$
   (E) $2x^2 + 16x + 34$

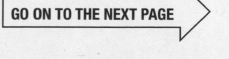

GO ON TO THE NEXT PAGE

32. If $\dfrac{9\left(\sqrt{x}-2\right)^2}{4}=6.25$, then x could equal which of the following?

   (A)   0.11
   (B)   2.42
   (C)   9.00
   (D) 10.24
   (E) 13.76

USE THIS SPACE FOR SCRATCHWORK.

33. If $0° < \theta < 90°$, then $\left(\dfrac{1}{\cos\theta}-\dfrac{\sin\theta}{\tan\theta}\right)\left(\cos\theta\right)=$

   (A) $\cos\theta$
   (B) $\sin\theta$
   (C) $\tan\theta$
   (D) $\sin^2\theta$
   (E) $\tan^2\theta$

34. If $f(x) = 2x^5$, then which of the following must be true?

   I. $f(x) = f(-x)$

   II. $f(-x) = -f(x)$

   III. $\dfrac{1}{2}f(x) = f\left(\dfrac{1}{2}x\right)$

   (A) I only
   (B) II only
   (C) I and III only
   (D) II and III only
   (E) I, II, and III

35. What is the domain of $f(x) = \dfrac{(x-3)^2}{5x\sqrt{x+10}}$?

   (A) All real numbers
   (B) All real numbers less than 2
   (C) All real numbers between −10 and 0
   (D) All real numbers greater than −7
   (E) All real numbers greater than −10 except 0

GO ON TO THE NEXT PAGE

36. How many distinct 3-digit numbers contain only nonzero digits?

    (A) 909
    (B) 899
    (C) 789
    (D) 729
    (E) 504

USE THIS SPACE FOR SCRATCHWORK.

37. At what points does the circle given by the equation $(y - 3)^2 + (x - 2)^2 = 16$ intersect the y-axis?

    (A) $(0, -5.66)$ and $(0, 5.66)$
    (B) $(0, -0.46)$ and $(0, 6.46)$
    (C) $(0, -1.00)$ and $(0, 7.00)$
    (D) $(-0.65, 0)$ and $(4.65, 0)$
    (E) $(-2.00, 0)$ and $(6.00, 0)$

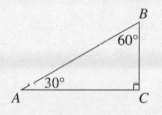

Figure 5

38. In Figure 5, $\angle ABC$ can be rotated around either leg to form a cone. Which of the following could be the ratio of the volumes of these cones?

    (A) $|n| : 1$
    (B) $2 : 1$
    (C) $3 : 1$
    (D) $4 : 1$
    (E) $9 : 1$

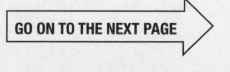

GO ON TO THE NEXT PAGE

USE THIS SPACE FOR SCRATCHWORK.

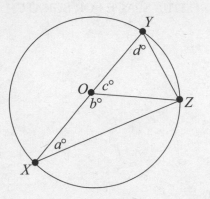

Figure 6

39. In Figure 6, in the circle with center O, which of the following is equal to c ?

(A) $\dfrac{b}{2}$

(B) d

(C) $2a$

(D) $\dfrac{a+d}{2}$

(E) $b - 90$

40. A researcher finds that an ant colony's population increases by exactly 8% each month. If the colony has an initial population of 1,250 insects, which of the following is the nearest approximation of the population of the colony 2 years later?

(A) 7,926
(B) 5,832
(C) 3,650
(D) 2,400
(E) 1,458

GO ON TO THE NEXT PAGE

USE THIS SPACE FOR SCRATCHWORK.

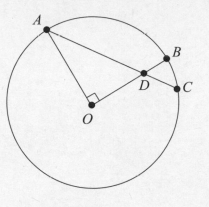

Figure 7

41. In Figure 7, if the circle with center O has a radius of 4 and $OD = 3DB$, then sin $\angle A =$

    (A) 0.60
    (B) 0.71
    (C) 0.80
    (D) 0.87
    (E) 1.00

42. Which of the following represents the solution set of $\left| x^3 - 8 \right| \leq 5$?

    (A) $-1.71 \leq x \leq 1.71$
    (B) $\quad 0 \leq x \leq 3.21$
    (C) $0.29 \leq x \leq 3.71$
    (D) $1.44 \leq x \leq 2.35$
    (E) $6.29 \leq x \leq 9.71$

43. Six congruent circles are arranged so that each circle is externally tangent to at least two other circles. The centers of these six circles are then connected to form a polygon. If each circle has a radius of 2, then what is the perimeter of this polygon?

    (A) 6
    (B) 12
    (C) 24
    (D) 36
    (E) 48

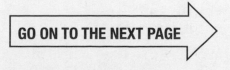

GO ON TO THE NEXT PAGE

44. What is the distance between the *x*-intercept and the *y*-intercept of the line given by the equation $2y = 6 - x$?

    (A) 3.67 (B) 6.32 (C) 6.71 (D) 7.29 (E) 8.04

USE THIS SPACE FOR SCRATCHWORK.

45. The point $(5, -10)$ is at a distance of 26 from point Q, and the point $(2, -10)$ is at a distance of 25 from Q. Which of the following could be the coordinates of Q ?

    (A) $(-5, 14)$
    (B) $(-3, 18)$
    (C) $(-1, 19)$
    (D) $(0, 21)$
    (E) $(2, 16)$

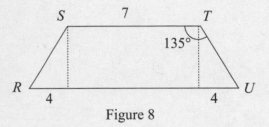

Figure 8

Note: Figure not drawn to scale.

46. In Figure 8, what is the area of isosceles trapezoid *RSTU* ?

    (A) 12
    (B) 18
    (C) 24
    (D) 44
    (E) 56

47. Which of the following has the greatest value?

    (A) 1.73^{999}
    (B) 2^{799}
    (C) 3^{500}
    (D) 4^{400}
    (E) 250^{100}

GO ON TO THE NEXT PAGE

48. If $f(x) = 4x^2 + 4x + 4$, which of the following is equal to $f(-3.5)$?

   (A) $f(-14)$
   (B) $f(-7)$
   (C) $f(-0.5)$
   (D) $f(0.5)$
   (E) $f(2.5)$

USE THIS SPACE FOR SCRATCHWORK.

49. A fair cube is one that is labeled with the numbers 1, 2, 3, 4, 5, and 6, such that there is an equal probability of rolling each of those numbers. If Jade rolls two fair cubes at the same time, then what is the probability that the product of the two numbers she rolls will be greater than 18 ?

   (A) 0.222
   (B) 0.278
   (C) 0.5
   (D) 0.6
   (E) 0.778

50. If $z = \log_x (y^x)$, then $x^z =$

   (A) x^x
   (B) y^x
   (C) xy^x
   (D) y^{2x}
   (E) $x^2 y$

STOP

IF YOU FINISH BEFORE TIME IS CALLED, YOU MAY CHECK YOUR WORK ON THIS TEST ONLY.
DO NOT WORK ON ANY OTHER TEST IN THIS BOOK.

HOW TO SCORE THE PRINCETON REVIEW
PRACTICE SAT MATH SUBJECT TEST

When you take the real exam, the proctors will collect your test booklet and bubble sheet and send your bubble sheet to New Jersey where a computer looks at the pattern of filled-in ovals on your bubble sheet and gives you a score. We couldn't include even a small computer with this book, so we are providing this more primitive way of scoring your exam.

Determining Your Score

STEP 1   Using the answers on the next page, determine how many questions you got right and how many you got wrong on the test. Remember: Questions that you do not answer don't count as either right answers or wrong answers.

STEP 2   List the number of right answers here.

STEP 3   List the number of wrong answers here. Now divide that number by 4. (Use a calculator if you're feeling particularly lazy.)

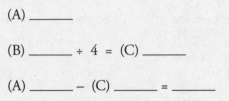

(A) _____

(B) _____ ÷ 4 = (C) _____

(A) _____ − (C) _____ = _____

STEP 4   Subtract the number of wrong answers divided by 4 from the number of correct answers. Round this score to the nearest whole number. This is your raw score.

STEP 5   To determine your real score, take the number from Step 4 above and look it up in the left column of the Score Conversion Table on page 380; the corresponding score on the right is your score on the exam.

MATHEMATICS LEVEL 1 SUBJECT TEST FORM A

Answer Key

1.	B	11.	E	21.	D	31.	E	41.	A
2.	A	12.	E	22.	C	32.	A	42.	D
3.	C	13.	B	23.	E	33.	D	43.	C
4.	D	14.	D	24.	C	34.	B	44.	C
5.	D	15.	A	25.	B	35.	E	45.	A
6.	A	16.	D	26.	C	36.	D	46.	D
7.	C	17.	D	27.	A	37.	B	47.	D
8.	B	18.	E	28.	B	38.	A	48.	E
9.	E	19.	E	29.	B	39.	C	49.	A
10.	E	20.	C	30.	B	40.	A	50.	B

MATHEMATICS SUBJECT TEST
SCORE CONVERSION TABLE

Raw Score	Scaled Score	Raw Score	Scaled Score	Raw Score	Scaled Score
50	800	25	530	0	330
49	780	24	520	−1	320
48	770	23	510	−2	310
47	760	22	510	−3	300
46	740	21	500	−4	300
45	730	20	490	−5	290
44	720	19	480	−6	280
43	710	18	480	−7	270
42	700	17	470	−8	260
41	690	16	460	−9	260
40	680	15	450	−10	250
39	670	14	440	−11	240
38	660	13	430	−12	230
37	650	12	430		
36	640	11	420		
35	630	10	410		
34	610	9	400		
33	600	8	390		
32	590	7	380		
31	580	6	370		
30	570	5	370		
29	560	4	360		
28	550	3	350		
27	550	2	340		
26	540	1	340		

Chapter 14
Mathematics Level 1
Practice Test Form B

MATHEMATICS LEVEL 1 TEST FORM B

For each of the following problems, decide which is the BEST of the choices given. If the exact numerical value is not one of the choices, select the choice that best approximates this value. Then fill in the corresponding oval on the answer sheet.

Notes: (1) A scientific or graphing calculator will be necessary for answering some (but not all) of the questions on this test. For each question, you will have to decide whether or not you should use a calculator.

(2) The only angle measure used on this test is degree measure. Make sure that your calculator is in degree mode.

(3) Figures that accompany problems on this test are intended to provide information useful in solving the problems. They are drawn as accurately as possible EXCEPT when it is stated in a specific problem that its figure is not drawn to scale. All figures lie in a plane unless otherwise indicated.

(4) Unless otherwise specified, the domain of any function f is assumed to be the set of all real numbers x for which $f(x)$ is a real number. The range of f is assumed to be the set of all real numbers $f(x)$, where x is in the domain of f.

(5) Reference information that may be useful in answering the questions on this test can be found below.

THE FOLLOWING INFORMATION IS FOR YOUR REFERENCE IN ANSWERING SOME OF THE QUESTIONS ON THIS TEST.

Volume of a right circular cone with radius r and height h:
$$V = \frac{1}{3}\pi r^2 h$$

Lateral area of a right circular cone with circumference of the base c and slant height ℓ: $S = \frac{1}{2}c\ell$

Volume of a sphere with radius r: $V = \frac{4}{3}\pi r^3$

Surface area of a sphere with radius r: $S = 4\pi r^2$

Volume of a pyramid with base area B and height h:
$$V = \frac{1}{3}Bh$$

---

1. Rob and Sherry together weigh 300 pounds. Sherry and Heather together weigh 240 pounds. If all three people together weigh 410 pounds, then what is Sherry's weight in pounds?

   (A) 110
   (B) 115
   (C) 120
   (D) 130
   (E) 145

USE THIS SPACE FOR SCRATCHWORK.

2. If the point $(5, 2)$ is reflected across the x-axis, then what are the coordinates of the resulting point?

   (A) $(5, 0)$
   (B) $(0, 2)$
   (C) $(5, -2)$
   (D) $(-5, 2)$
   (E) $(2, 5)$

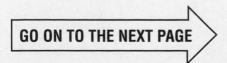
GO ON TO THE NEXT PAGE

3. If $r = \dfrac{2}{3}$ and $s = 6$, then $\dfrac{s}{r} + \dfrac{4}{r^2} =$

USE THIS SPACE FOR SCRATCHWORK.

(A) 4
(B) 6
(C) 9
(D) 12
(E) 18

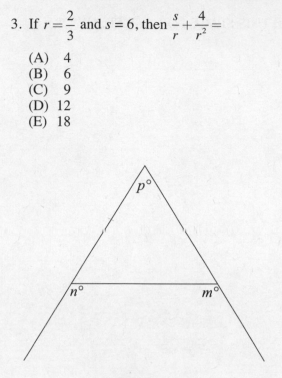

Figure 1

4. In Figure 1, what is the value of p in terms of m and n ?

(A) $m + n - 180$
(B) $m + n + 180$
(C) $m - n + 360$
(D) $360 - (m - n)$
(E) $360 - (m + n)$

5. After 8:00 p.m., a ride in a taxi costs $2.50 plus $0.30 for every fifth of a mile traveled. If a passenger travels b miles, then what is the cost of the trip, in dollars, in terms of b ?

(A) $2.5 + 0.3b$
(B) $2.5 + 1.5b$
(C) $2.8b$
(D) $30 + 250b$
(E) $250 + 30b$

GO ON TO THE NEXT PAGE

6. If $|y - 3| = 4y - 7$, then which of the following could be the value of y ?

(A) $\dfrac{3}{4}$

(B) 1

(C) $\dfrac{5}{4}$

(D) 2

(E) 5

USE THIS SPACE FOR SCRATCHWORK.

7. What is the slope of the line given by the equation
$y + 3 = \dfrac{5}{4}(x - 7)$?

(A) $-\dfrac{4}{5}$

(B) $-\dfrac{2}{3}$

(C) $\dfrac{3}{7}$

(D) $\dfrac{2}{3}$

(E) $\dfrac{5}{4}$

8. If $a = \cos\theta$ and $b = \sin\theta$, then for all θ, $a^2 + b^2 =$

(A) 0

(B) 1

(C) 2

(D) $(\cos\theta + \sin\theta)^2$

(E) $(\cos\theta \cdot \sin\theta)^2$

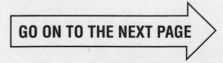

GO ON TO THE NEXT PAGE

USE THIS SPACE FOR SCRATCHWORK.

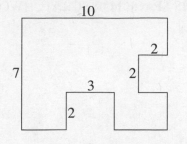

Figure 2

9. In Figure 2, if every angle in the polygon is a right angle, then what is the perimeter of the polygon?

(A) 34
(B) 42
(C) 47
(D) 52
(E) 60

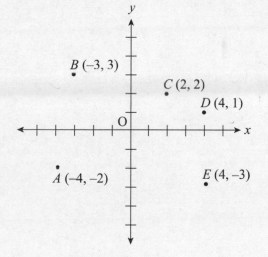

Figure 3

10. For which of the points shown in Figure 3 is $|x + y| > 5$?

(A) A
(B) B
(C) C
(D) D
(E) E

GO ON TO THE NEXT PAGE

Questions 11-12 refer to the chart below, which shows the monthly sales made by a salesperson in 1996.

USE THIS SPACE FOR SCRATCHWORK.

Keri's Monthly Sales for 1996

◯ =100 units

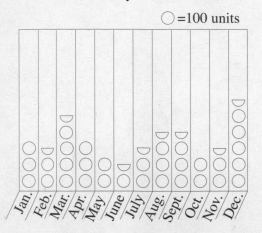

11. As a saleswoman, Keri receives a $10.00 commission for each unit she sells. In any month in which she sells more than 300 units, she receives an additional bonus of $1,000.00. What was the total amount Keri received in bonuses in 1996 ?

(A) $3,000.00
(B) $4,000.00
(C) $5,000.00
(D) $6,000.00
(E) $8,000.00

12. In 1996, Keri had the greatest total income from commissions and bonuses in what three-month period?

(A) January, February, March
(B) February, March, April
(C) March, April, May
(D) July, August, September
(E) October, November, December

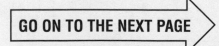

GO ON TO THE NEXT PAGE

13. If a varies directly as b^2, and $a = 14$ when $b = 2$,
then what is the value of a when $b = 5$?

   (A) 3.6
   (B) 14
   (C) 35
   (D) 70
   (E) 87.5

USE THIS SPACE FOR SCRATCHWORK.

14. If $\dfrac{1}{x} = \dfrac{4}{5}$, then $\dfrac{x}{3} =$

   (A) 0.27
   (B) 0.33
   (C) 0.42
   (D) 0.66
   (E) 1.25

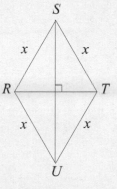

Figure 4

15. In Figure 4, $\sin \angle RSU$ must be equal to which of
the following?

   (A) $\cos \angle RTU$
   (B) $\cos \angle TSU$
   (C) $\sin \angle SRT$
   (D) $\sin \angle STR$
   (E) $\sin \angle TRU$

GO ON TO THE NEXT PAGE

16. If $y = \sqrt{x} + \dfrac{1}{x-3}$, then which of the following

    statements must be true?

    I. $x > 1$
    II. $x \neq 3$
    III. $x \neq -3$

    (A) I only
    (B) II only
    (C) I and III only
    (D) II and III only
    (E) I, II, and III

USE THIS SPACE FOR SCRATCHWORK.

17. Sphere O is inscribed in cube A, and cube B is inscribed in sphere O. Which of the following quantities must be equal?

    (A) An edge of A and the radius of O
    (B) The diameter of O and the longest
        diagonal in A
    (C) An edge of B and the diameter of O
    (D) An edge of B and the radius of O
    (E) An edge of A and the longest diagonal in B

18. If $a - x = 12$, $b - y = 7$, $c - z = 15$, and $a + b + c = 50$, then $x + y + z =$

    (A) 16   (B) 18   (C) 34   (D) 66   (E) 84

GO ON TO THE NEXT PAGE

19. A jeep has four seats, including one driver's seat and three passenger seats. If Amber, Bunny, Cassie, and Donna are going for a drive in the jeep, and only Cassie can drive, then how many different seating arrangements are possible?

    (A)   3
    (B)   6
    (C) 12
    (D) 16
    (E) 24

USE THIS SPACE FOR SCRATCHWORK.

20. If $\dfrac{1}{2}x - 3 = 2\left(\dfrac{x-1}{5}\right)$, then $x =$

    (A) 9   (B) 11   (C) 13   (D) 22   (E) 26

21. Line l passes through the origin and point (a, b). If $ab \neq 0$ and line l has a slope greater than 1, then which of the following must be true?

    (A) $a = b$
    (B) $a > b$
    (C) $a^2 < b^2$
    (D) $b - a < 0$
    (E) $a + b > 0$

GO ON TO THE NEXT PAGE

USE THIS SPACE FOR SCRATCHWORK.

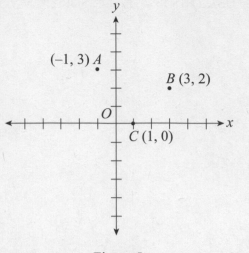

Figure 5

22. In Figure 5, points *A*, *B*, and *C* are three vertices of a parallelogram, and point *D* (not shown) is the fourth vertex. How many points could be *D* ?

(A) 1
(B) 2
(C) 3
(D) 4
(E) 5

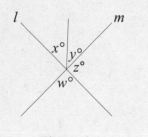

Figure 6

Note: Figure not drawn to scale.

23. In Figure 6, lines *l* and *m* intersect as shown. If $y = \dfrac{2}{3}x$ and $w = 2z$, then $x =$

(A) 30 (B) 40 (C) 48 (D) 60 (E) 72

GO ON TO THE NEXT PAGE

24. Circle O has a radius of r. If this radius is increased by t, then which of the following correctly expresses the new area of circle O ?

(A) πt^2

(B) $2\pi(r + t)$

(C) $\pi(t^2 + r^2)$

(D) $\pi(r^2 + 2rt + t^2)$

(E) $4\pi(r^2 + 2rt + t^2)$

USE THIS SPACE FOR SCRATCHWORK.

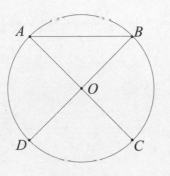

Figure 7

25. In Figure 7, AC and BD are perpendicular diameters of the circle with center O. If the circle has an area of 9π, what is the length of AB ?

(A) 2.12
(B) 3.36
(C) 4.24
(D) 6.36
(E) 8.48

26. If $x < |x|$ and $x^2 + 2x - 3 = 0$, then $2x + 4 =$
(A) –2   (B) 2   (C) 6   (D) 8   (E) 10

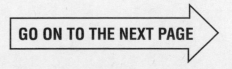

GO ON TO THE NEXT PAGE

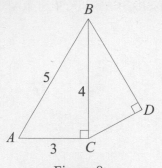

Figure 8

USE THIS SPACE FOR SCRATCHWORK.

27. In Figure 8, triangles *ABC* and *CBD* are similar.
    What is the area of triangle *CBD* ?

    (A) 3.07
    (B) 3.84
    (C) 5.24
    (D) 7.68
    (E) 9.60

28. If $i = \sqrt{-1}$, then $(5 - 3i)(4 + 2i) =$

    (A) $14 - 2i$
    (B) 16
    (C) 24
    (D) $26 - 2i$
    (E) 28

29. If $f(x) = x^2 - 5x$ and $f(n) = -4$, then which of the
    following could be the value of *n* ?

    (A) –5
    (B) –4
    (C) –1
    (D) 1
    (E) 5

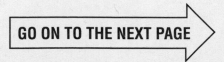

GO ON TO THE NEXT PAGE

30. Two identical rectangular solids, each of dimensions $3 \times 4 \times 5$, are joined face to face to form a single rectangular solid with a length of 8. What is the length of the longest line segment that can be drawn within this new solid?

   (A) 8.60
   (B) 9.90
   (C) 10.95
   (D) 11.40
   (E) 12.25

USE THIS SPACE FOR SCRATCHWORK.

31. Which of the following most closely approximates $\left(5.5 \times 10^4\right)^2$?

   (A) 3.0×10^5
   (B) 3.0×10^6
   (C) 3.0×10^7
   (D) 3.0×10^8
   (E) 3.0×10^9

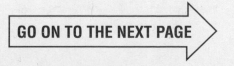

GO ON TO THE NEXT PAGE

USE THIS SPACE FOR SCRATCHWORK.

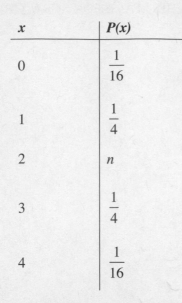

x	$P(x)$
0	$\dfrac{1}{16}$
1	$\dfrac{1}{4}$
2	n
3	$\dfrac{1}{4}$
4	$\dfrac{1}{16}$

32. If a fair coin is flipped four times, the probability of the coin landing heads-side-up x times is shown in the table above. What is the value of n ?

(A) $\dfrac{1}{8}$

(B) $\dfrac{3}{16}$

(C) $\dfrac{5}{16}$

(D) $\dfrac{3}{8}$

(E) $\dfrac{1}{2}$

33. A sample of metal is heated to 698°C and then allowed to cool. The temperature of the metal over time is given by the formula $n = 698 - 2t - 0.5t^2$, where t is the time in seconds after the start of the cooling process, and n is the temperature of the sample in degrees Celsius. After how many seconds will the temperature of the sample be 500°C ?

(A) 16 (B) 18 (C) 20 (D) 22 (E) 24

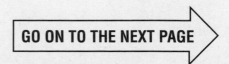

GO ON TO THE NEXT PAGE

34. Perpendicular lines *l* and *m* intersect at $(4, 5)$. If line *m* has a slope of $-\dfrac{1}{2}$, which of the following is an equation for line *l* ?

USE THIS SPACE FOR SCRATCHWORK.

(A) $y = \dfrac{1}{2}x - 1$

(B) $y = \dfrac{1}{2}x + 3$

(C) $y = \dfrac{1}{2}x + 5$

(D) $y = 2x - 1$

(E) $y = 2x - 3$

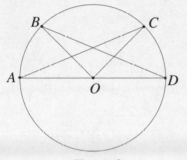

Figure 9

35. In Figure 9, points *A, B, C,* and *D* are all on the circle with center *O*. If $\angle BDA$ measures $25°$, and $\angle CAD$ measures $32°$, what is the measure of $\angle BOC$ in degrees?

(A) 33
(B) 66
(C) 123
(D) 147
(E) 303

36. If $4^{x+2} = 48$, then $4^x =$

(A)   3.0
(B)   6.4
(C)   6.9
(D) 12.0
(E) 24.0

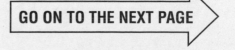

GO ON TO THE NEXT PAGE

37. If $r(x) = 6x + 5$ and $s(r(x)) = 2x - 1$, then $s(x) =$

USE THIS SPACE FOR SCRATCHWORK.

(A) $-4x - 6$

(B) $\dfrac{x - 2}{3}$

(C) $\dfrac{x - 8}{3}$

(D) $3x - 6$

(E) $4x + 4$

38. Of the 850 stores in Noel-Bentley County, 250 have alarm systems and 450 have guard dogs. If 350 stores have neither alarm systems nor guard dogs, then how many stores have both alarm systems and guard dogs?

(A) 100
(B) 150
(C) 200
(D) 500
(E) 700

39. If $\log_9 27 = n$, then $n =$

(A) $\dfrac{1}{3}$

(B) 1

(C) $\dfrac{3}{2}$

(D) $\sqrt{3}$

(E) 3

GO ON TO THE NEXT PAGE

40. A cylindrical cup has a height of 3 inches and a radius of 2 inches. How many such cups may be completely filled from a full rectangular tank whose dimensions are $6 \times 7 \times 8$ inches?

    (A)   8
    (B)   9
    (C) 12
    (D) 17
    (E) 28

USE THIS SPACE FOR SCRATCHWORK.

41. Line segments AC and BD intersect at point O, such that each segment is the perpendicular bisector of the other. If $AC = 7$ and $BD = 6$, then $\sin \angle ADO =$

    (A) 0.16
    (B) 0.24
    (C) 0.39
    (D) 0.76
    (E) 0.85

42. Which of the following boxplots represents the data set with the greatest interquartile range?

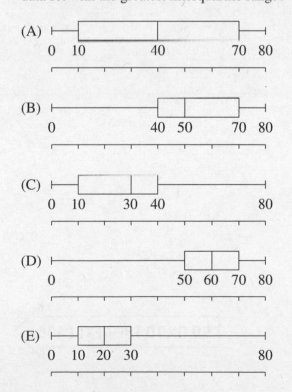

(A)   0 10   40   70 80

(B)   0   40 50   70 80

(C)   0 10   30 40   80

(D)   0   50 60 70 80

(E)   0 10 20 30   80

GO ON TO THE NEXT PAGE

43. If $f(x) = kx$, where k is a nonzero constant, and $g(x) = x + k$, then which of the following statements must be true?

    I. $f(2x) = 2f(x)$
    II. $f(x + 2) = f(x) + 2$
    III. $f(g(x)) = g(f(x))$

(A) I only
(B) II only
(C) I and II only
(D) I and III only
(E) I, II, and III

USE THIS SPACE FOR SCRATCHWORK.

44. A rectangular room has walls facing due north, south, east, and west. On the southern wall, a tack is located 85 inches from the floor and 38 inches from the western wall, and a nail is located 48 inches from the floor and 54 inches from the western wall. What is the distance in inches between the tack and the nail?

(A) 21.0
(B) 26.4
(C) 32.6
(D) 37.0
(E) 40.3

45. If $f(x) = \sqrt{12 - x^2}$, then which of the following is the domain of f?

(A) $\{x:\ x \neq \sqrt{12}\}$

(B) $\{x:\ x \geq 0\}$

(C) $\{x:\ -\sqrt{12} \leq x \leq \sqrt{12}\}$

(D) $\{x:\ 0 < x < \sqrt{12}\}$

(E) $\{x:\ 0 \leq x \leq 144\}$

GO ON TO THE NEXT PAGE

"If a tree falls in the forest,
a sound is heard."

USE THIS SPACE FOR SCRATCHWORK.

46. If the statement above is true, then which of the following CANNOT be true?

    (A) No tree falls in the forest, but a sound is heard.
    (B) No sound is heard as a tree falls in the forest.
    (C) A sound is heard as a tree falls in the forest.
    (D) No tree falls in the forest, and no sound is made.
    (E) A sound is heard in the forest as no tree falls.

47. At a dance competition, each of six couples must compete against the other five couples in a dance-off three times before the winning couple can be declared. How many such dance-offs will occur?

    (A) 12
    (B) 33
    (C) 45
    (D) 60
    (E) 63

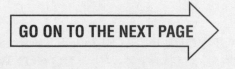

GO ON TO THE NEXT PAGE

USE THIS SPACE FOR SCRATCHWORK.

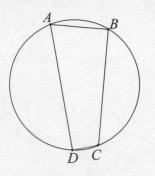

Figure 10

Note: Figure not drawn to scale.

48. In Figure 10, $AB = 4$, $BC = 7$, and $CD = 1$.
If AC is a diameter of the circle, then what is the
length of AD ?

    (A) 3
    (B) 6
    (C) 8
    (D) $\sqrt{65}$
    (E) 10

49. $(0, 0)$ and $(-2, 2)$ are the coordinates of two vertices of an equilateral triangle. Which of the following could be the coordinates of the third vertex?

    (A) $(-2.0, 0)$
    (B) $(-0.73, 2.73)$
    (C) $(-0.73, 0.73)$
    (D) $(0, 2.0)$
    (E) $(0.73, 2.73)$

50. What is the distance between the two x-intercepts
of the graph of $y = x^2 - 9x + 19.25$?

    (A)   2.0
    (B)   3.5
    (C)   5.5
    (D) 10.25
    (E) 28.25

STOP

IF YOU FINISH BEFORE TIME IS CALLED, YOU MAY CHECK YOUR WORK ON THIS TEST ONLY.
DO NOT WORK ON ANY OTHER TEST IN THIS BOOK.

HOW TO SCORE THE PRINCETON REVIEW PRACTICE SAT MATH SUBJECT TEST

When you take the real exam, the proctors will collect your test booklet and bubble sheet and send your bubble sheet to New Jersey where a computer looks at the pattern of filled-in ovals on your bubble sheet and gives you a score. We couldn't include even a small computer with this book, so we are providing this more primitive way of scoring your exam.

Determining Your Score

STEP 1   Using the answers on the next page, determine how many questions you got right and how many you got wrong on the test. Remember: Questions that you do not answer don't count as either right answers or wrong answers.

STEP 2   List the number of right answers here.

STEP 3   List the number of wrong answers here. Now divide that number by 4. (Use a calculator if you're feeling particularly lazy.)

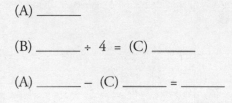

(A) _____

(B) _____ ÷ 4 = (C) _____

(A) _____ − (C) _____ = _____

STEP 4   Subtract the number of wrong answers divided by 4 from the number of correct answers. Round this score to the nearest whole number. This is your raw score.

STEP 5   To determine your real score, take the number from Step 4 above and look it up in the left column of the Score Conversion Table on page 403; the corresponding score on the right is your score on the exam.

MATHEMATICS LEVEL 1 SUBJECT TEST FORM B

Answer Key

1.	D	11.	B	21.	C	31.	E	41.	D
2.	C	12.	D	22.	C	32.	D	42.	A
3.	E	13.	E	23.	E	33.	B	43.	A
4.	A	14.	C	24.	D	34.	E	44.	E
5.	B	15.	A	25.	C	35.	B	45.	C
6.	D	16.	D	26.	A	36.	A	46.	B
7.	E	17.	E	27.	B	37.	C	47.	C
8.	B	18.	A	28.	D	38.	C	48.	C
9.	B	19.	B	29.	D	39.	C	49.	E
10.	A	20.	E	30.	B	40.	A	50.	A

MATHEMATICS SUBJECT TEST
SCORE CONVERSION TABLE

Raw Score	Scaled Score	Raw Score	Scaled Score	Raw Score	Scaled Score
50	800	25	530	0	330
49	780	24	520	−1	320
48	770	23	510	−2	310
47	760	22	510	−3	300
46	740	21	500	−4	300
45	730	20	490	−5	290
44	720	19	480	−6	280
43	710	18	480	−7	270
42	700	17	470	−8	260
41	690	16	460	−9	260
40	680	15	450	−10	250
39	670	14	440	−11	240
38	660	13	430	−12	230
37	650	12	430		
36	640	11	420		
35	630	10	410		
34	610	9	400		
33	600	8	390		
32	590	7	380		
31	580	6	370		
30	570	5	370		
29	560	4	360		
28	550	3	350		
27	550	2	340		
26	540	1	340		

Chapter 15
Mathematics Level 2
Practice Test Form A

MATHEMATICS LEVEL 2 TEST FORM A

For each of the following problems, decide which is the BEST of the choices given. If the exact numerical value is not one of the choices, select the choice that best approximates this value. Then fill in the corresponding oval on the answer sheet.

Notes: (1) A scientific or graphing calculator will be necessary for answering some (but not all) of the questions on this test. For each question, you will have to decide whether or not you should use a calculator.

(2) For some questions in this test you may have to decide whether your calculator should be in the radian mode or the degree mode.

(3) Figures that accompany problems on this test are intended to provide information useful in solving the problems. They are drawn as accurately as possible EXCEPT when it is stated in a specific problem that its figure is not drawn to scale. All figures lie in a plane unless otherwise indicated.

(4) Unless otherwise specified, the domain of any function f is assumed to be the set of all real numbers x for which $f(x)$ is a real number. The range of f is assumed to be the set of all real numbers $f(x)$, where x is in the domain of f.

(5) Reference information that may be useful in answering the questions on this test can be found below.

THE FOLLOWING INFORMATION IS FOR YOUR REFERENCE IN ANSWERING SOME OF THE QUESTIONS ON THIS TEST.

Volume of a right circular cone with radius r and height h:
$$V = \frac{1}{3}\pi r^2 h$$

Lateral area of a right circular cone with circumference of the base c and slant height ℓ: $S = \frac{1}{2}c\ell$

Volume of a sphere with radius r: $V = \frac{4}{3}\pi r^3$

Surface area of a sphere with radius r: $S = 4\pi r^2$

Volume of a pyramid with base area B and height h:
$$V = \frac{1}{3}Bh$$

1. If $r - s > r + s$, then which of the following must be true?

   (A) $r > s$
   (B) $s < 0$
   (C) $r < 0$
   (D) $r < s$
   (E) $s > 0$

USE THIS SPACE FOR SCRATCHWORK.

2. If $f(x) = |x| + 10$, for which of the following values of x does $f(x) = f(-x)$?

   (A) −10 only
   (B) −10 and 10 only
   (C) All real x
   (D) All real x except 10
   (E) All real x except −10 and 10

GO ON TO THE NEXT PAGE

3. $\dfrac{15!}{13!2!} =$

USE THIS SPACE FOR SCRATCHWORK.

(A) 0   (B) 0.58   (C) 1   (D) 105   (E) 210

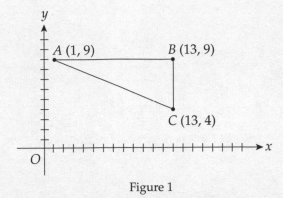

Figure 1

4. In Figure 1, $\sin \angle BAC =$

(A) $\dfrac{5}{13}$

(B) $\dfrac{5}{12}$

(C) $\dfrac{12}{13}$

(D) $\dfrac{12}{5}$

(E) $\dfrac{13}{5}$

5. Which of the following is the complete solution set of the system:

$A = \{(x, y): x^2 + y^2 = 25\}$ and
$B = \{(x, y): y = x + 1\}$?

(A) $\{(5, 5)\}$
(B) $\{(16, 9)\}$
(C) $\{(-4, -3)\}$
(D) $\{(-4, -3), (3, 4)\}$
(E) $\{(-3, -4), (4, 3)\}$

GO ON TO THE NEXT PAGE

USE THIS SPACE FOR SCRATCHWORK.

6. If $jk \neq 0$, then $\dfrac{jk - \dfrac{j}{k}}{\dfrac{j}{k}} =$

(A) $k^2 - \dfrac{j}{k}$

(B) $j^2 - \dfrac{j^2}{k^2}$

(C) $jk - 1$

(D) $j^2 - 1$

(E) $k^2 - 1$

7. All of the following can be formed by the intersection of a cube and a plane EXCEPT

(A) a triangle
(B) a point
(C) a rectangle
(D) a line segment
(E) a circle

8. If $f(x) = \sqrt[3]{x}$ and $g(x) = \dfrac{1}{2}\sqrt{x} + 1$, then $f(g(2.3)) =$

(A) 0.1
(B) 1.2
(C) 1.3
(D) 1.8
(E) 2.3

9. If $x \bmod y$ is the remainder when x is divided by y, then $(61 \bmod 7) - (5 \bmod 5) =$

(A) 2
(B) 3
(C) 4
(D) 5
(E) 6

GO ON TO THE NEXT PAGE

10. Which of the following must be true?

    I. $\sin(-\theta) = -\sin \theta$
    II. $\cos(-\theta) = -\cos \theta$
    III. $\tan(-\theta) = -\tan \theta$, where $\tan \theta$ is defined

(A) I only
(B) II only
(C) III only
(D) I and III only
(E) I, II, and III

USE THIS SPACE FOR SCRATCHWORK.

11. If for all real numbers x, a function $f(x)$ is defined
by $f(x) = \begin{cases} 2, x \neq 13 \\ 4, x = 13 \end{cases}$, then $f(15) - f(14) =$

(A) –2 (B) 0 (C) 1 (D) 2 (E) 4

12. If $\dfrac{x^5}{25} = 25$, then $x =$

(A) 1.00
(B) 1.90
(C) 2.19
(D) 3.62
(E) 5.00

13. If the ratio of $\sec x$ to $\csc x$ is $1 : 4$, then the ratio
of $\tan x$ to $\cot x$ is

(A) 1 : 16
(B) 1 : 4
(C) 1 : 1
(D) 4 : 1
(E) 16 : 1

GO ON TO THE NEXT PAGE

USE THIS SPACE FOR SCRATCHWORK.

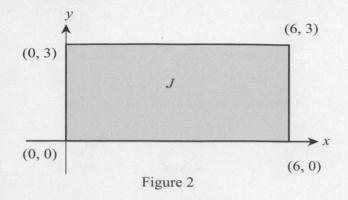

Figure 2

14. In Figure 2, rectangle J contains all points (x, y). What is the area of a rectangle that contains all points $(2x, y - 1)$?

    (A) 12
    (B) 18
    (C) 24
    (D) 36
    (E) 48

15. In right triangle ABC, $\angle B$ measures $90°$, $\angle C$ measures $27°$, and $AB = 9$. What is the length of the hypotenuse of $\triangle ABC$?

    (A)   4.1
    (B) 10.1
    (C) 17.7
    (D) 19.8
    (E) 21.2

16. Which of the following is a zero of $f(x) = x^2 + 6x - 12$?

    (A) −15.16
    (B) −7.58
    (C)   0.67
    (D)   3.16
    (E)   7.58

GO ON TO THE NEXT PAGE

17. If $\sin x = m$ and $0 < x < 90°$, then $\tan x =$

USE THIS SPACE FOR SCRATCHWORK.

(A) $\dfrac{1}{m^2}$

(B) $\dfrac{m}{\sqrt{1-m^2}}$

(C) $\dfrac{1-m^2}{m}$

(D) $\dfrac{m}{1-m^2}$

(E) $\dfrac{m^2}{\sqrt{1-m^2}}$

18. If $\log_y 2 = 8$, then $y =$

(A) 0.25
(B) 1.04
(C) 1.09
(D) 2.83
(E) 3.00

19. If $\sin\theta = \dfrac{1}{3}$ and $-\dfrac{\pi}{4} \le \theta \le \dfrac{\pi}{4}$, then $\cos(2\theta) =$

(A) $-\dfrac{7}{9}$

(B) $-\dfrac{2}{3}$

(C) $\dfrac{2}{3}$

(D) $\dfrac{7}{9}$

(E) 1

GO ON TO THE NEXT PAGE

20. If $f(x) = \sqrt{x} - 1$, for all $x > 0$, then $f^{-1}(x) =$

    (A) $(x+1)^2$
    (B) $x^2 + 2$
    (C) $x^2 + 1$
    (D) $(x-1)^2$
    (E) $(x+2)^2$

USE THIS SPACE FOR SCRATCHWORK.

21. When $4x^2 + 6x + L$ is divided by $x + 1$, the remainder is 2. Which of the following is the value of L ?

    (A) 4
    (B) 6
    (C) 10
    (D) 12
    (E) 15

22. What is the length of the major axis of the ellipse given by the equation $\dfrac{x^2}{10} + \dfrac{y^2}{20} = 1$?

    (A)   3.2
    (B)   4.5
    (C)   8.9
    (D) 10.0
    (E) 20.0

GO ON TO THE NEXT PAGE

23. If $f(x) = [x]$, where $[x]$ is the greatest integer less than or equal to x, which of the following is a graph of $f\left(\dfrac{x}{2}\right) - 1$?

USE THIS SPACE FOR SCRATCHWORK.

(A)

(B)

(C)

(D)

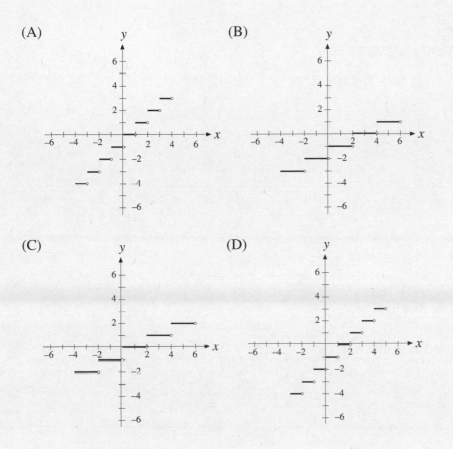

(E)

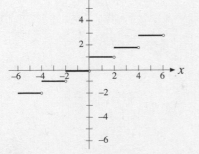

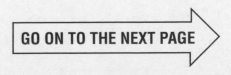
GO ON TO THE NEXT PAGE

24. Which of the following is equal to the positive value of $\sec(\cos^{-1}(0.3527))$?

(A) 0.01
(B) 0.94
(C) 1.69
(D) 2.84
(E) 69.35

USE THIS SPACE FOR SCRATCHWORK.

25. If $f(x) = x^2 + 5x + 6$, for what value of x will $f(x)$ have its minimum value?

(A) -3

(B) $-\dfrac{5}{2}$

(C) -2

(D) 0

(E) $\dfrac{5}{2}$

26. If the 20th term of an arithmetic sequence is 20 and the 50th term is 100, what is the first term of the sequence?

(A) -33.33
(B) -30.67
(C) 1.00
(D) 2.00
(E) 2.67

27. The polar equation $r \sin \theta = 1$ defines the graph of

(A) a line
(B) a circle
(C) an ellipse
(D) a parabola
(E) a hyperbola

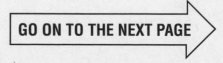
GO ON TO THE NEXT PAGE

28. For which of the following functions f is f^{-1} a function?

    I. $f(x) = x^2$

    II. $f(x) = x^3$

    III. $f(x) = |x|$

  (A) I only
  (B) II only
  (C) I and III only
  (D) II and III only
  (E) I, II, and III

USE THIS SPACE FOR SCRATCHWORK.

29. What is $\lim\limits_{x \to -1} \dfrac{x^3 - x}{x + 1}$?

  (A) -2
  (B) -1
  (C) 1
  (D) 2
  (E) The limit does not exist.

30. If $f(x) = \dfrac{e^{7x} + \sqrt{3}}{2}$, and $g(f(x)) = x$, then $g(x) =$

  (A) $\dfrac{\ln\left(2x - \sqrt{3}\right)}{7}$

  (B) $\dfrac{2x - \sqrt{3}}{e^7}$

  (C) $\dfrac{2x - \sqrt{3}}{7}$

  (D) $7 \ln(2x - \sqrt{3})$

  (E) $\dfrac{\left(2x - \sqrt{3}\right) \ln e}{7}$

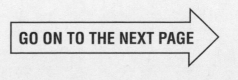

GO ON TO THE NEXT PAGE

31. A cube is inscribed in a sphere of radius 6. What is the volume of the cube?

    (A) $36\sqrt{3}$ (B) 36π (C) 216 (D) $192\sqrt{3}$ (E) $216\sqrt{3}$

USE THIS SPACE FOR SCRATCHWORK.

32. A right circular cone has height h and radius r. If the cone is cut into two pieces by a plane that passes through the midpoint of the height and is parallel to the base, then the volume of the larger of the two resulting solids is

    (A) $\dfrac{\pi r^2 h}{6}$

    (B) $\dfrac{\pi r^2 h}{3}$

    (C) $\dfrac{\pi r^2 h}{2}$

    (D) $\dfrac{2\pi r^2 h}{3}$

    (E) $\dfrac{7\pi r^2 h}{24}$

33. If $e^x \neq 1$ and $e^{x^2} = \dfrac{1}{\sqrt{3}^{\,x}}$, then $x =$

    (A) -1.73
    (B) -0.55
    (C) 1.00
    (D) 1.10
    (E) 1.73

34. If the graph of the equation $y = 2x^2 - 6x + c$ is tangent to the x-axis, then the value of c is

    (A) 3 (B) 3.5 (C) 4 (D) 4.5 (E) 5

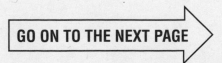
GO ON TO THE NEXT PAGE

35. If $x = i - 1$, then $x^2 + 2x + 2 =$

    (A) $2i + 4$
    (B) $4 + 2i$
    (C) 0
    (D) i
    (E) -2

USE THIS SPACE FOR SCRATCHWORK.

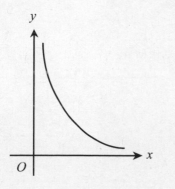

Figure 3

36. The curve shown in Figure 3 could represent a portion of the graph of which of the following functions?

    (A) $y = e^x$
    (B) $y = e^{-x}$
    (C) $y = 100 - x$
    (D) $y = x^2 - 3x + 2$
    (E) $xy = 3$

37. If two coins are removed at random from a purse containing three nickels and eight dimes, what is the probability that both coins will be dimes?

    (A) $\dfrac{14}{55}$ (B) $\dfrac{49}{110}$ (C) $\dfrac{28}{55}$ (D) $\dfrac{64}{121}$ (E) $\dfrac{32}{55}$

GO ON TO THE NEXT PAGE

38. A function $g(x)$ is odd if $g(-x) = -g(x)$ for all x and even if $g(x) = g(-x)$ for all x. Which of the following is the graph of a function that is both odd and even?

USE THIS SPACE FOR SCRATCHWORK.

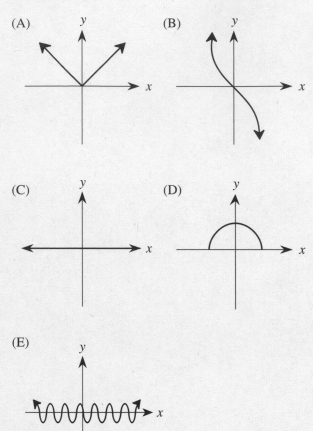

(A)

(B)

(C)

(D)

(E)

39. Points A and B lie on the edge of a circle with center O. If the circle has a radius of 5, and if the measure of $\angle AOB$ is 70°, what is the length of chord AB ?

(A) 2.9
(B) 4.7
(C) 5.0
(D) 5.7
(E) 9.4

GO ON TO THE NEXT PAGE

USE THIS SPACE FOR SCRATCHWORK.

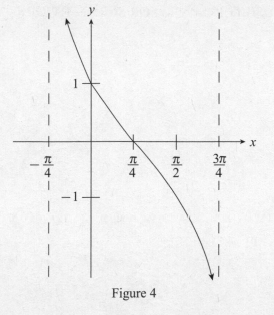

Figure 4

40. If the graph of $y = f(x)$ is shown in Figure 4, then which of the following could be true?

(A) $f(x) = \tan\left(x - \dfrac{\pi}{4}\right)$

(B) $f(x) = \cot\left(x - \dfrac{\pi}{4}\right)$

(C) $f(x) = \tan\left(x + \dfrac{\pi}{2}\right)$

(D) $f(x) = \cot\left(x + \dfrac{\pi}{4}\right)$

(E) $f(x) = \tan\left(x + \dfrac{\pi}{4}\right)$

41. Vectors v and w have components $(-3, 4)$ and $(12, 5)$, respectively. If $z = -(v + w)$, then z has components

(A) $(-9, -9)$

(B) $(5, 13)$

(C) $(-5, 13)$

(D) $(9, 9)$

(E) $\left(\dfrac{9}{2}, \dfrac{9}{2}\right)$

GO ON TO THE NEXT PAGE

42. If $f(x) = \dfrac{1}{\sqrt{2\pi}} e^{-\frac{x^2}{2}}$, then for which of the follow-

    ing values of x does $f(x) = 0.33$?

    (A) 0.62
    (B) 0.71
    (C) 1.36
    (D) 3.93
    (E) 4.95

USE THIS SPACE FOR SCRATCHWORK.

43. The system of equations given by
    $$2x + 3y = 7$$
    $$10x + cy = 3$$
    has solutions for all values of c EXCEPT

    (A) −15
    (B) −3
    (C)   3
    (D) 10
    (E) 15

44. If $f(x, y) = \dfrac{xy}{3}$ for all $x, y, f(a, b) = 15, f(b, c) =$

    20, and $f(a, c) = 10$, which of the following could

    be the product of a, b, and c ?

    (A)   18.26
    (B)   54.77
    (C)   284.60
    (D)   1,800.00
    (E)   3,000.00

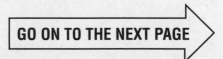

GO ON TO THE NEXT PAGE

45. If $x > 0$ and $y > 1$, then $\log_{x^2} y =$

    I. $\log_x y^2$

    II. $\log_x \sqrt{y}$

    III. $\log_x \left(\dfrac{y}{2} \right)$

  (A) I only
  (B) II only
  (C) III only
  (D) I and II only
  (E) II and III only

USE THIS SPACE FOR SCRATCHWORK.

46. Carlos is filling a spherical balloon with water. If he increases the volume of the balloon from 4,188.79 cubic centimeters to 14,137.167 cubic centimeters in 12 seconds, then what is the average rate at which he has increased the balloon's surface area?

  (A) 130.9 square centimeters per second
  (B) 314.159 square centimeters per second
  (C) 829.031 square centimeters per second
  (D) 1,570.796 square centimeters per second
  (E) 9,948.377 square centimeters per second

47. What is the value of $|6 - 3i|$?

  (A) -3

  (B) $3\sqrt{2}$

  (C) $3\sqrt{5}$

  (D) 9

  (E) 15

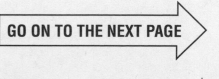

GO ON TO THE NEXT PAGE

48. The menu of a certain restaurant lists 10 items in column A and 20 items in column B. A family plans to share 5 items from column A and 5 items from column B. If none of the items are found in both columns, then how many different combinations of items could the family choose?

    (A)   25
    (B)   200
    (C)   3,425
    (D)   3,907,008
    (E) 5.63×10^{10}

USE THIS SPACE FOR SCRATCHWORK.

49. y varies directly as the square of x. When $y = 2.5$, $x = 0.5$. If $y = 80$, then x could equal

    (A) $-2\sqrt{2}$
    (B) -8
    (C) -10
    (D) -16
    (E) -64

50. Seven blue marbles and six red marbles are held in a single container. Marbles are randomly selected one at a time and not returned to the container. If the first two marbles selected are blue, what is the probability that at least two red marbles will be chosen in the next three selections?

    (A) $\dfrac{5}{33}$ (B) $\dfrac{5}{11}$ (C) $\dfrac{6}{11}$ (D) $\dfrac{19}{33}$ (E) $\dfrac{2}{3}$

STOP

IF YOU FINISH BEFORE TIME IS CALLED, YOU MAY CHECK YOUR WORK ON THIS TEST ONLY.
DO NOT WORK ON ANY OTHER TEST IN THIS BOOK.

HOW TO SCORE THE PRINCETON REVIEW
PRACTICE SAT MATH SUBJECT TEST

When you take the real exam, the proctors will collect your test booklet and bubble sheet and send your bubble sheet to New Jersey where a computer looks at the pattern of filled-in ovals on your bubble sheet and gives you a score. We couldn't include even a small computer with this book, so we are providing this more primitive way of scoring your exam.

Determining Your Score

STEP 1 Using the answers on the next page, determine how many questions you got right and how many you got wrong on the test. Remember: Questions that you do not answer don't count as either right answers or wrong answers.

STEP 2 List the number of right answers here.   (A) _____

STEP 3 List the number of wrong answers here. Now divide   (B) _____ ÷ 4 = (C) _____
that number by 4. (Use a calculator if you're feeling
particularly lazy.)   (A) _____ − (C) _____ = _____

STEP 4 Subtract the number of wrong answers divided by 4 from the number of correct answers. Round this score to the nearest whole number. This is your raw score.

STEP 5 To determine your real score, take the number from Step 4 above and look it up in the left column of the Score Conversion Table on page 425; the corresponding score on the right is your score on the exam.

MATHEMATICS LEVEL 2 SUBJECT TEST FORM A

Answer Key

1.	B	11.	B	21.	A	31.	D	41.	A
2.	C	12.	D	22.	C	32.	E	42.	A
3.	D	13.	A	23.	B	33.	B	43.	E
4.	A	14.	D	24.	D	34.	D	44.	C
5.	D	15.	D	25.	B	35.	C	45.	B
6.	E	16.	B	26.	B	36.	E	46.	A
7.	E	17.	B	27.	A	37.	C	47.	C
8.	B	18.	C	28.	B	38.	C	48.	D
9.	D	19.	D	29.	D	39.	D	49.	A
10.	D	20.	A	30.	A	40.	D	50.	D

MATHEMATICS LEVEL 2 SUBJECT TEST
SCORE CONVERSION TABLE

Raw Score	Scaled Score	Raw Score	Scaled Score	Raw Score	Scaled Score
50	800	25	630	0	350
49	800	24	630	−1	330
48	800	23	620	−2	320
47	800	22	610	−3	300
46	800	21	600	−4	280
45	800	20	590	−5	270
44	800	19	590	−6	250
43	800	18	580	−7	230
42	790	17	570	−8	220
41	780	16	560	−9	200
40	770	15	560	−10	200
39	760	14	540	−11	200
38	750	13	530	−12	200
37	740	12	520		
36	730	11	500		
35	720	10	490		
34	710	9	470		
33	700	8	460		
32	690	7	440		
31	690	6	430		
30	680	5	400		
29	670	4	400		
28	660	3	380		
27	650	2	370		
26	640	1	360		

Chapter 16
Mathematics Level 2
Practice Test Form B

MATHEMATICS LEVEL 2 TEST FORM B

For each of the following problems, decide which is the BEST of the choices given. If the exact numerical value is not one of the choices, select the choice that best approximates this value. Then fill in the corresponding oval on the answer sheet.

Notes: (1) A scientific or graphing calculator will be necessary for answering some (but not all) of the questions on this test. For each question, you will have to decide whether or not you should use a calculator.

(2) For some questions in this test you may have to decide whether your calculator should be in the radian mode or the degree mode.

(3) Figures that accompany problems on this test are intended to provide information useful in solving the problems. They are drawn as accurately as possible EXCEPT when it is stated in a specific problem that its figure is not drawn to scale. All figures lie in a plane unless otherwise indicated.

(4) Unless otherwise specified, the domain of any function f is assumed to be the set of all real numbers x for which $f(x)$ is a real number. The range of f is assumed to be the set of all real numbers $f(x)$, where x is in the domain of f.

(5) Reference information that may be useful in answering the questions on this test can be found below.

THE FOLLOWING INFORMATION IS FOR YOUR REFERENCE IN ANSWERING SOME OF THE QUESTIONS ON THIS TEST.

Volume of a right circular cone with radius r and height h:

$$V = \frac{1}{3}\pi r^2 h$$

Lateral area of a right circular cone with circumference of the base c and slant height ℓ: $S = \frac{1}{2}c\ell$

Volume of a sphere with radius r: $V = \frac{4}{3}\pi r^3$

Surface area of a sphere with radius r: $S = 4\pi r^2$

Volume of a pyramid with base area B and height h:

$$V = \frac{1}{3}Bh$$

---

1. If $xy \neq 0$ and $3x = 0.3y$, then $\dfrac{y}{x} =$

   (A) 0.1   (B) 1.0   (C) 3.0   (D) 9.0   (E) 10.0

2. If $f(x) = \left(3\sqrt{x} - 4\right)^2$, then how much does $f(x)$ increase as x goes from 2 to 3 ?

   (A) 1.43
   (B) 1.37
   (C) 1.00
   (D) 0.74
   (E) 0.06

USE THIS SPACE FOR SCRATCHWORK.

GO ON TO THE NEXT PAGE

3. What is the equation of a line with a y-intercept of 3 and an x-intercept of -5 ?

   (A) $y = 0.6x + 3$
   (B) $y = 1.7x - 3$
   (C) $y = 3x + 5$
   (D) $y = 3x - 5$
   (E) $y = -5x + 3$

USE THIS SPACE FOR SCRATCHWORK.

4. For what positive value of a does $a - \sqrt{5a + 18}$ equal -4 ?

   (A) 0.56
   (B) 1.00
   (C) 1.12
   (D) 2.06
   (E) 4.12

5. If the second term in an arithmetic sequence is 4, and the tenth term is 15, what is the first term in the sequence?

   (A) 1.18
   (B) 1.27
   (C) 1.38
   (D) 2.63
   (E) 2.75

6. If $g(x) = \left| 5x^2 - x^3 \right|$, then $g(6) =$
   (A) -54 (B) -36 (C) 36 (D) 216 (E) 396

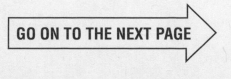
GO ON TO THE NEXT PAGE

7. Which of the following graphs of functions is symmetrical with respect to the line $y = x$?

USE THIS SPACE FOR SCRATCHWORK.

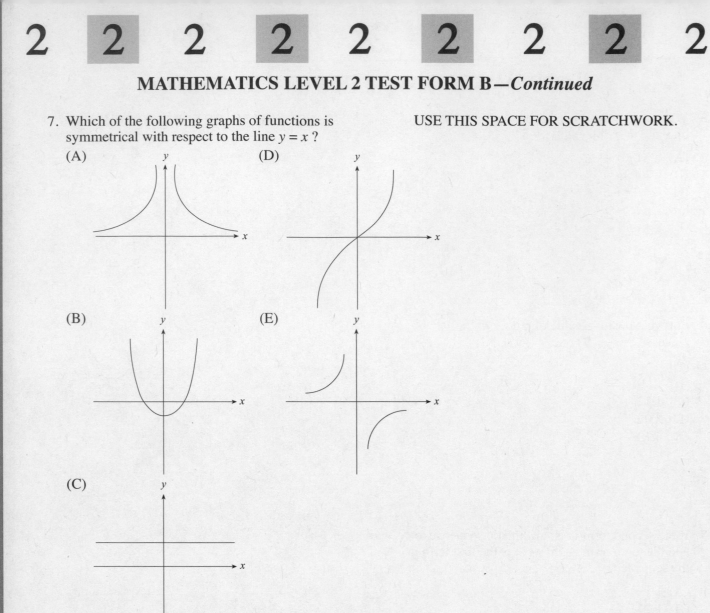

8. If $0° \le A \le 90°$ and $\sin A = \dfrac{1}{3} \sin 75°$, then $A =$

(A) 12.9° (B) 18.8° (C) 25.0° (D) 32.2° (E) 45.0°

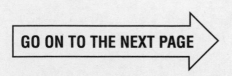
GO ON TO THE NEXT PAGE

9. If $f(x) = \dfrac{1}{2}x^2 - 6x + 11$, then what is the minimum value of $f(x)$?

USE THIS SPACE FOR SCRATCHWORK.

(A) −8.0
(B) −7.0
(C)   3.2
(D)   6.0
(E) 11.0

10. $\big| x \quad y \big| \, | \, \big| y \quad x \big| =$

(A) 0

(B) $x - y$

(C) $y - x$

(D) $2|x - y|$

(E) $2|x + y|$

$$0° \le A \le 90°$$
$$0° \le B \le 90°$$

11. If $\sin A = \cos B$, then which of the following must be true?

(A) $A = B$

(B) $A = 2B$

(C) $A = B + 45$

(D) $A = 90 - B$

(E) $A = B + 180$

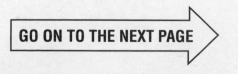
GO ON TO THE NEXT PAGE

USE THIS SPACE FOR SCRATCHWORK.

	Total Units Production	Flawed Units
April	569	15
May	508	18
June	547	16

Figure 1

12. Each month, some of the automobiles produced at the Carco plant have flawed catalytic converters. According to the chart in Figure 1, what is the probability that a car produced in one of the three months shown will be flawed?

(A) 0.01
(B) 0.02
(C) 0.03
(D) 0.04
(E) 0.05

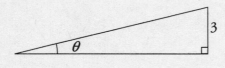

Figure 2

13. Adamsvillle building codes require that a wheelchair ramp must rise at an angle (θ) of no less than 5° and no more than 7° from the horizontal. If a wheelchair ramp rises exactly 3 feet as shown in Figure 2, which of the following could be the length of the ramp?

(A) 19.0 feet
(B) 24.0 feet
(C) 28.0 feet
(D) 35.0 feet
(E) 42.0 feet

GO ON TO THE NEXT PAGE

USE THIS SPACE FOR SCRATCHWORK.

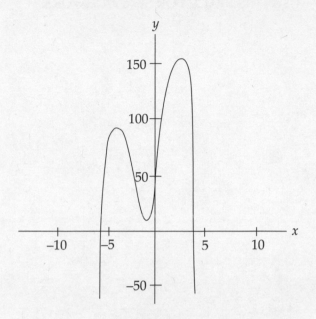

Figure 3

14. Figure 3 represents the graph of the function
$y = -x^4 - 4x^3 + 14x^2 + 45x - n$. Which of the following could be the value of n ?

(A) −50
(B) −18
(C)   50
(D) 100
(E) 150

15. What value does $\dfrac{x^2 - x - 6}{3x + 6}$ approach as x
approaches −2 ?

(A) −1.67
(B) −0.60
(C)   0
(D)   1.00
(E)   2.33

GO ON TO THE NEXT PAGE

16. In Titheland, the first 1,000 florins of any inheritance are untaxed. After the first 1,000 florins, inheritances are taxed at a rate of 65%. How large must an inheritance be, to the nearest florin, in order to amount to 2,500 florins after the inheritance tax?

   (A) 7,143
   (B) 5,286
   (C) 4,475
   (D) 3,475
   (E) 3,308

USE THIS SPACE FOR SCRATCHWORK.

17. In an engineering test, a rocket sled is propelled into a target. If the sled's distance d in meters from the target is given by the formula $d = -1.5t^2 + 120$, where t is the number of seconds after rocket ignition, then how many seconds have passed since rocket ignition when the sled is 10 meters from the target?

   (A) 2.58
   (B) 8.56
   (C) 8.94
   (D) 9.31
   (E) 11.26

18. $\sum\limits_{k=1}^{10} 3k - 2 =$

   (A) 25   (B) 28   (C) 145   (D) 280   (E) 290

19. If $e^x = 5$, then $x =$

   (A) 0.23
   (B) 1.61
   (C) 7.76
   (D) 148.41
   (E) 13.59

GO ON TO THE NEXT PAGE

20. If the greatest possible distance between two points within a certain rectangular solid is 12, then which of the following could be the dimensions of this solid?

    (A) $3 \times 3 \times 9$
    (B) $3 \times 6 \times 7$
    (C) $3 \times 8 \times 12$
    (D) $4 \times 7 \times 9$
    (E) $4 \times 8 \times 8$

USE THIS SPACE FOR SCRATCHWORK.

21. Runner A travels *a* feet every minute. Runner B travels *b* feet every second. In one hour, runner A travels how much farther than runner B, in feet?

    (A) $a - 60b$
    (B) $a^2 - 60b^2$
    (C) $360a - b$
    (D) $60(a - b)$
    (E) $60(a - 60b)$

22. A right triangle has sides in the ratio of $5 : 12 : 13$. What is the measure of the smallest angle in the triangle, in degrees?

    (A) 13.34
    (B) 22.62
    (C) 34.14
    (D) 42.71
    (E) 67.38

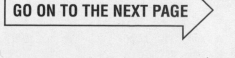

GO ON TO THE NEXT PAGE

23. If $f(x) = \dfrac{1}{x+1}$, and $g(x) = \dfrac{1}{x} + 1$, then $g(f(x)) =$

USE THIS SPACE FOR SCRATCHWORK.

(A) 2

(B) $x + 2$

(C) $2x + 2$

(D) $\dfrac{x+2}{x+1}$

(E) $\dfrac{2x+1}{x+1}$

24. If $f(x) = (x - \pi)(x - 3)(x - e)$, then what is the greatest possible distance between points at which the graph of $y = f(x)$ intersects the x-axis?

(A) 0.14
(B) 0.28
(C) 0.36
(D) 0.42
(E) 0.72

25. $\dfrac{x!}{(x-2)!} =$

(A) 0.5
(B) 2.0
(C) x
(D) $x^2 - x$
(E) $x^2 - 2x + 1$

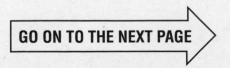

GO ON TO THE NEXT PAGE

USE THIS SPACE FOR SCRATCHWORK.

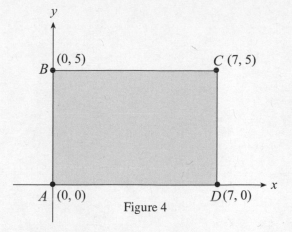

Figure 4

26. What is the volume of the solid created by rotating rectangle *ABCD* in Figure 4 around the *y*-axis?

    (A) 219.91
    (B) 245.00
    (C) 549.78
    (D) 769.69
    (E) 816.24

27. If $f(x, y) = \dfrac{x^2 - 2xy + y^2}{x^2 - y^2}$, then $f(-x, -y) =$

    (A) 1

    (B) $\dfrac{1}{x + y}$

    (C) $\dfrac{-x + y}{x + y}$

    (D) $\dfrac{-x + y}{x - y}$

    (E) $\dfrac{x - y}{x + y}$

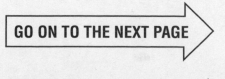
GO ON TO THE NEXT PAGE

28. In order to disprove the hypothesis, "No number divisible by 5 is less than 5," it would be necessary to

    (A) prove the statement false for all numbers divisible by 5
    (B) demonstrate that numbers greater than 5 are often divisible by 5
    (C) indicate that infinitely many numbers greater than 5 are divisible by 5
    (D) supply one case in which a number divisible by 5 is less than 5
    (E) show that a statement true of numbers greater than 5 is also true of numbers less than 5

USE THIS SPACE FOR SCRATCHWORK.

29. A parallelogram has vertices at $(0, 0)$, $(5, 0)$, and $(2, 3)$. What are the coordinates of the fourth vertex?

    (A) $(3, -2)$
    (B) $(5, 3)$
    (C) $(7, 3)$
    (D) $(10, 5)$
    (E) It cannot be determined from the information given.

30. The expression $\dfrac{x^2 + 3x - 4}{2x^2 + 10x + 8}$ is undefined for what values of x ?

    (A) $x = \{-1, -4\}$
    (B) $x = \{-1\}$
    (C) $x = \{0\}$
    (D) $x = \{1, -4\}$
    (E) $x = \{0, 1, 4\}$

GO ON TO THE NEXT PAGE

31. For which of the following functions is $f(x) > 0$ for all real values of x ?

    I. $f(x) = x^2 + 1$
    II. $f(x) = 1 - \sin x$
    III. $f(x) = \pi (\pi^{x-1})$

    (A) I only
    (B) II only
    (C) I and III only
    (D) II and III only
    (E) I, II, and III

USE THIS SPACE FOR SCRATCHWORK.

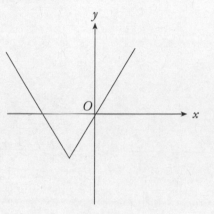

Figure 5

32. The graph of $y = f(x)$ is shown in Figure 5. Which of the following could be the graph of $y = -f(-x)$?

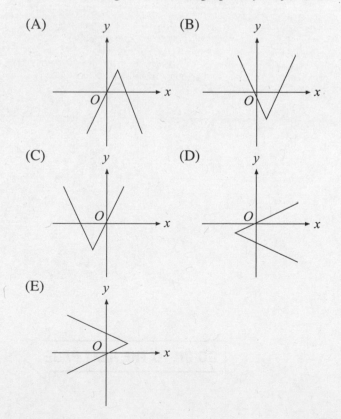

(A)

(B)

(C)

(D)

(E)

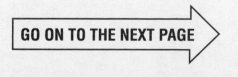
GO ON TO THE NEXT PAGE

33. A wire is stretched from the top of a two-foot-tall anchor to the top of a 50-foot-tall antenna. If the wire is straight and has a slope of $\frac{2}{5}$, then what is the length of the wire in feet?

    (A)   89.18
    (B)   120.00
    (C)   123.26
    (D)   129.24
    (E)   134.63

USE THIS SPACE FOR SCRATCHWORK.

34. If $\frac{3\pi}{2} < \theta < 2\pi$ and $\sec \theta = 4$, then $\tan \theta =$

    (A)   −3.93
    (B)   −3.87
    (C)   0.26
    (D)   3.87
    (E)   3.93

35. Circle O is centered at $(-3, 1)$ and has a radius of 4. Circle P is centered at $(4, -4)$ and has a radius of n. If circle O is externally tangent to circle P, then what is the value of n ?

    (A)   4.00
    (B)   4.37
    (C)   4.60
    (D)   5.28
    (E)   6.25

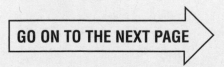

36. In triangle ABC, $\dfrac{\sin A}{\sin B} = \dfrac{7}{10}$ and $\dfrac{\sin B}{\sin C} = \dfrac{5}{2}$. If angles A, B, and C are opposite sides a, b, and c, respectively, and the triangle has a perimeter of 16, then what is the length of a ?

    (A) 2.7
    (B) 4.7
    (C) 5.3
    (D) 8.0
    (E) 14.0

USE THIS SPACE FOR SCRATCHWORK.

x	$h(x)$
-1	0
0	3
1	0
2	3

37. The table of values above shows selected coordinate pairs on the graph of $h(x)$. Which of the following could be $h(x)$?

    (A) $x(x + 1)(x - 1)$
    (B) $(x + 1)^2(x - 1)$
    (C) $(x - 1)(x + 2)^2$
    (D) $(x - 1)^2(x + 3)$
    (E) $(x - 1)(x + 1)(2x - 3)$

$$a + b + 2c = 7$$
$$a - 2b = 8$$
$$3b + 2c = n$$

38. For what values of n does the system of equations above have no real solutions?

    (A) $n \neq -1$
    (B) $n \leq 0$
    (C) $n \geq 1$
    (D) $n > 7$
    (E) $n = -15$

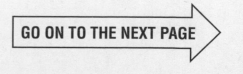

GO ON TO THE NEXT PAGE

USE THIS SPACE FOR SCRATCHWORK.

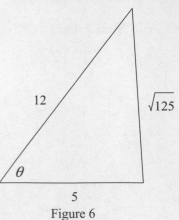

Figure 6

Note: Figure not drawn to scale.

39. In Figure 6, what is the value of θ in degrees?

(A) 62.00
(B) 65.38
(C) 65.91
(D) 68.49
(E) 68.70

40. If $\begin{vmatrix} l & m & n \\ p & q & r \\ s & t & u \end{vmatrix} = A$, then $\begin{vmatrix} 2l & 2m & 2n \\ 2p & 2q & 2r \\ 2s & 2t & 2u \end{vmatrix} =$

(A) $2A$
(B) $4A$
(C) $6A$
(D) $8A$
(E) $18A$

41. In the function $g(x) = A[\sin(Bx + C)] + D$, constants are represented by A, B, C, and D. If $g(x)$ is to be altered in such a way that both its period and amplitude are increased, which of the following constants must be <u>increased</u>?

(A) A only
(B) B only
(C) C only
(D) A and B only
(E) C and D only

GO ON TO THE NEXT PAGE

42. All of the elements of list M and list N are arranged in exactly 20 pairs, such that every element from list M is paired with a distinct element from list N. If in each such pair, the element from list M is larger than the element from list N, then which of the following statements must be true?

(A) The median of the elements in M is greater than the median of the elements in N.

(B) Any element of M is greater than any element of N.

(C) The mode of the elements in M is greater than the mode of the elements in N.

(D) The range of the elements in M is greater than the range of the elements in N.

(E) The standard deviation of the elements in M is greater than the standard deviation of the elements in N.

USE THIS SPACE FOR SCRATCHWORK.

43. If $3, 5, 8.333$, and 13.889 are the first four terms of a sequence, then which of the following could define that sequence?

(A) $a_0 = 3; a_{n+1} = a_n + 2$

(B) $a_0 = 3; a_{n+1} = 2a_n - 1$

(C) $a_0 = 3; a_n = a_{n-1} + \dfrac{40}{9}$

(D) $a_0 = 3; a_n = \dfrac{5}{3}a_{n-1}$

(E) $a_0 = 3; a_n = \dfrac{7}{3}a_{n-1} - \dfrac{40}{9}a_{n-1}$

44. If $0 \le n \le \dfrac{\pi}{2}$ and $\cos(\cos n) = 0.8$, then $\tan n =$

(A) 0.65
(B) 0.75
(C) 0.83
(D) 1.19
(E) 1.22

GO ON TO THE NEXT PAGE

45. The height of a cylinder is equal to one-half of n, where n is equal to one-half of the cylinder's diameter. What is the surface area of this cylinder in terms of n ?

(A) $\dfrac{3\pi n^2}{2}$

(B) $2\pi n^2$

(C) $3\pi n^2$

(D) $2\pi n^2 + \dfrac{\pi n}{2}$

(E) $2\pi n^2 + \pi n$

USE THIS SPACE FOR SCRATCHWORK.

46. If $(\tan\theta - 1)^2 = 4$, then which of the following could be the value of θ in radian measure?

(A) −0.785
(B) 1.373
(C) 1.504
(D) 1.512
(E) 3

47. Which of the following expresses the range of values of $y = g(x)$, if $g(x) = \dfrac{5}{x+4}$?

(A) $\{y:\ y \neq 0\}$
(B) $\{y:\ y \neq 1.25\}$
(C) $\{y:\ y \neq -4.00\}$
(D) $\{y:\ y > 0\}$
(E) $\{y:\ y \leq -1 \text{ or } y \geq 1\}$

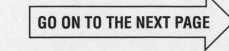
GO ON TO THE NEXT PAGE

48. If $\csc \theta = \dfrac{1}{3t}$, then where defined, $\cos \theta =$

    USE THIS SPACE FOR SCRATCHWORK.

    (A) $3t$

    (B) $\sqrt{1 - 3t^2}$

    (C) $\sqrt{1 - 9t^2}$

    (D) $\dfrac{3t}{\sqrt{1 - 3t^2}}$

    (E) $\dfrac{3t}{\sqrt{1 - 9t^2}}$

49. If $f(x, y) = \dfrac{xy + y}{x + y}$, then which of the following

    statements must be true?

    I. If $x = 0$ and $y \neq 0$, then $f(x, y) = 1$.
    II. If $x = 1$, then $f(x, x) = 1$.
    III. $f(x, y) = f(y, x)$

    (A) I only
    (B) II only
    (C) I and II only
    (D) I and III only
    (E) I, II, and III

50. A triangle is formed by the x-axis, the y-axis, and
    the line $y = mx + b$. If $m = -b^3$, then what is the
    volume of the cone generated by rotating this
    triangle around the x-axis?

    (A) $\dfrac{\pi}{9}$

    (B) $\dfrac{\pi}{3}$

    (C) π

    (D) 3π

    (E) 9π

STOP

IF YOU FINISH BEFORE TIME IS CALLED, YOU MAY CHECK YOUR WORK ON THIS TEST ONLY.
DO NOT WORK ON ANY OTHER TEST IN THIS BOOK.

HOW TO SCORE THE PRINCETON REVIEW PRACTICE SAT MATH SUBJECT TEST

When you take the real exam, the proctors will collect your test booklet and bubble sheet and send your bubble sheet to New Jersey where a computer looks at the pattern of filled-in ovals on your bubble sheet and gives you a score. We couldn't include even a small computer with this book, so we are providing this more primitive way of scoring your exam.

Determining Your Score

STEP 1 Using the answers on the next page, determine how many questions you got right and how many you got wrong on the test. Remember: Questions that you do not answer don't count as either right answers or wrong answers.

STEP 2 List the number of right answers here.

(A) _____

STEP 3 List the number of wrong answers here. Now divide that number by 4. (Use a calculator if you're feeling particularly lazy.)

(B) _____ ÷ 4 = (C) _____

(A) _____ – (C) _____ = _____

STEP 4 Subtract the number of wrong answers divided by 4 from the number of correct answers. Round this score to the nearest whole number. This is your raw score.

STEP 5 To determine your real score, take the number from Step 4 above and look it up in the left column of the Score Conversion Table on page 448; the corresponding score on the right is your score on the exam.

MATHEMATICS LEVEL 2 SUBJECT TEST FORM B

Answer Key

1.	E	11.	D	21.	E	31.	C	41.	A
2.	B	12.	C	22.	B	32.	A	42.	A
3.	A	13.	C	23.	B	33.	D	43.	D
4.	A	14.	A	24.	D	34.	B	44.	D
5.	D	15.	A	25.	D	35.	C	45.	C
6.	C	16.	B	26.	D	36.	C	46.	A
7.	E	17.	B	27.	E	37.	E	47.	A
8.	B	18.	C	28.	D	38.	A	48.	C
9.	B	19.	B	29.	E	39.	D	49.	C
10.	D	20.	E	30.	A	40.	D	50.	B

MATHEMATICS LEVEL 2 SUBJECT TEST
SCORE CONVERSION TABLE

Raw Score	Scaled Score	Raw Score	Scaled Score	Raw Score	Scaled Score
50	800	25	630	0	350
49	800	24	630	−1	330
48	800	23	620	−2	320
47	800	22	610	−3	300
46	800	21	600	−4	280
45	800	20	590	−5	270
44	800	19	590	−6	250
43	800	18	580	−7	230
42	790	17	570	−8	220
41	780	16	560	−9	200
40	770	15	560	−10	200
39	760	14	540	−11	200
38	750	13	530	−12	200
37	740	12	520		
36	730	11	500		
35	720	10	490		
34	710	9	470		
33	700	8	460		
32	690	7	440		
31	690	6	430		
30	680	5	400		
29	670	4	400		
28	660	3	380		
27	650	2	370		
26	640	1	360		

Chapter 17
Level 1 Practice Test
Form A
Answers and
Explanations

Question	Answer	Explanation
1	B	Make the bases on both sides of the equation the same. 81 is the same as 3^4. So $3^{4x} = 3^4$, which means that $x = 1$.
2	A	The fraction $\dfrac{b}{a}$ is the reciprocal of $\dfrac{a}{b}$; it's just flipped over. To find the numerical value of $\dfrac{b}{a}$, just flip the numerical value of $\dfrac{a}{b}$, which is 0.625. Your calculator will tell you that $\dfrac{1}{0.625} = 1.6$.
3	C	PITA, starting with (C). Use your calculator to see which value makes the equation true. The first one you try, (C), is correct. To solve the problem algebraically, isolate x one step at a time. First, multiply through by 3 on the right: $x - 3 = 3 - 3x$. Next, add $3x$ to each side, and then add 3 to each side, to get $4x = 6$. Divide each side by 4 to get $x = \dfrac{6}{4}$, or 1.5.
4	D	This one's much clearer if you draw it. You can think of segments AC and BD as overlapping segments, where BC is the amount of the overlap. The lengths of AC and BD add up to 27, but it's only a distance of 21 from A to D. The difference, a distance of 6, is the overlap. That's the length of BC.
5	D	Notice that the x-coordinate in both points is the same. So you just have to find the difference in the y-coordinates. The difference is $5 - (-12) = 17$.
6	A	The value at which a line intersects the y-axis is called the y-intercept. That's the y-coordinate of the point of intersection; the x-coordinate is zero at every point on the y-axis, so eliminate answers (D) and (E). If you put the line $3y + 5 = x - 1$ into the form $y = mx + b$, then b will be the y-intercept. The rearranged equation looks like $y = \dfrac{1}{3}x - 2$. The y-intercept is -2, and you know the x-coordinate must be 0, so the point of intersection has the coordinates $(0, -2)$.
7	C	 Figure 1 The fact that m and n are parallel tells you that Fred's theorem is at work here. That means that all the big angles are equal, all the small angles are equal, and any big angle plus any small angle equals 180°. The big angles measure 125°, so the small ones must measure 55°. Don't choose (B); it's a partial answer! Because d and f are both small angles, $d + f = 110°$.

Question	Answer	Explanation
8	B	Translate the words into math: $\sqrt[3]{\sqrt{x}} = 2$. Now peel away. First cube both sides: $\sqrt{x} = 8$. Now square both sides: $x = 64$. PITA works well, too.
9	E	When you're given two equations extremely similar in form, you're probably looking at classic ETS-style simultaneous equations. The best way to solve these? Rack 'em, stack 'em, add or subtract 'em! (Isn't that satisfying?) In this case, adding the two equations cancels out the b term, leaving you with the equation $8a = 16$, so $a = 2$.
10	E	Plug -3 into the function: $(-3^2) - 3(-3) = 18$.
11	E	Remember that the absolute value of something can be thought of as the distance on a number line between that value and zero. If the absolute value of some value is greater than 3, then that value must be more than 3 away from zero. In this case, you're dealing with y-coordinates and you want all points 3 units or more from the x-axis, where $y = 0$. Only (E) fits the bill. If this kind of reasoning is unclear to you, just try picking points in the shaded region of each graph, and seeing whether they make the equation $|y| \geq 3$ true. Any answer choice whose graph contains "illegal" points can be eliminated.
12	E	Direct variation between two quantities means that they always have the same quotient. In this case, it means that $\dfrac{m}{n}$ must always equal 5. To find the value of m when $n = 2.2$, set up the equation $\dfrac{m}{2.2} = 5$, and solve for m. You'll find that $m = 11$.
13	B	To find the slope of the line easily, get its equation into the form $y = mx + b$, where m will be the value of the slope. To express $3y - 5 = 7 - 2x$ in this form, just isolate y. You'll find that $y = -\dfrac{2}{3}x + 4$. Here, the slope of the line (m) is $-\dfrac{2}{3}$.
14	D	A quick review of exponent rules—when raising powers to powers, multiply exponents; when multiplying powers of the same base, add exponents; and when dividing powers of the same base, subtract exponents. For this problem, you have to do all three. Take the steps one at a time, following the rule of PEMDAS. $\dfrac{\left(n^3\right)^6 \times \left(n^4\right)^5}{n^2} = \dfrac{n^{18} \times n^{20}}{n^2} = \dfrac{n^{38}}{n^2} = n^{36}$.
15	A	Work from the inside out. $g(2) = 2^2 + 7 = 11$. Now put in 11 for x: $f(11) = 5 - 2(11) = -17$.

Question	Answer	Explanation
16	D	With few exceptions, logic questions on the Math Level 1 test you on the contra-positive. The idea is that, given a statement like "If *A*, then *B*," the only thing you automatically know is the contrapositive: "If not *B*, then not *A*." Here, you're told that no doctoral candidates graduate. In Cookie Monster language, that would read "If doctoral student, then no graduate." The contrapositive would be "If graduate, then not doctoral student." That's almost exactly what (D) says (since there are only engineers and doctoral candidates at this school, not being a doctoral candidate is the same as being an engineer). The other answer choices all talk about subjects you don't know anything about, like the number of students or the quality of their scholarly skills. You can eliminate those answer choices.
17	D	 Figure 2 There are a few simple rules for lines tangent to circles. Most important, a tangent line is always perpendicular to the radius it meets. That makes both $\triangle APO$ and $\triangle BPO$ right triangles. In each triangle, segment *PO* is the hypotenuse, so it's impossible for *PB* to be longer than *PO*. Statement I is therefore not true, and (A), (C), and (E) can be eliminated. Both of the remaining answers, (B) and (D), contain Statement II, so it must be true. Concentrate on Statement III. Both $\angle PAO$ and $\angle PBO$ are right angles, so $a + d = 180$. Since the other two angles, $\angle APB$ and $\angle AOB$, complete a quadrilateral, $(x + y)$ and $(b + c)$ must also add up to 180° (making a total of 360° in the quadrilateral). Statement III must also be true, and (D) is correct.
18	E	Plug In $x = 1,000$. Then Rodney has earned $4 \times 1,000 = \$4,000$ and spent \$200, so he has made a total of \$3,800. That's (E).
19	E	All the sides of a square are the same. So each side must be 15. Since the area of a square is (side)^2, the area must be 225.
20	C	Plug In 0.5 for *n*. Now $n^2 = 0.25$, $\sqrt{n} = 0.707$, $|n| = 0.5$, $-n = -0.5$, and $\frac{1}{n} = 2$. This makes (A), (B), (D), and (E) true. (C) is false because $\sqrt{3} = n$ whenever *n* is positive.
21	D	Move the equation around so that it's in $y = mx + b$ formula: $y = \frac{3}{2}x - 8$. So an equation perpendicular would have a slope of $-\frac{2}{3}$. The only one is (D).

Question	Answer	Explanation
22	C	You can just factor this one, and then cancel. $$\left(\frac{x^2-4}{4}\right)\left(\frac{8}{2x+4}\right)=$$ $$\left(\frac{(x+2)(x-2)}{4}\right)\left(\frac{2\times4}{2(x+2)}\right)=x-2$$ Alternatively, you could use Plugging In.
23	E	Use the formula for surface area of a sphere with radius r. In case you forget the equation, it is given in the reference information at the beginning of the test: $S = 4\pi r^2$. You are given S, so write $75 = 4\pi r^2$, and therefore $r = 2.443$. The formula for volume of a sphere with radius r is also given in the reference info; it's $V = \frac{4}{3}\pi r^3$. So plug $r = 2.443$ into the formula. $V = 61.075$.
24	C	Plug In 45° for each angle; this makes them complementary and congruent. Next, draw four lines intersecting at the same point, forming eight 45° angles; angles directly across from each other are vertical, and angles next to each other are adjacent. This shows that (A), (B), (D), and (E) can be true of acute angles. Acute angles measure *less* than 90°, so there's no way for two of them to add up to 180° and be supplementary.
25	B	To simplify the expression $\frac{(3-i)^2}{2}$, follow PEMDAS and do the exponent first—you'll need to use FOIL to square the binomial on top of the fraction. You should get $\frac{9-6i+i^2}{2}$. Since i is the square root of –1, the value of i^2 is –1, and $\frac{9-6i-1}{2} = \frac{8-6i}{2}$. Then just divide by 2 and get the expression in its simplest form, $4 - 3i$.

Question	Answer	Explanation
26	C

Figure 3

The diagram of this triangle gives you the length of the hypotenuse and the measure of an angle, and asks for the length of the side opposite that angle. That's enough to set up a simple equation using the SOHCAHTOA definition of the sine— $\sin \theta = \dfrac{O}{H}$. Plugging the values from this triangle into the equation gets you $\sin 38° = \dfrac{x}{4}$. Use your calculator to find the value of $\sin 38°$, and you get the equation $0.61566 = \dfrac{x}{4}$. Multiply both sides by 4 to get $x = 2.4626$. |
| 27 | A | The range of a function is the set of values the function can produce; on a graph, the range corresponds to the y-coordinates of the curve. Looking at this graph, you'll see that it seems to continue downward (in the negative y-direction) forever. The range doesn't seem to have a minimum value. (D) and (E) can therefore be eliminated. The graph has an apparent maximum value of 2. That makes (A) a strong contender. The function's graph is also a continuous curve; that means it occupies a range of values, not just a few specific ones. Only (A) describes such a range of values. |
| 28 | B | Use three average pies:

|
| 29 | B | This one isn't really vulnerable to shortcuts or techniques. You pretty much have to visualize the situation described in each answer choice and find the one that produces exactly eight points of intersection. When a cube is inscribed in a sphere, each of the cube's 8 corners touches the inside of the sphere. |

Question	Answer	Explanation
30	B	The median of ten numbers will be the average of the fifth and sixth numbers. Because the numbers are distinct, the fifth and sixth numbers cannot be the same, so the median will be between them. This makes II impossible—eliminate (C) and (E). Also, there is no mode because there are no repeated numbers. This makes III impossible—eliminate (D). Some creative Plugging In can make I work: 1, 2, 3, 4, 5, 6, 7, 8, 9, and 15 have a mean of 6, for example.
31	E	Since there are variables in the answer choices, you should Plug In. Try $x = 3$. We are trying to find $f(3 + 4) = f(7) = 2(7)^2 + 2$, which is 100, our target number. Now plug 3 in for x in the answer choices, to see which answer choice hits the target. Only (E) works.
32	A	PITA. Plug In values from the answer choices, and see which one makes the equation true. Only (A) does it. When solving this question algebraically, the trick is to isolate x one step at a time. The correct order is below. $$\frac{9\left(\sqrt{x}-2\right)^2}{4} = 6.25$$ $$9\left(\sqrt{x}-2\right)^2 = 25$$ $$\left(\sqrt{x}-2\right)^2 = \frac{25}{9}$$ $$\sqrt{x}-2 = \frac{5}{3} \text{ or } -\frac{5}{3}$$ $$\sqrt{x} = \frac{11}{3} \text{ or } \frac{1}{3}$$ $$x = \frac{121}{9} \text{ or } \frac{1}{9}$$ $$x = 13.44 \text{ or } 0.11$$ Only (A) represents a possible value of x.

Question	Answer	Explanation
33	D	Plug In 30° for θ and use your calculator; this makes the whole expression equal 0.25, which is $\sin^2(30°)$. (Remember that this means to find $\sin(30°)$ first, which is 0.5, and then square that result.) If you want to see how to simplify the expression, read on… The best place to start is usually with any tangent functions in the expression, using the fact that $\tan\theta = \dfrac{\sin\theta}{\cos\theta}$: $$\left(\frac{1}{\cos\theta} - \frac{\sin\theta}{\tan\theta}\right)(\cos\theta) =$$ $$\left(\frac{1}{\cos\theta} - \frac{\sin\theta}{\frac{\sin\theta}{\cos\theta}}\right)(\cos\theta) =$$ $$\left(\frac{1}{\cos\theta} - \left(\frac{\sin\theta}{1}\right)\left(\frac{\cos\theta}{\sin\theta}\right)\right)(\cos\theta) =$$ $$\left(\frac{1}{\cos\theta} - \cos\theta\right)(\cos\theta) =$$ $$\left(\frac{\cos\theta}{\cos\theta} - \cos^2\theta\right) =$$ $$1 - \cos^2\theta$$ Once you've simplified it this far, you can use a basic trigonometric identity to simplify the expression one step further: $1 - \cos^2\theta = \sin^2\theta$.
34	B	Plug In! Suppose $x = 2$. Then $f(x) = 64$ and $f(-x) = -64$, making Statement I not true. You can eliminate any answer choice containing I—(A), (C), and (E). Both of the remaining answer choices contain Statement II, so it must be true. Go straight to Statement III: $\frac{1}{2}f(2) = 32$ and $f\left(\frac{1}{2}(2)\right) = 2$. Statement III is also false, so the correct answer is (B).
35	E	Gaps in the domain occur in two situations—when taking even roots of negative numbers, and when dividing by zero. The denominator of the function will be zero if x is zero, so that's one hole in the domain. Eliminate (A), (B), and (D) because they include 0. The other problems occur when the expression inside the square root sign is negative, or zero, since you can't divide by zero. So we know that $x + 10 > 0$, which means $x > -10$. (E) points out both situations.
36	D	In a 3-digit number containing no zeros, there are nine possibilities for the first digit (1–9); nine possibilities for the second digit (1–9); and nine possibilities for the third digit (1–9). That makes a total of $9 \times 9 \times 9$ possible 3-digit numbers, or 729.

Question	Answer	Explanation
37	B	At all points on the *y*-axis of the coordinate plane, $x = 0$, so eliminate (D) and (E) right away. Then PITA. In this case, plug each point (x, y) from the answer choices into the equation, to see if it makes the equation true. If the first point in the answer choice works, then try the other point. If they both work, you've found the right answer. If either point fails, cross off that answer choice. Only the two points in (B) fit the given equation. Notice that (D) gives you the *x*-intercepts.
38	A	Plug In 1 for *BC* and $\sqrt{3}$ for *AC*. Rotating around *BC* makes the radius $\sqrt{3}$ and the height 1, so the volume is $\frac{1}{3}\pi\left(\sqrt{3}\right)^2(1)$. Rotating around *AC* makes the radius 1 and the height $\sqrt{3}$, so the volume is $\frac{1}{3}\pi(1)^2\left(\sqrt{3}\right)$. To find the ratio of the two volumes, either cancel common factors or enter each expression into your calculator. Your calculator will give you volumes of 3.1416 and 1.8138; their ratio is 1.7321, which is just about $\sqrt{3}$.
39	C	There are two ways to solve this one. The elegant way is to notice that *c* is a central angle intersecting the arc *YZ*. Since *a* is an inscribed angle that intersects the same arc, it must measure half of angle *c*. Therefore $2a = c$ (see Chapter 5 for central versus inscribed angles in circles). If that doesn't jump out at you, then just Plug In using triangle rules. Suppose, for example, that $c = 50$. The other two angles in $\triangle OYZ$ would then need to add up to 130°; since $\triangle OYZ$ is isosceles (two sides are radii), each of the other angles must equal 65°. That tells you that $d = 65$. Meanwhile, elsewhere in the triangle, the Rule of 180° tells you that $b = 130$, because $c = 50$. Then, since $\triangle OZX$ is also isosceles (two sides are radii), the other two angles must each measure 25°. That means that $a = 25$. This is just one possible set of numbers. Any number would work as long as you obeyed the rules of geometry. Go to your answer choices using $a = 25$, $b = 130$, $c = 50$, and $d = 65$. Using these values, you'll find that the only answer choice that equals *c* is (C).

Question	Answer	Explanation
40	A	This is a repeated percent-change question, basically the same as a compound interest question about a bank account. Remember the formula, Final = Original × (1 + Rate)$^{\text{# of changes}}$. This colony has an original size of 1,250 and increases by 8% (.08) every month. In two years, it will make 24 of these increases. That's all you need to fill in the formula, which would look like the following: Final = 1,250 × (1 + 0.08)^{24}. Paying careful attention to the order of operations, run that through your calculator. You should find that Final = 7,926.4759. That's very close to (A).
41	A	Figure 7 Both segments OA and OB have lengths of 4, because they're both radii. The ratio you're given, $OD = 3DB$, tells you that the lengths of OD and DB are 3 and 1, respectively. Consequently, you know you're looking at a right triangle with legs of lengths 3 and 4, so the length of the hypotenuse must be 5. Using the SOHCAHTOA definition of the sine function, you can determine that $\sin \angle A = \dfrac{3}{5}$, or 0.6.
42	D	PITA. In this situation, pick an easy number that is in some, but not all of the ranges in the answer choices. This will allow you to cross off the greatest number of answers. Let's try $x = 1$. This gives you $\left|(1)^3 - 8\right| \le 5$, which means $7 \le 5$. But that is false, so eliminate any answer choices that include 1 in their ranges: (A), (B), and (C). Now, the trick is to try a value that is in one of the two remaining answer choices, but not the other. Use $x = 2$. This produces $\left|(2)^3 - 8\right| \le 5$, which simplifies to $0 \le 5$. Since that's true, the correct answer must contain 2, and you should cross off any answer that doesn't contain 2. Cross off (E), and pick (D).
43	C	The best way to attack this question is just to try it. You'll find that no matter how you arrange the circles and connect them, the resulting polygon (which will be a hexagon) always has a perimeter of 24. That's because the polygon is always made up of two radii from each circle, for a total of 12 radii—each with a length of 2.

Question	Answer	Explanation
44	C	To find the y-intercept, just make $x = 0$ and solve for y. $y = 3$, so it's the point $(0, 3)$. To find the x-intercept, make $y = 0$ and solve for x. $x = 6$, so it's the point $(6, 0)$. To find the distance between the two points, sketch their positions on the coordinate plane. You'll see they form a right triangle with legs of lengths 3 and 6, in which the hypotenuse represents the distance between the two points. Use the Pythagorean theorem to find the length of the hypotenuse, 6.7082. That's the distance between the intercepts.
45	A	The simple, grinding way to do this one is to use the distance formula $\left(d = \sqrt{\left(x_2 - x_1\right)^2 + \left(y_2 - y_1\right)^2}\right)$ on the answer choices. Any answer choice that produces a distance other than 25 or 26 can be discarded immediately. Only (A) produces distances of 25 and 26 from the two points given.
46	D	 Figure 8 Note: Figure not drawn to scale. Because this is an isosceles trapezoid, you know that $\angle S$ is equal to $\angle T$, and so measures 135° as well. The four angles must total 360°, so $\angle R$ and $\angle U$ measure 45° each (you can also use Fred's theorem to figure that out, since the bases of the trapezoid are parallel lines). Divide the trapezoid into a rectangle and two triangles by drawing altitudes to S and T. Each of the triangles must be a 45°-45°-90° right triangle. Using the proportions of 45°-45°-90°, you can find the length of each of the triangle's sides: 4, 4, and $4\sqrt{2}$. So the area of each triangle is $\frac{1}{2} b \times h$, or $\frac{1}{2}(4)(7 + 15)$. The area of the rectangle is $7 \times 4 = 28$. $28 + 8 + 8 = 44$. Or, using the trapezoid area formula, you get $\frac{1}{2}(4)(7 + 15) = 44$.

Question	Answer	Explanation
47	D	No ordinary calculator can work with exponents this big, and there's no way to spot the biggest values here by looking at them; you've got to get tricky. The important fact about this question is that it's not necessary to find the exact value of any expression merely to compare them. The best way to compare these expressions is to get them into similar forms. To start with, rearrange as many answer choices as possible so that they have exponents of 100. (C) can be expressed as $(3^5)^{100}$, or 243^{100}; (D) can be expressed as $(4^4)^{100}$, or 256^{100}; and (E) is already there—250^{100}. Suddenly it's easy to see that (D) is the biggest of the three, and eliminate (C) and (E). Next, take a look at (A). The exponent 999 is approximately 1,000. The expression is therefore worth a little less than $(1.73^{10})^{100}$, or $(240.14)^{100}$. That's definitely smaller than (D), so you can eliminate (A) as well. Finally, take a look at (B). The expression 2^{799} is almost equal to 4^{400}. How can you tell? Well, 4^{400} can be written as $(2^2)^{400}$, or 2^{800}. That makes it clear that (D) is bigger than (A). Answer choice (D) reigns supreme.
48	E	If you have a graphing calculator, press the Y= key and enter the function. If you check the values of the TABLE, you can find that $f(-3.5)$ and $f(2.5)$ both equal 39. If you don't have a graphing calculator, you can PITA. It may take a while, but you'll get it.
49	A	To find the probability, first figure out the total number of possibilities, and then figure out how many meet the condition you want. Since there are 6 possible rolls on a fair cube, the total number of possibilities for two rolls is $6 \times 6 = 36$. Now you need to figure out all the ways to get a product greater than 18. If you roll a 1, 2, or 3 on the first cube, you're out of luck, since the most you could roll would be $3 \times 6 = 18$, but you want more than 18. The rolls that will work are 4×5, 4×6, 5×4, 5×5, 5×6, 6×4, 6×5, and 6×6. That's 8 rolls out of 36, which is a probability of $\frac{8}{36} = 0.222$.
50	B	If $\log_x(y^x) = z$, then z is the exponent that turns x into y^x. If you think about it that way, then it's clear that x raised to the power of z would be y^x. If that doesn't make sense to you, then review Chapter 3. If that doesn't work for you, then it's possible (but a little tricky) to Plug In. Do it this way. Plug 10 in for x so that you're working with a common logarithm, the kind your calculator can compute. Plug In 2 for y and you get: $\log_{10}(2^{10}) = z$. This can be written simply as $\log 1{,}024 = z$. Your calculator can then compute the value of z. $z = 3.0103$. You can then compute the value of x^z. You get 1,024. The only answer choice that equals 1,024 is (B).

Chapter 18
Level 1 Practice Test
Form B
Answers and
Explanations

Question	Answer	Explanation
1	D	All three people weigh 410 pounds, but Rob and Sherry weigh 300 pounds; therefore, Heather must weigh 410 − 300 = 110 pounds. Because Sherry and Heather weigh 240 pounds, Sherry must weigh 240 − 110 = 130 pounds. If you don't want to handle the question this way, you can simply PITA. That means starting with (C) and using the answer choices as Sherry's weight. For example, if Sherry's weight is 120 pounds, that makes Rob's weight 180 pounds and Heather's weight 120 pounds. Those three weights don't add up to 410 pounds, so move on and try the next answer choice. Answer choice (D) works.
2	C	Draw a rough sketch: The point (5, 2) is 2 units above the x-axis, so its reflection will be 2 units below the x-axis. Reflecting the point across the x-axis keeps the x-coordinate the same but changes the sign of the y-coordinate.
3	E	This is just Plugging In. Plug the values given for r and s into the equation. $$\frac{s}{r}+\frac{4}{r^2}=$$ $$\frac{6}{\frac{2}{3}}+\frac{4}{\left(\frac{2}{3}\right)^2}=$$ $$\frac{6}{\frac{2}{3}}+\frac{4}{\frac{4}{9}}=$$ $$\left(6\times\frac{3}{2}\right)+\left(4\times\frac{9}{4}\right)=$$ $$\frac{18}{2}+\frac{36}{4}=9+9=18$$

Question	Answer	Explanation
4	A	You're given variables and no numbers, so Plug In. Suppose $p = 60$. The other two interior angles of the triangle must then add up to 120°. For now, Plug In 50 and 70, making the angle above n a 50° angle, and the angle above m a 70° angle. Then, because there are 180° in a straight line, you know that $n = 130$ and $m = 110$. Now that you have values for each of the variables, you can go to the answer choices and see which one works. You're looking for the answer choice that is equal to p, or 60. Only (A) works, and that's the correct answer.
5	B	You've got variables in the question and the answer choices, so Plug In. Suppose that you're traveling 5 miles ($b = 5$). That means that your fare will include an original \$2.50 plus five \$0.30 charges (\$1.50) for each of the 5 miles traveled (which is \$7.50), for a total of \$9.00. To find the correct answer, plug $b = 5$ into the answer choices and see which one gives you a value of 9. Only (B) does the trick.
6	D	You have to set up two different equations. The first is if what's in the absolute value is nonnegative, and the other if what's inside the absolute value is negative. The first equation is $y - 3 = 4y - 7$, which simplifies to $y = \dfrac{4}{3}$. That's not in the answers. So let's set up the second equation: $-(y - 3) = 4y - 7$. This simplifies to $3 - y = 4y - 7$, which becomes $5y = 10$ and $y = 2$.
7	E	You may recognize that this is the point-slope form and that the slope is $\dfrac{5}{4}$. If you don't see that, rewrite the equation into slope-intercept form.
8	B	Substitute for a and b. So $a^2 + b^2 = \cos^2\theta + \sin^2\theta$. But you know the identity $\cos^2\theta + \sin^2\theta = 1$, so the answer is (B).

Question	Answer	Explanation
9	B	A friendly reminder—the perimeter is what you get when you add up all a polygon's sides. The most common careless mistake on perimeter questions is to calculate the area instead. Notice answer choice (E). Figure 2 In the end, this is a simple addition question. The polygon can be seen as a 7×10 rectangle with two notches cut into it. The notches add to the polygon's perimeter, but figuring out how much they add is the tricky part. A plain 7×10 rectangle has a perimeter of 34. The notch cut into the bottom of this rectangle adds 4 units to this perimeter, not 7. The three horizontal segments on the bottom of the figure must still add up to 10, the length of the rectangle; only the vertical segments add length. In the same way, the notch cut into the right side of the rectangle adds 4 units of length, not 6, because the vertical sides must still add up to 7, the rectangle's height; only the horizontal segments add length. The total perimeter is $34 + 4 + 4$, or 42.
10	A	The thing to be careful about here is taking the absolute value at the right time. To find $\lvert x + y \rvert$, you have to add x and y together first, and then take the absolute value. If you take the absolute value of each quantity before adding, you're likely to get a wrong answer. The only pair of coordinates whose sum has an absolute value greater than 5 is (A), because $-4 + -2 = -6$, and $\lvert -6 \rvert = 6$.
11	B	Keri sold more than 300 units in only four months in 1996: March, August, September, and December. That means four bonuses, for a total of $4,000.00.
12	D	The trick here is to remember the bonuses. In the 3-month periods shown in answer choices (A), (B), and (E), Keri sold 1,000 units, earning $10,000 in commissions. Each 3-month period also includes one bonus, raising her income for that period to $11,000.00. In the 3-month period shown in answer choice (D), however, Keri earns more. She sells 950 units, earning $9,500.00 in commissions, and also receives two bonuses, for a total of $11,500.00.
13	E	Set up a proportion: $\dfrac{14}{2^2} = \dfrac{a}{5^2}$. Simplify: $4a = 350$, and $a = 87.5$. You can also approximate. When b goes up, a goes up. So you can eliminate (A) and (B).

Question	Answer	Explanation
14	C	It's algebra time. Whenever two fractions are equal, you can cross-multiply. $$\frac{1}{x} = \frac{4}{5}$$ $$4x = 5$$ $$x = \frac{5}{4}$$ You're not done when you've solved for x, though. The question asks not for x, but for $\frac{x}{3}$. To produce the right answer, you have to divide by 3. $$x = \frac{5}{4}$$ $$\frac{x}{3} = \frac{5}{12} = 0.41666\ldots$$
15	A	The four right triangles inside the quadrilateral are congruent; they have legs and hypotenuses of equal length. The exact lengths of the segments don't matter. For convenience's sake, you can Plug In values for the lengths. Suppose that the right triangles are all 3-4-5 triangles. That makes the hypotenuses 5. The value of $\sin \angle RSU$, according to SOHCAHTOA, will now be $\frac{3}{5}$. The correct answer choice will be the one that also equals $\frac{3}{5}$. Answer choice (A) is correct.
16	D	There are two common sorts of nonreal numbers that are important on the Math Subject Tests. These are the square roots of negative numbers (imaginary numbers) and numbers divided by zero (undefined). The expression $\sqrt{x} + \frac{1}{x-3}$ will therefore be real only if x is zero or greater (so that the quantity under the radical isn't negative) and only if x doesn't equal 3 (so that the fraction's denominator isn't zero). You can see that x doesn't have to be greater than 1 ($x = 0$ is allowed, for example), so Statement I is out. This allows you to eliminate (A), (C), and (E). Statement II is definitely true because it is in both remaining answer choices. Statement III must also be true, since x must be greater than or equal to zero. The correct answer is (D).

Question	Answer	Explanation
17	E	Always sketch situations that are described but not shown. Here's the situation described in the question: Cube *A* is the outermost shape. Sphere *O* is inscribed inside it, and cube *B* is then inscribed within the sphere. You can use this simple sketch to check your answer choices. As you can see from your sketch, one edge of *A* is equal in length to the diameter of *O*, which in turn is equal to the diagonal of *B*. The correct answer is (E).
18	A	This is a fancy simultaneous-equations question. It's impossible to solve for the value of x, y, or z, but you can find the value of their sum. It's done by adding the equations, like $$\begin{aligned} a - x &= 12 \\ b - y &= 7 \\ c - z &= 15 \\ \hline a + b + c - x - y - z &= 34 \end{aligned}$$ This equation can be written as $(a + b + c) - (x + y + z) = 34$. And since the question tells you that $a + b + c = 50$, you can simplify the equation even further: $50 - (x + y + z) = 34$ $-(x + y + z) = -16$ $x + y + z = 16$
19	B	Since Cassie's stuck in the driver's seat, the number of permutations of the people in the car is simply determined by the possible arrangements of passengers in the 3 passengers' seats. The number of permutations of 3 items in 3 spaces is given by 3!, which equals $3 \times 2 \times 1$, or 6.
20	E	PITA. See which value of x in the answer choices makes the equation true. It's (E).

Question	Answer	Explanation
21	C	Remember that slope is equal to "rise" over "run." A line that has a slope greater than 1 is changing vertically (along the y-axis) faster than it's changing horizontally (along the x-axis). Line l might look like As you can see, a and b don't have to be equal—in fact, they can't be. You can also see that a doesn't have to be less than b—a will be less than b when they're both positive, but b will be less than a when they're negative. Of all the statements in the answer choices, only (C) must be true. Since b is always farther from zero than a, its square will always be greater than the square of a.
22	C	 Figure 5 This one is a little tricky. The best way to approach it is by experimenting with sketches. If you examine the possibilities carefully, you'll see that there are three possible locations of the missing vertex.
23	E	PITA works well on this one. Just take the values of x from the answer choices and fill in the values for the other angles using the formulas $y = \frac{2}{3}x$ and $w = 2z$. You'll know you've got the right answer when the values produced obey the Rule of 180°. If $x = 72$, then $y = \frac{2}{3}(72)$, or 48. The sum of x and y is then 120, which means that $w = 120$, since it's a vertical angle. The equation $w = 2z$ gives us $z = 60$. If you check all those numbers against the Rule of 180°, you'll see that (E) is the correct answer.

Question	Answer	Explanation
24	D	The new radius of circle O is $(r + t)$. To find the circle's area, just plug this quantity into the formula for the area of a circle, $A = \pi r^2$. To do this, you'll need to use FOIL. $$A = \pi(r + t)^2$$ $$A = \pi(r^2 + rt + rt + t^2)$$ $$A = \pi(r^2 + 2rt + t^2)$$ Alternately, you could Plug In something like $r = 5$ and $t = 3$. The new radius is 8, making your target answer $\pi(8)^2$ or 64π. Only (D) works.
25	C	You can find the radius of the circle from the area you're given, just by plugging the area into the formula and solving. $$A = \pi r^2$$ $$\pi r^2 = 9\pi$$ $$r^2 = 9$$ $$r = 3$$ Because OA and OB are both radii, each must have a length of 3. And because they're perpendicular, they must be legs of an isosceles right triangle. That means that $\triangle ABO$ has angles measuring 45°, 45°, and 90°, and must therefore have sides in the ratio $1 : 1 : \sqrt{2}$. The length of the hypotenuse, AB, is simply $3\sqrt{2}$, or 4.24.
26	A	Solving $x^2 + 2x - 3 = 0$ is just a matter of factoring. $$x^2 + 2x - 3 = 0$$ $$(x - 1)(x + 3) = 0$$ $$x = -3, 1$$ The funny looking equation $x < |x|$, however, tells you that x is negative. That means that x can only equal -3. To find the answer, just plug $x = -3$ into the expression $2x + 4$. $$2(-3) + 4 = -6 + 4 = -2$$

Question	Answer	Explanation
27	B	The corresponding parts of similar triangles are proportional. To figure out a value in one triangle from the corresponding value in the other, you need to know what the proportion is. Luckily, this question gives you the hypotenuse of both triangles—5 and 4, respectively. This allows you to set up this proportion. $$\frac{\text{any part of } \triangle ABC}{\text{the matching part of } \triangle CBD} = \frac{5}{4}$$ To find the area of $\triangle CBD$, you'll need to know the lengths of both of its legs. Use the proportion to find these lengths from the legs of the larger triangle. First, find the longer leg, BD: $$\frac{4}{BD} = \frac{5}{4}$$ $$5BD = 16$$ $$BD = \frac{16}{5} = 3.2$$ Then, find CD: $$\frac{3}{CD} = \frac{5}{4}$$ $$5CD = 12$$ $$CD = \frac{12}{5} = 2.4$$ Once you know that $\triangle CBD$ is a right triangle with legs 2.4 and 3.2, all you have to do is plug these lengths into the area formula for triangles. $$A = \frac{1}{2}bh$$ $$A = \frac{1}{2}(2.4)(3.2)$$ $$A = 3.84$$
28	D	For this question, you need to remember how FOIL works, and that i^2 can be replaced by -1. $$(5 - 3i)(4 + 2i) =$$ $$20 + 10i - 12i - 6i^2 =$$ $$20 - 2i - 6i^2 =$$ $$20 - 2i - 6(-1) =$$ $$20 + 6 - 2i =$$ $$26 - 2i$$
29	D	PITA. Plug each answer choice into the function for x, to see which one spits out -4. (D) works, because $f(1) = (1)^2 - 5(1) = 1 - 5 = -4$.

Question	Answer	Explanation
30	B	It's a good idea to sketch the situation that's described in this question: As you can see, only one dimension of this solid is doubled. It's now a rectangular solid of dimensions $3 \times 5 \times 8$. The longest segment that can be drawn within this solid is the long diagonal, which can be found using the Super Pythagorean theorem. $$d^2 = a^2 + b^2 + c^2$$ $$d^2 = 3^2 + 5^2 + 8^2$$ $$d^2 = 9 + 25 + 64$$ $$d^2 = 98$$ $$d = \sqrt{98} = 9.899$$ The correct answer is (B).
31	E	Type this into your calculator, being careful to use parentheses. You should get either 3025000000 or something like 3.025e9. To get 3025000000 into scientific notation, you need to move the decimal point 9 places to the left, which means your power of 10 will be 9; pick (E).
32	D	The probabilities must add up to 1; the probabilities shown in the table add up to $\frac{5}{8}$, so n must be $\frac{3}{8}$.
33	B	Don't let all the scientific talk scare you. All you're being asked to do is find the value of t for which $n = 500$. To do that, just PITA. Plug each answer choice in for t, to see which one makes $n = 500$. (B) works.
34	E	Perpendicular lines have opposite reciprocal slopes. That means that if line m has a slope of $-\frac{1}{2}$, line l, which is perpendicular to it, must have a slope of 2. That alone lets you eliminate the equations in (A), (B), and (C), all of which have the wrong slope. So the answer must be (D) or (E). Since the point $(4, 5)$ is on the line you're looking for, you can plug that point in for (x, y) in the equation of a line to see whether it makes the equation true. If you plug $(4, 5)$ into (D), you get $5 = 2(4) - 1$, which is wrong. Cross off (D)—the answer is (E).
35	B	For this question, it's important to remember the difference between central angles and inscribed angles. Central angles, like $\angle AOB$ and $\angle BOC$, are like pie slices that start at the circle's center. The arcs they intercept are equal in measure to the angles themselves. Inscribed angles, on the other hand, start on the edge of the circle, like $\angle BDA$ and $\angle CAD$. The arcs they intercept are twice as great in measure as the angles themselves. Since $\angle BDA$ is an inscribed angle measuring 25°, the arc it intercepts, AB, must measure 50°. For the same reason, the arc intercepted by $\angle BDA$ must measure 64°. That's a total of 114° out of the semicircle $ABCD$, which leaves 66° out of the 180° half-circle. That's the measure of arc BC. Since arc BC measures 66°, the central angle BOC must also measure 66°. The correct answer is (B).

Question	Answer	Explanation
36	A	This question tests your understanding of exponent rules. You're told that $4^{x+2} = 48$, but how do you solve for 4^x? Remember that when you multiply exponential terms that have a common base, you add the exponents. In the same way, you can express addition in an exponent as multiplication. $$4^{x+2} = 48$$ $$4^x \times 4^2 = 48$$ Once you've taken this step, solving is easy. $$4^x \times 16 = 48$$ $$4^x = 3$$
37	C	Just Plug In a number for x. If $x = 2$, the problem reads $r(2) = 17$ and $s(r(2)) = 3$. But that means you can substitute 17 for $r(2)$ in the second equation, so you know that $s(17) = 3$. Since the problem is asking for $s(17)$, and 3 is your target number, Plug In 17 for x in the answer choices, to see which answer choice hits 3. Only (C) works.
38	C	Use the Group Problem Formula, Total = Group 1 + Group 2 + Neither − Both. Here, you've got $850 = 250 + 450 + 350 −$ Both. So Both = 200. Pick (C). You need to memorize this formula!
39	C	Rearrange the equation to read $9^n = 27$, then change each base to 3: $(3^2)^n = 3^3$. So $3^{2n} = 3^3$, which means that the exponents are equal: $2n = 3$. Therefore, $n = \dfrac{3}{2}$.
40	A	The cylindrical cup has a radius of 2 and a height of 3. Its volume, given by $V = \pi r^2 h$, is $\pi(2)^2(3)$, or 12π. The volume of the rectangular tank, given by $V = lwh$, is $6 \times 7 \times 8$, or 336. To find out how many times the cup can be filled completely from the tank, just divide 336 by 12π using your calculator: $$\frac{336}{12\pi} = 8.913$$ As you can see, the cup can be filled almost 9 times, but can be filled *completely* only 8 times. The correct answer is (A).

Question	Answer	Explanation
41	D	Always sketch situations that are described but not shown. The situation described in this question would look something like this:

Segments AC and BD form right angles, and each cuts the other exactly in half. Segments BO and DO have lengths of 3, and segments AO and CO have lengths of 3.5. If you sketch segments AB, BC, CD, and DA, then you have four identical right triangles. You can use the Pythagorean theorem to find the length of each hypotenuse.

$$a^2 + b^2 = c^2$$
$$3^2 + 3.5^2 = c^2$$
$$9 + 12.25 = c^2$$
$$21.25 = c^2$$
$$c = 4.61$$

When you know the lengths of each side, you can use SOHCAHTOA to figure out the value of $\sin \angle ADO$. The side opposite $\angle ADO$ is AO, and the hypotenuse is AD. You can use the lengths of these segments to find the value of the trig function.

$$\text{sine} = \frac{\text{opposite}}{\text{hypotenuse}}$$

$$\sin \angle ADO = \frac{AO}{AD}$$

$$\sin \angle ADO = \frac{3.5}{4.61} = 0.76$$

Question	Answer	Explanation
42	A	The interquartile range is the difference between the third quartile and the first quartile; put simply, it's the width of the entire box in the middle of the boxplot. (A) has an interquartile range of $70 - 10 = 60$; no other choice comes close.

Question	Answer	Explanation
43	A	Plugging In can work wonders for you on this one. The constant k can be anything. Let's say it equals 3. If that's the case, $f(x) = 3x$, and $g(x) = x + 3$. Using these values makes it easy to plug into the function to test each of the three statements. Suppose $x = 2$, take a look at Statement I. Using your values, you can plug into the statement to see whether it must be true. $$f(2x) = 2f(x)$$ $$f(4) = 2f(2)$$ $$3 \times 4 = 2(3 \times 2)$$ $$12 = 12$$ Statement I works so far, so let's keep it and move on. Here's how Statement II looks with our values plugged into it. $$f(x + 2) = f(x) + 2$$ $$f(4) = f(2) + 2$$ $$3 \times 4 = (3 \times 2) + 2$$ $$12 = 8$$ Statement II is definitely NOT true, so you can eliminate it. That gets rid of answer choices (B), (C), and (E), leaving only (A) and (D). Since Statement I is present in both answers, you can forget about it. To pick the right answer, you need to check out Statement III. $$f(g(x)) = g(f(x))$$ $$f(g(2)) - g(f(2))$$ $$f(2 + 3) = g(3 \times 2)$$ $$f(5) = g(6)$$ $$3 \times 5 = 6 + 3$$ $$15 = 9$$ Statement III definitely isn't true either, so you can get rid of it. That eliminates answer choice (D), leaving only (A).

Question	Answer	Explanation
44	E	This is a Pythagorean theorem question disguised by a complicated physical description. Making a sketch of the southern wall can help clear this up.

As you can see, the nail and tack can be viewed as points on a coordinate plane. The coordinates of the points are given by their distances from the floor and the western wall. The coordinates of the tack are (–38, 85), and the coordinates of the nail are (–54, 48). These are larger coordinates than you're used to working with, but you can work with them normally. To find the distance between the tack and nail, use the distance formula.

$$d = \sqrt{\left(y_2 - y_1\right)^2 + \left(x_2 - x_1\right)^2}$$

$$d = \sqrt{\left(48 - 85\right)^2 + \left(-54 - (-38)\right)^2}$$

$$d = \sqrt{\left(-37\right)^2 + \left(-16\right)^2}$$

$$d = \sqrt{1369 + 256}$$

$$d = \sqrt{1625}$$

$$d = 40.31$$

Question	Answer	Explanation
45	C	The domain of the function $f(x)$ is the set of values that you're allowed to plug into the function in the x position. The only numbers not in a function's domain are those that make the function produce nonreal numbers—that is, fractions with zero in the denominator and even roots of negative numbers. There are no fractions in this function, so any values not in the domain of f will be those that make the square root negative. For $\sqrt{12 - x^2}$ to be a real number, the quantity under the radical, $12 - x^2$, must be zero or positive. To find the values of x that make $f(x)$ real, just write that as an inequality, and solve. $$12 - x^2 \geq 0$$ $$-x^2 \geq -12$$ $$x^2 \leq 12$$ $$-\sqrt{12} \leq x \leq \sqrt{12}$$ This is the domain of $f(x)$. The correct answer is (C). You could also PITA. Just pick numbers that are in some of the ranges in the answer choices, but not others, and plug them into the function to see if they work.
46	B	The basic rule of logic most commonly tested on the Math Subject Tests is the contrapositive. When you see any statement in the form "If A, then B," then you automatically know that the statement "If not B, then not A" is also true. That's the contrapositive statement. In this case, you're given the statement "If a tree falls in the forest, a sound is heard." The contrapositive of this statement is, "If no sound is heard, a tree doesn't fall in the forest." The question asks you to pick the logically impossible answer choice. That will be a statement that contradicts either the original statement or the contrapositive of the original statement. Answer choice (B) is directly opposed to the contrapositive.
47	C	The first couple must compete against 5 couples. The second couple has already faced the first couple, so they have to compete against only four new couples. The third couple has to compete against three new couples, and so on. This means that to make sure everyone competes in a dance-off with everyone else, there have to be 5 + 4 + 3 + 2 + 1 = 15 dance-offs. Multiply 15 by the 3 times this must happen, and you get 45.

Question	Answer	Explanation
48	C	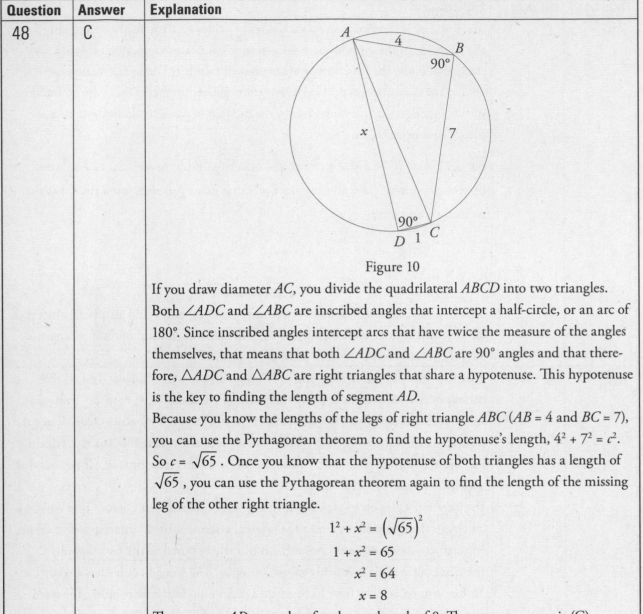

Figure 10

If you draw diameter AC, you divide the quadrilateral $ABCD$ into two triangles. Both $\angle ADC$ and $\angle ABC$ are inscribed angles that intercept a half-circle, or an arc of $180°$. Since inscribed angles intercept arcs that have twice the measure of the angles themselves, that means that both $\angle ADC$ and $\angle ABC$ are $90°$ angles and that therefore, $\triangle ADC$ and $\triangle ABC$ are right triangles that share a hypotenuse. This hypotenuse is the key to finding the length of segment AD.

Because you know the lengths of the legs of right triangle ABC ($AB = 4$ and $BC = 7$), you can use the Pythagorean theorem to find the hypotenuse's length, $4^2 + 7^2 = c^2$. So $c = \sqrt{65}$. Once you know that the hypotenuse of both triangles has a length of $\sqrt{65}$, you can use the Pythagorean theorem again to find the length of the missing leg of the other right triangle.

$$1^2 + x^2 = \left(\sqrt{65}\right)^2$$
$$1 + x^2 = 65$$
$$x^2 = 64$$
$$x = 8$$

The segment AD must therefore have a length of 8. The correct answer is (C). |

Question	Answer	Explanation
49	E	The segment from (0, 0) to (–2, 2) has a length of $2\sqrt{2}$, or 2.83 (you can think of it as the diagonal of a square with sides 2 units long, or the hypotenuse of a 45°-45°-90° triangle). If you sketch this line segment, you'll see that there are two possible locations for the third vertex of an equilateral triangle constructed from that segment.

Before you start doing more complicated calculations, make the best sketch you can of the situation that's described. You may find that you can eliminate a few answer choices just by looking at your sketch and guesstimating. On this question, if you can draw the figure accurately, the answer is obviously (E).

If not, there are a couple of ways to find the coordinates of these vertices, but the simplest way is to use trigonometry. Let's start with the upper vertex. Draw an altitude from this point to the x-axis to produce a right triangle.

Since the hypotenuse of this triangle is one side of the equilateral triangle, you know it has a length of $2\sqrt{2}$, or 2.83. The Rule of 180° also lets you figure out the measure of the lower acute angle in this right triangle. It must measure 75°, since it forms a straight line with the 45° and 60° angles. All you need to find the coordinates of the third vertex are the legs of this right triangle. Trigonometry is the easiest way to find them. The length of the horizontal leg, adjacent to the 75° angle, will be $(\cos 75°)(2\sqrt{2}) = (0.26)(2.83) = 0.73$. The length of the vertical leg will be $(\sin 75°)(2\sqrt{2}) = (0.97)(2.83) = 2.73$. The coordinates of the third vertex in this position will therefore be (0.73, 2.73). |

Question	Answer	Explanation
50	A	The x-intercepts of a graph are the places where $y = 0$. To solve $0 = x^2 - 9x + 19.25$, use the quadratic formula, $x = \dfrac{-b \pm \sqrt{b^2 - 4ac}}{2a}$. In the given equation, $a = 1$, $b = -9$, and $c = 19.25$. Plugging these values into the quadratic formula gives you $x = 3.5$ or 5.5. These points are both on the x-axis, so the distance between them is simply 2.0. Another way to approach this is to multiply the equation through by 4 to clear out the decimal, and then factor. You get $0 = 4x^2 - 36x + 77$, which factors to $0 = (2x - 7)(2x - 11)$. This makes the x-intercepts $\dfrac{7}{2}$ and $\dfrac{11}{2}$; their difference is 2. Perhaps the quickest method would be to graph $y = x^2 - 9x + 19.25$ on your calculator and see where the graph crosses the x-axis.

Chapter 19
Level 2 Practice Test
Form A
Answers and
Explanations

Question	Answer	Explanation
1	B	Algebraic manipulation is the easiest way to solve this one. Start by adding s to each side, producing the inequality $r > r + 2s$. Then subtract r from each side to get $0 > 2s$. If $2s < 0$, then $s < 0$ (just divide both sides by 2). This can also be solved by Plugging In, but since only certain values will make the original inequality true, it can take some time to Plug In enough different values to eliminate all the wrong answers. Algebraic manipulation is faster here.
2	C	You'll want to use Process of Elimination here to knock out some answer choices. The best numbers to plug into the function are the ones in the answer choices: 10 and -10. Start by finding out whether the statement $f(x) = f(-x)$ is true when $x = 10$. $f(10) = \lvert 10 \rvert + 10 = 20$. $f(-10) = \lvert -10 \rvert + 10 = 10 + 10 = 20$. Since $f(10)$ and $f(-10)$ are equal, $f(x) = f(-x)$ is true when $x = 10$, and every answer choice that does not include 10 can be eliminated. That gets rid of (A), (D), and (E). To choose between the remaining answers (B) and (C), Plug In a number included in (C) but not in (B). A simple number like zero works best. $f(0) = \lvert 0 \rvert + 10 = 10$. $f(-0) = \lvert -0 \rvert + 10 = 0 + 10 = 10$. You can see that $f(0) = f(-0)$, so zero must be part of the correct answer. (B) does not include zero, so you can eliminate it. (C) is correct.
3	D	Remember how factorials cancel out in fractions. If you expand the factorials in the fraction $\dfrac{15!}{13!2!}$, then you get $$\frac{15\times14\times13\times12\times11\times10\times9\times8\times7\times6\times5\times4\times3\times2\times1}{(13\times12\times11\times10\times9\times8\times7\times6\times5\times4\times3\times2\times1)(2\times1)}$$ You can see that every factor from 1 to 13 in the numerator is also in the denominator; these factors cancel out, leaving you with $\dfrac{15\times14}{2\times1}$, or $\dfrac{210}{2}$, which equals 105.
4	A	Remember the SOHCAHTOA definitions of the trigonometric functions. In a right triangle, the sine of an angle equals the length of the opposite side over the length of the hypotenuse. You can easily find the lengths of sides AB and BC, since they are horizontal and vertical, respectively. The hypotenuse's length can be found with the Pythagorean theorem, but you don't even need it if you recognize this as a 5-12-13 triangle. To find the sine of $\angle BAC$, then, you just need to find the value of $\dfrac{BC}{AC}$, which equals $\dfrac{5}{13}$.

Question	Answer	Explanation
5	D	A "system" is another way of describing a set of simultaneous equations. To find the complete solution set of a system of equations, you need to solve the equations simultaneously. Instead of doing the algebra here, however, you should notice that the answer choices all have numbers in them. That means you can PITA. Start with (C), which in this case is the coordinate pair $(-4, -3)$, since it appears in two answer choices. That will allow you to eliminate more efficiently. That makes $x = -4$ and $y = -3$. To PITA, put these numbers into both equations. These numbers work in the first equation, because $(-4)^2 + (-3)^2 = 16 + 9 = 25$. They also work in the second equation, because $-3 = -4 + 1$. That means that (A), (B), and (E) can be eliminated, because they do not contain the coordinate pair $(-4, -3)$. The only difference between (C) and (D) is the point $(3, 4)$. If you plug it into both equations, it works, so the answer is (D).
6	E	When there are variables in the question and the answer choices, Plug In. Remember to select numbers that make your math easy. In this case, it's important to choose numbers that make the fraction $\frac{j}{k}$ work out conveniently. Making $j = 4$ and $k = 2$ turns out well, because it makes $\frac{j}{k} = 2$. The expression $\dfrac{jk - \frac{j}{k}}{\frac{j}{k}}$ then works out to $\dfrac{(4)(2) - 2}{2} = \dfrac{8 - 2}{2} = \dfrac{6}{2} = 3$. To find the correct answer, just go quickly through the answer choices to find the one that also equals 3 when $j = 4$ and $k = 2$. Only (E) works out equal to 3. (E) is correct.

Question	Answer	Explanation
7	E	This is a visual perception question, and there's no hard and fast technique to follow to solve it. The best plan is to experiment with sketches in your test booklet and use common sense. Remember that this is an EXCEPT question, so you're looking for a shape that *can't* be made. Any time you find a way to make one of the shapes in the answer choices, that choice can be eliminated.

The intersection of a cube and a plane can be a triangle:

a point:

a rectangle:

or a line segment:

but there's no way to produce a circle, since none of a cube's edges or faces is curved. The correct answer is (E).

Question	Answer	Explanation
8	B	This is a compound-function question, in which you'll have to apply two functions in combination. The most important rule to remember is that you have to work from the inside out. Start by finding $g(2.3)$. That means putting the number 2.3 in place of the x in the definition of $g(x)$, $g(2.3) = \frac{1}{2}\sqrt{2.3} + 1 = \frac{1}{2}(1.52) + 1 = 0.76 + 1 = 1.76$. Once you know that $g(2.3) = 1.76$, you know that $f(g(2.3))$ is equal to $f(1.76)$, which is easily solved. $f(1.76) = \sqrt[3]{1.76} = 1.21$. The correct answer is (B).
9	D	Don't panic because you've never seen a term like "x mod y" before. This isn't something you slept through in math class. It's just one of those terms ETS throws at you sometimes. Some will be little-known math terms, and others will be made up. Either way, it doesn't matter whether you've seen it before, because ETS defines it for you. To find the value of any "x mod y," just take the number in the x position and divide it by the number in the y position. The remainder is the value of "x mod y" for those numbers. The value of 61 mod 7 is 5, because the remainder when 61 is divided by 7 is 5. The value of 5 mod 5 is 0, because the remainder when 5 is divided by 5 is zero. The expression (61 mod 7) − (5 mod 5) can be rewritten as 5 − 0, which equals 5. The correct answer is (D).
10	D	Plug In! Trying to solve this question by thinking through the trigonometric theory is a good way to give yourself a brain cramp. Just Plug In a few numbers on your calculator (angles between 0° and 90°) and see what happens. You'll soon find that Statements I and III always prove true, while it's easy to find an exception to Statement II. The correct answer is (D).
11	B	The statement $f(x) = \begin{cases} 2, x \neq 13 \\ 4, x = 13 \end{cases}$ can be read, "f of x equals 2 when x does not equal 13, and f of x equals 4 when x equals 13." Since neither of the values you're given equals 13, the function will always come out to 2. $f(15) - f(14) = 2 - 2 = 0$. The correct answer is (B).
12	D	You can PITA on this question if you get completely stuck, but algebraic manipulation is simpler and faster. Just isolate x. Start by multiplying both sides by 25, so that $\frac{x^5}{25} = 25$ becomes $x^5 - 625$. Then take the fifth root of each side to get x alone. On most calculators, you take the fifth root of a value by raising that value to the power of one-fifth, or 0.2. $x = \sqrt[5]{625} = 3.62$. The correct answer is (D).

Question	Answer	Explanation
13	A	On the Math Level 2, most trigonometry questions like this one are solved by using trigonometric identities to change the form of equations. Most often, the most successful strategy is to start by getting everything in terms of sine and cosine. The ratio you're given can be written in fractional form, like $\dfrac{\sec x}{\csc x} = \dfrac{1}{4}$. The secant and cosecant can also be expressed in terms of sine and cosine, $\dfrac{\frac{1}{\cos x}}{\frac{1}{\sin x}} = \dfrac{1}{4}$. This fraction simplifies to $\dfrac{\sin x}{\cos x} = \dfrac{1}{4}$, and since $\tan x = \dfrac{\sin x}{\cos x}$, this can be written as $\tan x = \dfrac{1}{4}$. The cotangent is the reciprocal of the tangent, so $\cot x = 4$. The ratio of $\tan x$ to $\cot x$ is therefore equal to $\dfrac{\frac{1}{4}}{4}$, or $\dfrac{1}{16}$. The correct answer is (A).
14	D	You can tell by looking at the figure that the x-coordinates of the points in region J include everything from $x = 0$ to $x = 6$. The y-coordinates of the points in the region include everything from $y = 0$ to $y = 3$. A rectangular region containing all points $(2x, y - 1)$ would therefore stretch from $x = 0$ to $x = 12$ (doubling both values) and from $y = -1$ to $y = 2$ (subtracting 1 from both values). The resulting region would look like this:

It would have a length of 12, a width of 3, and an area of 36. The correct answer is (D). |

Question	Answer	Explanation
15	D	Draw it! It's always a good idea to sketch any figure that is described but not shown. The triangle described here would look something like this: where h is the unknown length of the hypotenuse. As you can see, you're given the measure of an angle and the length of the opposite side in a right triangle, and you're trying to find the hypotenuse. The easiest way to find it is to use a trigonometric function that relates all these quantities. Since $\text{sine} = \dfrac{\text{opposite}}{\text{hypotenuse}}$, the sine is the function you want. Just plug the information you have into the formula, and solve for the missing piece, $\sin 27° = \dfrac{9}{h}$. To solve, start by isolating h. $h = \dfrac{9}{\sin 27°}$. Then use your calculator to find a numerical value: $h = \dfrac{9}{\sin 27°} = \dfrac{9}{0.454} = 19.82$.
16	B	PITA. Plug each answer choice in for x to see which one makes $f(x) = 0$. (B) works. Alternately, you could graph $y = x^2 + 6x - 12$ on your calculator and see where it crosses the x-axis.
17	B	There are variables in the answer choices, so it behooves you to Plug In. Pick a nice friendly angle for x like 30°. So $\sin 30° = 0.5 = m$, $\tan 30° = 0.577$, our target number. Now Plug In 0.5 for m to see which answer choice becomes 0.577. It's (B).
18	C	Use the definition of a logarithm to rewrite the equation $\log_y 2 = 8$ in exponential form, $y^8 = 2$. To find the value of y, take the eighth root of both sides. This can be done on your calculator by raising 2 to the power of one-eighth, or 0.125. You'll find that $y = 1.09$. The correct answer is (C). You can also PITA, starting with (C), which works.

Question	Answer	Explanation
19	D	An angle of $\dfrac{\pi}{4}$ radians is equivalent to an angle of 45°. You're therefore looking for an angle between 45° and −45° whose sine equals $\dfrac{1}{3}$. The easiest way to find this number is to enter the quantity $\dfrac{1}{3}$ into your calculator and take its inverse sine. This will show you the smallest positive angle whose sine is $\dfrac{1}{3}$. This angle, θ, is 19.47 degrees, or 0.34 radians. To find $\cos(2\theta)$, just double this value and take its cosine. You'll get 0.777..., or $\dfrac{7}{9}$. The correct answer is (D).
20	A	The best way to solve inverse-function questions on the Math Level 2 is to Plug In numbers. Be sure to pick a number that will work out neatly. For example, for the function $f(x) = \sqrt{x} - 1$, a good value for x would be 4. Then, $f(4) = \sqrt{4} - 1 = 2 - 1 = 1$. You can see that $f(x)$ turns 4 into 1. So $f^{-1}(1) = 4$. To find the correct answer, plug 1 into all of the answer choices. The correct answer will produce a value of 4. Only (A) comes out to 4, since $(1 + 1)^2 = 4$, and so (A) is the correct answer.
21	A	Don't bother doing long division with the polynomial. Just Plug In $x = 10$. The problem now reads, "When $460 + L$ is divided by 11, the remainder is 2." Well, 460 divided by 11 gives you 41.818. $11 \times 41 = 451$, and $11 \times 42 = 462$. To get a remainder of 2, you would divide 464 by 11. So $460 + L = 464$, and $L = 4$.

Question	Answer	Explanation
22	C	If you've studied the section of this book dealing with ellipses, then you can tell by looking at the formula that this is an ellipse centered at the origin. You can also tell that the ellipse's major axis is the vertical axis rather than the horizontal, because the constant under the y is larger than the one under the x. That means that the ellipse looks something like this: The major axis is the vertical axis of the ellipse. The endpoints of the major axis are the two points at which the ellipse intersects the y-axis. Since every point on the y-axis has an x-coordinate of 0, then all you have to do to find the coordinates of the endpoints is plug $x = 0$ into the equation of the ellipse, and see what y-coordinates that produces. $$\frac{0^2}{10} + \frac{y^2}{20} = 1$$ The zero causes the entire first term to equal zero, effectively eliminating it: $$0 + \frac{y^2}{20} = 1$$ $$\frac{y^2}{20} = 1$$ $$y^2 = 20$$ $$y = \pm\sqrt{20}$$ $$y = 4.472, -4.472$$ The endpoints of the ellipse's major axis are therefore $(0, -4.472)$ and $(0, 4.472)$. Because the points lie on a vertical line, it's not even necessary to use the distance formula to find the length of the segment between them. The distance between the points is equal to $4.472 - (-4.472)$, or 8.944. This is the length of the ellipse's major axis. The correct answer is (C).

Question	Answer	Explanation
23	B	Ah, functions with weird symbols. In this case, $[x]$ means the greatest integer less than or equal to x. In simple terms, that means that $[x]$ equals x if x is an integer, and if x isn't an integer, then $[x]$ is the next smallest integer. The number 2.75 becomes 2.0, –3.54 becomes –4.0, and so on. To find the graph of the function $f\left(\dfrac{x}{2}\right) - 1$, just Plug In numbers. Start with something very easy, like zero. $f\left(\dfrac{0}{2}\right) - 1 = [0] - 1 = 0 - 1 = -1$. The function $f\left(\dfrac{x}{2}\right) - 1$ must contain the point $(0, -1)$. Only (B) and (D) contain that point; answer choices (A), (C), and (E) may be eliminated (remember that a function does not include points marked by open circles). To choose between (B) and (D), Plug In another easy number, like 2. $f\left(\dfrac{2}{2}\right) - 1 = [1] - 1 = 1 - 1 = 0$. The function $f\left(\dfrac{x}{2}\right) - 1$ must therefore also contain the point $(2, 0)$. Only (B) contains that point—(D) contains the point $(2, 1)$ instead. The correct answer is (B).
24	D	Since $\cos \theta$ and $\cos^{-1} \theta$ are inverses, $\cos(\cos^{-1} \theta) = \theta$. If you also remember that the secant is the reciprocal of the cosine, then you can rewrite the given equation as $\dfrac{1}{\cos(\cos^{-1}(0.3527))} = \dfrac{1}{0.3527} = 2.8353$.
25	B	The function $f(x) = x^2 + 5x + 6$ is a quadratic function, which means that its graph will be a parabola. Since the coefficient of the x^2 term is positive, you know the parabola opens upward. The parabola therefore has a minimum value—its vertex. To find the value of x at which $f(x)$ reaches its minimum value, just find the x-coordinate of the parabola's vertex. You can do this by using the vertex formula. For any parabola in the form $y = ax^2 + bx + c$, the x-coordinate of the vertex equals $\dfrac{-b}{2a}$. For the parabola $f(x) = x^2 + 5x + 6$, that places the vertex at $\dfrac{-5}{2}$. The correct answer is (B). Of course, you can also PITA. Plug each answer choice into $f(x)$, to see which one gives you the lowest value.

Question	Answer	Explanation
26	B	An arithmetic sequence is one that increases by adding a constant amount again and again. The most important information to have when you're working with an arithmetic sequence is the size of the interval between any two consecutive terms in the sequence. Since the 20th term in the sequence is 20 and the 50th term is 100, you know that 30 steps in the sequence produce an increase of 80. That makes each step worth $\frac{80}{30}$, or $2.66\overline{6}$. To find the first term in the sequence, you can use the formula for the nth term in an arithmetic sequence, $a_n = a_1 + (n-1)d$, where n is the number of the term and d is the interval between any two consecutive terms. In this case, you know that $a_{20} = 20$, and that $d = 2.66\overline{6}$, or $\frac{8}{3}$. You can then fill those values into the formula, so $$20 = a_1 + (20-1)(2.66\overline{6})$$ You can then solve for the value of a_1. $$20 = a_1 + 19 \times 2.66\overline{6}$$ $$20 = a_1 + 50.66\overline{6}$$ $$a_1 = -30.66\overline{6}$$ The correct answer is (B).
27	A	This question is a lot simpler than it looks. ETS will never require you to do complex calculations with polar coordinates; you need to know only the basics. As you've seen in this book, polar coordinates can be converted to rectangular coordinates very simply, with the following two equations: $x = r \cos \theta$ and $y = r \sin \theta$. That means that the equation $r \sin \theta = 1$ simply translates to $y - 1$ in rectangular coordinates. And that's the equation of a horizontal line. The correct answer is (A).

Question	Answer	Explanation
28	B	Remember: A function is a relation in which every element in the domain corresponds to only one element in the range. Simply put, that means that there's only one y for every x. If you look at simple tables of values for the functions you're given, you can see that they obey the rule.

I. $f(x) = x^2$ II. $f(x) = x^3$ III. $f(x) = |x|$

x	$f(x)$	x	$f(x)$	x	$f(x)$
–2	4	–2	–8	–2	2
–1	1	–1	–1	–1	1
0	0	0	0	0	0
1	1	1	1	1	1
2	4	2	8	2	2

But the inverses of these functions will *reverse* these tables of values, switching the x and $f(x)$ values. After all, the inverse undoes the original function, turning all the $f(x)$ values back into the x values. If you reverse the tables of values for these three functions, you'll find that only one of them remains a function.

I. $f(x) = \pm\sqrt{x}$ II. $f(x) = \sqrt[3]{x}$ III. $f(x) = \pm x$

x	$f(x)$	x	$f(x)$	x	$f(x)$
0	0	–8	–2	0	0
1	1, –1	–1	–1	1	1, –1
4	2, –2	0	0	2	2, –2
		1	1		
		8	2		

The inverses of functions I and III are not functions themselves. In each case, some x values correspond to more than one $f(x)$ value. That is, there's more than one y for each x. The inverse of function II, however, *is* a function, because there's still only one y for every x. The correct answer is (B).

Question	Answer	Explanation
29	D	This is a classic ETS limit question. Ordinarily, to find the limit of an expression as x approaches a certain value, you just plug that value in for x, and *voilà*, there's your answer. This, however, is one of those annoying expressions that becomes undefined (zero in the denominator) when you Plug In the value. That could mean that the limit does not exist; but before you decide that, you've got to factor the top and bottom and see whether anything cancels out. In this case, the expression is factorable. $$\frac{x^3 - x}{x+1} =$$ $$\frac{x(x^2 - 1)}{x+1} =$$ $$\frac{x(x+1)(x-1)}{x+1} =$$ $$\frac{x(x-1)}{1} = x^2 - x$$ The whole expression reduces to $x^2 - x$. In order to find the value of $\lim\limits_{x \to -1} x^2 - x$, just Plug In -1 for x, $(-1)^2 - (-1) = 1 + 1 = 2$. The correct answer is (D).
30	A	Since there are variables in the answer choices, your best bet is to Plug In an easy number, like $x = 2$, and use your calculator. So $f(2) = 601{,}303$. $g(f(x)) = x$ tells you that f and g are inverses, so $g(601{,}303) = 2$, our target number. Plug $601{,}303$ into each answer choice to see which one turns into 2. The nice thing about Plugging In is that you can approximate and eliminate answer choices. You don't need to compute (B), (C), and (E) to see that they are way too big. Then just calculate the value of (A) and (D). The correct answer is (A).

Question	Answer	Explanation
31	D	When a figure is described but not shown, always sketch it. When a cube is inscribed in a sphere, the long diagonal of the cube is a diameter of the sphere. Since the sphere has a radius of 6 and a diameter of 12, you know that the sphere has a long diagonal of 12. The long diagonal of a cube is related to a side of the cube using the formula $d = s\sqrt{3}$. You can use that formula to find the length of a side: $s = \dfrac{d}{\sqrt{3}}$. In this case $s = \dfrac{12}{\sqrt{3}} = \dfrac{12}{1.732} = 6.93$. Once you know the length of one side of the cube, you can easily find the cube's volume using the formula $V = s^3$. You'll find that the cube has a volume of 332.55. Answers (A), (B), and (C) can immediately be eliminated by approximation. To choose between (D) and (E), just calculate the decimal value of one of them. Since $192\sqrt{3} = 332.55$, (D) is the correct answer.

Question	Answer	Explanation
32	E	When a figure is described but not shown, always sketch it.

In this problem, you're actually slicing a small cone off a bigger cone. To find the volume of the remaining solid, all you need to do is find the volumes of the two cones, and subtract the little one from the big one. Because you're given only variables in the question and answer choices, you'll be Plugging In your own values. Let's say the larger cone has a height of $h = 4$ and a radius of $r = 2$. Then you can find its volume using the formula $V = \frac{1}{3}\pi r^2 h$. In this case, you get $V = \frac{1}{3}\pi r^2 h = \frac{1}{3}\pi(2)^2(4) = \frac{16\pi}{3}$. To find the volume of the smaller cone, you first need to figure out its base and height. The height is easy—since the problem says the larger cone is cut "midway," you know that the smaller cone's height equals 2, or half of the larger cone's height. Because one cone is a piece of the other, they are proportional. The radius of the smaller cone must equal 1, or half of the larger cone's radius. Now you can find the volume of the smaller cone. $V = \frac{1}{3}\pi(1)^2(2) = \frac{1}{3}\pi(2) = \frac{2\pi}{3}$. Once you know the volumes of both cones, it's easy to subtract to find the volume of the leftover solid, $\frac{16\pi}{3} - \frac{2\pi}{3} = \frac{14\pi}{3}$. That's your target number. To find the right answer just plug $h = 4$ and $r = 2$ into the answer choices, and see which answer produces a value of $\frac{14\pi}{3}$. Only (E) does the trick.

Question	Answer	Explanation
33	B	The equation $e^{x^2} = \dfrac{1}{\sqrt{3}^x}$ looks very difficult to solve. Just PITA. Plug each answer choice in for x to see which makes both sides of the equation equal.
34	D	The equation $y = 2x^2 - 6x + c$ is in quadratic form, which means that its graph will be a parabola. If it's tangent to the x-axis, that means the vertex of the parabola lies on the x-axis (sketch it and you'll see that's the only way to get a point of tangency). You know that the y-coordinate of the vertex must therefore be zero. Since the quadratic has a "double root," that is, one distinct zero, then the discriminant in the quadratic formula must equal zero. In this case, $b^2 - 4ac = 0$ becomes $(-6)^2 - 4(2)c = 0$, so $c = 4.5$. The correct answer is (D). Another way to attack this is to PITA and graph each equation on your calculator.
35	C	You're dealing with imaginary numbers here, so your calculator won't be much use. To solve this problem, just plug $(i - 1)$ into the expression in place of x and do the math. $$x^2 + 2x + 2 =$$ $$(i - 1)^2 + 2(i - 1) + 2 =$$ $$(i - 1)(i - 1) + 2(i - 1) + 2 =$$ $$i^2 - 2i + 1 + 2i - 2 + 2 =$$ $$i^2 + 1 =$$ $$-1 + 1 = 0$$
36	E	With a graphing calculator, this is easy. Just type in the equations in the answer choices and see what their graphs look like. If you haven't got a graphing calculator, then you've got to proceed by Process of Elimination. The easiest way to eliminate answers is to observe that this curve does not appear to cross the x-axis or the y-axis. Any answer choice whose graph *does* intercept an axis can therefore be eliminated. That means plugging $x = 0$ and $y = 0$ into the answer choices to see what happens. You should know roughly what the graph of $y = e^x$ looks like (it appears earlier in this book). If you remember it, you'll recall that it crosses the y-axis. Even if you don't remember the shape of the graph, it's easy to discover that the curve crosses the axis just by Plugging In $x = 0$ and seeing that the equations in both (A) and (B) contain the point $(0, 1)$. That's a y-intercept, so you can eliminate both choices. Answer choice (C) can be eliminated because it's the equation of a line—no exponents. Answer choice (D) is the equation of a parabola, which might fit the graph you're given. But if you Plug In $x = 0$, you get $y = 2$. The point is clearly not on this graph. That leaves only (E), which is the equation of a hyperbola. You can easily tell from the equation that $x \neq 0$ and $y \neq 0$. That makes (E) the correct answer.

Question	Answer	Explanation
37	C	Remember that when you calculate the probability of multiple events, you've got to find the probabilities of the individual events and multiply them together. On the first drawing, the odds of getting a dime are $\frac{8}{11}$, because there are 8 dimes out of a total of 11 coins. On the second drawing, the odds of getting a dime are $\frac{7}{10}$, because there are 7 dimes remaining out of a total of ten remaining coins. The total probability of drawing two dimes, then, is $\frac{8}{11} \times \frac{7}{10} = \frac{56}{110}$ which reduces to $\frac{28}{55}$.
38	C	You can recognize the graph of an even function because it's symmetrical across the y-axis. The graphs in (A), (C), and (D) are symmetrical across the y-axis, making them even functions. Graphs (B) and (E) are not even, so you can eliminate them. You can recognize the graph of an odd function because it looks the same when rotated 180°. The only remaining graph that looks just the same when the page is turned upside-down is (C).

Question	Answer	Explanation
39	D	Always draw figures that are described but not shown. The diagram described in this question would look like this: The circle is just window-dressing here. The important thing in this problem is the triangle. You've got an isosceles triangle with two sides of length 5 that meet at a 70° angle. Your mission is to find the length x of the mystery side opposite the 70° angle. Estimation is the fastest way to choose the right answer. This is almost an equilateral triangle, but one angle is opened wider than 60°, making the other two angles smaller. Side x, opposite the big angle, must be bigger than 5 but much smaller than 10. Only (D) gives you such a number. Of course, it's also possible to find the exact value of x. For this, the Law of Cosines is your best tool, $c^2 = a^2 + b^2 - 2ab \cos C$. This formula contains the lengths of all three sides of a triangle (a, b, and c) and the measure of one angle C. To solve the problem, just plug the two sides and angle that you know into the formula, and solve for the unknown side. Remember that the unknown side in this case is opposite the 70° angle. $$x^2 = (5)^2 + (5)^2 - 2(5)(5) \cos 70°$$ $$x^2 = 25 + 25 - 50 \cos 70°$$ $$x^2 = 50 - 50(0.342)$$ $$x^2 = 50 - 17.10$$ $$x^2 = 32.90$$ $$x = \pm 5.74$$ All lengths must be positive, so the length of the missing side must be 5.74. The correct answer is (D).
40	D	Plug some points from the graph into the equation. For example, the point $(0, 1)$ is on the graph, so plug 0 in for x in the answer choices, to see if $f(0) = 1$ in any of them. Cross off (A), (B), and (C), since they don't work. Now pick another point on the graph. $\left(\frac{\pi}{8}, \frac{1}{2}\right)$ looks about right. But when you plug $\frac{\pi}{8}$ in for x in answer choice (E), you get 2.414, which can't be correct. Doing the same thing in (D) gives you 0.414, which looks right, so the correct answer is (D).

Question	Answer	Explanation
41	A	This is a vector addition question with a minor twist—the negative sign. Have no fear—just add the components. Simplifying the expression, you have $$z = -(v + w) =$$ $$-[(-3, 4) + (12, 5)] =$$ $$-[(-3 + 12, 4 + 5)] =$$ $$-(9, 9) =$$ $$(-9, -9)$$ So the answer is (A).
42	A	This question looks frighteningly complicated, but it's not actually that bad as long as you PITA. Plug each answer choice in for x, and use your calculator to see which one spits out 0.33. The correct answer is (A).
43	E	You could certainly try out all five answer choices, and solve five sets of simultaneous equations, but it's easier to think of the graphs of these simultaneous equations. Three things can happen with simultaneous equations. First, the two given equations may be identical (or one is simply a multiple of the other), which means they describe the same line. That results in infinite solutions, since there are infinite points on a line. Second, the lines are parallel, because one equation has the same slope as the other, but a different y-intercept. That results in zero solutions, since the lines never intersect. Third, the lines have different slopes, which means they will always intersect in one point. This results in one solution. In this problem, all the answer choices fit the third situation, except (E), which fits the second situation. If you look at the two equations that result $$2x + 3y = 7$$ $$10x + 15y = 3$$ you can see that the first equation can be multiplied by 5 to get $10x + 15y = 35$. This line is parallel to the line described by the second equation. Algebraically, you can see that $10x + 15y$ could be 3 or 35 for a given point (x, y), but it can't be both at the same time! The answer is (E).

Question	Answer	Explanation
44	C	The statements $f(a, b) = 15$, $f(b, c) = 20$, and $f(a, c) = 10$ can be rewritten as equations by inserting the definition of the function $f(x, y)$. $$\frac{ab}{3} = 15, \frac{bc}{3} = 20, \text{ and } \frac{ac}{3} = 10$$ These equations can be simplified easily by getting the 3 out of the denominator. $ab = 45$, $bc = 60$, and $ac = 30$ The easiest way to find the product of a, b, and c is to multiply these three equations together, like $$ab \times bc \times ac = 45 \times 60 \times 30$$ $$aabbcc = 81,000$$ $$a^2 b^2 c^2 = 81,000$$ $$abc = \sqrt{81,000}$$ $$abc = 284.60$$
45	B	You've got variables in the question and variables in the answer choices. That means it's time to Plug In. Pick numbers that make the calculation easy. In this case, let's say that $x = 3$ and $y = 81$. The expression $\log_{x^2} y$ then becomes $\log_{3^2} 81$, or $\log_9 = 81$, and is equal to 2—the exponent that turns 9 into 81. Since $\log_{3^2} 81 = 2$, the correct answer will be the one that also equals 2 when $x = 3$ and $y = 81$. Quickly reading through Statements I, II, and III, you'll find the following: Statement I isn't true, because $\log_3 81^2 \neq 2$ (you don't need to compute the value of $\log_3 81^2$; it's obviously not 2, because $3^2 \neq 81^2$). You can therefore eliminate (A) and (D). Statement II is true, because $\log_3 9 = 2$. Statement III isn't true, because $\log_3 \left(\frac{81}{2} \right) \neq 2$ (again, you don't have to compute the exact value of $\log_3 \left(\frac{81}{2} \right)$; it's clearly not 2). You can therefore eliminate answer choices (C) and (E). The correct answer is (B).
46	A	Use the formula for volume of a sphere with radius r, given in the reference information at the beginning of the test, $V = \frac{4}{3}\pi r^3$. Plug In the given volumes, and solve for the radii. When $V = 4188.79$, $r = 10$. When $V = 14137.167$, $r = 15$. Now use the given formula for surface area of a sphere with radius r, $S = 4\pi r^2$. Plugging In the values of r that you found, you discover that S increases from 1256.637 to 2827.433, an increase of 1570.796. Now divide this increase in surface area by 12 seconds to find the average rate at which the surface area is changing per second. It's 130.9, so the answer is (A).

Question	Answer	Explanation
47	C	This is a complex number, because it has both real and imaginary components. To find its absolute value, visualize the term $6 - 3i$ on the complex plane, where one axis represents real values and the other represents imaginary values.

The point representing $6 - 3i$ would be six steps along the positive real axis and 3 steps along the imaginary negative axis, as shown. The point's absolute value is its distance from the origin, which is simply the hypotenuse of a right triangle with legs of lengths 3 and 6, respectively. Just plug those values into the Pythagorean theorem, and you've got the absolute value.

$$h^2 = 3^2 + 6^2$$
$$h^2 = 45$$
$$h = 3\sqrt{5}$$

Question	Answer	Explanation
48	D	This is a combinations question, since rearranging the order of the dishes doesn't change the dinner. Since the dinner's being ordered in two parts (the part from column A and the part from column B), you should calculate the number of combinations in two parts. Start with the five dishes from column A. The number of permutations for five items selected from a group of ten is given by $10 \times 9 \times 8 \times 7 \times 6 = 30,240$. To find the number of combinations, divide that number by 5! $\dfrac{10 \times 9 \times 8 \times 7 \times 6}{5 \times 4 \times 3 \times 2 \times 1} = 252$. There are 252 possible combinations of five dishes from column A. You're also selecting five dishes from column B, which has twenty selections. The number of combinations for column B will therefore be given by $\dfrac{20 \times 19 \times 18 \times 17 \times 16}{5 \times 4 \times 3 \times 2 \times 1} = 15,504$. So there are 15,504 combinations of 5 dishes from column B. To find the total number of possible combinations, multiply these figures together, $15,504 \times 252 = 3,907,008$. The correct answer is (D).
49	A	If y varies directly as the square of x, that means that $\dfrac{y}{x^2}$ will always have the same value. So set up a proportion. $\dfrac{2.5}{(0.5)^2} = \dfrac{80}{x^2}$. Cross-multiply and solve. $x^2 = 8$, so $x = \pm 2\sqrt{2}$. The negative value is answer choice (A).

Question	Answer	Explanation
50	D	This probability question starts out with a trick. Since it *tells* you what happens in the first two drawings, they don't even enter into your calculations. Their outcome is certain. The real question starts after that. Given a container that holds 5 blue marbles and 6 red ones, what is the probability that three drawings will produce *at least* two red marbles? That "at least" is what makes the question difficult. It's relatively easy to find the probability of just one outcome—but look at all the ways you can get *at least* two red marbles in three tries—RRB, RBR, BRR, RRR. Each one of these is a separate outcome. To compute the total probability of getting at least two red marbles, you need to find the probability of each outcome that does the trick, and then add them up. Here's the probability of drawing RRB. $$\frac{6}{11} \times \frac{5}{10} \times \frac{5}{9} = \frac{150}{990} = \frac{5}{33}$$ There are 6 red marbles out of a total of 11 on the first drawing, 5 red marbles out of a total of 10 on the second, and 5 blue marbles out of a total of 9 on the third. The total probability of this outcome is $\frac{5}{33}$. Here's the probability of drawing RBR. $$\frac{6}{11} \times \frac{5}{10} \times \frac{5}{9} = \frac{150}{990} = \frac{5}{33}$$ And here's the probability of BRR. $$\frac{5}{11} \times \frac{6}{10} \times \frac{5}{9} = \frac{150}{990} = \frac{5}{33}$$ As you can see, RRB, RBR, and BRR are all equally probable. Only one other outcome remains, and that's RRR. $$\frac{6}{11} \times \frac{5}{10} \times \frac{4}{9} = \frac{120}{990} = \frac{4}{33}$$ You now know the probability of every outcome that produces at least two red marbles in three drawings. To find the total overall probability, add up all of the individual probabilities. $$\frac{5}{33} + \frac{5}{33} + \frac{5}{33} + \frac{4}{33} = \frac{19}{33}$$ The correct answer is (D).

Chapter 20
Level 2 Practice Test
Form B
Answers and
Explanations

Question	Answer	Explanation
1	E	The statement $xy \neq 0$ means that neither x nor y is zero. To find the value of $\frac{y}{x}$, rearrange the equation so that $\frac{y}{x}$ is isolated on one side of the equals sign; whatever's on the other side will be the answer. In this case, the easiest way to isolate $\frac{y}{x}$ is to divide each side of the equation by x, getting $3 = \frac{0.3\,y}{x}$, and then divide both sides by 0.3, getting $\frac{3}{0.3} = \frac{y}{x}$. Your calculator will tell you that $\frac{3}{0.3}$ is equal to 10.
2	B	To find the increase in $f(x)$ as x goes from 2 to 3, calculate $f(2)$ and $f(3)$ by plugging those numbers into the definition of the function. You'll find that $f(2) = 0.0589$ and $f(3) = 1.4308$. The increase in $f(x)$ is the difference between these two numbers, 1.3719.
3	A	 Since you are given the two intercepts, draw a rough sketch like the one above and approximate. The slope is positive, but less than 1, since the line has a slope smaller than 45°. Only answer choice (A) matches your description. You could also notice that since the y-intercept is 3, the equation of the line (in slope-intercept form) must look like $y = mx + 3$, which narrows it down to (A) or (E). But (E) has a negative slope, which doesn't fit your sketch, so it's (A).
4	A	PITA. Starting with (C), Plug In the values from the answer choices for a in the original expression. If the value makes the equation true, you've got the right answer. If not, then pick another answer choice and try again.

Question	Answer	Explanation
5	D	An arithmetic series is one that increases by a constant added amount. From 4 to 15 is a total increase of 11, which happens from the second term in the arithmetic series to the tenth, taking 8 steps. This means that each step is worth one-eighth of 11, $\frac{11}{8}$, or 1.375. That's the constant amount added to each term in the series to get the next term. To find the first term in the series, just take one step backward from the second term, that is, subtract 1.375 from 4. You get 2.625.

You can also solve this equation by using the formula for the nth term of an arithmetic sequence: $a_n = a_1 + (n-1)d$. You'd start by figuring out d (the difference between any two consecutive terms) just as you did above, finding that $d = 1.375$. Then, take one of the terms you're given (for example, $a_2 = 4$, in which case $n = 2$) and use these values to fill in the formula, $4 = a_1 + (2-1)(1.375)$. Then just solve for a_1. Once again you'll find that $a_1 = 2.625$. |
| 6 | C | This simple function question just requires you to plug 6 into $g(x)$. You can start by eliminating (A) and (B), because the entire function is contained within an absolute value sign, so it can't produce negative values. To find the exact value of $g(6)$, Plug In the number. You get $\left|5(6)^2 - (6)^3\right|$, or $\left|-36\right|$, which equals 36. |
| 7 | E | The line $y = x$ is shown above. A graph symmetrical across this line will look like it is reflected in this line as though it were a mirror. Another way to think about it is that the two halves of a curve symmetrical across the line $y = x$ would meet perfectly if you folded the paper along that line. Of the five choices, only (E) has this kind of symmetry. |

Question	Answer	Explanation
8	B	Just use your calculator. $$A = \sin^{-1}\left(\frac{1}{3}\sin 75°\right) =$$ $$\sin^{-1}\left(\frac{1}{3}(0.9659)\right) =$$ $$\sin^{-1}(0.3220) =$$ $$18.8°$$
9	B	This is the equation of a parabola which opens upward. The minimum value will be the y-value of the vertex, which you can find using the vertex formula. The x-coordinate of the vertex is given by $x = \dfrac{-b}{2a}$, which gives you $x = 6$ in this case. Plug this value back into the equation to get the y-coordinate of the vertex, $\frac{1}{2}(6)^2 - 6(6) + 11 = -7$. The function's minimum value is -7.
10	D	This is a great question for Plugging In. Plug In a couple of simple values, like $x = 3$ and $y = 5$, and solve. $|3 - 5| + |5 - 3| = |-2| + |2| = 2 + 2 = 4$. The correct answer must also equal 4. Using $x = 3$ and $y = 5$, you'll find that only (D) gives you the correct value.
11	D	Plugging In works very well here. Find simple values that make the original equation true, like $A = 90°$ and $B = 0°$, so $\sin 90° = 1$ and $\cos 0° = 1$. Then go through the answer choices to find the one that is also true when $A = 90°$ and $B = 0°$. In this case, only (D) works. In fact, (D) states a basic trigonometric identity, $\sin A = \cos(90° - A)$.
12	C	To figure out a probability, divide the number of things you're looking for (in this case, flawed automobiles) by the total (all automobiles produced). |	Total Units Production	Flawed Units
April	569	15
May	508	18
June	547	16 | Figure 1 Since you're calculating the odds for the entire three-month period, you have to add up the two columns of the chart. You find that 49 flawed automobiles were produced out of a total of 1,624. Divide 49 by 1,624 to find the probability, 0.03.

Question	Answer	Explanation
13	C	 Figure 2 The easiest way to find the possible ramp lengths is to find the shortest and longest legal lengths. The length of the ramp is the hypotenuse of a right triangle. Using the SOHCAHTOA definition of sine $\left(\sin = \dfrac{O}{H}\right)$, you can set up equations to find the lengths of a 5°-ramp and a 7°-ramp. $\sin 5° = \dfrac{3}{H}$ and $\sin 7° = \dfrac{3}{H}$. Solve for H in each case, and you'll find that the shortest possible hypotenuse has a length of 24.62, while the longest has a length of 34.42. Only (C) is between these limits.
14	A	This question is simpler than it looks. The constant term $-n$ represents the y-intercept (where $x = 0$) of the whole complicated function. Just look to see where the function crosses the y-axis. It does so at $y = 50$. That means that $-n$, the y-intercept, equals 50. Just plain n, however, equals -50. Watch out for (C), a trap answer!
15	A	Here's a classic limit question. You can't just plug the x-value in the question into the function, because it makes the denominator equal zero, which means the function is undefined at that point. To find the limit of the function approaching that point (assuming the limit exists), try to cancel out the troublesome term. First, factor the top and bottom of the function, $\dfrac{(x+2)(x-3)}{3(x+2)}$. As you can see, the term $(x+2)$ occurs in the numerator and the denominator, so you can cancel it out. You're left with $\dfrac{(x-3)}{3}$. Now you can plug $x = -2$ into the function without producing an undefined quantity. The result, -1.67, is the limit of the function as x approaches -2.

Question	Answer	Explanation
16	B	This is a great PITA question. When you receive an inheritance in Titheland, you get the first 1,000 florins free and clear. After that, you get only 35% of the remaining amount; the government keeps the other 65%. To find the right answer, take the numbers from the answer choices and see which one would give you 2,500 florins after taxes. Answer choice (C) is 4,475 florins. Starting with that amount, you'd get 1,000 florins free and clear, and 3,475 would be taxed. The government would take 65% of 3,475, or 2,258.75. That would leave you with 1,216.25 plus the first 1,000, for a total of 2,216.25 florins after taxes—not enough. Your next step is to select the next larger answer choice and try again. Answer choice (B) is 5,286 florins, which will give you 1,000 untaxed and 4,286 taxed. That means the government takes 65% of 4,286, or 2,785.9 florins, leaving you with 1,500.1. Add the untaxed 1,000, and you've got a total of 2,500.1 florins after taxes—right on the money.
17	B	PITA. Plug each answer choice into the equation for t, to see which one makes $d = 10$. (B) works.
18	C	Plug In 1 for k in the expression $3k - 2$; then repeat for 2, 3, 4, etc., all the way up to 10, and add up all the results. This gives us $1 + 4 + 7 +\ldots+ 28$. This is clearly an arithmetic sequence where you keep adding 3. The formula for the sum of the first n terms of an arithmetic sequence is $\text{sum} = n\left(\dfrac{a_1 + a_n}{2}\right)$, which, in this case, gives us $\text{sum} = 10\left(\dfrac{1+28}{2}\right) = 145$. The answer is (C).
19	B	It may not be obvious at first, but this is a natural logarithm question. The equation $e^x = 5$ can be rewritten in logarithmic form: $\log_e 5 = x$. A logarithm to the base e is called a natural logarithm, which can be written as $\ln 5 = x$. And that's something you can just punch into your calculator. The natural logarithm of 5 is 1.60944, which rounds to 1.61. The correct answer is (B). You can also PITA, starting with (C), to see which value, when plugged in for x, makes the equation true.
20	E	The greatest distance within a rectangular solid is the length of the long diagonal—the line between diagonally opposite corners, through the center of the solid. The length of this line can be determined using the Super Pythagorean theorem, $a^2 + b^2 + c^2 = d^2$, where a, b, and c are the dimensions of the solid, and d is the length of the diagonal. To find the possible coordinates of the box, use the Super Pythagorean theorem on each of the answer choices, and find the one that gives a diagonal of 12. Only (E) produces the right number, $4^2 + 8^2 + 8^2 = d^2$, and so $d = \sqrt{144}$, or 12.

Question	Answer	Explanation
21	E	The variables in the answer choices tell you that this is a perfect Plugging In question. Pick a rate for each runner. Say runner A travels 100 feet every minute ($a = 100$) and runner B travels 1 foot every second ($b = 1$). In one hour, that means A travels 60×100 feet, or 6,000 feet, while B travels $3,600 \times 1$ foot, or 3,600 feet. In this case, A travels 2,400 feet farther than B. This makes 2,400 your target number—the number the correct answer will equal. Only (E) equals 2,400 using these values.
22	B	This question is easier when you draw the triangle. This right triangle has a hypotenuse of 13 and legs of 5 and 12. The smallest angle will clearly be the angle opposite the side of length 5. Knowing this, you can use SOHCAHTOA to figure out the angle (let's call it θ). $\sin \theta = \dfrac{5}{13} = 0.3846$. Take the inverse sine of both sides, and you get $\theta = 22.62°$.
23	B	Plugging In makes this question easy. Suppose, for example, that $x = 2$. To evaluate the expression $g(f(2))$, start on the inside, $f(2) = \dfrac{1}{2+1}$, or $\dfrac{1}{3}$. Then, work with the outside function, $g\left(\dfrac{1}{3}\right) = \dfrac{1}{\frac{1}{3}} + 1$, or $3 + 1$, which equals 4. That's the value of $g(f(2))$. The correct answer choice will be the one that gives the same value (4) when you Plug In $x = 2$. Answer choice (B) is the only one that does.
24	D	The roots of an expression are the values that make that expression equal to zero. In this case, there are three roots—π, 3, and e. To figure out which are the greatest and least roots, use your calculator to find the values of π (3.14159…) and e (2.71828…). These are the greatest and least roots, so subtract them to find their difference, 0.42331. (Hint: If your calculator doesn't have an e key, get one that does.)
25	D	Plug In! Suppose that $x = 4$, for example. Then $\dfrac{x!}{(x-2)!} = \dfrac{4!}{2!} = \dfrac{4 \times 3 \times 2 \times 1}{2 \times 1} = 12$. The correct answer will be the one that equals 12 when $x = 4$.

Question	Answer	Explanation
26	D	 Figure 4 A rectangle rotated around one edge generates a cylinder. This rectangle is being rotated around the vertical axis, so the cylinder will have a radius of 7 and a height of 5. Just plug these values into the formula for the volume of a cylinder, $V = r^2 h$. $$V = \pi(7)^2(5)$$ $$= \pi \times 49 \times 5$$ $$= 245\pi$$ $$= 769.69$$
27	E	To make this problem easier, simplify the original function. You can do this by factoring the top and bottom of the fraction: $f(x,y) = \dfrac{(x-y)(x-y)}{(x-y)(x+y)}$. You can cancel out an $(x-y)$ term on the top and bottom, producing the simplified function $f(x,y) = \dfrac{(x-y)}{(x+y)}$. Then, to answer the question, just Plug In $(-x)$ for x and $(-y)$ for y: $f(-x,-y) = \dfrac{(-x)-(-y)}{(-x)+(-y)} = \dfrac{-x+y}{-x-y}$. Then, just multiply by $\left(\dfrac{-1}{-1}\right)$ to flip the signs on the top and bottom of this fraction, $\left(\dfrac{-x+y}{-x-y}\right) \times \left(\dfrac{-1}{-1}\right) = \dfrac{x-y}{x+y}$.

Question	Answer	Explanation
28	D	In order to disprove a rule, it's only necessary to find one exception. That's what (D) is saying. Even if you didn't know that, however, there are still ways to eliminate wrong answers here. Use POE and some common sense. Answer choices (A), (C), and (E) are all pretty much impossible—they each require you to accomplish an enormous or even endless task. Answer choice (B) is more reasonable, but it doesn't relate to the question, which asks about numbers *less* than 5. Answer choice (D) is the only one that is both possible and relevant to the question.
29	E	Careful with this one. Given three corners of a rectangle, you know for sure where the fourth one is. But this is just a parallelogram—capable of having many different shapes. You could place the fourth vertex at $(-3, 3)$, $(3, -3)$, or $(7, 3)$, and still have a parallelogram. You don't know for sure where the fourth vertex is.
30	A	An expression is undefined when its denominator equals zero. To find out what values might do that wicked deed, factor the expression. You'll find it equals $\frac{(x+4)(x-1)}{2(x+4)(x+1)}$. Two values will make this expression undefined—$x = -1$ and $x = -4$, both of which make the denominator equal to zero. (A) is correct. [Note: It's true that the term $(x + 4)$ cancels out of the factored expression. That doesn't mean that the original expression is defined at $x = -4$, however. It just means that you can calculate the limit of the expression as x approaches -4. Don't confuse the existence of a limit with the defined/undefined status of an expression.] You can also PITA to see which values from the answer choices cause problems for the expression. In this case, pick an easy value that shows up in 2 or 3 answer choices, so you can eliminate the greatest number of them. Try $x = 0$. Plugging this in gives you $-\frac{1}{2}$, that is fine. So eliminate answer choices that contain 0: Cross off (C) and (E). Let's try $x = -1$. This causes the denominator to become 0, so you know that -1 is in the correct answer. Therefore, eliminate answer choices that don't contain 1: Cross off (D). The only difference between (A) and (B) is -4. When you test $x = -4$, the denominator again becomes 0, so -4 must be in the correct answer, which is (A).

Question	Answer	Explanation
31	C	In a I, II, III question, tackle the statements one at a time and remember the process of elimination. The expression in Statement I is always positive, because x^2 must be positive and adding 1 can only increase it. That means that (B) and (D) can be eliminated, because they don't include Statement I. Statement II is trickier. The sine of an expression can be anywhere from –1 to 1, inclusive. That means that most values of $(1 - \sin x)$ will be positive. If $\sin x = 1$, however, then the expression equals zero—not a positive value. Statement II is out, and you can eliminate (E). Finally, Statement III can be simplified. $\pi(\pi^{x-1}) = \pi^{x-1+1} = \pi^x$. Since π is positive, and no exponent can change the sign of a base, π^x is always positive. (A) is out, and (C) is the correct answer. Graphing each function on your calculator may be easier, as long as you look carefully when you check Statement II.
32	A	 Figure 5 Changing the sign of x in the expression $f(x)$ will flip the function's graph around the x-axis. Changing the sign of the whole function to produce $y = -f(-x)$ will flip the graph over the y-axis as well. The graph in answer choice (A) represents the original graph flipped both horizontally and vertically.
33	D	It's helpful to draw this one. The wire has a slope of $\frac{2}{5}$, meaning that it rises 2 feet for every 5 feet it runs. Since its total rise is 48, or (2×24), its total run must be 120, or (5×24). Don't pick answer choice (B), though. The question asks for the length of the wire, not the distance between the anchor and antenna. The wire's length is the hypotenuse of a right triangle with legs 48 and 120. The Pythagorean theorem will tell you that its length is 129.24.

Question	Answer	Explanation
34	B	To start, you can do some useful elimination. The statement $\frac{3\pi}{2} < \theta < 2\pi$ tells you that you're working in the fourth quadrant of the unit circle, where the tangent is negative. You can immediately eliminate (C), (D), and (E). If $\sec \theta = 4$, then $\cos \theta = 0.25$, because, by definition, $\sec\theta = \frac{1}{\cos\theta}$. Here you have to be careful. If you take the inverse cosine of 0.25, your calculator will display a value whose cosine equals 0.25—in radians, you should get 1.3181; but remember that different angles can produce the same cosine. In this case, you know that $\frac{3\pi}{2} < \theta < 2\pi$, which means that the angle in question is in the fourth quadrant of the unit circle. The angle in that quadrant with an equivalent cosine can be expressed in radians as -1.3181, or as $2\pi - 1.3181 = 4.9651$. Take the tangent of either of these values, and you'll get -3.8730.
35	C	Drawing this one is helpful. You'll find that the radii of the two circles have to add up to the distance between the circles' centers. You can find that distance using the distance formula, $d = \sqrt{(x_2 - x_1)^2 + (y_2 - y_1)^2}$. You'll find that the two centers are separated by a distance of 8.6023. Since one circle has a radius of 4, the other must have a radius of 4.6023.
36	C	The equations in the beginning of this question can be rearranged into the Law of Sines. A little algebraic manipulation gets you $\frac{\sin A}{7} = \frac{\sin B}{10}$ and $\frac{\sin B}{5} = \frac{\sin C}{2}$. These equations can be combined into $\frac{\sin A}{7} = \frac{\sin B}{10} = \frac{\sin C}{4}$, which is the Law of Sines. This tells you that the lengths of the triangle's sides are in a ratio of 7:10:4. So, you can call the sides $7x$, $10x$, and $4x$. They add up to 16, so $21x = 16$, and $x = 0.7619$; side a has length $7x$, which equals 5.3333. The answer is (C).
37	E	 | x	$h(x)$
---	---
-1	0
0	3
1	0
2	3	 Test each expression with the values from the table. The easiest one to use is 0; when you make $x = 0$, the function should equal 3. Only (D) and (E) equal 3 when $x = 0$. Then, notice that the function is equal to zero when $x = 1$ or -1. These values must be roots of the function. Only (E) contains both 1 and -1 as roots. It's the right answer.

Question	Answer	Explanation
38	A	This is a tricky simultaneous-equations problem. After some experimentation, you might notice that the second and third equations can be added together, $a + b + 2c = n + 8$, which is very similar to the first equation, $a + b + 2c = 7$. From this, you can determine that $n + 8 = 7$. If n is any value other than -1, this is impossible—no values of a, b, and c can make this system of equations true. There is no solution for this system if $n \neq -1$.
39	D	 Figure 6 Note: Figure not drawn to scale. When you know all three sides of a triangle, and you need to determine the measures of the angles, it's time to use the Law of Cosines, $c^2 = a^2 + b^2 - 2ab \cos C$. Just Plug In the lengths of the sides, making sure that you make c the side opposite θ. $\sqrt{125}^2 = (12)^2 + (5)^2 - 2(12)(5) \cos \theta$. Simplifying this gives you the equation $\cos \theta = 0.3667$. Taking the inverse cosine of both sides shows that $\theta = 68.4898°$.
40	D	The formula for the determinant of a 3×3 matrix tells you that $A = lqu + mrs + npt - mpu - lrt - nqs$. This is easy to see if you take the first two columns of the matrix and recopy them to the right of the original matrix, and make diagonal lines connecting the elements. Now do the same thing with the second matrix, and you find that the determinant is $8lqu + 8mrs + 8npt - 8mpu - 8lrt - 8nqs$. Factor out 8, and it's clear that this determinant is $8A$. The answer is (D). Want an easier way to solve this? Go to the MATRIX menu on your graphing calculator and enter a random 3×3 matrix, like $\begin{bmatrix} 9 & 2 & 5 \\ 3 & 4 & 0 \\ 6 & 8 & 1 \end{bmatrix}$. Your calculator will tell you that the determinant of this matrix is 30. Now enter the matrix with each entry doubled: $\begin{bmatrix} 18 & 4 & 10 \\ 6 & 8 & 0 \\ 12 & 16 & 2 \end{bmatrix}$. The determinant of this matrix is 240. This is 8 times the determinant of the original matrix, making (D) the answer once again.

Question	Answer	Explanation
41	A	This is a little tricky; you've got to pay attention to that underlined word, "increased." The values in the equation $g(x) = A[\sin(Bx + C)] + D$ that determine amplitude and period are A and B, respectively. Quantities C and D do not have to change to alter the amplitude or period, so (C) and (E) are out. The trick is that while you increase the amplitude by increasing A, you increase the period by *decreasing* B. If the amplitude and period of the curve both increase, that means that A increases and B decreases.
42	A	All the fancy language in this question basically boils down to this: List M and list N each contains 20 elements; each element in list M is larger than the corresponding element in list N.
		Once you have a clear idea of what that means, tackle the answer choices one at a time. Since the middle two values of M are bigger than the middle two values of N, the median of M must be greater, and (A) is correct. If you don't see this right away, you can always eliminate the other answer choices. You can eliminate (B) because it's quite possible that the largest value in list N is larger than the smallest value in list M. You don't know anything about the modes of the two lists, so cross off (C). For (D), suppose that each element in M is exactly 1 greater than the corresponding element in N. The ranges would be identical, so you can cross off (D). In that same situation, the standard deviations of the two lists would be identical, so you can cross off (E).
43	D	This problem looks scary, but it's really just a matter of Plugging In. Each answer choice says that the first term is 3, and then each one gives a different definition of the sequence. In the given sequence $a_0 = 3$, $a_1 = 5$, $a_2 = 8.333$, and $a_3 = 13.889$. This obviously isn't an arithmetic sequence, because the difference between the terms is not consistent. So Plug In values of n to see if the terms you are given fit the equations in each answer choice. If you plug $n = 0$ into answer choice (A), you get $a_{0+1} = a_0 + 2$. Well, $5 = 3 + 2$, so this seems to work. Now plug $n = 1$ into answer choice (A). This gives $a_{1+1} = a_1 + 2$. But $8.333 \neq 5 + 2$, so (A) doesn't define the sequence. In (B), Plug In $n = 0$ again, which gives $a_{0+1} = 2a_0 - 1$. This works, because $5 = 2(3) - 1$. But when you try $n = 1$, you get $a_{1+1} = 2a_1 - 1$, which is wrong, because $8.333 \neq 2(5) - 1$. Cross off (B). Repeating this process for answer choice (C), Plug In $n = 1$, which fails. Choice (D) works for all the terms given. It turns out that this is a geometric sequence with a constant factor of $\frac{5}{3}$.

Question	Answer	Explanation
44	D	The statement $0 \le n \le \dfrac{\pi}{2}$ tells you that you're working in the first quadrant of the unit circle where both sine and cosine are never negative. The unit $\dfrac{\pi}{2}$ also tells you that you'll be working with angles in radians, not degrees. Make sure your calculator is in the correct mode. The question tells you that the cosine of the cosine of n is 0.8. To find n, just take the inverse cosine of 0.8, and then take the inverse cosine of the result. You should get 0.8717—that's n. If you get an error, your calculator is probably in degree mode. Finally, take the tangent of 0.8717. You should get 1.1895.
45	C	This cylinder has a radius of n (because n is half the diameter) and a height of $\dfrac{n}{2}$. Just plug these values into the formula for the surface area of a cylinder, $SA = 2\pi r^2 + 2\pi rh$. You get $2\pi n^2 + \pi n^2$, or $3\pi n^2$.
46	A	PITA. Plug In each answer choice for θ to see which one makes the equation true. Make sure your calculator is in radian mode. Only (A) works.
47	A	A good way to tackle this one is by trying to disprove each of the answer choices. If you start with (A), you're lucky. There's no way to divide 5 by another quantity and get zero; it's the right answer. Even if you weren't sure, the other answer choices are pretty easy to disprove. Just set $\dfrac{5}{x+4}$ equal to a quantity prohibited by each answer choice, and solve for x. If there's a real value of x that solves the equation, then the value *is* in the range after all, and the answer choice is incorrect. Another method is to graph the function on your calculator and see what y-values seem impossible.
48	C	$\csc\theta = \dfrac{1}{\sin\theta}$, so rewrite the given equation as $\dfrac{1}{\sin\theta} = \dfrac{1}{3t}$. That means $\sin\theta = 3t$. Now, Plug In an easy number for θ, such as 30°. So you have $\sin 30° = 3t$. Therefore, $t = 0.167$. The question asks for cos 30°, which is 0.866, the target number. Now, Plug In 0.167 for t in the answer choices to see which one becomes 0.866. Choice (C) is the only one that comes close.

Question	Answer	Explanation
49	C	There's no sophisticated math here. It's just an annoying function question with a lot of steps. As usual with I, II, III questions, tackle the statements one at a time and remember the Process of Elimination. Statement I must be true—if $x = 0$, then the function comes out to $\frac{y}{y}$, which equals 1 no matter what y is (since y can't be zero). Answer choice (B) can be eliminated since it doesn't contain Statement I. Statement II must be true; since the value 1 is being plugged into the function in the x and y positions, the function will always equal $\frac{2}{2}$, or 1. Answer choices (A) and (D) can be eliminated because they don't include Statement II. Finally, Statement III is not necessarily true; $f(x, y) = \frac{xy + y}{x + y}$, and $f(y, x) = \frac{xy + x}{x + y}$. If x and y have different values, then these expressions will not be equal. Answer choice (E) can thus be eliminated, because Statement III is false. That leaves only (C).
50	B	Plug In! Since no numerical values are assigned to m and b, you can Plug In whatever you want. For example, say $m = -8$ and $b = 2$. The line's equation is then $y = -8x + 2$. The x-intercept is $\frac{1}{4}$ and the y-intercept is 2. The triangle formed by this line and the axes has a base of length $\frac{1}{4}$ and a height of length 2 (it's helpful to sketch this). If you rotate this triangle around the x-axis to generate a cone, the cone will have a radius of 2 and a height of $\frac{1}{4}$. Plug those values into the formula for the volume of a cone, $V = \frac{1}{3}\pi r^2 h$. You'll find that the volume equals $\frac{\pi}{3}$. This immediately eliminates answers (A), (C), and (D). Things look pretty good for (B), but you can't be sure it's not (E) until you've tried another set of numbers. If you try $m = -1$ and $b = 1$, you get a line with the equation $y = -x + 1$. This line has an x-intercept of 1 and a y-intercept of 1. The cone generated by rotation would then have a radius of 1 and a height of 1. Plug those numbers into the volume formula and you will once again get $\frac{\pi}{3}$. That's proof enough, the answer's clearly (B). That's the power of Plugging In.

Level 2 Practice Test Form B Answers and Explanations | 515

Index

Symbols

Group questions, statistical, 275–276
Guessing, 13

H

Height, in solid geometry, 130, 133–136, 138, 143, 149
Heptagon, 118
Hexagon, 118, 124
Hyperbola, 174–175
Hypotenuse, 99, 105–106
    in trigonometry, 180–181, 183, 186–187, 190, 192

I

i
    computing powers of, 304
    doing algebra with, 304
    as imaginary unit, 305–306
Imaginary axis, 305
Imaginary numbers, 20, 303–304, 306–307
    in complex numbers, 304–307
Increase, percentage, 31
Independent variable, 219–221, 228, 232
Indirect variation. *See* inverse variation
Inequalities
    algebraic, 64–65
    linear, 166
Infinite geometric sequence, sum of, 293
Inscribed, 91
Inscribed angle, 122–123
Inscribed solids, 143–145
Integers, 20
Intersection, 137, 154, 155, 177, 289
Interval, 232–233
Inverse functions, 225–227
Inversely proportional quantities, 69–70
Inverse variation, 70–71
Irrational numbers, 20
Isosceles right triangle, 105
Isosceles triangles, 97, 105, 146

J

Joe Bloggs answers, 15–17

L

Lateral area, of cone, 135
Law of cosines, 205–207
Law of sines, 204–205
Legs, of right triangle, 99, 146, 208
Length
    in changing dimensions, 148–150
    in solid geometry, 130–131
Limits, 295–298
Line, 90
    basic rules, 91

equation of, 156–158
    parallel, 90, 93
    perpendicular, 91, 123
    rotation around, 145–148
    tangent, 123
Linear inequalities, 166
Line of symmetry, rotation around, 146
Line segment, 90, 163–165
Logarithms, 280–287
    change of base, 280, 283
    common, 282
    in exponential equations, 282–284
    natural, 284–287
    rules, 281–282
    simplification, 282
Logic, 301–303
Long diagonal
    of cube, 132–133
    of rectangular solid, 131

M

Magnitude
    of complex number, 306
    of vectors, 297–300
Major arc, 122
Math Level 1 Test, 1–4, 6
Math Level 2 Test, 1–4, 6
Math Subject Tests, 2
    calculator use, 4, 18
    scoring strategy, 9–13
    topics included per level, 2
    when to take, 3–4
    which level to take, 3
Matrix, 309–310
Mean, 260
    arithmetic, 21
Median, 21, 260
Memorization, for scoring, 17
Midpoint, 90
    of a line segment, 165
Minor arc, 122, 124
Mode, 21, 260–261
Multiples, 23–24
Multiplication, 25
    in algebraic equations, 52–53
    of binomials, 78–79
    of exponents, 42–43
    in PEMDAS, 27–28
    in quadratic equation, 80–81
    of ranges, 68
    in repeated percent change, 33–35
    of roots, 44
    in simultaneous equations, 75–78

N

Natural logarithms, 284–287
Negative exponents, 46–47
Negative numbers, 25–27
    square root, 228–229
    in trigonometric functions, 193–198
Negative reciprocal, 161
Negative root, 44, 228–230
Negative slope, 159
Nonnegative function, 216, 230
Non-right triangles, 204–207
Nth-degree function, 255
Nth term
    of an arithmetic sequence, 290–291
    of a geometric sequence, 292
Numbers
    basic manipulations, 27
    even and odd, 25
    exponent effects, 42–43
    positive and negative, 25–26
    term definitions, 20–21

O

Obtuse angle, 180
Octagon, 118
Odd function, 216
Odd numbers, 24–25
One, as exponent, 45
Origin, 154
Origin symmetry, 247–248
Outcomes, in probability, 263–268

P

Pacing, for scoring, 10–11
Pair of values, 219
Parabola, 167–169
    as function, 235–239
    general equation, 168
    standard equation, 167
Parallel lines, 90, 93
    slope, 161
Parallelograms, 113
Parentheses, in PEMDAS
    for algebra, 53–55
    for arithmetic, 27–28
PEMDAS
    in algebra, 215
    in arithmetic, 27–28
    calculator use with, 27–28
Pentagon, 118
Percentages
    conversions, 29–31

repeated conversions, 33–37
    word-problem translation, 29–30
Percent change
    calculating, 31–33
    repeated, 33–37
    up *vs.* down, 32–33
Percentile score, 3
Percent sign, 29–30
Perimeter, 90
Period, 216
Periodic functions, 216, 250
Permutations, 260
    advanced, 270
    in combination calculation, 270–272
    simple, 269–270
Perpendicular lines, 91
    slope, 161
Personal order of difficulty (POOD), 12
Pi (π) constant, 284
    in degree to radian conversion, 199–201
    in trigonometric graphs, 202–203
PITA (Plugging In the Answers), 62–64
Plane, 90
Plane geometry, 89–128
    approximation, 91
    line and angle rules, 91–95
    other polygons, 118–119
    quadrilaterals, 112–117
    term definitions, 90–91
    test level, 2, 89
    triangles, 96–112
Plugging In 57–61
    algebraic functions, 242, 251
    polynomial division, 307–308
    range questions, 232
Plugging In the Answers (PITA), 62–64
POE (Process Of Elimination), 13
Polar coordinates, 208–211
Polygons, 90
    other, 118–119
    in pyramids, 138
    regular, 90, 118
Polynomial, 52
    quadratics as, 80
Polynomial division, 307–308
POOD (personal order of difficulty), 12
Positive difference, 21
Positive numbers, 25–27
    exponent effects, 42–43
    in trigonometric functions, 192–198
Positive root, 44, 230
Positive slope, 159

Power
    fractional, 45
    of *i*, 304
    raising of exponents, 43
Power rule, 281–282
Prime factorization, 21–23
Prime numbers, 20
Prisms, 130
    rectangular, 130–131
Probability, 263–268
    of multiple events, 264–266
Problem-solving tools, 13–18, 27–28
Process of Elimination (POE). *See* POE
Product, 20
Product rule, 281–282
Proportion
    in algebraic equations, 69–71
    of triangles, 96, 108–109
    in trigonometry, 180, 204–205
Pyramids, 138
Pythagorean theorem, 99
    in coordinate geometry, 163–164, 297
    in plane geometry, 104–107
    in solid geometry, 131, 134, 139
    super, 131, 139
    in trigonometry, 182
Pythagorean triplets, 104–107, 182

Q

Quadrants, 154–155
Quadratic equation, 80
Quadratic formula, 83–85
Quadratic identities, 81–83
Quadratics, 52, 80–81
    factoring, 80–81
    special identities, 81–82
Quadrilaterals, 90, 113–116
    parallelograms, 112–114
    rectangles, 114–115
    squares, 114–115
    trapezoids, 115–116
Quotient, 20
Quotient rule, 281

R

Radian
    conversion from degrees, 199–201
    in trigonometric graphs, 202–203
    mode on calculator, 183
Radical, 44
Radius, 90
    in coordinate geometry, 170, 172
    in plane geometry, 90, 120–122

radian *vs.*, 199
    in solid geometry, 133–137, 146
    of unit circle, 192–193
Raising power to power, of exponents, 43
Range
    algebraic, 216, 230–232
        graphing, 240–243
        intervals and, 232–234
    statistical, 260–261
    of values, 66–68
Range notation, 231
Rational numbers, 20
Ray, 90
Real axis, 305
Real numbers, 20
    in algebra questions, 240–242
    in complex numbers, 305–306
Reciprocal, 21, 46
    negative, 161
    trigonometric functions, 189–191
Rectangles, 114–115
Rectangular coordinate system, 154–155
    polar coordinates *vs.*, 208, 213
Rectangular prism, 130–131
Rectangular solids, 130–133
    changing dimensions, 148–149
    inscribed, 143
    triangles, 139
Regular polygon, 90, 118
Remainder, 21
Repeated percent change, 33–37
Reverse FOIL, 80–81, 307
Right angle, 91, 99, 113–114, 123
Right triangles, 99–100, 126–127
    isosceles, 105
    in trigonometry, 182–191, 210, 306
    rotation and, 146
Rise over run, 160
Root, 44, 52
    in algebraic functions, 216, 228–230
    in arithmetic functions, 31, 44
    cube, 44
    of functions, 245
    in PEMDAS, 27
    in quadratic equation, 80–81
Rotation, 145–148
Rule of 180°, 96

S

Scoring, 3
    strategy for, 9–18
Scoring curve, 3
Secant, 189–191

Second-degree function, 254
Sector, 90, 122
Sequences
    arithmetic, 290–291, 294
    geometric, 292–294
Series, 291
Sets
    combinations, 260, 269–272
    statistical, 260–261
    of values, 228–231
Sigma (Σ), 291
Similar triangles, 108–112
Simplification
    of algebraic functions, 219
    of logarithms, 282
    of radicals, 44
    of trigonometric functions, 186–191
Simultaneous equations, 75–78
Sine, 181
    graphing, 192–198, 202–203
    law of, 204–205
Sixth-degree function, 253
Slant height, 135
Slope, 154, 160–162
Slope formula, 160
Slope-intercept formula, 156
SOHCAHTOA, 180–181, 183, 186, 190
Solid geometry, 129–152
    changing dimensions, 148–150
    cones, 135–136
    cubes, 132–133
    cylinders, 133–134
    inscribed solids, 143–145
    prisms, 130
    pyramids, 138
    rectangular solids, 130–133
    rotation and, 145–148
    spheres, 137
    test level, 2, 129
    triangles in rectangular solids, 139
    volume, 130–133, 135, 137–138, 140–141,
        151–152
Solutions
    of the function, 245
    in quadratic equation, 80–81
Space, coordinate, 175–176
Space diagonal, 131
Special exponents, 45–46
Speed, average, 73–75
Spheres, 137
    changing dimensions, 148–149
    inscribed, 143–144
    rotation and, 145–146

Split function, 220
Square root, 44–45
    domain and, 228–230
    of negative numbers, 228–230
Squares, 114–115
Standard deviation, 260–262
Standard form of the equation of a circle, 170
Standard form of the equation of a parabola, 167
Statistics
    combinations, 270–272
    factorials, 269–270, 273
    group questions, 275
    permutations, 269–270
    probability, 263–268
    term definitions, 260
    working with, 260–263
Straight angle, 92
Study plan, 5
Subtraction, 20–21, 25–27
    in algebraic equations, 53, 76, 78
    of exponents, 42–43
    in logarithms, 281–282
    in PEMDAS, 27
    of ranges, 67–68
    in repeated percent change, 33–36
    of roots, 44
    in simultaneous equations, 75–77
    of vectors, 299–300
Sum, 20
    of arithmetic sequence, 291
    of geometric sequence, 292
    of infinite geometric sequence, 293
Summation, 291
Super Pythagorean theorem, 131, 139, 151
Supplementary angles, 90
Surface area
    of cone, 136
    of cube, 132
    of cylinder, 134
    of rectangular solid, 131
    of sphere, 137
Symbols, in functions, 216–217
Symmetry
    in algebraic functions, 246–249
    axis of, 146, 167–168
    rotation around line of, 145–146

About the Authors

Jonathan Spaihts was born in 1970. He is a graduate of Princeton University, and by pure coincidence works for The Princeton Review as a teacher, researcher, and writer. In that capacity, he has helped to develop Princeton Review courses for the SAT Math Subject Tests and a number of other standardized tests. He may also be seen in thrilling full-motion video on The Princeton Review's Inside the SAT and Inside the GRE CD-ROMs. When not working for The Princeton Review, Jonathan creates various arcane writings of his own.

Graham Sultan is a Master Trainer who has trained and tutored thousands of teachers and students in nineteen subjects, including SAT, SAT Subject Tests, PSAT, and ACT. Graham loves weird job titles, and firmly believes that he who dies with the most certifications wins. He has the unusual habit of taking multiple-choice tests early on Saturday mornings, which has helped him write seven of The Princeton Review's retail books, four of its courses, and zillions of practice tests. Occasionally, he actually sleeps.

Alexandra Schaffer took New York by storm five days after graduating from Oberlin College. Two months later she was a Princeton Review employee and has been ever since. She is a Master Tutor and Trainer, and has tutored thousands of students in many subjects, including the PSAT, SAT, SAT Subject Tests, GMAT, and GRE. She also works part-time as an editor. She has helped develop courses, including our SAT program and SAT/ACT for Sophomores. Alexandra can sometimes be seen on screens big and small. She currently resides in Los Angeles, with her cat.

1.

YOUR NAME: _____
(Print)
        Last   First   M.I.

SIGNATURE: _____   DATE: ___ / ___ / ___

HOME ADDRESS: _____
(Print)
        Number and Street

        City   State   Zip Code

PHONE NO.: _____
(Print)

5. YOUR NAME

First 4 letters of last name				FIRST INIT	MID INIT
Ⓐ	Ⓐ	Ⓐ	Ⓐ	Ⓐ	Ⓐ
Ⓑ	Ⓑ	Ⓑ	Ⓑ	Ⓑ	Ⓑ
Ⓒ	Ⓒ	Ⓒ	Ⓒ	Ⓒ	Ⓒ
Ⓓ	Ⓓ	Ⓓ	Ⓓ	Ⓓ	Ⓓ
Ⓔ	Ⓔ	Ⓔ	Ⓔ	Ⓔ	Ⓔ
Ⓕ	Ⓕ	Ⓕ	Ⓕ	Ⓕ	Ⓕ
Ⓖ	Ⓖ	Ⓖ	Ⓖ	Ⓖ	Ⓖ
Ⓗ	Ⓗ	Ⓗ	Ⓗ	Ⓗ	Ⓗ
Ⓘ	Ⓘ	Ⓘ	Ⓘ	Ⓘ	Ⓘ
Ⓙ	Ⓙ	Ⓙ	Ⓙ	Ⓙ	Ⓙ
Ⓚ	Ⓚ	Ⓚ	Ⓚ	Ⓚ	Ⓚ
Ⓛ	Ⓛ	Ⓛ	Ⓛ	Ⓛ	Ⓛ
Ⓜ	Ⓜ	Ⓜ	Ⓜ	Ⓜ	Ⓜ
Ⓝ	Ⓝ	Ⓝ	Ⓝ	Ⓝ	Ⓝ
Ⓞ	Ⓞ	Ⓞ	Ⓞ	Ⓞ	Ⓞ
Ⓟ	Ⓟ	Ⓟ	Ⓟ	Ⓟ	Ⓟ
Ⓠ	Ⓠ	Ⓠ	Ⓠ	Ⓠ	Ⓠ
Ⓡ	Ⓡ	Ⓡ	Ⓡ	Ⓡ	Ⓡ
Ⓢ	Ⓢ	Ⓢ	Ⓢ	Ⓢ	Ⓢ
Ⓣ	Ⓣ	Ⓣ	Ⓣ	Ⓣ	Ⓣ
Ⓤ	Ⓤ	Ⓤ	Ⓤ	Ⓤ	Ⓤ
Ⓥ	Ⓥ	Ⓥ	Ⓥ	Ⓥ	Ⓥ
Ⓦ	Ⓦ	Ⓦ	Ⓦ	Ⓦ	Ⓦ
Ⓧ	Ⓧ	Ⓧ	Ⓧ	Ⓧ	Ⓧ
Ⓨ	Ⓨ	Ⓨ	Ⓨ	Ⓨ	Ⓨ
Ⓩ	Ⓩ	Ⓩ	Ⓩ	Ⓩ	Ⓩ

IMPORTANT: Please fill in these boxes exactly as shown on the back cover of your test book.

2. TEST FORM

6. DATE OF BIRTH

Month	Day		Year	
◯ JAN				
◯ FEB	⓪	⓪	⓪	⓪
◯ MAR	①	①	①	①
◯ APR	②	②	②	②
◯ MAY	③	③	③	③
◯ JUN		④	④	④
◯ JUL		⑤	⑤	⑤
◯ AUG		⑥	⑥	⑥
◯ SEP		⑦	⑦	⑦
◯ OCT		⑧	⑧	⑧
◯ NOV		⑨	⑨	⑨
◯ DEC				

3. TEST CODE   **4. REGISTRATION NUMBER**

⓪	Ⓐ	Ⓙ	⓪	⓪	⓪	⓪	⓪	⓪	⓪	⓪
①	Ⓓ	Ⓚ	①	①	①	①	①	①	①	①
②	Ⓒ	Ⓛ	②	②	②	②	②	②	②	②
③	Ⓓ	Ⓜ	③	③	③	③	③	③	③	③
④	Ⓔ	Ⓝ	④	④	④	④	④	④	④	④
⑤	Ⓕ	Ⓞ	⑤	⑤	⑤	⑤	⑤	⑤	⑤	⑤
⑥	Ⓖ	Ⓟ	⑥	⑥	⑥	⑥	⑥	⑥	⑥	⑥
⑦	Ⓗ	Ⓠ	⑦	⑦	⑦	⑦	⑦	⑦	⑦	⑦
⑧	Ⓘ	Ⓡ	⑧	⑧	⑧	⑧	⑧	⑧	⑧	⑧
⑨			⑨	⑨	⑨	⑨	⑨	⑨	⑨	⑨

7. SEX
◯ MALE
◯ FEMALE

The Princeton Review

Form A

Start with number 1 for each new section.
If a section has fewer questions than answer spaces, leave the extra answer spaces blank.

1. Ⓐ Ⓑ Ⓒ Ⓓ Ⓔ
2. Ⓐ Ⓑ Ⓒ Ⓓ Ⓔ
3. Ⓐ Ⓑ Ⓒ Ⓓ Ⓔ
4. Ⓐ Ⓑ Ⓒ Ⓓ Ⓔ
5. Ⓐ Ⓑ Ⓒ Ⓓ Ⓔ
6. Ⓐ Ⓑ Ⓒ Ⓓ Ⓔ
7. Ⓐ Ⓑ Ⓒ Ⓓ Ⓔ
8. Ⓐ Ⓑ Ⓒ Ⓓ Ⓔ
9. Ⓐ Ⓑ Ⓒ Ⓓ Ⓔ
10. Ⓐ Ⓑ Ⓒ Ⓓ Ⓔ
11. Ⓐ Ⓑ Ⓒ Ⓓ Ⓔ
12. Ⓐ Ⓑ Ⓒ Ⓓ Ⓔ
13. Ⓐ Ⓑ Ⓒ Ⓓ Ⓔ
14. Ⓐ Ⓑ Ⓒ Ⓓ Ⓔ
15. Ⓐ Ⓑ Ⓒ Ⓓ Ⓔ
16. Ⓐ Ⓑ Ⓒ Ⓓ Ⓔ
17. Ⓐ Ⓑ Ⓒ Ⓓ Ⓔ
18. Ⓐ Ⓑ Ⓒ Ⓓ Ⓔ
19. Ⓐ Ⓑ Ⓒ Ⓓ Ⓔ
20. Ⓐ Ⓑ Ⓒ Ⓓ Ⓔ
21. Ⓐ Ⓑ Ⓒ Ⓓ Ⓔ
22. Ⓐ Ⓑ Ⓒ Ⓓ Ⓔ
23. Ⓐ Ⓑ Ⓒ Ⓓ Ⓔ
24. Ⓐ Ⓑ Ⓒ Ⓓ Ⓔ
25. Ⓐ Ⓑ Ⓒ Ⓓ Ⓔ
26. Ⓐ Ⓑ Ⓒ Ⓓ Ⓔ
27. Ⓐ Ⓑ Ⓒ Ⓓ Ⓔ
28. Ⓐ Ⓑ Ⓒ Ⓓ Ⓔ
29. Ⓐ Ⓑ Ⓒ Ⓓ Ⓔ
30. Ⓐ Ⓑ Ⓒ Ⓓ Ⓔ

31. Ⓐ Ⓑ Ⓒ Ⓓ Ⓔ
32. Ⓐ Ⓑ Ⓒ Ⓓ Ⓔ
33. Ⓐ Ⓑ Ⓒ Ⓓ Ⓔ
34. Ⓐ Ⓑ Ⓒ Ⓓ Ⓔ
35. Ⓐ Ⓑ Ⓒ Ⓓ Ⓔ
36. Ⓐ Ⓑ Ⓒ Ⓓ Ⓔ
37. Ⓐ Ⓑ Ⓒ Ⓓ Ⓔ
38. Ⓐ Ⓑ Ⓒ Ⓓ Ⓔ
39. Ⓐ Ⓑ Ⓒ Ⓓ Ⓔ
40. Ⓐ Ⓑ Ⓒ Ⓓ Ⓔ
41. Ⓐ Ⓑ Ⓒ Ⓓ Ⓔ
42. Ⓐ Ⓑ Ⓒ Ⓓ Ⓔ
43. Ⓐ Ⓑ Ⓒ Ⓓ Ⓔ
44. Ⓐ Ⓑ Ⓒ Ⓓ Ⓔ
45. Ⓐ Ⓑ Ⓒ Ⓓ Ⓔ
46. Ⓐ Ⓑ Ⓒ Ⓓ Ⓔ
47. Ⓐ Ⓑ Ⓒ Ⓓ Ⓔ
48. Ⓐ Ⓑ Ⓒ Ⓓ Ⓔ
49. Ⓐ Ⓑ Ⓒ Ⓓ Ⓔ
50. Ⓐ Ⓑ Ⓒ Ⓓ Ⓔ

The Princeton Review

1.

YOUR NAME: _____
(Print)
         Last   First   M.I.

SIGNATURE: _____   DATE: ___ / ___ / ___

HOME ADDRESS: _____
(Print)
        Number and Street

_____
   City   State   Zip Code

PHONE NO.: _____
(Print)

IMPORTANT: Please fill in these boxes exactly as shown on the back cover of your test book.

2. TEST FORM

3. TEST CODE

4. REGISTRATION NUMBER

5. YOUR NAME

First 4 letters of last name				FIRST INIT	MID INIT

6. DATE OF BIRTH

Month	Day		Year	
JAN				
FEB	0	0	0	0
MAR	1	1	1	1
APR	2	2	2	2
MAY	3	3	3	3
JUN		4	4	4
JUL		5	5	5
AUG		6	6	6
SEP		7	7	7
OCT		8	8	8
NOV		9	9	9
DEC				

7. SEX

MALE
FEMALE

The Princeton Review

Form B   Start with number 1 for each new section.
If a section has fewer questions than answer spaces, leave the extra answer spaces blank.

1. A B C D E
2. A B C D E
3. A B C D E
4. A B C D E
5. A B C D E
6. A B C D E
7. A B C D E
8. A B C D E
9. A B C D E
10. A B C D E
11. A B C D E
12. A B C D E
13. A B C D E
14. A B C D E
15. A B C D E
16. A B C D E
17. A B C D E
18. A B C D E
19. A B C D E
20. A B C D E
21. A B C D E
22. A B C D E
23. A B C D E
24. A B C D E
25. A B C D E
26. A B C D E
27. A B C D E
28. A B C D E
29. A B C D E
30. A B C D E

31. A B C D E
32. A B C D E
33. A B C D E
34. A B C D E
35. A B C D E
36. A B C D E
37. A B C D E
38. A B C D E
39. A B C D E
40. A B C D E
41. A B C D E
42. A B C D E
43. A B C D E
44. A B C D E
45. A B C D E
46. A B C D E
47. A B C D E
48. A B C D E
49. A B C D E
50. A B C D E

The Princeton Review

Completely darken bubbles with a No. 2 pencil. If you make a mistake, be sure to erase mark completely. Erase all stray marks.

1.

YOUR NAME: _____
(Print)   Last   First   M.I.

SIGNATURE: _____   DATE: ___ / ___ / ___

HOME ADDRESS: _____
(Print)   Number and Street

_____
City   State   Zip Code

PHONE NO.: _____
(Print)

IMPORTANT: Please fill in these boxes exactly as shown on the back cover of your test book.

2. TEST FORM

3. TEST CODE

4. REGISTRATION NUMBER

5. YOUR NAME

First 4 letters of last name | FIRST INIT | MID INIT

6. DATE OF BIRTH

Month	Day	Year
JAN		
FEB	0 0	0 0
MAR	1 1	1 1
APR	2 2	2 2
MAY	3 3	3 3
JUN	4 4	4
JUL	5 5	5
AUG	6 6	6
SEP	7 7	7
OCT	8 8	8
NOV	9 9	9
DEC		

7. SEX

○ MALE
○ FEMALE

The Princeton Review

Form A

Start with number 1 for each new section.
If a section has fewer questions than answer spaces, leave the extra answer spaces blank.

1. Ⓐ Ⓑ Ⓒ Ⓓ Ⓔ
2. Ⓐ Ⓑ Ⓒ Ⓓ Ⓔ
3. Ⓐ Ⓑ Ⓒ Ⓓ Ⓔ
4. Ⓐ Ⓑ Ⓒ Ⓓ Ⓔ
5. Ⓐ Ⓑ Ⓒ Ⓓ Ⓔ
6. Ⓐ Ⓑ Ⓒ Ⓓ Ⓔ
7. Ⓐ Ⓑ Ⓒ Ⓓ Ⓔ
8. Ⓐ Ⓑ Ⓒ Ⓓ Ⓔ
9. Ⓐ Ⓑ Ⓒ Ⓓ Ⓔ
10. Ⓐ Ⓑ Ⓒ Ⓓ Ⓔ
11. Ⓐ Ⓑ Ⓒ Ⓓ Ⓔ
12. Ⓐ Ⓑ Ⓒ Ⓓ Ⓔ
13. Ⓐ Ⓑ Ⓒ Ⓓ Ⓔ
14. Ⓐ Ⓑ Ⓒ Ⓓ Ⓔ
15. Ⓐ Ⓑ Ⓒ Ⓓ Ⓔ
16. Ⓐ Ⓑ Ⓒ Ⓓ Ⓔ
17. Ⓐ Ⓑ Ⓒ Ⓓ Ⓔ
18. Ⓐ Ⓑ Ⓒ Ⓓ Ⓔ
19. Ⓐ Ⓑ Ⓒ Ⓓ Ⓔ
20. Ⓐ Ⓑ Ⓒ Ⓓ Ⓔ
21. Ⓐ Ⓑ Ⓒ Ⓓ Ⓔ
22. Ⓐ Ⓑ Ⓒ Ⓓ Ⓔ
23. Ⓐ Ⓑ Ⓒ Ⓓ Ⓔ
24. Ⓐ Ⓑ Ⓒ Ⓓ Ⓔ
25. Ⓐ Ⓑ Ⓒ Ⓓ Ⓔ
26. Ⓐ Ⓑ Ⓒ Ⓓ Ⓔ
27. Ⓐ Ⓑ Ⓒ Ⓓ Ⓔ
28. Ⓐ Ⓑ Ⓒ Ⓓ Ⓔ
29. Ⓐ Ⓑ Ⓒ Ⓓ Ⓔ
30. Ⓐ Ⓑ Ⓒ Ⓓ Ⓔ

31. Ⓐ Ⓑ Ⓒ Ⓓ Ⓔ
32. Ⓐ Ⓑ Ⓒ Ⓓ Ⓔ
33. Ⓐ Ⓑ Ⓒ Ⓓ Ⓔ
34. Ⓐ Ⓑ Ⓒ Ⓓ Ⓔ
35. Ⓐ Ⓑ Ⓒ Ⓓ Ⓔ
36. Ⓐ Ⓑ Ⓒ Ⓓ Ⓔ
37. Ⓐ Ⓑ Ⓒ Ⓓ Ⓔ
38. Ⓐ Ⓑ Ⓒ Ⓓ Ⓔ
39. Ⓐ Ⓑ Ⓒ Ⓓ Ⓔ
40. Ⓐ Ⓑ Ⓒ Ⓓ Ⓔ
41. Ⓐ Ⓑ Ⓒ Ⓓ Ⓔ
42. Ⓐ Ⓑ Ⓒ Ⓓ Ⓔ
43. Ⓐ Ⓑ Ⓒ Ⓓ Ⓔ
44. Ⓐ Ⓑ Ⓒ Ⓓ Ⓔ
45. Ⓐ Ⓑ Ⓒ Ⓓ Ⓔ
46. Ⓐ Ⓑ Ⓒ Ⓓ Ⓔ
47. Ⓐ Ⓑ Ⓒ Ⓓ Ⓔ
48. Ⓐ Ⓑ Ⓒ Ⓓ Ⓔ
49. Ⓐ Ⓑ Ⓒ Ⓓ Ⓔ
50. Ⓐ Ⓑ Ⓒ Ⓓ Ⓔ

1.

YOUR NAME: _____
(Print)   Last   First   M.I.

SIGNATURE: _____ DATE: ___ / ___ / ___

HOME ADDRESS: _____
(Print)   Number and Street

_____
City   State   Zip Code

PHONE NO.: _____
(Print)

IMPORTANT: Please fill in these boxes exactly as shown on the back cover of your test book.

2. TEST FORM

3. TEST CODE

4. REGISTRATION NUMBER

5. YOUR NAME

First 4 letters of last name				FIRST INIT	MID INIT

6. DATE OF BIRTH

Month	Day		Year	
JAN				
FEB	0	0	0	0
MAR	1	1	1	1
APR	2	2	2	2
MAY	3	3	3	3
JUN		4	4	4
JUL		5	5	5
AUG		6	6	6
SEP		7	7	7
OCT		8	8	8
NOV		9	9	9
DEC				

7. SEX

○ MALE
○ FEMALE

The Princeton Review

Form B

Start with number 1 for each new section.
If a section has fewer questions than answer spaces, leave the extra answer spaces blank.

1. A B C D E
2. A B C D E
3. A B C D E
4. A B C D E
5. A B C D E
6. A B C D E
7. A B C D E
8. A B C D E
9. A B C D E
10. A B C D E
11. A B C D E
12. A B C D E
13. A B C D E
14. A B C D E
15. A B C D E
16. A B C D E
17. A B C D E
18. A B C D E
19. A B C D E
20. A B C D E
21. A B C D E
22. A B C D E
23. A B C D E
24. A B C D E
25. A B C D E
26. A B C D E
27. A B C D E
28. A B C D E
29. A B C D E
30. A B C D E

31. A B C D E
32. A B C D E
33. A B C D E
34. A B C D E
35. A B C D E
36. A B C D E
37. A B C D E
38. A B C D E
39. A B C D E
40. A B C D E
41. A B C D E
42. A B C D E
43. A B C D E
44. A B C D E
45. A B C D E
46. A B C D E
47. A B C D E
48. A B C D E
49. A B C D E
50. A B C D E

NOTES

NOTES

Ace the APs:

Cracking the AP Biology Exam, 2013 Edition (Revised)
978-0-307-94633-1 • $18.99/$21.99 Can.
eBook: 978-0-307-94580-8

Cracking the AP Calculus AB & BC Exams, 2013 Edition
978-0-307-94486-3 • $19.99/$23.99 Can.
eBook: 978-0-307-94451-1

Cracking the AP Chemistry Exam, 2013 Edition
978-0-307-94488-7 • $18.99/$21.99 Can.
eBook: 978-0-307-94452-8

Cracking the AP Economics Macro & Micro Exams, 2013 Edition
978-0-307-94509-9 • $18.00/$21.00 Can.
eBook: 978-0-307-94581-5

Cracking the AP English Language & Composition Exam, 2013 Edition
978-0-307-94511-2 • $18.00/$21.00 Can.
eBook: 978-0-307-94582-2

Cracking the AP English Literature & Composition Exam, 2013 Edition
978-0-307-94512-9 • $18.00/$21.00 Can.
eBook: 978-0-307-94583-9

Cracking the AP Environmental Science Exam, 2013 Edition

Cracking the AP Spanish Exam with Audio CD, 2013 Edition
978-0-307-94518-1 • $24.99/$28.99 Can.

Cracking the AP Statistics Exam, 2013 Edition
978-0-307-94519-8 • $19.99/$23.99 Can.

Cracking the AP U.S. Government & Politics Exam, 2013 Edition
978-0-307-94520-4 • $18.99/$21.99 Can.
eBook: 978-0-307-94587-7

Cracking the AP U.S. History Exam, 2013 Edition
978-0-307-94490-7 • $18.99/$21.99 Can.
eBook: 978-0-307-94447-4

Cracking the AP World History Exam, 2013 Edition
978-0-307-94491-7 • $18.99/$21.99 Can.
eBook: 978-0-307-94445-0

Essential AP Biology (Flashcards)
978-0-375-42803-6 • $18.99/$20.99 Can.

Essential AP Psychology (Flashcards)
978-0-375-42801-2 • $18.99/$20.99 Can.

Essential AP U.S. Government & Politics (Flashcards)
978-0-375-42804-3 • $18.99/$20.99 Can.

Essential AP U.S. History (Flashcards)
...75-42800-5 • $18.99/$20.99 Can.

Essential AP World History (Flashcards)
...75-42802-9 • $18.99/$20.99 Can.

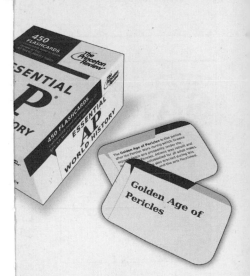

4/1/2013

...re sold
and at PrincetonReviewBooks.com

The Princeton Review

939a